Major Alexander St. Clair-Abrams

The Unparalleled Career
OF THE
Perfect Southern Gentleman

For Mary
Thank you
Bob Grenier
'22

D1528005

Major Alexander St. Clair-Abrams:
The Unparalleled Career of the Perfect Southern Gentleman
By Bob Grenier

Copyright © 2022 Bob Grenier

ISBN 978-0-9746626-4-0

Front cover design by Gene Packwood

Printed in the United States of America

DEDICATED TO

MY DAD

ROBERT A. GRENIER

"History and historians are generally supposed to be truthful and impartial; narrating events as they occur, giving praise even to an enemy, when he deserves it."

Alexander St. Clair-Abrams, 1863

CONTENTS

INTRODUCTION
By Richard Lee Cronin

I was thrilled to learn Bob Grenier was writing a biography of Alexander St. Clair-Abrams, and truly honored when asked to write an introduction to his book. A consummate historian, Bob is likewise an exceptional researcher - two essential ingredients for a biographer intent on capturing the amazing life story of the little-known 19th century visionary, Alexander St. Clair-Abrams.

Those who had encountered the man either admired or despised him. There was no middle of the road when describing the provocative St. Clair-Abrams, although such feelings, good or bad, likely stemmed from the fact that St. Clair-Abrams himself never accepted middle of the road solutions to turning his mega-dreams into reality. He always went big and refused to settle for mediocrity. St. Clair-Abrams dove headfirst into his every venture - *adventures* for the flamboyant Alexander, and there were many such adventures throughout his lifetime. Warrior, author, attorney, publisher, builder, politician, citrus grower, canal builder, steamboat operator, railroad builder, town founder, schemer, and dreamer - no challenge, no matter how big or small, was off limits to St. Clair-Abrams.

Founder of Tavares of Lake County, Florida, is likely the man's best-known achievement, although the town itself was merely one small fragment of his immense plan. St. Clair-Abrams had envisioned a railroad hub, where every passenger and every piece of freight coming into or going out of Central and South Florida would pass through his downtown Tavares. He planned to relocate Florida's Capital from Tallahassee to the new central town of Tavares - yet another part of his vibrant new city.

Florida's capital remains at Tallahassee, and yet the accomplishments of Alexander St. Clair-Abrams are easily visible today, beginning with the County of Lake itself. It took the Tavares founder three elections and a courthouse battle before his town was awarded the title County Seat, but ultimately, the unwavering St. Clair-Abrams got his way. And those who knew the man assumed that he would.

At the height of his time at the Lake County seat, St. Clair-Abrams had enticed five different railroads, including two of his own, to route twenty-two trains daily through downtown Tavares.

Prior to St. Clair-Abrams ever stepping foot in the wilderness of central Florida he had imprinted his very own trademark on the Vicksburg, Mississippi, battlefield; in the burnt ruins of a General Sherman's Atlanta, Georgia; and as a notable reporter of world affairs in New York City.

Although not always good marks, Alexander St. Clair-Abrams' climb to fame is a lesson from which we can all benefit. A participant on the Confederate side of our Nation's tragic Civil War, Alexander St. Clair-Abrams mustered out a bitter enemy of the Union. In 1875, he then became part of an amazing story of America's Civil War Veterans of Orange County, Florida. Retired warriors, both Union and Confederate, laid down arms and took up homesteads in a remote central Florida wilderness. Former enemies became neighbors, farmers, town builders, railroad builders, civic leaders, and even friends.

Perhaps no single event exemplifies the evolution of St. Clair-Abrams' transition to peacetime citizen of this nation than the day Clermont celebrated the arrival of its first train from Tavares. Alexander, arriving aboard his train, was welcomed by the town's founder, Arthur Wrotnowski. Two decades earlier, the same two men had participated in the Siege of Vicksburg, Mississippi - but on opposing sides.

Alexander St. Clair-Abrams was indeed a fascinating individual, and in my view, one characteristic of the man that all who knew him would agree on was his love of family. By all accounts, he was devoted to his wife Joanna, daughter Irma, and son Alfred. The sun rose each day over Lake Joanna, adorned Alfred and Irma Streets in downtown Tavares with the warmth only the Florida sun can provide, and then set each night with Alexander enjoying the company of those he loved most.

This is the Alexander St. Clair-Abrams I came to know from researching his past. I am truly looking forward to reading Bob Grenier's biography.

PROLOGUE

"The perfect Southern gentleman; an unswerving friend; a charming and persuasive politician; an implacable enemy; an explosively hot-headed Portuguese; and a ruthless competitor who gave no quarter."

This is the description friends, rivals, business associates, and casual acquaintances gave Major Alexander St. Clair-Abrams, according to notable Lake County, Florida, historian Kenneth Sears, who was an avid admirer of St. Clair-Abrams and who lived in the St. Clair-Abrams house in Tavares, Florida.

As accurate as the description above was of St. Clair-Abrams, I have discovered, in studying this unique man that there is so much more to describe his character. He was extremely loyal to those who were loyal to him; compassionate to those who were less fortunate; courageous in the heat of battle; a clever and creative wordsmith and storyteller; a dynamically convincing salesman; a remarkable visionary; a devout Catholic, who had great faith in God; and a devoted husband to his wife Joanna.

In 1992, Mr. Sears added that Alexander St. Clair-Abrams was, "an unusual and brilliant man, who probably had more influence on the development of Central Florida than any other…and had a career that is without parallel." The *Tampa Tribune* said at his passing in June 1931, "A varied, unusual, important career was his."

On April 20, 1882, The *Winfield Courier* in Kansas printed a letter from their correspondent visiting Florida that read, "On the shores of Lake Joanna, resides with his family…Col. Alex. St. Clair-Abrams, a true, generous, noble-hearted gentleman of Southern birth, a distinguished lawyer…his abilities, indomitable energy and perseverance, have made him one of the most notable and, perhaps, the best known of anyone in the State."

He was recognized as a "Great Floridian" in 2000 by the Florida Department of State, Division of Historical Resources, through the efforts of the Historical Society of Tavares. In researching the entire embodiment of the life of Alexander St. Clair-Abrams, I believe that the passage of time has made him one of Florida's - and the United States - forgotten pioneers. The fast-paced, high-profile life and career of St. Clair-Abrams quieted substantially during his retirement years and prior to his passing in 1931, which may have sent him into the forgotten pages of the history books. The *Tampa Tribune* in 1931 wrote, "Notice of his death served to remind older Floridians that there was a notable career which passed out in virtual oblivion; yet which, while at its zenith, counted for much in the larger affairs of the state."

He lived a lifetime of tremendous personal and professional successes and accomplishments, along with some obstacles and disappointments, with fortunes made, lost, and re-made, as a lawyer, soldier, army correspondent, author, statesman, orator, newspaper editor, manufacturer, railroad magnate, citrus grower, city and county founder and builder, and much more. Alexander St. Clair-Abrams, throughout his life, was written about in stories and editorials in newspapers coast to coast; having left his mark as an innovator, builder, and influencer not only in the state of Florida, but throughout the South, the Midwest, and the Eastern United States, especially in Louisiana, Mississippi, Alabama, Georgia, New York, and Washington D.C. He was well-connected internationally with royalty, military leaders, and powerful business and political friends in Europe.

Alexander St. Clair-Abrams was born on March 10, 1845, in the busy and energetic Mississippi River port city of New Orleans, Louisiana. As a lad, Alex, as he preferred to be called, attended a private Catholic school, and then soon after, began his ambitious and influential life by becoming a law student; self-studied and well-versed in the Louisiana required common law treatises, as well as apprenticing at a local law office.

On April 12, 1861, sixteen-year-old Alexander St. Clair-Abrams' life, like hundreds of thousands of Americans, would drastically change with the bombardment of Fort Sumter, South Carolina, and the beginning of the War Between the States. In late April 1862, after a year of unexpected, bitter, and extremely unpleasant warfare had already passed, with battles in places such as Manassas, Mill Springs, Fort Donelson, and Shiloh, the ominous guns of Admiral David Glasgow Farragut's Union Navy fleet were aimed at the Confederacy's largest city – New Orleans. It is at this point in the most written about and controversial period in our American history that we begin his biography.

ONE

Signed "One of the Garrison"

On April 25, 1862, sixty-year-old Navy veteran, Admiral David Farragut, flag officer of the Federal fleet known as the West Gulf Blockading Squadron, anchored along the Mississippi shoreline of New Orleans. The day before, Farragut had passed through Fort St. Philip and Fort Jackson, the principal defense fortresses seventy-five miles below New Orleans. His fleet of twenty-one mortar ships, under the command of his adoptive brother David D. Porter, had inflicted heavy damage to the structures and armaments. A Confederate fleet of sixteen gunboats had guarded the city. Also, there was the converted steamship to ironclad ram, *Manassas*, and two yet to be finished ironclads, *Louisiana* and *Mississippi*. But all three of these ships were incapable of any defense. And despite the gallant efforts of unseasoned Confederate defenders, Admiral Farragut had the city of New Orleans, a place he had lived a good portion of his youth, ready to be captured and occupied by 15,000 troops under the command of the political commander, Major General Benjamin Franklin Butler.

The military force in the city of New Orleans consisted of only three thousand local militiamen, who signed for only ninety days of service. Just over half of those guardsmen shouldered shotguns. The command was just too insufficient for the heavily criticized commander of this military unit, Major General Mansfield Lovell. Prior to April 25, he had withdrawn his men northward to assist in fighting in the interior of Louisiana, Mississippi, and Tennessee. Later, on May 1, Butler disembarked Farragut's ships and took command of the city.

Soon after General Lovell abandoned the city, he did offer to return with his troops, knowing full well that it would be a futile attempt to defend against overwhelming man-power. He sent a dispatch to New Orleans mayor, John T. Monroe, stating if "the people of New Orleans were desirous of signalizing their patriotism and devotion to the cause by permitting the bombardment and burning of their city, I would return with my troops and not leave as

Illustration of Admiral David Farragut's fleet anchored on the
Mississippi River at New Orleans in April 1862.

long as one brick remained upon another." Mayor Monroe and several leading advisors declined the general's offer. The *loyal to the Cause* women of New Orleans, including diarist and author Julia LeGrand were all in support of Lovell's return. LeGrand wrote that the women were "all in favor of resistance no matter how hopeless that resistance might be."

Mayor Monroe had ordered the state flag of Louisiana hoisted over city hall on April 25. Admiral Farragut sent two of his Navy officers ashore to demand of the mayor to formally surrender the city and lower the flag. Mayor Monroe replied that he had no authority to surrender the city and that General Lovell is the proper official to receive and reply to that demand. The mayor also told the officers to inform the admiral that he would not lower the flag. Subsequently, he sent for Lovell, who returned with aids and a detail. He, in turn, refused to surrender the city and returned the responsibility of surrender back to Monroe.

After four days of political haggling and temperamental skirmishes, Farragut sent a detachment of sailors and marines into the city to raise the United States flag over the mint and customhouse and strongly requested that the mayor have the Louisiana state flag lowered from city hall, as he thought that responsibility fell to those who raised the state flag. Admiral Farragut, tired of negotiations, deployed Butler and his troops into the city.

General Butler became the military governor of New Orleans and was hated by the citizenry. Edward A. Pollard, editor of the *Richmond Examiner* during the War Between the States, wrote about Butler, "The immediate sufferers of the disaster of New Orleans were the people of that city. The acts of the tyrant of New Orleans surpassed all former atrocities and outrages of the war. In frequent instances, citizens, accused by Butler of contumacious disloyalty, were confined at hard labor, with balls and chains attached to their limbs; and sometimes this degrading punishment was inflicted upon men whose only offense was that of selling medicines to the sick soldiers of the Confederacy. Helpless women were torn from their homes and confined in prison."

General Butler held the female population of New Orleans in resentful contempt. On May 15, 1862, believing the ladies of New Orleans to be disrespectful to the men of his command, issued Order

Major General
Benjamin Franklin Butler
USA

Major General
Mansfield Lovell
CSA

No. 28, which stated, "that when any female shall by word, gesture, or movement insult or show contempt for any officer or soldier of the United States she shall be regarded and held liable to be treated as a woman of the town plying her avocation."

Northern newspapers supported Butler; however, he was replaced in December 1862 by Major General Nathaniel Banks. Though it was believed that Butler's conduct politically, and towards the people of New Orleans, was the reason for his recall, Banks informed him that it was President Abraham Lincoln who made the decision. Butler, though, suspected it was Secretary of State William Henry Seward.

The buildings, structures, and landscape of New Orleans did not suffer much damage when the Union took control of the city from April 25 through May 1. There were no major casualties on either side during that period as well. The only casualty was the spirit of the residents of New Orleans. It was the human tragedy of hate, greed, torture, persecution, and torment that replaced respect, courtesy, compassion, morality, and Christian values that followed the occupation of New Orleans that had a great effect on a young fledgling lawyer named Alexander St. Clair-Abrams.

A CAJUN RECRUIT ENLISTS IN MISSISSIPPI.

Alexander St. Clair-Abrams enlisted in the Confederate Army on March 22, 1862. Presenting his age to be nineteen, the seventeen-year-old dark-haired, blue-eyed, Louisiana recruit, who stood over six feet tall, reported to a camp near Jackson, Mississippi, on May 22, 1862. He listed his occupation as a clerk and signed for three years of service.

The 1st Mississippi Light Artillery regiment was assembled under wealthy, Kentucky-born, Colonel William Temple Withers. Withers would finance much of the accoutrements and supplies needed to outfit his new command. The regiment, made up of mostly Mississippians from Hinds and Madison counties, would be known as Withers Light Artillery and was attached to Brigadier General Carter Littlepage Stevenson's Division. Withers' command was divided into eleven companies. St. Clair-Abrams, one of a handful of Louisianians in this predominate Mississippi camp, was assigned

Colonel William
Temple Withers
CSA

Major General
William Wing Loring
CSA

Captain Samuel
Jones Ridley
CSA

Major General
Carter Littlepage Stevenson
CSA

to Company A, Ridley's Battery, also referred to as the Jackson Light Artillery.

Samuel Jones Ridley, like St. Clair-Abrams, was a tall man who stood six foot three inches tall. He was an affluent planter from Madison County, Mississippi. He too enlisted on March 22; accompanied by his personal servant known as *Old Bill*. He overwhelmingly was elected captain of Company A when camp assembled in May. He was a strict disciplinarian, who drilled his men continuously until they became highly proficient gunneries. Ridley would be killed on May 16, 1863, at the Battle of Baker's Creek, also known as the Battle of Champion Hill, during the Vicksburg campaign. He was posthumously awarded the Confederate *Medal of Honor* for his heroic actions in defense of his position where he enfiladed the advance of the Union troops before he alone stood and fell.

Within a couple of days, Company A found themselves forty miles from camp in Vicksburg. The picket lines protecting the city were reinforced by batteries of Withers Light Artillery. On May 25, Ridley's Battery, supported by infantry and cavalry, were posted toward Warrenton, a swampy village located about five miles south of Vicksburg tucked between the Mississippi River and a tributary called Big Bayou Pierre.

In his report of the defense of Vicksburg during the bombardment, May 26 - July 27, 1862, Major General Earl Van Dorn said: *"Withers Light Artillery was placed in such position as to sweep all near approaches."*

By July 1862, the roll of Withers' command showed 24 officers and 399 men on duty and a combined 877 present and absent. On August 1, the regiment returned to camp at the Marshall place. The men referred to their encampment as "Camp Parker," named for their Lieutenant Colonel James P. Parker.

COLONEL WILLIAM TEMPLE WITHERS.

Colonel Withers was a well-respected and valued commander and received high praise from his superior officers. General John Pemberton, who led the Army of Mississippi, complimented Withers and the First Mississippi Artillery as one of the commands "entitled to the highest distinction." After the pivotal battle at

Baker's Creek on May 15, 1863, Pemberton reported, "Col. W. T. Withers, Chief of Field Artillery, with the army, was active and attentive to his duties and prompt in the execution of orders."

Colonel Withers, during intense fighting, had personally assisted bringing up General Winfield Scott Featherston, commander of the 2nd Brigade in Major General William Wing Loring's Division. Loring witnessed this action and said, "It was a scene ever to be remembered, when the gallant Withers and his brave men, with their fine part of artillery, stood unflinchingly amid a shower of shot and shell before the approach of the enemy in overwhelming force, after his supports had been driven back, trusting that a succoring command would arrive in time to save the batteries."

Colonel Withers was born in Kentucky on January 8, 1825. He had volunteered to fight in the Mexican War in 1846. He was wounded while leading a charge in the Battle of Buena Vista. Considered a mortal wound when the musket ball entered his right side and drove his sword chain into his body, he recovered. After the war he married Martha Sharkey and became a lawyer. He joined the law practice of his wife's father, Judge Sharkey.

After General Ulysses S. Grant seized Vicksburg in 1863, he had heard of Colonel Withers valiant efforts and rewarded him with safe passage to Alabama. He later returned to service and was promoted to general. He had lost everything after the war. But soon, after various jobs and enterprises, he began rebuilding his wealth. He moved his family back to Lexington, Kentucky, in 1874, and invested in ranchland. He began raising trotting horses on his land he called Fairlawn Stock Farm and built a fortune. His former rival, Grant, and many other dignitaries from around the world, visited him at Fairlawn. General Withers passed away on June 16, 1889.

SOLDIER, PRISONER, AND AUTHORING THE SIEGE OF VICKSBURG.

St. Clair-Abrams was present for the July and August roll calls at Camp Parker, but sometime in August he went on sick leave. He returned briefly, but on September 14, 1862, was discharged for a disability. In August, St. Clair-Abrams began experiencing severe spasms that didn't seem to subside heading into September. The regimental surgeon, Dr. M. W. Boyd, declared him incapable to perform the duties of a soldier. He had diagnosed epilepsy, and in his medical report added that his complexion was sallow.

St. Clair-Abrams received a certificate of disability for discharge, and being unable to return to *occupied* New Orleans, he obtained a position as a soldier correspondent in the office of the *Vicksburg Whig* newspaper. In Vicksburg, he could remain near his regiment and very close to what he knew would be the center of a great battle. The *Vicksburg Whig*, also known as the *Vicksburg Daily Whig*, was created and published by M. Shannon and W. H. M'Cardle from 1839 through 1863, with the number of weekly editions ranging from three to six issues a week, excluding Sunday. The newspaper ceased publication when it's offices and printing house were burned in May of 1863, at the beginning of Major General Ulysses Simpson Grant's forty-seven-day Siege of Vicksburg and defeat of Lieutenant General John Clifford Pemberton.

St. Clair-Abrams was present on the front lines throughout the Siege of Vicksburg as a member of the Whig's staff. And though the newspaper was destroyed the month prior to the city's fall on July 4, he continued to write his accounting in his journal. On that Independence Day, soldier and army correspondent, Alexander St. Clair-Abrams, was one of over 29,000 Confederate soldiers who marched out of their lines, stacked their rifles, furled their flags, and became prisoners. The garrison then were released on parole on July 11 to travel to any destination beyond the Federal lines they choose.

St. Clair-Abrams quickly made his way to Mobile, Alabama, where he submitted his Vicksburg accounting to the *Mobile Advertiser and Register*. The articles were published on July 14, 1863. He stayed in Mobile for a day and continued his journey to Atlanta, Georgia, where he settled. His reputation as a front-line army correspondent preceded him and he was immediately, upon arrival, hired by the *Atlanta Intelligencer*.

It was here, In Atlanta, that St. Clair-Abrams wrote and published his first book, *A Full and Detailed History of the Siege of Vicksburg*. In the book he noted the criticisms, both good and bad, that he received from his accounting of the siege in the articles published in the Mobile newspaper. But the determined eighteen-year-old author clearly and without fear, wrote his thoughts, opinions, criticisms, and commentary as he saw it. He certainly was quite qualified to write his version of the siege for, as he states in his book, "that he was at that point, in Company A, Withers Light Artillery, as a private, when the first gun was fired in its defense, and served as such until the raising of the first siege."

War correspondent John H. Linebaugh of the *Mobile Register* reviewed St. Clair-Abrams' book and wrote that it was the "fullest and most intelligent account that had been published."

To provide the reader with a personal first-hand account of the actions and events that took place throughout the siege, I have included in this biography, at the end of this first chapter, the entire text of Mr. A. S. Abrams of New Orleans's *The Full and Detailed History of the Siege of Vicksburg.*

REPORTING CHICKAMAUGA AND THE CHATTANOOGA CAMPAIGN.

After two years of the war, hardship and devastation had touched much of the country. Newspaper publishing became increasingly difficult in the south. There were many challenges to overcome. The destruction of newspaper buildings destroyed presses and type sets. Obtaining paper had become extremely problematic. Paper from mills in Virginia and the Carolinas were, for the most part, blockaded, so many publishers used wallpaper. Machinery came from manufacturers' supply houses in Pennsylvania and New York, so purchasing new equipment would prove impossible.

Atlanta was the hub of the Southern media in the autumn of 1863. Newspapermen from major daily and tri-weekly publications in Charleston, Memphis, Columbia, Savannah, Richmond, and Knoxville, as well as contributing freelance writers and soldier correspondents covering the war, would gather at the headquarters of the *Press Association of the Confederate States of America*. The association, referred to as *Thrasher's Confederate Press Association* because of its experienced general manager, John Sydney Thrasher, was the best place to receive news through telegraph wire reports and dispatches that arrived from association agents posted in the camps of the Confederate Army.

In late August, 1863, St. Clair-Abrams was in Chattanooga with Major General Braxton Bragg's Army of Tennessee when Major General William Starke Rosecrans's Army of the Cumberland began shelling the city as a diversion to allow his troops time to cross

16

the Tennessee River. Bragg earlier had been reluctant to press and go on the offensive against Rosecrans, even after having been offered reinforcements by President Jefferson Davis's War Department. Bragg cited the terrain, and General Ambrose Everett Burnside's army near Knoxville, as his reasons for staying in position in Chattanooga. On September 4, after two weeks of bombardment, the bulk of Rosecrans's Union troops were across the river and southeast of the city. Four days later, Bragg evacuated Chattanooga and Rosecrans and his army of sixty thousand men secured the town and the railroads, and then began the pursuit. He had his sights on Atlanta, and St. Clair-Abrams anticipated this in his reporting, though at this time, he downplayed in his articles the fear of Atlanta being attacked. He was confident of a *turning tide* that would keep the Federal troops from moving nearer to the city. His newspaper reports were critical of the decisions made by several of the Confederate commanders, including General Bragg. Bragg, falling back into the mountainous terrain of north Georgia, was dealing with insubordinate commanders who were ignoring orders to engage the Federal columns. Relief came in mid-September when two divisions from Mississippi, who were in the Vicksburg campaign, plus a division and several brigades from the Department of East Tennessee, and two divisions numbering twelve thousand men under Lieutenant General James Longstreet, arrived.

General Rosecrans, who was still in pursuit, was unaware of the huge support that had arrived for Bragg. On September 19 and 20, near Chickamauga Creek, with the advantage of superior numbers, General Bragg engaged the Union forces. The following day, Bragg ordered Lieutenant General Leonidas Polk to make a sunrise attack on the Federal left flank, which was commanded by Major General George Henry Thomas. Longstreet was to assist Polk once he heard the sound of Polk's guns. The sun rose, and Longstreet heard not a sound. As some time went by, Bragg sent an officer from his staff to check on Polk. The officer found him two miles from his troops preparing to eat his breakfast claiming he did not know why the attack hadn't begun as he had ordered. This delay allowed Rosecrans time to fortify his position on his left.

Lieutenant General James Longstreet, CSA

By strengthening his left, Rosecrans had weakened his right. He also gave a careless order that opened a gap in the center of his lines. This allowed the Confederates to pour through the gap and overwhelm the right flank. The Union Virginian, General Thomas, was able to hold back a total rout. His Twenty-Fourth Corps was supported by Major General Gordon Granger's Reserve Corps, who reinforced Thomas without receiving an order to do so. Both Thomas and Granger received high praise for their stand against the Confederate troops. Thomas's men called him "Slow Trot," because as an instructor at West Point, he had restrained his cadets from galloping their elderly mounts. After this battle, he received the moniker, "Rock of Chickamauga."

General Rosecrans returned to Chattanooga. This was the *turning of the tide* that St. Clair-Abrams expected and reported back to Atlanta. He felt the Confederates could still regain Chattanooga. But at the same time, the idealistic soldier-reporter still maintained a sense of apprehension. He had earlier reported that the morale of the troops was poor, but now with the recent victory, reported that morale was improving. He continued to include in his dispatches that Atlanta was not in any serious urgency from an attack.

General Rosecrans's depleted Union Army was entrapped in Chattanooga. While Bragg's troops were camped outside of the city, Longstreet and several other officers felt that Bragg needed to be replaced. After they sent a message to President Davis, the president traveled to Bragg's headquarters and had a meeting with the dissatisfied generals, with Bragg in attendance. President Davis retained him as commander.

Meanwhile, General Grant arrived in Chattanooga to evaluate and reorganize. Major General Joseph Hooker's corps of 23,000 men arrived after a six-day trip by rail from Alexandria, Virginia. Also, Grant sent for recruitments from Major General William Tecumseh Sherman's command in Mississippi. Grant replaced Rosecrans with Thomas. Grant then had a bridge laid over the Tennessee River that allowed Hooker to march across and into position at the base of Lookout Mountain.

While the Union was reenforcing Chattanooga, Bragg was very complacent in dispersing his troops. He sent Longstreet and his

20,000 men - a third of his force - to head off Burnside at Knoxville, Tennessee.

Even while the Confederates held strategic positions and much of the high ground around Chattanooga, the Union, with 61,000 troops, outmanned and outgunned the Confederates 40,000 troops. Starting on November 23, 1863, and over the following two days, the Confederates suffered three demoralizing defeats against Hooker, Sherman, and Thomas at Chattanooga, Lookout Mountain and Missionary Ridge. With these three battles and General Longstreet unable to take Knoxville, the road to Atlanta had opened.

General Bragg's Army of Tennessee retreated to Dalton, Georgia. He had lost the respect and confidence of his men, and in response, he felt his commanders had let him down by disobedience, drunkenness, and being unfit for duty. He asked to be relieved of command on December 1, 1863, and his request was granted. He returned to Richmond to be an advisor to President Davis and was replaced by General Joseph Eggleston Johnston.

Prior to reporting Johnston's appointment to his new command, St. Clair-Abrams returned to Dalton, approximately 80 miles from Atlanta, where the Army of Tennessee camped for the winter of 1863-1864. St. Clair-Abrams had traveled to Atlanta to write a series of columns about the disaster of Chattanooga and the replacement of General Bragg. Bragg was somewhat uncooperative with army correspondents and St. Clair-Abrams didn't hold back criticisms regarding his temperamental mood towards the press.

While many special reports were more willing to expose vandalism and other misbehavior on the part of Confederate cavalrymen than to report mistreatment of the soldiers by their officers, near the end of 1863, assistant editor St. Clair-Abrams wrote an angry letter to his newspaper. He wrote of acts of cruelty by officers that he had witnessed as punishment for minor infractions of discipline. He wrote he had observed several soldiers "riding rails" for nothing more than failing to respond to roll call at morning muster. One such incident that triggered his angry letter was regarding a soldier who had been sentenced to wear a barrel shirt as a punishment for absenting himself without leave for some weeks. When St. Clair-Abrams inquired about the cause which led to desertion, he heard that the soldier's wife had written to him to say she and their children were in a destitute situation and in a deplorable position.

He continued the letter, "I also learned that the commander of the battalion was in the habit of inflicting such punishment as 'rail toting', 'rail riding', 'post whipping', 'stump digging', and 'thumb lifting' for the slightest offense and then without waiting for the order of a court martial, but on his own responsibility…I abstained this time from mentioning the name of the officer referred to above, but should he continue such unauthorized acts after this notice of them comes to his knowledge (which I shall take good care it does) I shall not only call his name, but make it my business to call the attention of Lieutenant General Hardee to this usurpation of power, as I feel certain neither the Lieutenant General nor his subordinates are aware of such acts being committed in the army or approve of them."

While in Dalton, St. Clair-Abrams wanted to check on the morale of the troops and write a series of columns based on interviews of the enlisted men. He surprisingly wrote that the morale and attitude of the men were greatly improved over what had been recently reported. He wrote that an emotional desire for revenge had replaced the humiliation of defeat at Missionary Ridge. These series of columns about the positive morale of the troops may not have reflected his true findings or feelings, but possibly he may have felt pressured by editor John Steele to report it that way.

St. Clair-Abrams asked the soldiers their view and opinions about the recent change of command from Bragg to Johnston. And though much of the response had been that the troops were satisfied, many soldiers told him they would have preferred General P. G. T. Beauregard.

It was a few months later, on May 2, 1864, that another army correspondent, in contradiction to St. Clair-Abrams, wrote that the army was a "demoralized wreck" and that General Johnston considered the valley they were scattered about to be militarily untenable. The reporter also wrote that Johnston reluctantly remained in Dalton rather than risk further depressing public morale by surrendering more territory to the enemy.

Throughout 1863, St. Clair-Abrams wrote his personal rebuttal and commentary regarding attacks made by *Richmond Examiner* principal editor, Edward Alfred Pollard, in his newspaper and in

public. Pollard was the author of several books, mainly about the causes and events of the war, including the *Southern History of the War, The Lost Cause: A New Southern History of the War of the Confederates,* and *The Lost Cause Regained.* He was a strong proponent of secession and quite extreme in his ideas of class and aristocratic life in the South. Pollard wrote a continuous stream of negative articles about Jefferson Davis and his cabinet members, and in 1869 published a highly critical biography of the Confederate president.

Edward Alfred Pollard

St. Clair-Abrams admitted he wasn't a partisan of Jefferson Davis, but felt the attacks by Pollard were unwarranted. Pollard was very hard on Secretary of War, James Seddon, as well. St. Clair-Abrams wrote a widely distributed twenty-page pamphlet that he had published in Atlanta in 1864 titled *President Davis and His Administration - Being a Review of the "Rival Administrations."* The publication was written to defend the Davis administration against Pollard's onslaught of negative press. The following excerpts are taken from the small booklet published under the name A. S. Abrams.

PREFACE – The object of this pamphlet is purely to review the late attack on the administration, and to do justice to those who have been placed in charge of the government, believing that Mr. Pollard has acted very unjustly towards the President and his Cabinet.

It having been said, by those who have seen the within pages, while in manuscript, that they may be construed into a personal attack on the author of the Rival Administrations, the author of this review, while declaring that his purpose is simply to defend the administration from Mr. Pollard's charges of incapacity, takes occasion to say that *should* the object of this work be misrepresented [erratum: for the word "misrepresented" read deemed offensive] he holds himself personally responsible for every word contained therein.

CHAPTER I – The following pages are not intended as a praise of the President. We are no partisan of the administration, as the thousands who have read the "History of the Siege of Vicksburg," and "Review of the War," can testify. Ours is but to defend from a gross and unmanly assault the President who, with all his faults, is universally acknowledged to be the most able man in the Confederate States. That he has erred in some instances we will not deny, but that his errors have been so serious as to warrant the attack made on him by the author of

"The Rival Administration," we not only deny, but endeavor to proof our denial.

CHAPTER II - Mr. Pollard says that "the civil administration of Mr. Davis has fallen to a low ebb." This is emphatically false. The President has ever been looked upon by the masses of the people as an able and efficient servant of the Confederacy, and as the only man in the South who could fill the office he holds with as much success. We speak the sentiments of the *people*, not the private opinions of a partisan feeling. That the administration possesses the confidence of the people, was made apparent on the tour of the President though the different States, a short time after the battle of Chickamauga. His reception was enthusiastic, and we cannot conceive how he would have been so well received by them, if his administration had fallen to so low an ebb.

Nor has the "history of this war proved one proposition," "that in all its subjects of congratulation the 'statesmanship' of Richmond had little part in it." We also "deny the justice of this historical (?) judgment, which refuses to attribute to the official authorities of this government, such success as we have had in this war." No "history" of this war has yet been written. In the two volumes issued, and the pamphlet now before us, we find a narrative of the different civil and military operations compiled together, for the purpose of covering an unmanly attack upon the President. And when the assertion is broadly made that no success achieved by the South in this contest can be attributed to the administration, we not only deny it, but come prepared to show where the administration is worthy of, and has received the heartfelt praises of the country.

CHAPTER III – It is generally the case that after an enigma has been solved, all parties find out how simple it was, and one party will wonder at the dullness of another in not solving it, forgetful at the time that he was one of those whose want of penetration prevented its solution. This is the case with Mr. Pollard when he gravely tells the people that "it is mortifying indeed to look back upon the currents of our history, to observe the blindness and littleness of mind, the conceit, the perversity, the shortsighted management, in all which we have drifted into this present vastness of war and depths of distress." "Blindness and littleness of mind" are not appropriate terms, for neither the one nor the other was shown. To the contrary, as soon as all hope for peace had departed, a powerful army was raised and put in the field. Jefferson Davis assumed control of a government, or rather revolutionary party, without it having any form of government. With the skill of a statesman, he moulded that revolutionary party into a model government, in a few short weeks. Civil and military departments were put in operation with astonishing energy and rapidity. He measured the necessity of the South by the strength of the North. The President saw not before him a war of indefinite duration; no one saw it. It was a gift of far-sightedness which only the craven hearted and *soi disant* patriots possessed. None else saw it.

It is charged by Mr. Pollard that the administration, to have exhibited any marks of statesmanship, should have discovered that this war would be one of several years' duration, but he gives no one instance where such far-seeing statesmanship has been shown. Not on this continent, for Calhoun and Webster, the two farthest-seeing statesmen that America ever had, could never see a greater calamity occurring to this continent, than the disruption of the Union. They never saw war resulting from it. Nor can we find in European history any evidence of such far-seeing statesmanship as that desired by Mr. Pollard.

CHAPTER V – The next subject which comes under Mr. Pollard's notice, "is the disclosure from the Confederate Secretary of War, Mr. James Seddon, that the effective force of the army was not more than a half, never two-thirds of the numbers in the ranks," and this fact is attributed wholly and solely to the Secretary or to use Mr. Pollard's word, "the fault of his own administration, the remissness of discipline, the weak shunning of the death penalty in our armies, and that poultry quackery which proposed to treat the great evil of desertion with 'proclamations and patriotic appeals.'"

CHAPTER VII – When we look on the work performed by the administration, and the successes which have attended it, all the errors committed become insignificant. The formation of this government in the midst of an excitement consequent upon the secession of the different States; the organization of armies which have become the terror of enemies, the wonder of the world, and the pride of friends; and last, though the most important of all, the long list of brilliant victories which have crowned the banners of the Confederacy, are proof enough of the ability and energy of the administration.

Jefferson Davis

At some other time, we may be induced to give to the public the causes which have led to this gross abuse of President Davis and his administration; at present we will close this brief work by observing that it would be preferable for the North to overrun twice as much Southern soil as she already has, than for Confederacy to lose the services of Jefferson Davis. With all his faults there is none in the Confederacy who possesses the high administrative talent that he does, and though the voice of malice and censure may endeavor for awhile to deprive him of that praise he has so well merited by his successful administration of the government, the time will surely come when he will receive the thanks and blessings of a free people, and he looked upon as the SECOND WASHINGTON of the Southern States of America.

General Sherman's Military Division of the Mississippi was on the move. Following the Battle of Rocky Face Ridge in Whitfield County from May 7-13, 1864, General Johnston withdrew and repositioned his Army of Tennessee to the mountains around Resaca. Assistant editor St. Clair-Abrams was now traveling with the new commanding general, who wasn't any more cooperative with the press than General Bragg.

At Resaca, the fighting between Sherman and Johnston continued. Sherman had over 98,000 men to Johnston's 60,000. On May 13, there was minor skirmishing and gun fire exchanged, but on the following day, heavy fighting commenced. On May 15, the combatants were fighting with no side taking a clear advantage until Sherman sent forces across the Oostanaula River. Johnston was not able to stop the advance and withdrew, having burnt the railroad spans and a bridge on the morning of May 16. The Union repaired the bridge and Sherman's pursuit continued.

St. Clair-Abrams wrote of the repeated charges by the Federal troops against the Confederate defenses at Resaca, "The Minnie balls of the Yankees poured over our line in an increasing stream, and in such numbers that the air seemed black with them. The sharp and musical whiz they emit was no longer heard; it was an angry and discordant imitation of a peal of thunder rolling along the clouds while the booming of the artillery and the bursting of the shells as they came flying over our line, formed a fire unequaled, perhaps, since nations first made war upon each other."

St. Clair-Abrams added that if the Federal forces had not fired too high, Confederate troops would have suffered fearful losses.

He made a quick trip to the *Intelligencer* office in Atlanta and then traveled back to meet up with the army in Allatoona. But in Cartersville, he ran into some difficulty when he could not locate the officer to whom he had entrusted his horse when he left Adairsville. He discovered that his horse had been taken to Marietta by mistake. He managed to procure a mule and made it back to the front.

The continued retreating by the Confederates was getting increasingly difficult to explain to the readers. St. Clair-Abrams wrote that the necessity of retreating was a means to counter the enemy's flanking strategy, as well as Johnston's unwillingness to risk a general engagement. Retreats were being referred to as "retrograde movements." St. Clair-Abrams felt confident that a battle would soon be fought between the Etowah and Chattahoochee Rivers, and that it would halt the Yankee invasion.

The retreating not only played on the nerves of the civilians, but the soldiers as well. Soon, Johnston began to censor press dispatches. When the army fell back to Adairsville, the general manager of the Press Association went to Atlanta to see what could be done about restoring daily press services from the front. On a visit to Johnston, the general was unreceptive to the Press Association's pleas. Unable to receive telegrams, the only way to receive news reports were from letters, visits to Atlanta by reporters, interviews of wounded soldiers brought to Atlanta for care, and unreliable reports from railroad passengers. St. Clair-Abrams and Henry Watterson of the *Augusta Constitutionalist* were the only full-time Georgia correspondents covering the battles in the state by this time. Several publications used soldier correspondents.

General Sherman shifted east and toward the line of the railroad, with Johnston keeping pace with a parallel movement. On June 5, St. Clair-Abrams reported that to keep his right flank from being turned, Johnston had withdrawn to a new line about ten miles long from Lost Mountain to the railroad north of Kennesaw Mountain. St. Clair-Abrams was having trouble with the transmission of his telegraphic and letter correspondence to the *Intelligencer*. Yet, at the same time, he was impatient with the *Confederate Associated Press* because of its "glaring misrepresentations."

On June 9, Governor Joseph E. Brown, who would in the future have an ongoing feud with St. Clair-Abrams, visited General Johnston. Governor Brown was there to discuss the military defense of the state. The governor, who had made several visits, was a strong partisan of Johnston. St. Clair-Abrams and other correspondents reported these conferences.

General Sherman's march toward Atlanta was a series of flanking maneuvers, which were successful in making the Confederates withdraw from positions they had solidly fortified. These flanking movements allowed the march to advance with few casualties. On June 27, Sherman ran into heavy fortification on Kennesaw Mountain, and ordered a major frontal assault, a tactical change in his plan.

Johnston was able to hold against Sherman and won the battle, but the success was short-lived as Sherman restarted his flanking maneuvers, causing Johnston to fall back and evacuate Kennesaw Mountain and Marietta.

Johnston pleaded for several weeks with Richmond to send Lieutenant General Nathan Bedford Forrest's and Lieutenant General Stephen Dill Lee's cavalries to halt Sherman's railroad communications. Jefferson Davis, along with his new advisor, General Bragg, refused the requests, explaining the need is more urgent in Mississippi.

The *Atlanta Intelligencer* had written articles that predicated General Johnston would be flanked to the Gulf and then to Richmond. Other newspapers wondered why General Wheeler's cavalry was not sent to stop Sherman's communications, unaware that Wheeler's corps were needed to guard Johnston's flanks and keep him informed of Sherman's movements. There were several publications that were quite critical of General Wheeler, despite his gallantry. Wheeler wrote a letter to Bragg that explained why Johnston would not allow him to go to the enemy's rear and that the papers were abusing him for not doing so. He continued in his letter to Bragg by saying that General Johnston told him not to mind the papers, but that those things are disagreeable.

St. Clair-Abrams was a partisan and admirer of General Wheeler and wrote that he formed a much more favorable opinion of Wheeler during the campaign than he had had before he gained firsthand knowledge of the general's capabilities.

TRIALS OF THE SOLDIER'S WIFE.

On April 20, 1864, nineteen-year-old Alexander St. Clair-Abrams published his second book titled, *The Trials of the Soldier's Wife: A Tale of the Second American Revolution.* As with his first book, he utilized the steam power presses of the *Atlanta Intelligencer.*

St. Clair-Abrams wrote in the Preface of the new book that the first thought of this story came in December of 1862. He had heard a story of a soldier from his hometown of New Orleans, who had escaped from Camp Douglas in Chicago, who arrived in Jackson, Mississippi, just in time to see his wife die.

He noted that the press made no notice of the soldier's story, but thought it made a fit subject for a literary work. He continued by saying that if the picture drawn in the following pages appears exaggerated to our readers, they will at least recognize the moral it contains as truthful.

St. Clair-Abrams realized there were defects in the text, especially as he attempted to phonetically spell the vernacular speech and accents of several of the characters. But he also stated in the Appendix that at the time the book was in press he was with the Army of Tennessee performing his duties, which prevented him from reading the proof sheets and correcting all mistakes which crept in during composition. He requested of the public that the readers will overlook the story's defects and hopes there will be found in his little book sufficient interest to while away the idle hours.

I have included at the end of this book the entire text of Mr. Alex St. Clair-Abrams *The Trials of the Soldier's Wife: A Tale of the Second American Revolution.*

JOANNA AND JONESBOROUGH.

St. Clair-Abrams's schedule was extremely busy. He spent much of his time with the army on the battlefield and in isolated camps. However, he did find the time while he resided and worked in Atlanta, to meet sixteen-year-old Joanna Immel.

Joanna, sometimes spelled Johanna, was the daughter of baker and manufacturer Phillip Immel. Phillip, born in Bavaria in 1823, arrived in the United States on August 1, 1837. He was received in Augusta, Georgia, by Mr. T. F. Diel. Phillip married Emily Gardner of Maryland in Richmond County, Georgia, on October 8, 1845. On February 22, 1848, daughter Joanna was born. By 1850, the Immels moved to Atlanta, where Phillip and other family members were bakers. In addition, he was a manufacturer and printer, and in their large home, Phillip and Emily took in boarders.

Phillip Immel died on September 10, 1861, and was buried at the Atlanta Graveyard, also called the City Burial Place. Later, in 1872, the city renamed it the Oakland Cemetery. His widow, Emily, then married Marcus Roberts and had a daughter, Joanna's half-sister, named Kate.

Joanna Immel St. Clair-Abrams

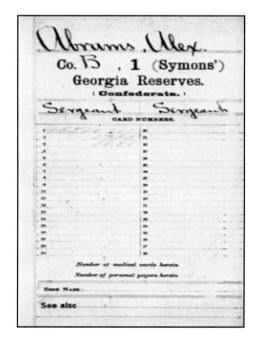

On April 16, 1864, prior to returning to the Army of Tennessee at Resaca, St. Clair-Abrams had traveled to Savannah to enlist in a reserve regiment to get into the fight should Atlanta be threatened, and he was sure at this time that it would be. He was appointed fifth sergeant of Company B, First Georgia Reserves, under the command of Major William R. Symons. His company commander was Captain John Cunningham. In July, he was promoted to third sergeant, and was present for both July and August roll call. He noticed that the majority of the reserve enlistees were boys sixteen years of age and younger and men well over forty years of age - and some even in their sixties.

On August 24, St. Clair-Abrams married Joanna in Macon, Bibb County, Georgia. Just days after his marriage, St. Clair-Abrams shouldered a rifle and re-joined his reserve unit. On the day the young couple were getting married, General Sherman's cavalry tried to cut the Macon & Western Railroad. After several failed attempts, Sherman left the Twentieth Corps at the Chattahoochee and with six corps, marched southwest of Atlanta. On August 25, he turned his entire army east in an attempt to cut the railroad before Jonesborough.

Cavalry units of General John Bell Hood relayed messages to him on August 27 that a large number of Union infantry were marching toward Fairburn. The next day, supplied with that information, Hood ordered two brigades to travel by rail to Jonesborough, about thirty miles east of Fairburn. At this time, Hood estimated the Union strength at two or three corps. By the 29th, he figured there to be five or six corps – possibly General Sherman's entire army.

General Hood ordered General S. D. Lee to East Point, about sixteen miles north of Jonesborough and General William Hardee four miles south of Lee to Rough and Ready way station about twelve miles north of Jonesborough.

On August 30, Hood received a report from the cavalry that a large force eight miles west of Jonesborough, was moving against them. Two Union corps had destroyed railroad lines and were heading to Hardee's location, while Union Major General Oliver O. Howard corps were headed directly for Jonesborough. Howard fought through some minor skirmishing with Southern cavalry, but continued toward Jonesborough. Sherman had approved for him to halt his march, but Howard needed water and wanted to get his men to the Flint River.

Meanwhile, Hood received a wire that the Federal troops were just a mile from Jonesborough. Without delay, Hood ordered generals Hardee and Lee to Jonesborough. The small force already at the town were ordered to hold their position at all hazards.

Hood still underestimated the strength that marched toward Jonesborough. He assumed it to be three corps and wanted Hardee and Lee to drive them out. On the afternoon of August 31, General Hardee ordered Major General Patrick Cleburne's division to attack the Union right, with Lee's division to advance after Cleburne. The Confederates were outnumbered almost three to one, and suffered a huge number of casualties.

St. Clair-Abrams and his Georgia reserve unit fell into Major General Henry Rootes Jackson's brigade of Major General William Brimage Bates's division, who, while recuperating from a wound, was commanded by Major General John Calvin Brown.

On the night of August 31 and into the morning of September 1, Bate's Division, under Brown, was positioned in the center of a north-south defensive line along the Macon & Western Railroad. He had Cheatham's Division on his left and Cleburne on his right. The line of the three divisions formed a salient. Cleburne had Brigadier General Absalom Baird in front of him. Baird ordered, and personally led, a brigade in a bayonet charge against Brigadier General Daniel Govan's brigade, who were positioned closest to Baird. Hand-to-hand combat ensued. Govan and nearly six-hundred men in his command were captured. As the Federals broke though the lines, the Confederate troops were able to support, fill the gaps, and hold.

By nightfall of September 1, General Hardee was able to withdraw the army south about eight miles to Lovejoy Station without much contention and confusion. The Union scored a major victory at Jonesborough that ended the Atlanta Campaign as General William Tecumseh Sherman's army captured the city of Atlanta the following day - September 2, 1864.

At the Battle of Jonesborough, there was a young enlisted soldier in Cleburne's command, who would cross paths with St. Clair-Abrams twenty years into the future, and forge a friendship of over thirty years. They would be forever linked in the Florida history books. His name was Henry Holcomb Duncan.

HENRY HOLCOMB DUNCAN.

Henry Holcomb Duncan, known to everyone as H. H., was born in Springfield, Illinois. When he was sixteen years old, he enlisted in the Confederate Army. He mustered into the 45th Alabama Infantry, Company C, in May 1862.

Described as slight in form, modest and gentle, yet possessing an indomitable will with the courage of a lion, he survived an apparently mortal wound to his left lung from a Minie ball in the Battle of Stones River in Murfreesboro, Tennessee, on the foggy, cold morning of January 2, 1863. Convalescing in a field hospital, H. H. was captured three days after he received his wound and was sent to City Point, Virginia. After prisoner exchange, he traveled back home to Eufala, Alabama, for the summer, and then rejoined his compatriots, now under the command of General Patrick Cleburne, in time to participate in the Battle of Chickamauga.

During the battle, while shooting through a loophole in the breastworks that his company defended, H. H. took a bullet under his shoulder blade. Again, the resilient young eighteen-year-old recovered and two months later was in the Battle of Missionary Ridge, and other skirmishes, as the Confederate troops fell back toward Atlanta. One of those battles was at Jonesborough, Georgia, twenty miles south of Atlanta.

On November 30, 1864, H. H. performed a heroic feat at the Battle of Franklin, Tennessee. He volunteered to leave the cover of the woods to go out into the open and hand out ammunition to the soldiers who defended in the redoubts as Minie balls flew all around him; and he did this several times. His Union counterparts applauded his valor. Shortly thereafter, in another act of bravery, he was captured as he and others in Company C charged at the Battle of Franklin. He was sent to Camp Douglas Prison in Chicago, Illinois. In the bitter cold of Chicago's winter, he had only a thin blanket for warmth and a strong will to survive.

General Patrick Cleburne, who was extremely admired by H. H. Duncan, fell at the Battle of Franklin on November 30, 1864.

Lieutenant General
Ulysses Simpson Grant
USA

Major General
William Tecumseh Sherman
USA

General Edmund Kirby-Smith
Commander of the Trans-
Mississippi Department,
Vicksburg Campaign
CSA

The First Georgia Reserves fell back seventy miles and regrouped in Macon. They had lost much of their strength at Jonesborough. St. Clair-Abrams received a wound but was able to continue, assuming the position of second sergeant. They remained in Macon through the months of September and October.

General Sherman, meanwhile, remained in Atlanta for over two months, well aware that General John Bell Hood's Army of Tennessee and General Nathan Bedford Forrest's cavalry were still near and could disrupt his intentions to make "Georgia howl" as he boldly and unpleasantly stated.

Sherman issued special field order No. 67 on September 14, 1864 that required all the residents of Atlanta to vacate the city, and travel either north or south. Joanna and her family went as far as Macon, as that is where her husband would be.

On November 12, 1864, Sherman issued an order that the business district of Atlanta be destroyed. Atlanta, though not as big as Augusta and Savannah at this time in history, was a prime supply route and commercial center. Newspapers and communications ran through the city and it served as a base for military operations. Three days later, on November 15, Sherman's forces burned nearly the entire city of Atlanta.

Sherman divided his army into two wings and began his two hundred fifty-mile march to Savannah. The Army of the Tennessee, commanded by Major General Oliver O. Howard, were on the right wing.

In late November, the Georgia reserves prepared to move to Augusta, Georgia, having received an order that they were to support in the defense of the city. The Confederate command believed that's where Sherman was headed, so the reserve militia began their one-hundred-mile journey to Augusta.

On November 21, ten miles east of Macon, near a factory town called Griswoldville, Union cavalry apprehended a train full of military supplies. Before moving on, they burned a saw mill, a grist mill, a cotton gin factory, as well as factories that manufactured furniture and soap.

On the morning of the following day, the 22nd, Brigadier General Charles Carroll Walcutt was ordered by Howard to make a move toward Macon to find out where the Confederate troops were headed. It did not take long before Walcutt ran into General Wheeler's cavalry and an engagement commenced. After some skirmishing, Brigadier General Charles R. Woods ordered Walcutt to fall back and take a position at the Duncan farm and fortify it with artillery and barricades in case the Confederates made a counterattack.

It was there, on that afternoon, about two o'clock, that St. Clair-Abrams, marching with three brigades of Georgia militia on their way to Augusta, were ordered by Brigadier General Pleasant J. Philips to attack the fortified farm. They formed three tight lines and advanced toward Walcutt. They were met with heavy canister shot. The Georgia reserves made it to a ravine, reformed, and attempted three charges. All three charges failed and they were driven back. The militiamen then tried to turn the Union flanks, but the cavalry protected those. Falling back to the ravine, they remained there until dark, and then withdrew. 472 Confederate soldiers were wounded in this battle, including St. Clair-Abrams. It was enough of an injury to end his service in the reserves. He convalesced with the regiment as they fell back to Macon, where he reunited with Joanna. He would not join the remaining reserves on their trek to South Carolina.

The Battle of Griswoldville was considered the first battle of Sherman's March to the Sea. He reached Savannah on December 21, just over a month after he left Atlanta.

By the end of November, many residents, including St. Clair-Abrams and Joanna, began to return to Atlanta. An estimated three-quarters of the city was destroyed and in ashes, but the citizens did not waste time in re-building. The *Atlanta Intelligencer* was still in operation, though only a one-page publication. The newspaper reported that the city was "still viable, but at the same time silent, except for a few howling dogs." Another article written on December 22, 1864, read, "As you reach the city limits, you see the awful effects of one vast extended conflagration. A city destroyed by FIRE! Two-thirds at least devoured by flames. Doomed to utter desolation, one-third of Atlanta still lives. This will be the nucleus, the cornerstone, the foundation upon which the city will again be restored. Of this, more anon."

In early December 1864, Atlanta had an election for mayor, of which James Calhoun was reelected. Also, a new city council was elected and held their first meeting on January 6, 1865. The city's treasury had $1.64. By April 1865, five churches began to hold services. A large inflow of people continued to return to Atlanta through May of 1865. Federal troops, under Major General John Pope, returned after the war during the Reconstruction period. Atlanta began a renaissance, steady and sure, towards prosperity.

Joanna's family businesses had endured heavy damage, except for a warehouse that contained various equipment, including print machines. The burning of Atlanta would not be the last time Joanna would suffer through a massive and devastating fire that would destroy a city. The emotional effect of Atlanta would take a tragic toll on her and St. Clair-Abrams over thirty years in the future.

The war took a turn for the worse for the Confederate army in late 1864. Battles in North Carolina, South Carolina, Florida, and Georgia depleted ammunition, food, supplies and man-power. On April 2, 1865, Richmond was seized and Jefferson Davis evacuated to Georgia and eventually was captured near Irwinville on May 10. On April 9, General Robert E. Lee, not wanting any more bloodshed, surrendered his Army of Northern Virginia to Ulysses S. Grant. On April 26, eleven days after President Lincoln was shot by actor John Wilkes Booth at Ford's Theatre, Johnston surrendered to Sherman. On May 26 in Texas, after he received word about Lee and Johnston, General Edmund Kirby-Smith surrendered the Trans-Mississippi Army. Finally, on June 23 in Oklahoma, Brigadier General Chief Stand Watie, who commanded the First Indian Brigade of the Army of the Trans-Mississippi, surrendered.

And with that, the sun had set on the Confederate States of America, and as author Clement Eaton wrote, "The dying Confederacy passed into the emotional realm of the 'lost cause.'"

Atlanta Intelligencer offices September-October 1864
after General Sherman entered the city.

A FULL

AND

DETAILED HISTORY

OF THE

SEIGE OF VICKSBURG

BY A.S. ABRAMS
OF NEW ORLEANS

ATLANTA, GEORGIA:
INTELLIGENCER STEAM POWER PRESSES
1863

TO

MAJOR GENERAL WM. LORING

THIS HISTORY IS RESPECTFULLY DEDICATED,

IN HUMBLE APPRECIATION OF

HIS SKILL AS AN OFFICER,

THE AUTHOR.

AUTHOR'S PREFACE

Soon after my arrival from Vicksburg, where I was taken prisoner, I contributed two articles to the "Advertiser and Register," of Mobile, Alabama, under the signature of "ONE OF THE GARRISON." One of these articles was an account of the Battle of Baker's Creek and Big Black, and the other a condensed account of the Siege of Vicksburg. The statements made in these two articles were from my own personal observation, and information received from sources of undoubted veracity.

The appearance of my two articles became the theme of criticisms by the press. Some of which were favorable, but others bitterly denounced the author as having acted through a feeling of prejudice against General Pemberton. Aware, as I am, that none in the Confederacy acted in a more cordial manner towards that General's control of the Army of Vicksburg than I did, I did not notice the many denunciatory remarks made, at the time, but compiled the work presented for the purpose of showing, that instead of being as censorious as the case allowed, I had kept silent in many things, which, had they been made public, would have raised a clamor against General Pemberton of a far more violent nature than what was hurled at him.

The author claims the right of knowing as much about the siege of Vicksburg as any one residing in that town, from the fact that he was at that point, in Company A, Withers' Light Artillery, as a private, when the first gun was fired in its defense, and served as such until the raising of the first siege. In September, 1862, he was discharged from the army on account of sickness, and being unable to return to his home, (New Orleans) obtained a position in the office of the "Vicksburg Whig," where he remained until its destruction by fire in the early part of May, 1863, and was taken prisoner and paroled after the surrender.

All the statements made in this work were either the result of the Author's observation, or obtained from parties whose standing in the Army warrants the Author in saying that the statements are beyond dispute, and, did not military law prevent it, the names of *many* prominent officers could be called in corroboration of all that is written in this work. My remarks are not only my own opinions, but the conclusions to which nine-tenths of the officers comprising the garrison of Vicksburg arrived at some time before the attack on Grand Gulf, and verified by the results following.

All that has been said or written, in defense of Gen. Pemberton's campaign, is fairly laid before the public, at the same time the Author brings forward all the evidence possible to prove that the defense is not one to which any credence can be attached. He, however, leaves it to the judgment of the reader, whether the defense made is sufficiently strong to falsify his assertions.

In conclusion the Author would say, that although aware of the many criticisms that a work of this nature will be subject to, he gives it to the public without fearing the censure of any. To those *not interested* in defending Gen. Pemberton from the errors he committed during the campaign, the work presented to the public will be recognized as, if a severe, at least a just account of all that transpired in Mississippi; and to those who *are interested* in defending Gen. Pemberton, as soon as the censure of this work is made public, the Author flatters himself of his ability *to lay bare the motives which prompted the defense.* Conscious that this work has been written in the firm belief of its truth, favorable criticism will be welcome; but the censure and denunciations of the press will not cause the least regret that he has given truths and facts to the public as they occurred.

A. S. ABRAMS

ATLANTA, GEORGIA, NOVEMBER, 1863.

THE SIEGE OF VICKSBURG.

CHAPTER I.
THE FIRST SIEGE, IN 1862.

On the 18th day of May, 1862, the advance division of Commodore Farragut's fleet, under Lieutenant Lee, United States Navy, arrived below Vicksburg, from New Orleans, and demanded the surrender of the city. (It may be proper to state, that as soon as New Orleans fell, the heights of Vicksburg were fortified, it is said by advice of Gen. Beauregard.) The demand was refused, and the Federal commander gave twenty-four hours' notice for the women and children to quit the town.

In accordance with the notice, Major General, then Brigadier General, M. L. Smith, commanding the defenses, ordered all non-combatants to leave the town, and actively prepared for the enemy. At this time the garrison consisted of the following regiments: the 26th, 27th, 28th, 30th, 31st and 4th Louisiana infantry; the 1st regiment and 8th battalion of Louisiana heavy artillery; 1st Tennessee heavy artillery; 3rd Mississippi battalion of infantry; Withers' light artillery regiment of two batteries, and Stark's regiment of cavalry.

On the 26th of May the first bombardment took place, and was continued with little or no damage to the forts, until the departure of the fleet.

The enemy's land forces, under Brigadier General Williams, occupied the Louisiana shore, nearly opposite Warrenton, and about twelve miles below Vicksburg, to the number of 6,000, but attempted no demonstration against the city, being kept there more as a corps of observation, than for the purpose of making an offensive movement.

It had been a matter of surprise to a great many persons, that Vicksburg was not then attacked by land, as from the feeble nature of our defenses, and the small number of men defending it, we could easily have been defeated in a pitched battle and driven out; but General Butler lacked both the capacity and force to attempt an enterprise of so bold a nature. Besides which, Memphis being in our possession then, and Beauregard confronting Halleck with an army of tried veterans, any serious attack on Vicksburg, if defeated, would have placed Butler in New Orleans and Halleck before Corinth, in a very dangerous position, so that, taking all things into consideration, it is now evident that the enemy was not then prepared to take Vicksburg, and the bombardment was only to keep us on the *quivive*, and compel us to mass troops there; thus either weakening, or preventing reinforcements from going to, Beauregard, so that Halleck would be enabled to overpower and destroy the only barrier to his sweeping through Mississippi, Tennessee and Alabama. That that was the plan, after events made evident.

The capture of New Orleans was an event less expected by the enemy than by our people. The attack on the forts was for the same purpose as the after bombardment of Vicksburg, viz: to keep us on the alert, and prevent any troops from being sent to Beauregard. The capture of New Orleans did them more harm than good, and had we neglected to fortify Vicksburg, and held Memphis, the result would have been greatly in our favor; for, by sending the 10,000 or 12,000 troops defending Vicksburg to Corinth, Beauregard would have been able to assume the offensive and drive Halleck from Tennessee. Butler's force in Louisiana was scarcely more than enough to hold the city of New Orleans; therefore, no attempt of a serious nature would have been made to penetrate the interior of the State of Mississippi. But to resume our account of the first siege.

On the 28th of June, 1862, the first serious assault was made by the enemy on water. At about two o'clock on the morning of that day, seven of the enemy's boats advanced in front of the city, and attempted to pass the batteries. A terrific bombardment ensued, but in consequence of our having only seven guns mounted at that time, the attempt was successful, and the fleet passed up.

Soon after the commencement of the siege, Major General Earl Van Dorn was sent to Vicksburg, and placed in command over Brigadier General M. L. Smith. His arrival was hailed with joy by the people of Mississippi, as an advent of success to our arms, Gen. Van Dorn having the reputation of being a "fighting man." Soon after his arrival, the garrison was reinforced by Major General Breckinridge's division, from Beauregard's army.

The bombardment progressed slowly until the 15th of July, when the Confederate ram *Arkansas* successfully run the gauntlet, through thirty of the enemy's gun and mortar boats. This feat, in point of daring, was the most brilliant and successful of the war, and reflected great credit on Lieutenant Brown, the commander. In referring to this boat, we cannot resist, making a few observations on the folly of Gen. Van Dorn in sending her to Baton Rouge, as, if she had been kept at Vicksburg, after the occupation of Port Hudson, she would have been the means of keeping the river open between that place and Vicksburg. Not a single Yankee transport would have dared to pass our batteries, though fear of being captured or destroyed by her, and those gunboats which had the temerity to venture past, would have fallen an easy prey to her, aided as she would have been by the gunboats Webb and Beatty. The end of this famous ram was her destruction near Baton Rouge, where she had gone for the purpose of co-operating with the land forces under Van Dorn. Her machinery is said to have been damaged on the trip, and she was blown up to prevent her falling into the hands of the enemy.

At about seven o'clock on the morning of the same day that the *Arkansas* ran past the Yankee fleet, five of their gun boats came down and endeavored to cut the Arkansas from her moorings under our batteries. The effort was unsuccessful, and they were compelled to hasten down the river, two of their boats having been severely damaged by our guns.

Nothing of interest transpired from that time until the 25th of July, 1862, when the two fleets retired, having accomplished nothing more than keeping eight or ten thousand men idle at that point.

It was during this siege that the Confederate troops discovered the comparative harmlessness of mortar shells. Heretofore these missiles had been looked upon with great awe by our army. The gunboat panic also died away at this time, it having been found by long experience that they were not half so formidable as fear had pictured them.

During this siege, which lasted six weeks, the entire number of shells thrown from the enemy's boats, were estimated at from 25,000 to 30,000. The casualties resulting from this large number were surprisingly small; there being but twenty-two soldiers killed and wounded, and one female and a negro killed. The female referred to was a most estimable lady named Mrs. Gamble, who had won the esteem of all who knew her, by her many amiable qualities, and among the soldiers was looked upon with great respect and friendship, for her constant and untiring kindness to them.

It was during the first siege of Vicksburg that the heroism of Southern women was fully illustrated. On the morning the 28th of June, when the enemy's fleet passed our batteries, going up the river, and shells were falling thick as hail in the streets of the city, crowds of ladies could have been seen on the "Court House," "Sky Parlor," and other prominent places in the city, gazing upon, as they termed it, the "magnificent scene."

On the departure of the United States fleet from Vicksburg, Gen. Breckinridge's division, together with the 4th Louisiana regiment, departed from Vicksburg for Baton Rouge.

Thus ended the first siege of Vicksburg, in which nothing was gained by the Confederate forces to have warranted the amount of consequence placed upon its successful defense. The enemy never attempted any attack by land on it, and the demonstrations of the fleet, even had they been successful, would have been of no avail without a corresponding success on the part of their land forces. It is true that the importance of the position was as much magnified in the North as it was in the South, and the failure to capture the city, made them as despondent as it made us rejoice.

CHAPTER II.
INTERIM BETWEEN THE FIRST AND SECOND SIEGE.

After the departure of the enemy's fleet, business in a great measure resumed its wonted activity. Port Hudson having been occupied by the Confederate forces, had been fortified, thus giving us control of the river from that point to Vicksburg; trade revived with Red River, and steamboats regularly arrived. It was at this time that the city should have been placed in a position to sustain a protracted siege, as there was always a sufficient supply of beeves in Texas to have enabled us to procure any number without difficulty; corn was also in abundance, and could have been bought cheap at that time.

Soon after the fatal battle of Corinth, Major Gen. Earl Van Dorn was removed from command, and Major Gen. Pemberton was placed in command of the Department of Mississippi and East Louisiana, and in consequence of his being out-ranked by both Gen.

Van Dorn and Gen. Lovell, was soon after appointed a Lieutenant General. With almost a unanimous voice, his appointment to such a responsible position was the subject of regret. It had been known that Gen. Pemberton was in favor of evacuating all points held by our forces on the water, and had actually recommended the destruction of the works in Charleston harbor, and the evacuation of the city. It was, therefore, a matter of great surprise, when it was announced that he was appointed to command a place that, since the fall of Memphis, had been universally acknowledged as one of the most important positions in the Confederacy. Gen. Pemberton was not a man that had won a name for capacity during the war. He had never been on a battle-field, and bore no reputation as a commander. And here it was that the President made the only grave error that has given cause to censure his administration.

During the time that elapsed from the departure of the enemy's fleet to the arrival of Lieutenant General Pemberton, several additional batteries had been erected above the town, and breastworks had been thrown up from Chickasaw Bayou to Snyder's Bluff on the Yazoo river, which point had also been fortified, for the purpose of preventing the enemy's boats from ascending the river.

The number of guns mounted at this time, along the river, did not exceed eighteen, and of these not more than four or five were of large calibre.

On the arrival of Lieutenant General Pemberton, the people anticipated that immediate steps would have been taken to procure a number of the heaviest kind of guns, and that new batteries would have been immediately erected. To their utter astonishment the Lieutenant General remained in Jackson, and except an occasional visit, appeared to forget that such a place existed as Vicksburg. Absolutely nothing was done for the further defense of the city. Not a single additional gun was mounted and no means whatever taken to strengthen our position, until after the battle of Chickasaw Bayou, when the Lieut. General appeared for a moment to awake from his lethargy

It was reasonably supposed, while we held possession of the river, from Port Hudson to Vicksburg, that prompt measures would have been taken to transport all the provisions possible from Louisiana and Texas to Vicksburg, but such was not the case. Boat after boat arrived, and nothing could be seen but sugar and molasses.

Ostensibly all that arrived (or nearly all) was for the government, but if the assertions of many respectable men can be believed, such was not the case, for a great deal of it belonged to private individuals, who had it transported on government boats for a share of the profits accruing from its sale. The importance of provisioning Vicksburg was forgotten in the thirst for speculation.

In the month of December, it was announced through the Northern press that Major General McClernand was entrusted with the opening of the Mississippi river, and although the people of Mississippi had become thoroughly disgusted with the gross mismanagement of the department, many believed that the warning would avail, and prompt measures would be taken to place Vicksburg in an efficient state of defense; but it was not so. Still the same apathy was evinced by Lieutenant General Pemberton, and nothing was done. This fact was well known to the press of Vicksburg, but from fear of its giving aid to the enemy, nothing was said in condemnation of the course pursued. Once or twice, when some disgraceful circumstance had occurred, the voice of censure would be heard; but as this was of rare occurrence, in this way the public outside of Vicksburg were led to believe that everything necessary had been performed for its defense. None supposed, with the fall of New Orleans before him, that Lieutenant General Pemberton would neglect to perform those duties apparent to the meanest private in the army. To the disgrace of the country be it known, that the work of throwing up fortifications, provisioning the city, and procuring a proper supply of ammunition, was left solely to the superintendence of subordinate officers.

We strive in vain to find one single act of Lieutenant General Pemberton that can entitle him to praise. Everything that comes before us wears an aspect of incompetency; and from the facts before us we are compelled to say, that had a Lee, a Beauregard, a Bragg, or a Johnston been appointed to defend it, Vicksburg would never have fallen, as those Generals would never have been guilty of the gross ignorance that characterized the movements of Lieutenant General Pemberton.

There are five things that occurred in the control of his department, for which we look in vain for some excuse, whereby we can in some measure remove the responsibility from General Pemberton's shoulders. First. The cause of there not being enough provisions to have lasted a siege of six months, stored away in the city. Second. The neglect to reinforce Brigadier General Bowen with sufficient troops to hold the enemy in check until Johnston could arrive with reinforcements. Third. The cause of our fortifications around Vicksburg not being completed during the five months preceding the siege. Fourth. The reason of the works being so defective, that the damage done to them in the day, from the fire of the enemy, could not be fully repaired by a large force of laborers in the night. Fifth. The cause of our army remaining on the west of Big Black river, while the enemy were marching, with their rear exposed, towards Jackson, and the majority of our officers favored an advance movement; and why it was that the advance was not made when General Johnston ordered it. We look in vain for some excuse to palliate these errors, and are compelled, however reluctantly, to come to the conclusion, that it was through gross neglect of duty that Vicksburg was not provisioned largely; that it was through mismanagement that we lost the battle of Baker's Creek; that it was through incompetency that Bowen was not reinforced; that it was through a proper want of skill and energy that the works around the city were not completed before our army fell back into Vicksburg; and that it was through a want of generalship that the enemy was allowed to march towards Jackson without General Pemberton promptly attacking him in the rear.

To every one of these errors, we find circumstances of so glaring a character that nothing said will ever satisfy the people that they were unavoidable. With respect to the provisioning of Vicksburg, we must emphatically deny that there was any difficulty in provisioning it. Many of the planters voluntarily offered their crops to the government for a small price, or *free of charge*. Among these are Col. Benson Blake, now in the Confederate Army, Col. Auter, Dr. P. H. Cook, and others, all men of standing and respectability in the State; and a short time before the investment, a committee of three planters arrived in Vicksburg, with an offer from the planters of the Yazoo and Deer Creek districts, to give the government all their crops *free of charge*, if the officials at Vicksburg would haul it away. These gentlemen, on arriving, went from one quartermaster to the other, and from one commissary to the other, but each of the parties thus applied to, disclaimed being the proper one to receive their offer, and stated that they were unable to inform the committee who the proper person was. The committee, after using their best endeavors to find someone to deliver the offer to, and seeing that the utmost indifference was manifested by the parties to whom they tendered their offer, whether it was accepted or not, became disgusted and returned home.

With respect to the reinforcing of Bowen at Grand Gulf, we can only say that it was the almost unanimous opinion of' our Generals that the battle of Vicksburg ought to have been fought there, and it is the general belief that had our entire army been massed at that point, we could have defeated Grant, and driven him into the river.

The battle of Baker's Creek, and the defect in our works around Vicksburg, will be referred to in another portion of this book.

CHAPTER III.
INTERIM BETWEEN FIRST AND SECOND SIEGE (continued.)

During the period elapsing between the first and second siege, the city had assumed a busy appearance; numerous stores were opened, and business, in a great measure, resumed its wonted activity.

The entire strength of our river batteries, at this time, did not exceed twenty-three guns, mounted along a space of several miles from near the Village of Warrenton to a place called Mint Spring, above the city. This small number of guns was inadequate to prevent the passage of the enemy's boats, as was afterwards proven by the safe running past of the *Queen of the West*, *Indianola, Monarch* and *Lancaster*, and the passage of the enemy's fleet of gunboats and transports, on the night of the twenty-second of April. While acknowledging that the number of guns was insufficient to prevent their passage entirely, we insist that had a proper degree of vigilance been exercised by the officers commanding our batteries, the enemy could never have succeeded in passing his boats without having at least one-half of them destroyed; but no vigilance was exercised, no discipline kept up among the officers; it was one constant scene of merriment among those who were not devotees to Bacchus, and one uninterrupted course of drunken brawls among those that were. Any quantity of officers, dressed up in all the toggery of gold lace and brass buttons, could be seen promenading the streets, and a civilian could scarcely enter a private residence without finding three or four of these gentry on a visit. So outrageous had this laxity of discipline become, that the press of Vicksburg was at last compelled to call attention to it. The censure had little or no effect, and the same course was pursued.

On the commencement of the month of December, the movements of the United States army plainly indicated that the storm, which had been so long gathering, would soon burst upon the devoted city, and the first intimation received was the landing of Sherman's corps on the Yazoo, and which resulted in the battles of the 28th, 29th and 30th of December, and known as the battles of Chickasaw Bayou, an account of which we will give in the following chapter.

CHAPTER IV.
THE BATTLES OF CHICKASAW BAYOU.

Chickasaw Bayou is situated about three miles above Vicksburg, and is a low and swampy portion of the County of Warren, in Mississippi. When the Yazoo river rises and overflows its banks, the water runs over that section of the county, and forms the Bayou from whence its name is derived.

A long line of breastworks and rifle-pits had been built at this place, extending in a zigzag line from our river batteries, above Vicksburg, to the fortifications on the Yazoo river, near Snyder's Bluff. The position was of great natural strength, being largely intersected with creeks and swamps, and offered great impediment to the advance of hostile forces.

On the morning of the 28th of December, the enemy having landed commenced driving in our pickets, and threw forward a body of infantry to throw a pontoon bridge across a creek that lay between them and our works. The building of the pontoon was stoutly resisted for some time, but artillery having been brought to bear upon our men they were forced to retire, and the enemy crossed over that night. Skirmishing lasted all day, with few or no casualties to the Confederate forces.

On the morning of the 29th the enemy, in strong force, advanced on our works, with the intention of storming them. They marched up with great regularity and firmness to the charge, and as soon as they arrived within one hundred yards from our works, gave a cheer and rushed on. They were gallantly met by our forces under Brigadier General, now Major General, Stephen D. Lee, of South Carolina, composed of a brigade of Louisianians, and after a severe engagement repulsed with great slaughter. Our army, a few days previous, had been reinforced by General Stephenson, with a division composed of Tennesseans, Georgians and Alabamians, who aided greatly in repulsing the enemy. The fighting of the 28th and 17th Louisiana was of the most gallant character possible. Although this battle was the first one in which the 28th was engaged, and the first time they had been under fire, they withstood several severe assaults of the enemy, repulsing him each time, and holding their position throughout the day. The fighting of the 17th Louisiana was also splendid. Unaided, these gallant men, under the command of the brave Richardson, defeated and put to flight three full regiments of the enemy, led by Brig. General Blair of the United States army.

On the morning of the next day (the 30th) the enemy made a desperate assault on our right wing, with a body of picked men, numbering, it is estimated, from 8,000 to 10,000. They advanced with courage, and made the attack with spirit. Our forces met them with equal gallantry, and very soon a desperate struggle for mastery commenced. The enemy made desperate efforts to storm our lines, but was resisted with success by our forces. Three times he appeared upon the point of carrying the works, and as many times, by dint of great exertion and heroism, was driven back with heavy loss. The battle continued long and desperate. Wherever the danger was greatest, the gallant Lee could be seen urging on his men, and inspiring them with fresh courage. At last, a flank movement was made by our forces, sallying from the breastworks and attacking the enemy on his flank, routing him, and compelling him to leave some four hundred prisoners in our hands. This *coup de etat* put an end to the battle, the enemy having been punished too severely to attempt another assault. Soon after his defeat, the enemy sent in a flag of truce, requesting permission to bury their dead. Under cover of this, many of the prisoners escaped.

Our loss in these battles did not exceed one hundred and twenty in killed and wounded. Among our killed was Captain Hamilton Paul, Assistant Adjutant General, on Brig. General S. D. Lee's staff.

He was a young man of great promise, and had gained the esteem and friendship of all who knew him.

The loss of the enemy is roughly estimated at twenty-five hundred killed and wounded, and about four hundred prisoners. In the last day's battle, we captured five stands of colors from the enemy, as well as all the small arms left by them in their retreat.

After the battle of the 30th, no engagement of any magnitude took place; the next night the enemy re-embarked in their boats, and returned to Memphis.

CHAPTER V.
RETURN OF THE ENEMY.

Vicksburg is situated on the Mississippi river, about five hundred and thirty miles from the Gulf of Mexico, and is built on a plateau of hills rising about two hundred feet above the water. These hills slope gradually upwards from the banks of the river, except in the upper portion of the city, where they rise precipitously and form cliffs, towering over the banks of the river. Northward, above the city, are a tier of hills generally known as the "Walnut Hills." The Mississippi river takes an abrupt turn at this point, forming a peninsula of that portion of Louisiana, opposite Vicksburg, for about two miles, when it makes another abrupt angle. Nine miles above this second curve in the river, the Yazoo empties itself. The rear of the city is a succession of hills, and the general feature of the country is broken and largely intersected with ravines. It is also greatly cut up by bayous and creeks, formed by the rain and overflow of the numerous springs which are to be found over the whole country.

Below Vicksburg, at Warrenton, the country is low and marshy for about six hundred yards from the banks of the river, when it makes an abrupt rise, forming a line of almost mountainous heights.

The country around Vicksburg is very fruitful. Large crops of cotton were usually made, and at the time we are speaking of, a very extensive crop of corn and other cereals had been planted. A large quantity of corn and bacon fell into the hands of the enemy on their march to Vicksburg; so large, in fact, that from Gen. Grant's official report, the entire Yankee army subsisted for eight days on what they found in the different plantations around Vicksburg, and during the entire siege their horses and mules used no other corn but that of the surrounding planters.

From the time the attack on our works on Chickasaw Bayou was made, to the return of the enemy, but little or nothing was done to strengthen our position. The fortifications in the rear of the city were commenced, but progressed slowly. It was not anticipated that they would be required, but to use the words of a prominent officer there, were "only thrown up to satisfy the public." In another portion of this book, we will make further remarks on the line of defenses that encircled Vicksburg.

On the 22nd of January, 1863, intelligence was received that fifty gunboats and transports had passed Greenville, coming down, and the following day a large fleet laden with troops arrived at the bend of the river above Vicksburg, known as "Young's Point." As soon as the boats arrived, the enemy landed on the Louisiana shore, at a place called " White's Plantation," which in a few hours became dotted with tents. The gigantic plan of cutting a canal through the lower end of the peninsula was then put in motion, with what success we shall hereafter relate. No demonstration was attempted against the city, until the morning of the 1st of February, when the ram *Queen of the West* ran past the batteries in open daylight.

CHAPTER VI.
RUNNING OF THE BATTERIES BY THE RAM
QUEEN OF THE WEST.

At about half past four o'clock on the morning of the 1st of February, a black smoke was observed moving slowly down the river, and shortly after, one of the enemy's cotton-clad rams, which was afterwards discovered to be the *Queen of the West*, was seen turning the point above the city. Not a shot having been fired at her, she slowly continued her course, and had almost got out of range of the water batteries above the city, known as the "Mint Spring battery," before a gun was fired. Just as she was on the point of going round the bend, the guard gave the alarm, and the water battery opened on her. Only a few rounds were fired, when she steamed across the river, and hugged the Mississippi shore, thus getting out of range of the water battery. From the great height of the hill batteries, the guns could not be depressed sufficiently to bear upon the ram, until she had gone some distance. At that time no guns had been mounted in front of the city, so that she continued her course without receiving any material damage, until she had arrived opposite where the hull of the steamer *Vicksburg* lay, when, reversing her engines, she made a dash at the boat with the intention of sinking it, her officers being under the impression that we were building a gunboat. The current of the river caused her to sheer off without doing any damage to the boat. She immediately tacked about, and was about to repeat the blow, when a shot from one of our batteries near the railroad depot struck her on the prow, evidently causing some damage, as she relinquished her purpose, and continued her way down the river.

The batteries by this time were in full play, and belched out a constant and rapid stream of shot and shell, but without any effect, as the most of the balls fell short of the boat. The *Queen of the West* steamed slowly down the river, and in a few minutes had safely passed out of range of our lower batteries. That she had sustained some injury was evident, as she remained several days moored up to the Louisiana shore, receiving repairs. Reports from the United States say that she was struck eleven times.

The neglect of duty in permitting the *Queen of the West* to turn the point above the city before a shot was fired at her, and the dilatory manner in which all the batteries acted, raised a cry of indignation among the citizens of Vicksburg, who were well aware of the cause. The statement that we now give, was witnessed by the author, who can vouch for its truth. As soon as the first gun was fired from our batteries on the ram, a party of men, wearing the uniform of officers, were seen issuing from a building on Washington street, known as the "Apollo Hall." This building is a theater, the rooms of which are constantly open. The men referred to were officers in command of our batteries, *who had been in this building all night on a drunken spree.*

The same day that the *Queen of the West* passed our batteries, ten deserters from the 31st Wisconsin regiment, came across the river and reported Grant's army as numbering from 50,000 to 60,000 men. They also stated that great dissatisfaction existed among the troops on the peninsula, the majority of them being desirous of return in to Memphis. These statements, coming from deserters, did not gain much credit.

CHAPTER VII.
PASSAGE OF THE INDIANOLA AND HER CAPTURE.

A few nights after the running of our batteries by the *Queen of the West*, a black object was descried moving down the river. The night was extremely dark, so dark in fact that the peninsula opposite our batteries could scarcely be distinguished. Our guns, however, opened fire on the object, but without being able to take aim with any accuracy. After firing a few rounds our cans ceased, there being an opinion among the officers that the object seen was nothing but a tree floating down the river. Two or three days after it was discovered to be the iron-clad gunboat *Indianola* that had passed down.

The *Queen of the West* had, by this time, been captured by our batteries on Red River. She was soon repaired, and starting up to Vicksburg with the ram *Webb* and gunboat *Beatty,* effected the destruction of the *Indianola*. The battle that took place between her and the Confederate boats was a short but spirited one. The immense superiority in strength, and the size of her guns, gave the *Indianola* a physical advantage over her opponents, which were wooden boats.

The *Indianola* had been chased up the river, to a short distance above Grand Gulf, when she stopped and offered battle. The challenge was quickly accepted. Our little fleet advanced in the following manner: The *Queen of the West* first, the *Webb* second, and the *Beatty* bringing up the rear. The *Queen of the West* ran rapidly pass the *Indianola*, pouring a broadside into her, but without effect. The *Webb*, reversing her engines, made a dart upon the *Indianola*, striking her full on the stern, below water mark. The *Indianola* had been making a gallant resistance all the time, but on being pierced by the ram of the *Webb*, commenced sinking rapidly. She then struck her colors and surrendered to the Confederate fleet. Her officers and crew were transported to the *Beatty*, and soon after sent to Vicksburg.

All the damage sustained by our little fleet, was the twisting of the *Webb's* ram, in her endeavor to extricate herself from the *Indianola* after striking her. All effort to save the *Indianola* was unavailing, and she now lies sunk in twenty feet of water. The loss in killed and wounded on both sides, during the engagement, was small.

CHAPTER VIII.
CUTTING THE CANAL - YAZOO PASS EXPEDITION - SECOND SHELLING OF VICKSBURG.

While these events were transpiring, Grant was hard at work cutting a Canal through the peninsula. The work was prosecuted with great vigor, day and night, for nearly two months, without accomplishing the desired object, namely: the turning of the current of the Mississippi river. It was stated, by deserters, that not less than six thousand soldiers and negroes were kept constantly at work widening the ditch and making it deeper, but without any effect, as not more than three or four feet of water entered the Canal.

Finding this project a failure, the Yazoo pass expedition was undertaken, but that also resulted in a failure, the enemy being repulsed at "Fort Pemberton" by the Confederate forces under Major General Loring. Although this movement may be regarded as a portion of the operations against Vicksburg, but few notes were taken by us, hence the meagre account we give.

Having been repulsed in their Yazoo pass exhibition, the enemy's boats returned in the early part of March, and on the ninth day of that month, two of their gunboats steamed down to the Louisiana shore, on the west side of the peninsula, and commenced throwing shells in the city; nearly all of them, however, fell short, and those that did fall in the streets did no damage to the soldiers or citizens.

On the same day, two dredge boats were observed for the first time in the canal. Our canal batteries opened fire as soon as they were perceived, and after a sharp cannonading, compelled the enemy to remove the boats. The fire from our battery, bearing upon the mouth of the canal, was then kept up constantly, with great effect, the enemy being prevented from working the boats.

During this week, large bodies of Federal troops were observed massing on the Louisiana shore, opposite Warrenton, and the idea became strong, that the long looked-for offensive movement was at last in progress.

CHAPTER IX.
OCCUPATION OF GRAND GULF.

A short time before the naval engagement at Port Hudson, which resulted in the passage of the United States steamers, *Hartford* and *Albatross*, the town of Grand Gulf was occupied by the Confederate forces, under Brigadier General Bowen, and a battery of six guns mounted on the banks of the river. A line of breastworks had also been made around the position.

Grand Gulf is situated on the East bank of the Mississippi river, immediately below the mouth of the Big Black river. Southeast of Grand Gulf is Port Gibson, and below Grand Gulf, Northwest of Port Gibson, on the banks of the river, is Bruinsburg.

The position at Grand Gulf was defended by two brigades of Missouri and Arkansas volunteers, under Brigadier General Bowen, of Missouri. This officer, a native of Georgia, but for many years an adopted son of Missouri, was one of the bravest officers in the Confederate army, and his fighting qualities had won for him a favorable name throughout the Confederacy. This gallant man, having passed unscathed through the siege of Vicksburg, died at Clinton on his way from Vicksburg to Brandon, Mississippi, on the 24th of July, 1863, from a disease contracted during the siege. His gallantry and ability as an officer had just been rewarded by a Major General's commission.

The position at Grand Gulf was naturally strong; and but for the flank movement of the enemy, and the want of reinforcements, could have been held for an indefinite period.

CHAPTER X.
ATTEMPTED PASSAGE OF THE RAMS,
LANCASTER AND MONARCH.

On the morning of the 25th of March, two of the enemy's rams, afterwards ascertained to be the *Lancaster* and *Monarch*, made an attempt to pass our batteries. For the first time, everything was prepared for them; and as soon as they commenced turning the bend of the river above the city, our batteries opened a terrific fire. At the same moment, two buildings on the crest of the peninsula were set on fire by our pickets, and, the light spreading a ray across the river, gave our gunners full view of the two boats. With increased rapidity, solid shot was hurled at them, but they calmly and slowly continued their way, as if certain they could not be destroyed. Our men at the batteries worked with the determination that they should not run the gauntlet uninjured, and redoubled their energies. It was apparent to the spectators, that both boats had been struck; but as they still steamed on their way, it was not believed that the damage done was of any consequence.

This engagement was a grand and magnificent spectacle. The day was just breaking, and the mimic thunder from our guns, the flash of light as they were fired, the piercing scream of the missiles as they sped through the air, blended with the soft light of the breaking day, and formed one of the greatest pyrotechnical displays ever witnessed.

The boats proceeded slowly down the river, followed by a constant stream of shot and shell from our batteries, but still they steamed down as if unhurt. A deep feeling of humiliation pervaded the spectators and men at the batteries, and curses loud and deep were spoken. At last, just as one of them came opposite our batteries at the railroad depot, a well-aimed shot from a ten-inch gun pierced her, and she ceased moving. In a few moments, she commenced to sink amid the cheers of the gunners and the crowd that were looking on. The *Lancaster*, for that was the name of the ram, continued slowly sinking for about fifteen minutes, when she careened, and soon nothing was seen but a dark speck on the water to denote what had become of the once boastful and defiant enemy. As soon as she commenced sinking, her officers and crew took to her boats and escaped to the peninsula, but nothing else was saved from her.

The remaining ram, the *Monarch*, having been struck repeatedly, soon became disabled, but not enough to sink her. She slowly floated down the river, under a heavy fire from our lower batteries, and, in a few minutes, had passed out of range. As soon as she had escaped the fire of our batteries, the *Albatross*, which had come up from Port Hudson with the *Hartford*, met and towed her to the landing on the Louisiana shore, opposite Warrenton. The damage done to this boat was of so severe a nature, that new machinery had to be transported across the peninsula for her; and it took several days before she could be repaired.

The damage done to these two boats, in this attempt to pass our batteries, fully sustained the opinion that we could always inflict great injury on the enemy in these demonstrations, if the necessary amount of vigilance was exercised by the officers commanding our batteries. The result of this engagement, in such glaring contrast with that of the *Queen of the West*, became a subject of remark; and all in Vicksburg anticipated that hence forth the officers would dispense with frivolities, and recollect they were engaged in war with the enemy then before them.

CHAPTER XI.
FAILURE OF THE CANAL - CHANGE OF PLANS.

Strenuous efforts had, meantime, been made by the Federals to succeed in their canal, but the "Father of Waters" remained obstinate, and would not consent to "change his base." Finding all efforts fruitless, the work was abandoned; and, the enemy despairing of capturing Vicksburg, decided upon abandoning their operations, and returning to Memphis. Preparations were made for their departure, and all their tents struck, when Major General Thomas, Adjutant General of the United States, and a renegade Southerner, arrived at Big Black. He immediately countermanded the order to return, and formed a plan which resulted in the downfall of Vicksburg.

This plan was to ran a fleet of transports pass the batteries, and cross troops from the Louisiana shore below Vicksburg to Mississippi, and then march their army through the country to the rear of Vicksburg. This plan, although the most dangerous of all yet conceived, and apparently the fruits of despair, was adopted, and a move on Vicksburg was immediately resolved upon. On the night of the 22nd of April, the first demonstration was made in accordance with the newly-formed plan by the running pass our batteries of three gunboats and seven transports, an account of which we will give in the next chapter.

CHAPTER XII.
PASSAGE OF THE ENEMY'S FLEET,
AND ATTACK ON GRAND GULF.

This successful demonstration, while it does credit to the enemy, reflects the deepest dishonor on the Confederate arms. Repeated warnings had failed to impress upon the minds of our officers the fact that that time was not one intended for mirth and revelry. They still continued to pursue the course which had been the subject of censure; and on the night the enemy's fleet passed down, a large number of officers were attending a ball given in the city, and not until our upper batteries opened fire, were they aware of the proximity of the enemy's fleet.

The passing of our batteries by the enemy, took place on Wednesday night, the 22nd of April, at about half past twelve o'clock. At this hour the Yankee fleet, consisting of three gunboats and seven transports, was observed moving down the river. Our pickets, on the peninsula opposite, promptly gave the alarm, and at the same time set fire to two buildings in De Soto, the name of the village on the peninsula, for the purpose of illuminating the river. From some cause unknown, the fire burned badly. Instead of issuing in a bright blaze, it sent up a dense smoke which enveloped the river, and, with the exception of one beam reflected across the river, completely obscured the boats. Our guns, however, opened a heavy fire on them, but without doing any damage of consequence. One small boat was set on fire and burnt in front of the city, but the others, aided by the darkness, and the unusually random firing of our men, succeeded in passing safely.

The fleet, after getting out of range of our guns, which by this time, was increased to the number of twenty-eight, moved to the Louisiana shore, opposite Warrenton, where they remained for three or four days. We own that there were many obstacles to our preventing the enemy from making the passage, but give it as our opinion that considerable more damage could have been done to them had the officers been at their post.

We omitted to mention in our description of the passage of the fleet, that all the transports were protected by bales of Cotton and Hay lashed to both sides, and almost obscuring the boats. This was another drawback to our doing any damage, for we had not the means at our disposal to set the Cotton and Hay on fire.

As soon as the enemy's fleet had passed, the Yankee plan of campaign became fully developed, and all anticipated an attack on Grand Gulf. In confirmation of this belief, on the 28th day of April, the fleet, having previously gone down the river, attacked our batteries at that place. An engagement between the gunboats and our land batteries then took place, and after lasting for six and a half hours, the enemy retired, foiled in his attempt to silence them. Our loss on that day was twelve killed and wounded. Among the former was Col. Wade, Chief of Artillery for Bowen's division, and a gallant officer.

The next day the enemy's fleet, consisting of two gunboats and six transports, lashed together, ran past the batteries under a terrific fire, but which did them but little damage, our guns not being large enough. They then proceeded down until they came to the Louisiana shore, opposite Bruinsburg, Miss. The enemy's troops had previously been marched through Louisiana to the vicinity of St. Joseph, opposite Bruinsburg. They were then transported across the river, numbering, as was estimated by themselves, between fifty thousand and sixty thousand men. To oppose this force, Brigadier General Bowen's command did not exceed three thousand. The brigades of General Baldwin from Smith's division, and Colonel, now Brig. Gen., Reynolds from Stephenson's, were placed at his disposal as reinforcements, but remained in Vicksburg until called for.

CHAPTER XIII.
LANDING OF THE ENEMY AND
BATTLE OF PORT GIBSON.

Bruinsburg, Mississippi, is situated on the banks of the Mississippi river, about twelve miles below Grand Gulf, and at the mouth of Bayou Pierre. At this point the enemy landed between fifty and sixty thousand men on the 30th of April, and prepared for an advance movement.

As soon as General Bowen received information of their landing, he crossed Bayou Pierre and advanced towards Port Gibson, situated several miles southeast of Grand Gulf. In the vicinity of this place, General Bowen met the enemy advancing in full force, and immediately prepared for battle, having previously telegraphed to Vicksburg for reinforcements.

The enemy, confident in numbers, advanced with spirit and resolution, hoping to crush our small force with superior numbers. Their assaults were gallantly met by our men, and each attack repulsed. The battle raged with great fury, until about the middle of the day, when our forces, worn out by their almost superhuman exertions, were about to fall back. The enemy perceiving their exhaustion pressed them heavily, and would have eventually broke our line but for the timely arrival of Baldwin's brigade from Vicksburg. These gallant men, tired and exhausted as they were, after a forced march of over twenty miles, were ordered to advance to the support of Bowen. They advanced in splendid order, and with loud yells double quicked to the battle field. The Missourians and Arkansians observing them made renewed exertion, and recovered a part of the ground they had lost during the day. At about three o'clock the battle was raging with awful fury. Our men, as if inspired with demoniac strength, fought with a desperation unknown before. Large bodies of the enemy could be seen making a flank movement, and fresh troops were thrown on our line of battle as fast as others were repulsed. In the early part of the engagement, Wade's battery of Virginia Artillery was captured by the enemy, but in the evening a determined charge, made by Green's brigade of Missouri and Arkansas troops, recaptured the lost guns, and brought them safely off. The battle raged with great violence until nightfall, when darkness put an end to the contest, neither party laying claim to a victory.

The loss on both sides was very heavy, and our casualties were greatly disproportioned to the number of men engaged, our total loss having exceeded one thousand out of about six thousand effective men. The loss of the enemy was estimated, by those present, at between four and five thousand in killed, wounded and captured.

As soon as the fighting ceased, General Bowen sent in a flag of truce to General Grant, requesting his permission to bury that portion of our dead that lay in his lines. The demand was refused by Grant, who promised, however, that our dead should be buried, and our wounded well cared for.

That night, no reinforcements arriving as was expected, the Confederate army fell back and crossed Bayou Pierre, burning the bridges after them. The retreat was conducted with order and regularity, every effective man being brought off safely, except one company of Mississippians, left by mistake. They were captured, but afterwards made their escape and rejoined their regiment. Col. Pettus, of the 20th Alabama, now Brigadier General, was also taken prisoner, but made his escape by a ruse.

On the morning after the Confederate army retreated from Port Gibson, the enemy commenced throwing pontoons across the creek, and skirmishing lasted all day. Towards evening, information was brought to General Bowen that the enemy was landing above Grand Gulf, with the intention of cutting him off from Vicksburg. The gallant Major General Loring had arrived at Bowen's headquarters by this time, but without any troops; the order to reinforce having been given at too late an hour for them to arrive with him. A council of war was immediately held, and it was unanimously determined to evacuate the position, as from the disparity of numbers, and the want of rations and ammunition, it could not be held for twenty-four hours.

In compliance with the resolution to evacuate, prompt measures were taken. Everything was destroyed that could not be removed - the guns spiked and the magazines blown up. Our army then rapidly fell back to the Big Black; and, crossing the river at Baldwin's Ferry, formed a junction with the main body of our army under Lieutenant General Pemberton.

CHAPTER XIV.
MARCH OF THE ENEMY TO JACKSON, AND BATTLE OF BAKER'S CREEK.

The position of the enemy, after the evacuation of Grand Gulf, was one of extreme peril. On one flank was Gen. Joseph E. Johnston with a force, whose strength was unknown to General Grant; and on the other was Lieutenant General Pemberton, with an army between 30,000 to 35,000 strong. To have remained at Grand Gulf would have ruined the Federal army; and with this knowledge Grant determined to make a feint movement on Pemberton, and by that means detain him on the West bank of the Big Black, while he marched rapidly on Jackson, Mississippi, with his entire force. The object of the Federal commander was to make sure of no enemy being in his rear when he marched on Vicksburg.

The ruse succeeded. Whether General Pemberton took any means of knowing what force the enemy had confronting him or not, we cannot tell; but this much we do know: that he remained on the West bank of the Big Black, near Bovina, Mississippi, with the main body of his army, until the evening of the 15th of May, when he received a telegram from General J. E. Johnston, ordering him to advance immediately and attack the enemy in the rear, while he (Johnston) would attack him in front with what forces he had.

It is said that Lieutenant General Pemberton was opposed to crossing the Big Black, preferring to await the advance of the enemy but that he was overruled by the majority of his subordinate Generals. This statement is made in defence of his campaign; but we cannot see in what way it serves to remove the responsibility from his shoulders. The great error was in not advancing, on the 12th, when the rear of Grant's arm was exposed to us, and offered every inducement for an attack, The idea of General Pemberton desiring to advance after the enemy had penetrated into the country, and cut him off from the river, for the purpose of starving him out, was a gigantic error, as, from General Grant's official report, there was enough provision found in the country through which he marched to have supplied his army for three months; besides which, Vicksburg would have been left in a very exposed position by such a movement.

A majority of the general officers having decided, on the receipt of General Johnston's dispatch to advance and attack the enemy, preparations were made to move forward, and on the l5th of May, the Confederate army took up its line of march, the troops being positioned as follows: Major General Stephenson's division, composed of the brigades commanded by Brigadier Generals Lee, Barton and Cummings, and Colonel, now Brigadier General Reynolds, in front; General Loring's division, composed of the brigades commanded by Brigadier Generals Tilghman, Featherstone, and others, in the centre; and Bowen's division, composed of two brigades under Brigadier General Green and Colonel Cochran. There was also one brigade commanded by Brigadier General Baldwin, detached from Major General M. L.

Smith's division, Waul's legion of Texians and Wirt Adam's Cavalry regiment, the whole making an effective force of between 23,000 and 26,000 fighting men.

The Confederate army marched that day to Baker's Creek, no one being aware of the close proximity of the enemy, who having intercepted the dispatch ordering Pemberton to advance, divided his forces, and, marching rapidly with one body on Jackson, drove Johnston across Pearl river, and marched the other towards Big Black, for the purpose of surprising Pemberton. On the evening of the 15th of May, the Confederate army moved forward in the same position as they occupied the day before; and, after marching some distance, discerned a thick line of the enemy's skirmishers. The army immediately fell back to Baker's Creek, and, the enemy following, prepared to give battle. The troops bivouacked that night on the battle field. All the pickets thrown out that night by our forces, consisted of a few cavalry on the roads, while our flank and rear were left entirely unprotected. The next morning skirmishing commenced, and the artillery of Stephenson's division was ordered to advance and open fire. In compliance with this command, the different batteries advanced and unlimbered their pieces. As soon as the gunners had taken their proper places and opened fire, a terrific volley of musketry was poured in upon them by a large body of the enemy concealed in the woods not fifty yards distant, which killed and wounded a large number of the gunners and horses. The fighting then became severe, and resulted in the repulse of our infantry, who, having but little or no artillery support, were compelled to meet the attacks of the enemy unsupported. In a few hours, nearly the whole of Stephenson's artillery was captured, and the enemy, advancing on his flank, soon broke the different brigades. The men of this division fought with great courage and determination, but were compelled to fall back before overwhelming numbers.

Sometime after the firing commenced, Major General Loring's division moved rapidly forward, and was advancing to attack the enemy, when a battery of light artillery, commanded by one Captain Cowan, of Vicksburg, was subjected to the same terrific fire from the enemy's infantry, killing nearly all the horses, and placing *hors de combat* a majority of the gunners. The guns were immediately taken by hand and hauled a considerable distance, but were finally left in a swamp, from which they could not be extricated.

General Loring, perceiving that Stephenson had lost all his artillery, and that his infantry, after making a stubborn resistance, was compelled to retreat, leaving his flank exposed, determined to cut his way through to Jackson, where he could be of greater service to the Confederacy than falling back to Vicksburg. Accordingly, the division was ordered to cross the creek to the right of where the enemy was posted in large numbers. The movement was made with celerity and dispatch, but not before the gallant Brigadier General Floyd Tilghman, of Fort Henry renown, had met his death wound while bravely fighting. His body was carried to Vicksburg, where it was interred in a garden.

After crossing the creek and moving off on the enemy's right flank, we are unaware what movement was made by General Loring that enabled him to escape with safety, but from the nature of the country and the large force of the enemy, we must acknowledge that his safe escape, with his entire division, was one of the most brilliant feats of the war, and displayed, on the part of Major General Loring, military skill of high order.

While this movement was being made by Loring's division, the forces under Brigadier General Bowen moved quickly forward on the right, and met the enemy just as Stephenson's division was rapidly falling back. General Bowen rapidly threw his brigades in front, and then commenced one of the most desperate struggles recorded this war. The entire force under General Bowen did not exceed five thousand, and opposed to him was a force, variously estimated, at from forty to sixty thousand men. Our line of battle was rapidly formed, and the attack of the enemy awaited. Then it was that McPherson's entire corps advanced on this small body of troops, and endeavored, by force of numbers, to crush them. Each charge was met with almost superhuman courage, and repulsed. The Missouri troops fought like demons, with the hope of retrieving the day and gaining a victory. So desperately did this division fight, that had there been anything like organization among Stephenson's division, and they had supported Bowen, the battle might have been won. But there was nothing like order among the majority of Stephenson's division. They had, after fighting for several hours with the most determined courage without artillery, and against overwhelming odds, been over powered, and were straggling in a demoralized condition towards Big Black. In justice to the gallant

Major General Stephenson and his subordinate Brigadier Generals, we would say, that every exertion was made on their part to rally the men, but with little success. The brunt of the battle then fell on Bowen's division and the few men of Stephenson's force, who remained intact.

Several desperate charges were made by these troops on the enemy, but, from the large numbers brought against them, without success. One of these charges was made by Gen. Green's brigade of Missouri and Arkansas troops, not numbering over eleven hundred men. These heroes advanced with the utmost coolness upon the enemy's forces, consisting of two batteries of artillery, supported by an entire division. They charged up to within thirty yards of the artillery, when the Yankee gunners, who were laying aside of their pieces, drew the string attached to the friction primers, discharging their guns, and poured in such a severe volley of canister, as to compel our men to fall back. So gallantly did these troops behave themselves that Major General McPherson, in conversation after the fall of Vicksburg, is reported to have said, in reference to this charge, that he almost "thought it a sin to fire on such brave men."

Lieutenant General Pemberton is reported to have lost all confidence after the capture of our artillery. He is said to have crossed the bridge over Baker's Creek, exclaiming to those around him, "I call upon you, gentlemen, to witness that I am not responsible for this battle – I am but obeying the orders of General Johnston." The battle was, in fact, fought without any one commander. It was left to the Major and Brigadier Generals to do their best, and which they did; but, from want of a general co-operation, effected nothing.

About dusk the Confederate army fell back towards the line of works erected on the Big Black river. In the retreat almost every step of the way was contested by the gallant Bowen and his brave men; every endeavor on the part of the enemy to flank us, being repulsed with heavy loss. Our forces arrived in safety to the works, which they immediately occupied with what troops remained in any state of organization, while the enemy, evidently exhausted at the determined resistance given him by our troops during the day, made no demonstration that night.

Our total loss in the battle did not exceed six thousand in killed, wounded and missing, while that of the enemy could not have been less than ten thousand. This great disparity in casualties, arose from the nature of the ground preventing any large line, and the enemy being compelled to mass his troops in dense columns, when making a charge, the fire from our infantry into their serried ranks was very destructive.

Our loss in artillery was large, not less than thirty pieces having been captured. Among the different batteries were:

Co. A. - Withers' 1st Mississippi Artillery, 2 pieces.
Cowan's of " " " " 6 "
Co. C. " " " " 6 "
Botetourt (Virginia) Artillery 6 "
Wofford's of Withers' 1st Miss. Artillery 4 "

We are unable to name the other batteries captured on this day. Nearly the whole of Stephenson's was captured. One of his brigades succeeded in bringing off its artillery safely, and that was a brigade of Tennesseans, commanded by Colonel, now Brigadier General, Reynolds. This gallant officer acted with great skill from the evacuation of Grand Gulf to the fall of Vicksburg. On the retreat from Grand Gulf, he was placed in command of the entire baggage train, and although the enemy twice got in his rear, he eluded them each time, and succeeded in bringing the wagons across Big Black without the loss of one.

The retreat from, and yielding up of the field, put an end to the battle. It cannot be denied that this engagement resulted in a most disastrous defeat to our arms, and one that could have resulted differently had competent generalship been displayed.

CHAPTER XV.
BATTLE OF BIG BLACK.

On Sunday morning, 17th May, (the day after the battle of Baker's Creek) the enemy advanced in force against the works erected on the Big Black. (These works were erected on the East side of the river, with the object, it is said, of defending two bridges, and of protecting Snyder's Bluff.) The attack on our right and left was repulsed, but a panic breaking out in a brigade on the centre, the men deserted their works and left the line exposed. As soon as the enemy perceived this they commenced pouring over the deserted works, thus compelling our right and left to fall back, which they did rapidly. Nearly all the artillery saved the day before was lost here, among which was two batteries belonging to Bowen's division, which, for want of horses, could not be moved in time. Our army then retreated towards the river, and, after crossing, set the bridge on fire. This, for a while, impeded the pursuit of the enemy, who were compelled to build pontoons before they could cross the river.

Our loss in this engagement was about 1,000, in killed, wounded and missing. A large number of small arms and knapsacks were thrown away by our men in their precipitate retreat from the breastworks. The retreat across the Big Black ended the engagement - an engagement that can scarcely be dignified with the name of battle.

CHAPTER XVI.
RETREAT FROM BIG BLACK TO VICKSBURG.

Soon after crossing Big Black, our army became a demoralized body of men; no order or discipline was observed during the march; the men were scattered for miles along the road. The sight of such a large body of men, retreating in the disorder that they were, was enough to create a panic in the strongest mind. A feeling of despondency could be observed among the troops, and curses, loud and deep, were hurled at Lieutenant General Pemberton for his mismanagement of the army - many of the troops declaring their willingness to desert rather than serve under him again.

At about ten o'clock on Sunday night, the main body of the Confederate forces commenced entering Vicksburg, and then ensued a scene that almost beggars description. Many planters, living near the city, with their families, abandoned their homes and entered our lines with the Confederate forces. We were among the troops when they entered, and never in our life beheld anything to equal the scene. As if by magic, the stillness of the Sabbath night was broken in upon, and an uproar, in which the blasphemous oath of the soldier, and the cry of the child, mingled and formed a sight which the pen cannot depict. It was a scene, which, once beheld, cannot be forgotten. There were many gentle women and tender children, torn from their homes by the advance of a ruthless foe, and compelled to fly to our lines for protection; and mixed up with them, in one vast crowd, were the gallant men who had left Vicksburg three short weeks before, in all the pride and confidence of a just cause, and returning to it a demoralized mob and a defeated army, all caused through one man's incompetency.

CHAPTER XVII.
INVESTMENT OF VICKSBURG.

On the arrival of our army within the fortifications at Vicksburg, prompt measures were taken to gather the men together and re-organize the demoralized body of men. Our officers worked hard, and, by two o'clock on Monday afternoon, had succeeded in placing the troops in position behind the breastworks.

On Sunday, Snyder's Bluff and Chickasaw Bayou were evacuated, and the troops brought to Vicksburg. The works on Snyder's Bluff consisted of about sixteen heavy guns, of which number six were brought away, our forces not having time to remove the balance. A good deal of stores, heavy artillery, ammunition and baggage, were left at the above-named points for want of transportation.

The position occupied by the different divisions, were as follows: Major General M. L. Smith's division, composed of Brigadier Generals Shoup, Baldwin, Vaughn, and Buford's brigades, on the left; Major General J. H. Forney's division, composed of Brigadier Generals Moore's and Hebert's brigades, in the centre; Major General C. L. Stephenson's division, composed of Brigadier Generals Barton's, Cummings', and Lee's, and Colonel, now Brigadier General Reynolds' brigades, on the right; and Brigadier General Bowen's division, composed of Brigadier General Green's and Colonel Cochran's brigades, held in reserve. Waul's legion of Texas cavalry was dismounted, and served as infantry on Stephenson's line.

When our forces entered the city on Saturday night, our line of defences was not yet completed, and the men, tired and worn out as they were, after the privations, marchings and counter-marchings of the past fortnight, were immediately set to work on the fortifications. On Monday, at 12 meridian, they were completed, and the men took their positions to await the approach of the enemy.

At about two o'clock, the enemy's skirmishers appeared in front of our works and opened fire, but without doing any damage to the Confederate forces. By dusk they had planted several batteries of artillery in position, about four hundred yards from our line, but abstained from using them. The sharp shooting was, however, continued until dark, when it ceased, and quiet reigned over the city and fortifications.

On Tucsday morning, by daylight, the enemy opened a terrific fire on our line of works, which was quickly responded to by our guns with fine effect; the enemy being compelled to shift his batteries several times. The enemy then endeavored to throw forward a body of sharpshooters, but a severe fire from our infantry drove them back, and prevented the execution of the design. Towards noon the enemy made their first attack on that portion of our line held by Brigadier Generals Shoup and Baldwin's brigades. They threw forward a large column, which, giving a loud cheer, charged upon the works. Our men withheld their fire until the Yankees had approached to within fifty yards, when they poured in a terrific and destructive volley of musketry, doing considerable execution in the serried ranks of the foe. The enemy wavered a moment, and their indecision giving our men time to reload; when they charged again, they were met with a more, galling fire than the first one, which caused them to break and retire precipitately behind the cover of the friendly hills. The loss of the enemy in this charge must have been severe, as the dead in front of our lines lay in large numbers. Our loss was very slight.

No other serious attack was attempted during the remainder of the day. The attack narrated above, was looked upon more as an endeavor to "feel" the strength of our forces, than to gain any important advantage. Artillery firing and sharpshooting continued for about three hours, when Lieutenant General Pemberton rode up and ordered our men to cease firing, as he desired no artillery duels. In obedience to this order the men ceased firing, but the order resulted very badly for us, as the next morning the enemy, emboldened by our silence, advanced their artillery one hundred yards nearer than they had them the day previous.

After their repulse in the morning, the enemy kept up a constant fire on our line from their artillery and sharpshooters, dismounting several of our guns, and compelling us to mask the remainder by hauling them from their position behind the works to the rear of the hills. The enemy evidently observed the effects of their fire; for as soon as a gun was removed from its position, or dismounted, they would send up a loud cheer of joy, much to the chagrin of our forces. In one instance, however, the laugh was turned on them by Brigadier General Louis Hebert, of Louisiana, who, observing the enemy taking particular aim at a fine Parrott gun on the right of his line, gave orders that as soon as a shell struck the parapet near the gun, and obscured it with dust, to remove the piece and make it appear as if it had been dismounted. A few minutes after the order was given, a thirty-pound Parrott shell, from the enemy's gun, struck the parapet, completely enveloping the gun with dust. The piece was promptly removed, and as soon as the dust had cleared away, the enemy, not seeing it any more, set up a loud cheering, which was heartily responded to by our men, who enjoyed the ruse highly.

On Wednesday morning, May 20th, at about three o'clock in the morning, the enemy opened a terrific fire, from their artillery, upon our line. The fire was absolutely fearful. Shell after shell came in such rapid succession, that the air seemed alive with them. The noise made by their shrieks, the loud explosion when they bursted, and the silvery sound they made when the fragments were falling, created an uproar almost deafening. This severe cannonading lasted until nearly five o'clock, when it slackened down to an occasional shot. Firing continued slowly from their artillery for the balance of the day, while their sharpshooters increased their fire perceptibly.

Towards the middle of the day, the enemy's mortars, which had been placed in position opposite Vicksburg, opened on the city. These mortars were mounted on large rafts, constructed for the purpose, and lashed to the west bank of the peninsula on the Louisiana shore. A brisk fire was kept up by them until about four o'clock in the evening, when they ceased and remained silent until next morning.

On Thursday morning at three o'clock the enemy opened the same heavy fire as they had done the day previous, and kept it up for about a similar length of time, when it decreased, but not as much as before. During the day they continued firing, increasing its rapidity to some extent, while their sharpshooters swept our breastworks with a constant stream of Minie balls. Several additional guns were also brought to bear upon us, their fire beginning to have some effect on our works.

The mortars on the peninsula opened fire in the morning and kept up a constant and rapid fire all day, but providentially injuring no one. The city at this time was filled with women and the only protection afforded them from the shells, was a number of caves built in the sides of the hills. General Pemberton had made several requests that they should quit the city, but without effect, as they declared themselves willing to risk the horrors of a siege rather than leave their homes.

Besides the residents of the city, there were many women and children, the families of planters, living near Vicksburg, who entered the city with our army on their retreat from Big Black. To their credit, be it said, that severe as was the hardships and sufferings they experienced, all these ills were endured uncomplainingly, their only desire being the successful defence [sic] of the city.

On the evening of the 21st, the enemy ceased firing from their artillery on our breastworks, but kept up a severe fire from their sharpshooters all night; the mortars also shelled the city all night from the peninsula opposite.

CHAPTER XVIII.
CONTINUATION OF THE INVESTMENT – GENERAL ATTACK ON OUR WORKS, AND REPULSE OF THE ENEMY.

On Friday morning, the 22nd of May, at about three o'clock, the enemy opened on the works, their fire exceeding, in severity, that of any previous morning. Every available gun appeared to have been brought to bear on our works, and the cannonading continued with unabated fury until eleven o'clock, when it suddenly ceased. This bombardment was the most terrible endured during the siege and, we believe, the most terrific ever known in civilized warfare. Nothing could be heard but one continual shrieking of the shells, as they came cutting through the air, and the sharp fiz of the Minie balls as they came by hundreds whizzing past.

Notwithstanding the severity of this fire, the casualties were small - a fact which almost seems a miracle, as, from the exposed condition of our defences, the enemy had enfiladed us on all sides, and had gained on us a fire in reverse.

At eleven o'clock, as soon as the firing had ceased, the enemy were discovered forming a line of battle with heavy columns of infantry. It was in this instance that the bad policy of ordering our men to cease firing on the enemy's sharpshooters was observed. Had we kept up a fire on them during the days previous to this attack, they would have been compelled to keep at a further distance, and our gunners would have been able to open a severe fire upon the columns then forming in line of battle, and prevented the charge; but as it was, the sharpshooters, being allowed to come within one hundred yards of our position, kept up such a rapid and galling fire on our works, that the cannoneers could scarcely raise from their position to load their pieces. With these advantages in their favor, the enemy formed their line of battle, and advanced to the charge with but little or no resistance from our artillery.

At about noon, the enemy advanced steadily, and in good order, pouring in a volley, which did but little or no damage, our men being protected by the rifle-pits and breastworks, reserving their fire until the enemy had approached near enough to feel its effects. As soon as they had approached to a distance of about fifty yards from our line of entrenchments, our men rose from their reclining positions behind the works, and gave them such a terrible volley of musketry, that they were compelled to fall back, which they did, however, in pretty good order. On the lines occupied by the brigades of Baldwin, Shoup, Hebert, Moore and Lee, the heaviest and most determined assaults were made.

The enemy, after being twice repulsed on Lee's line, were reinforced, and made a third charge. Force of numbers gained for them a momentary advantage, and several of their men entered our works, but the gallant and chivalrous Lee quickly rallied his men, and, after a severe fight, drove them back with immense loss. All of those who entered our line were shot. The enemy, foiled by the desperate lighting of the brave Georgians and Alabamians, made no further demonstration on this line of a like nature. Several charges were attempted, but each was repulsed, with great gallantry, by our men.

The charges on Moore's brigade were heavy and determined, but were all repulsed with great slaughter to the enemy. So desperate were the attacks, and so heroically were they made, that one of the enemy's flags was actually planted on the edge of the line of breastworks, occupied by the second Texas. The color-bearer who planted it was immediately shot dead by one of the men, and the colors captured. The Texans acted with their usual valor, and the Alabamians in this brigade behaved admirably, keeping up so galling a fire on the enemy as to prevent their approaching near the line occupied by them.

The fighting on Brigadier General Hebert's line was protracted and desperate, particularly on the immediate right and left of the Jackson road, occupied by the third and consolidated twenty-first and twenty-third Louisiana regiments. Their position was one which the enemy desired to obtain above all others, as, from the nature of the defences, had they carried the road, Vicksburg would have been lost. Several desperate charges were made on this line during the day, and had been successfully resisted. As often as the enemy were repulsed, they would return to the charge with fresh troops, and endeavor to carry the works; but the gallant men comprising the above-named regiments, held their ground manfully, and repulsed every attack.

The last charge on the line occupied by the twenty-first and twenty-third Louisiana, was made by the seventeenth Wisconsin regiment, composed entirely of Irishmen, and bearing the green flag of Erin. With their entire front rank carrying scaling-ladders, they rushed upon the works and endeavored to scale them, the fortifications at that point being erected on a very precipitous hill. Three times they essayed to plant, but a sweeping fire from our infantry compelled them to face back. At the last charge, they approached within twenty yards of our works, but such a terrible volley was poured into their ranks, that they broke and retreated in confusion, leaving their dead in large numbers lying in front of our line. The Mississippians in this brigade acted very handsomely, repulsing every charge made on their line.

The engagement on Shoup's line was conducted with the same bravery and success as on the others. The fighting on Baldwin's line was also severe, and was attended with the same success. On every portion of the line, the enemy was repulsed with heavy loss, although their attacks were not so desperately made on every portion as they were on those portions specially mentioned. Louisianians, Georgians, Alabamians, Mississippians, Texans and Tennesseans, behaved with the same valor and success. The service rendered by

Bowen's division of Missourians and Arkansians, was signal and glorious. With their usual valor, they reinforced all points threatened by the enemy, and aided greatly in repulsing them.

The loss of the enemy in this day's engagement, could not have been less than from 8,000 to 10,000 in killed and wounded. Their dead lay in large numbers before our works, while thousands of wounded men were carried off as soon as they fell. Our total loss did not exceed eight hundred.

A description of this day's fight would be a task too difficult to undertake. It was a continual booming of artillery, and a constant rattle of musketry. As each charge was repulsed or made, the lines would resound with the loud yells of our men at their success, or the cheer of the enemy as he made the charge.

Nightfall presented a sad spectacle. Small as our loss had been, in comparison with that of the enemy, and the severity of the conflict, many of our best and bravest officers and soldiers had fallen - many of the noblest and most devoted patriots had yielded their life on the altar of their country, and had fought their last battle in defence [sic] of their cause.

While the battle was raging at the breastworks, an attack was made on our water batteries by the gunboats, and, after a short contest, they were repulsed, and did not renew the engagement again that day. The mortars also kept up a rapid fire on the city, but without any other effect than partially destroying two or three buildings.

During this tremendous bombardment throughout the day, stores in the city were opened as usual, and the streets promenaded by women and children, as if no missiles of death were filling the air and bursting and scattering the fragments around. It was a miracle that so few were injured in the city that day. Nothing but the arm of Providence could have shielded the inhabitants from death.

CHAPTER XIX.
CONTINUATION OF THE INVESTMENT.
BURIAL OF THE ENEMY'S DEAD.

The day following the general assault and repulse of the enemy was ushered in with comparative silence by the enemy. Only an occasional shot was fired, and their sharpshooters relaxed their fire considerably. This gave great relief to our men, who were very much exhausted by the severe engagement of the day previous, and enabled them to move about behind the works, without running as much risk from the enemy's shells and bullets as before.

The enemy were evidently very much disheartened at the terrible repulse they had met with the day previous, and evinced no disposition to renew the attack; in anticipation of which, all the necessary preparations had been made. So humiliated was Grant at the successful defense made by our forces, deeming them, as he did, demoralized and broken in spirit, that he made no request to bury his dead. Many who were dangerously wounded remained in front of our works, groaning from pain and calling for help, without any one being able to come to their assistance. Our men would have assisted them, but the fire of the enemy prevented their showing themselves above the parapet. They were thus left to die through the inhumanity of their commander; but this brutal and unchristian spirit having been manifested so often by our foe, no one felt surprised at it.

Sunday morning at daylight the enemy opened fire on us from his Parrott and other guns, keeping it up all day without inter-mission, and continuing the fire all night. From the defective nature of our defences the casualties on our side began to grow larger, although strenuous exertions were made during the night, by the Major and Brigadier Generals, to repair the works injured by the fire of the enemy, and to strengthen them sufficiently to meet any future cannonading. The line occupied by Brigadier Generals Hebert, Moore, Shoup and Baldwin's brigades was the particular object at which the enemy directed their fire; a majority of their guns being concentrated at this point.

The mortars on the peninsula opened a steady fire on the city until the afternoon, when they increased it, and poured in thirteen-inch shells with great rapidity until the following morning. The number of mortars by this time had been increased to five, and a party sent over the river at night, for the purpose of making observations, reported the enemy busily engaged constructing works for large siege guns.

On Monday morning, the 25th of May, the enemy opened the same heavy fire from their artillery and sharpshooters, until eleven o'clock, when they ceased. The reason for a cessation of hostilities, was a flag of truce, which had been sent in by Lieutenant General

Pemberton, offering an armistice until eight o'clock that evening, for the purpose of giving Grant an opportunity to bury his dead.

From the first engagement on Tuesday to this day, the enemy's dead, to the estimated number of three thousand, had remained on the field in front of our works, while many of their wounded, left by them in their precipitate retreat from the last charge on Friday, had died from want of proper attendance. One of their wounded, (a captain) after remaining on the ground in front of Shoup's line for nearly two days, was removed in the night by several noble-hearted men of our forces, who crossed over the rifle pits with a litter, at the imminent peril of their lives, and bore him safely within our works. On examination, it was found that his thigh was shattered by a ball, and mortification had ensued. Before he died, he delivered some money and papers into the hands of the surgeons who attended him, with his name and address, and requested that after the siege was over, they should be forwarded to his wife - a request that was honorably complied with. After lingering a short time, he died.

The object of General Pemberton in making the offer to Grant to bury his dead was, to save our men from sickness. The dead bodies, beneath the influence of a burning sun, had become decomposed, and filled the air with an awful stench. From their proximity to our works, the men were considerably affected by the unwholesome air they were compelled to breathe, and great fears were entertained that it would result in an epidemic, unless some measures were taken to have the dead buried. Although *our* requesting Grant to bury his dead, was, in a measure, yielding somewhat to the enemy, the circumstances under which the deviation from dignity occurred, made the request perfectly right.

The offer for a cessation of hostilities for eight hours having been accepted, the dead were removed by a party detailed from our army, and carried to the enemy's picket lines, where they were buried. While the dead were being removed, many of our officers left our line, and going to the neutral ground, between the two armies, engaged the Federal officers in conversation. While out there, newspapers, and other small articles, were exchanged by our men for tobacco. The author of this work, in company with Dr. E. McD. Coffey, Chief Surgeon of Bowen's division, went out with the other officers, and held a conversation with a party of Federal officers, of about a half hour's duration. They expressed themselves very much dissatisfied at the result of Friday's engagement, and observed that, from our repeated defeats, they had not anticipated any attempt on our part to hold the city. They, however, appeared confident in their ability to starve us out, and said, on our observing that there was no chance of such a thing occurring: "Oh, we know that you cannot hold out longer than two months at furthest." On our remarking that we could hold out until Johnston advanced to our relief, they observed that we were depending on a broken reed, as they were well aware of the strength of our forces under Johnston, and they knew he had not men enough to attack them with; besides, said they, "we are looking for reinforcements daily, and they will arrive long before Johnston can organize an army, even if he intends doing so. Our reinforcements, with the aid of the Big Black river, will be ample to hold him in check until you are starved out."

As soon as the time agreed upon for a cessation of hostilities had expired, the enemy renewed their artillery firing and sharpshooting, but in a very feeble manner. The mortars on the peninsula in front of the city kept up a heavy fire, throwing their shells to the rear of our works, and by that way cross their fire with that of the besieging army in the rear.

The usual amount of firing continued on Tuesday, with little or no loss to the garrison, which by this time had become perfectly indifferent to the missiles falling continually around them. They had become so used to the shells bursting around them, that they were made rather a subject of jest than of fear. The only missiles from which they apprehended danger, were the hundreds of Minie balls constantly whizzing past them.

About this period the first courier that managed to elude the Federal army entered Vicksburg with dispatches from General Joseph E. Johnston to General Pemberton. On the receipt of the dispatch a circular was issued by the Lieutenant General commanding, giving a synopsis of the news, which was to the effect that "General Johnston was at Canton, Mississippi, with an organizing force;" that "he requested the Lieutenant General to hold out as long as he could, &c." It was also stated in the circular that a portion of General Bragg's army was ordered to General Johnston, and that they were then moving towards Jackson, Mississippi. The circular also gave our forces the first intelligence they had, from

Southern sources, of the capture of Winchester by Lieutenant General Ewell, and the invasion of Pennsylvania.

As might be supposed, the receipt of this intelligence, with the hope of relief that it held out, lent new vigor to the garrison, and although they had already been reduced to quarter rations, they were cheerful, and evinced a fresh determination to hold the works until the siege could be raised by Johnston.

The firing from the peninsula on the city had perceptibly increased; eight mortars and siege guns were now playing on Vicksburg; the enemy had erected strong breastworks in front of our line in the rear of the city, and had brought a large number of guns to bear upon us, while the bombardment and sharpshooting continued unceasingly.

CHAPTER XX.
SINKING OF THE IRON-CLAD CINCINNATI-MINING OPERATIONS OF THE ENEMY-HARDSHIPS OF THE SIEGE.

Wednesday morning, the 27th of May, was ushered in with the same unceasing stream of shells and Minie balls pouring over the breastworks, our men looking on their advent as a matter of course. The firing from the mortars still continued, with little or no intermission, from the peninsula, while fragments of, and thirteen-inch shells could be seen scattered in every part of the town.

At about ten o'clock on this morning, several of the enemy's gunboats below the city advanced a short way up the river, and opened a rapid fire on our lower batteries, but without doing any particular damage. While this bombardment was going on, one of the enemy's boats, the iron-clad ram *Cincinnati*, steamed down from the fleet, behind the peninsula, and opened fire on our water battery above the city. As soon as she had got in range of our guns, we opened fire. She replied with remarkable rapidity, pouring broadside after broadside of grape and canister at the battery. The men at the guns stood up to their posts gallantly, firing shot and shell at the *Cincinnati* as fast as possible. Their guns, however, being too small, had little or no effect upon the iron sides of the ram, all of them that struck her glancing off like an india rubber ball.

On the hill below the water battery was a battery containing one eight-inch Brooks gun, under the command, we think, of Captain

Johnson, of the 1st Tennessee heavy artillery regiment. This gun was one of the finest pieces of ordnance in Vicksburg, and had obtained the *soubriquet* of "Whistling Dick," from the shrill whistle of its shells as they sped through the air. Soon after the *Cincinnati* had steamed down and opened fire on the water battery, "Whistling Dick" was brought to bear upon her, and the shrill whistle of its shells was soon heard. The engagement had lasted several minutes, the firing on both sides increasing in rapidity, and still the iron-clad continued to pour volley after volley into the water battery, upon the holding of which depended the safety of the extreme left of our line; at last, a well-directed shot from a "Whistling Dick" pierced her armor, and, as if fortune had changed in favor of our forces, several other shots in rapid succession went crashing through her iron plating. In a few moments she was disabled and in a sinking condition. She immediately backed up the river, being afraid to turn and expose her broadside to our guns, and ran aground on the Mississippi shore, in full range of our guns, but within the enemy's picket line. Our batteries continued firing on her until she hopelessly disabled, when they ceased.

As soon as the *Cincinnati* was run aground, her officers and crew took to their boats and escaped, with the exception of a few, who fell into our hands. They reported that the attack by the *Cincinnati* had been made in accordance with the request of Major General Sherman, who had said that if she could silence the water battery, and shell our men from their works, there would be no difficulty in his entering the city, as the battery was the only obstacle in his path. This statement was no doubt correct, as Sherman's entire corps rested on their arms during the engagement, as if waiting for the battery to be silenced, for them to storm the works. No attempt was made, however, on the line, in consequence of the sinking of the *Cincinnati.*

After the destruction of this boat, the enemy's fleet made no demonstration of the like nature during the remainder of the siege. The enemy being satisfied, no doubt, of the inability of iron-clad boats to remain in one position and engage land batteries. This engagement proved the superiority of land batteries over war vessels, even when iron clad. Had the *Cincinnati* desired it, she could have run past the batteries, without being injured in the least, but all her modern improvements failed when she stood up squarely to give and receive a broadside. During the engagement between the iron-clad and our batteries, nothing transpired on the line, beyond the usual amount of artillery firing and sharpshooting.

After their repulse on the 22nd of May, the enemy, finding that our position could not be taken by storm, commenced mining. The reason of the enemy's coming so close to our works as to be able to dig under them, was the want of foresight in Gen. Pemberton's order prohibiting the expenditure of ammunition. Not being permitted to use the artillery, or to return the fire of the sharpshooters, our men were compelled to see the enemy approach nearer every day, until they had worked their way to within thirty yards of our breastworks. That this could have been prevented, was the opinion of many prominent officers of the garrison, who favored our throwing out a body of picked men every day to act as sharpshooters, and prevent the enemy from making his approaches. If this could not have prevented them entirely from approaching, it could have, at least, prevented their mining our works.

The enemy, having been permitted to approach as near as above described, went vigorously to work, mining our line of entrenchments at various places, the principal point being on the left of the Jackson road, held by the third Louisiana, of Hebert's brigade. The means at our disposal for annoying them in their labor, were limited to throwing a few hand grenades at their working parties, but these had little or no effect, as the fuses attached to them being very often too long, the enemy would pick them up before they exploded, and throw them back. The enemy, at first, worked only in the night, but pushed on their operations with untiring energy and determination. Had the sharpshooting been less severe, some effort would have been made to drive them out with musketry; but the Minie balls swept the line of entrenchments night and day, making it almost certain death for any of the men to show their bodies above the parapet of our works; at the same time, the greater portion of our artillery had been dismounted or disabled by the fire of the enemy. This was occasioned from the open condition of our works, the positions for the guns being all exposed, while the guns themselves were all *en barbette*, which rendered them easily dismounted by the fire of the enemy, and prevented our gunners from working them.

These circumstances, discouraging as they were, did not cause the least fear on the part of the men; and although they were well aware that as soon as the enemy completed their mines, the works would be blown up, their patriotic ardor remained unabated; the garrison was filled with enthusiasm for their cause, and expressed the same unflinching determination - as they had done before the works were mined - to maintain their position so long as they could fire a gun. In fact, the spirit of our men seemed to rise with the danger; their confidence in their ability to repulse the enemy, should he attack again, was still the same; all had but one desire: the successful defense of the city they had so long been fighting to hold.

It was about this period that the hardships and privations of a siege began to be comprehended and experienced. From the smallness of the garrison, and the extent of our line, it required every available man to occupy the works. The troops were thus compelled to remain behind the breastworks and in the rifle-pits for weeks without removing from their crouching positions, and subject to the different changes of weather. Very often a storm would rise, and the rain come pouring down, drenching them to the skin, and they would be unable to leave the works for the purpose of changing their clothing, but were compelled to remain in their damp and unhealthy garments, until the sun shone again and dried them. It is, therefore, no surprise that the list of sick in the garrison was large and daily increasing. Their food had to be cooked by details of men from each company, and brought to them at the breastworks, and they remained for weeks together without either washing their clothes or bathing themselves. Under this accumulation of hardships, they bore themselves manfully; and although it was apparent that the life they were then leading would soon break down their constitutions, and weaken them beyond the powers of endurance, not a murmur was heard, or a voice raised expressing discontent.

For a period of about five days after the siege commenced, the garrison was pretty comfortable so far as food was concerned, as they were allowed full rations. At the expiration of that time, however, Major General C. L. Stephenson, who had been appointed Chief of Subsistence, perceived that the supply of provisions on hand at that time would not last many days, if the soldiers continued to receive the allowance provided for them by the regulations. The rations were then gradually reduced, until it reached the following small amount of food, daily issued to each man as rations for twenty-four hours:

Flour, or meal................... 4 ounces.
Bacon............................. 4   "
Rice..............................1½ "
Peas, (scarcely eatable).........2   "
Sugar.............................3   "

the whole making a total of fourteen and a half ounces of food per day, or less than one-quarter the amount of rations usually issued to the men as full allowance. This small amount naturally brought the men to the verge of starvation, and was entirely inadequate to supply the cravings of nature. Though the men felt that such was the case, and saw that, under this partial starvation, their strength would soon fail, all cheerfully submitted to the inexorable necessity that had reduced them to such a strait.

CHAPTER XXI.
SORTIES ON THE ENEMY'S LINE - ERECTION OF "LOGAN FORT" BY THE ENEMY.

The days intervening from the twenty-seventh of May to the first of June, were devoid of any movement, on the part of the enemy, of interest. The cannonading and sharpshooting continued at times severely; while at other times it would slacken considerably. Several sorties were made by details from the different brigades in our army, which, in a measure, relieved the monotonous life our soldiers were leading. One of these sorties was a brilliant affair. It was made by Brigadier General Lee, and resulted in the capture of nearly two hundred of the enemy belonging to an Indiana regiment. The attack was made with great skill and caution, and took the enemy completely by surprise, as they never imagined we would venture on any such undertaking.

Shut up as the garrison was, and completely surrounded by the enemy, we were completely ignorant of everything transpiring outside of the city, except on the safe arrival of a courier in our lines. As these were of rare occurrence, we remained in profound ignorance of the true state of affairs outside nearly all the time. As will be found in all places, rumors of every kind and any quantity were circulated among the garrison, tending for a while to elate them with the hope of a speedy relief, all of them however turned out false, much to the chagrin of the soldiers whom the reports had deceived.

In the night the pickets of both armies would abstain from firing, and would sit down and engage in conversation, each bragging of their ability to whip the other. Many of these interviews were very amusing, and the incidents that occurred were the source of much laughter to our men, who would show their wit at every opportunity, for the purpose of exasperating the enemy. At one time, so familiar had the pickets become, that they would meet one another on the neutral ground between the two armies and discuss the merits of the war. The defense on both sides would be carried on with considerable vehemence, until argument failed on one side or the other, when they would separate to avoid, as a Yankee told one of our men who had argued him beyond reply, any fighting over the subject! As soon as this familiarity was discovered, strict orders were given to prohibit its continuation, and in a measure, it was stopped, nevertheless some "good joke" occurring between them would leak out now and then, but as the parties with whom it took place could never be discovered, the officers were obliged to laugh at the joke, and leave the disobedient party unpunished. In these conversations the different motives which occupied the opposing forces and impelled them to fight, would be apparent and form a striking contrast. The conversation of the Yankee would be principally directed to the fine country they had gone through, and its capacity for making money, while that of the Confederate soldier would be a defense of his country, and his determination never to go back into their accursed Union. We do not mention this from prejudice to the Yankee, or from what was reported to us by other parties, but from the strict character of Grant's army, and the sordid motives actuating them, and their conversation with us after the surrender.

On the first of June the enemy kept up a heavy fire, both in front and rear, from his mortars, Parrott's and other guns, and his sharpshooters poured thousands of Minie balls into our line. The enemy's sharpshooters were all splendid marksmen, and effectually prevented any of our men from rising above the parapet on pain of certain death, while it was an utter impossibility for our cannoneers, to load the guns remaining in position on our line, without being exposed to the aim of a dense line of sharpshooters.

Our line of works, as planned by Major General M. L. Smith, was as good as could be desired, but the execution of his plans was the most miserable ever performed by men claiming to be engineers. There were several faults in the construction of these works, the principal of which were: first, they were not high enough; second, they were not built sufficiently thick; and third, the bastions on which the guns rested were entirely too much exposed, and afforded no protection to the gunners.

There was a hill on the immediate left of the Jackson road, which ought to have been occupied by our forces, as it commanded that portion of our works afterwards held by the third Louisiana regiment. Brigadier General Louis Hebert, one of our ablest and most gallant officers, desired to hold this hill at the commencement of the siege, and before the enemy had invested us, but was prevented from so doing, we suppose, by order of his superior officers. This hill was afterwards occupied by the enemy, and a fort, known as "Logan Fort," erected on it. This position appears to have been entirely overlooked by our engineers, or its importance was very much undervalued.

So badly were the works erected, that three days after the siege commenced the enemy had enfiladed us, and a few days after that, opened a fire in reverse. We were thus subject to a continual fire from all quarters. The number of pieces of artillery brought to bear upon our defenses, could not have been less than from two hundred and fifty to three hundred of all descriptions and calibres. This large number of guns, keeping up a constant fire on our lines, naturally created an uproar almost deafening, and as a result, thousands of shells were poured into our works. There was no portion of the space of ground in our lines but where whole shells and fragments of shells could be seen, while at the line, and about one hundred yards from it, thousands upon thousands of Minie balls covered the road and woods. Enough of these little missiles could have been picked up in half an hour to have supplied our army for a day.

CHAPTER XXII.
SPIES IN THE CITY. CONDITION OF THE CITY. FIGHT BETWEEN THE ENEMY AND A TENNESSEE REGIMENT.

On Tuesday, the second of June, it was expected that the enemy would make a second general assault on our works, from certain suspicious movements of theirs the night previous. In accordance with this, preparations were immediately made to meet the threatened attack, and to give the enemy a warm reception on his assault. The day passed, however, without their attempting anything more than the customary bombardment, except on the peninsula, where the enemy appeared to slacken their fire somewhat, not caring to strain their mortars too much.

On the night of the first of June, several buildings in the city, on Washington street, were set on fire by incendiaries, and burnt down, while the parties who set them on fire were never discovered. That there were spies and emissaries of the enemy in the city is beyond a doubt true; as we were informed by a gentleman of reliability, that two or three days before the incendiarism narrated above took place, a man clad in the enemy's uniform, and to all appearance a stranger in Vicksburg, was observed walking about the city; several questions he propounded excited the suspicions of the party to whom he addressed them, and after answering them in an evasive manner, the party hastened to give information to the provost guard respecting the singular appearance of this man, and the suspicious questions he had asked. A guard was immediately started after him, and after a while discovered him walking up one of the streets. As soon as he observed them approaching him with the party he had previously questioned, he must have defined what they were coming for, for he immediately started off at a run, pursued by the guard for some distance, until he arrived at some deserted buildings, which he entered. When the guard arrived, they went into the building after him, but he could not be discovered. That he was a spy is evident, and we feel sure that he was well acquainted with the buildings he entered, otherwise he would have been captured.

The damage done to the city up to this date was small, when we consider the amount of shells that had been thrown into it. It is true that a great many buildings had been struck, but none demolished; all of those struck were still tenable, and were occupied by the different families during the brief moments that the enemy's mortars were silent. After the first excitement was over, the citizens became quite hopeful of the result, and from the exaggerated reports brought by couriers of the strength of Johnston's army, it was confidently believed that the day of relief would soon come, and that the siege would be shortly raised. Not the slightest fear was expressed of the city ever falling into the hands of the enemy; not a man, woman or child believed such an event at all likely to occur, but all anticipating the defeat and destruction of Grant's army as soon as Johnston arrived with the fifty thousand men he was reported to have under his command.

The same course of shelling and sharpshooting continued, without anything of importance being attempted by the enemy. They had now decided on a regular investment of the city, and determined upon making gradual approaches by means of their engineers and sappers and miners, until they could come up close to our works, when they would make another endeavor to storm our lines; if unsuccessful, they would then keep us penned up until starvation compelled the garrison to capitulate. That such was their idea we were repeatedly informed by their pickets.

Until the twenty-fifth of June, nothing of interest transpired, except at one or two points along our lines, and an occasional sortie by the garrison on the enemy's works. One night, a sharp skirmish took place beyond our picket lines, between a body of the enemy and a regiment of Tennesseans belonging to Reynolds' brigade. The regiment had gone out for the purpose of cutting wood for fuel and cane tops for the horses, they being compelled to subsist wholly on that, all the fodder being exhausted, and the corn ground into meal for the soldiers. As was customary, they carried their arms with them, so as to be prepared in case of emergency. "While in the midst of their work, the Yankee pickets opened fire on them. As this act of the enemy was contrary to their usual habit, it so exasperated the men that, throwing down their axes, they seized their arms and drove in the pickets. The enemy, alarmed at this demonstration, quickly threw forward a large body of their infantry, who met the Tennesseans just as they were driving in the pickets. A brisk fight ensued, in which the Tennesseans behaved very gallantly, and succeeded in cutting off and capturing a large number of the enemy. On another occasion a sortie made by our forces resulted very successfully, our men capturing Lt. Col. Cann, of an Illinois regiment, and several of the enemy, besides spiking one of their guns.

Instead of encouraging these expeditions, Lieutenant General Pemberton appeared disposed to stop them. An expedition was organized one night for the purpose of storming the enemy's works on the peninsula opposite Vicksburg, and throwing the mortars and guns into the river, by that way saving the city considerable injury from the enemy's shells, and the inhabitants from annoyance. A letter was sent in to Lieutenant General Pemberton, requesting his permission for the party to cross the river on the first dark night, and make the attempt, but the General refused his consent, on the ground that it was too dangerous an experiment; besides which, he was certain it could not be successful. Had the permission been granted we are pretty certain it would have resulted favorably to us, as the party who would have attempted it were picked men, of daring and courage, and men upon whom reliance could have been placed. After this reply, however, the idea was abandoned, and was not again thought of during the remainder of the siege.

CHAPTER XXIII.
CONDITION OF VICKSBURG. CONDUCT OF THE INHABITANTS. SPIRIT OF THE WOMEN.

By the middle of June, Vicksburg was in a deplorable condition. There was scarcely a building but what had been struck by the enemy's shells, while many of them were entirely demolished. The city had the appearance of a half-ruined pile of buildings, and on every street unmistakable signs of the fearful bombardment it had undergone, presented themselves to the observer.

Many families of wealth had eaten the last mouthful of food in their possession, and the poor class of non-combatants were on the verge of starvation. The situation of the latter was indeed terrible; for while the former class of population were able to buy what little food remained in the hands of the heartless speculators, at such prices as they - money-grasping and unpatriotic creatures - would demand, the poor people were without money, and consequently their sufferings were terrible.

It is true there was not much provision in the city; in fact, there was scarcely any. At the same time, the prices charged for what was there, were such as to make a man wonder whether the sellers had the slightest touch of pity in them. Shut up, as they were in our lines, with a knowledge that at any moment one, of the hundreds of shells falling around them, might end their existence, their thirst for money remained unabated and the holders of what food there was, actually asked and received the following prices: Flour, five dollars per pound, or nearly one thousand dollars per barrel; meal, one hundred and forty dollars per bushel; molasses, ten and twelve dollars per gallon; and beef, (very often oxen killed by the enemy's shells, and picked up by the butchers) at two dollars and two dollars and a half per pound. As we are unacquainted with the names of these infamous parties, we are unable to publish them to world, to receive the scorn their conduct merits.

The military authorities assisted these poor unfortunates as much as they possibly could, and Lieutenant General Pemberton gave them the privilege to grind all the corn they could get at the government mills; but this assistance went but a small way to relieve their wants, and they would undoubtedly have perished but for the benevolent and generous conduct of the wealthier classes of citizens, who set to work for the purpose of averting the horrors which threatened them. Among those who aided with their time and means in this highly meritorious work, we take great pleasure in giving the names of W. H. Stevens, Rev. Rutherford, of the Methodist Church; Victor F. Wilson, and a German by the name of J. Kaiser. This last-named gentleman acted nobly. He had several hundred bushels of corn at his residence, which he handed over to a committee appointed for the purpose, reserving for himself *just enough* to last his family during the siege. We make particular mention of his conduct, because it was an act of charity rarely met with in his nation, and the exception, on his part, deserves more than a passing notice. There were many other citizens of Vicksburg who acted liberally towards the half-starved poor of the city, but we have not been able to obtain their names.

We cannot frame words of sufficient eloquence to express our admiration for the noble manner in which the women in the city acted during the siege. Never, we believe, did the Carthaginian women evince more patriotism during the siege of Carthage, than did the spirited and noble-hearted women of Vicksburg. It is true that they were not called upon to make as many sacrifices as the women of Carthage were, a fact which only arose from the different ages in which they lived. Among the poorer classes of women; the feeling of patriotism was strong, and the desire for a successful defense was apparent in their conversation, while the feeling among the wealthier class of women almost amounted to a wild enthusiasm. Never, during this war, have their devotion to, and interest in, the cause been so severely tested, and never has the bright light of patriotism shone in mankind with as much brilliancy as it did in the hearts of the women of Vicksburg, during the forty-seven days the siege lasted. Amid the stream of mortar and Parrott shells that came pouring on the devoted city, bursting around them, and creating an uproar, as if all the demons of hell had broken loose, and were ascending to earth, these heroic women remained unawed. On the 22nd of May, when the enemy endeavored to storm our works, the anxiety, on their part, that we should succeed in repulsing them, and the joy they evinced at learning we had gained the day, were of the most striking nature, while, on the day of the engagement with the *Cincinnati,* a large number of them congregated on the most prominent points in the city to witness the fight, regardless of the shells bursting above them, and the fragments falling around.

As might be expected, several of the women and children were killed or wounded during the siege; among those who were unfortunately struck by the balls and shells, we only recollect the following as killed: Miss Holly, Mrs. Cescie, and a Miss Jones. Among those who were wounded are a Mrs. Hazzard, Mrs. C. W. Peters, Mrs. W. H. Clements, Mrs. Major T. B. Read, Miss Lucy Rawlings, Miss Margaret Cook, and a Miss Hassley. These are only a portion of those who got injured, the remaining names we were unable to procure.

Notwithstanding the heavy list of casualties among the women and children, their spirit remained unbroken, and the same desire was expressed among them, that the city should be successfully defended. Even those who were wounded, half forgot their pains in the height of their patriotism, and suffering as they were from their wounds, their unanimous desire was, that the city should be held until relief should come, even if they had to die for it. The conduct of these heroic women should be remembered long after the independence of the South is achieved, and though their names will never be known, the future historian of our struggle for freedom, should delight to honor and praise the exalted heroism and patriotic virtues of these women, many of whom, delicately nurtured, and reared amid all the luxuries that wealth could afford, preferred to suffer the pangs of hunger and live in damp caves, or endure the pains of wounds inflicted by the missiles of the enemy, which even strong men have groaned under, rather than see the home of their nativity surrendered to the enemy of their country; and we believe that, had it been necessary, they would have been found at our entrenchments ready to aid, as much as their feeble powers could afford, in the defense of Vicksburg. Though the pen of the writer of this work, cannot indite words sufficient to portray the nobleness they exhibited during the memorable siege of forty-seven days duration, in future days he trusts that someone, more gifted than himself, will show to the world, as examples of feminine patriotism and endurance, the HEROINES OF VICKSBURG.

CHAPTER XXIV.
EXPLOSION OF ONE OF THE ENEMY'S MINES - PARTIAL DESTRUCTION OF A PORTION OF OUR WORKS - SEVERE ENGAGEMENT AND REPULSE OF THE FOE.

On discovering that the enemy were engaged in mining our works, and seeing our inability to prevent the prosecution of their work, measures were immediately taken to countermine and blow up the working parties of the enemy. These attempts however were not successful, as the inadequate means at our command, and the position of the hills on which our works were erected, rendered any undertaking of this nature very difficult. On one portion of the line occupied by Major General M. L. Smith, the countermining was partially successful, several of the enemy having been killed when it was blown up; even this, we cannot vouch for, not having been present at the explosion, although the information was received from a very good source.

The enemy, by means of their sappers and miners, had gradually approached, until they had erected powerful works within thirty yards of some portions of our line. On the left of the Jackson road, they had occupied the hill, mentioned in a previous chapter, and erected a large fort on it. This hill was on the immediate left of the road, about thirty yards distant from the line of fortifications occupied by the third Louisiana, of Hebert's brigade. As we stated before, it was a very high and strategic position, entirely overlooking our works, and which Brig. General Hebert desired to hold, on the Monday his troops were placed in position, being apprehensive of the enemy taking possession of it, which would have enabled them to have kept up a destructive fire on the third Louisiana, and also enfilade the road held by the consolidated twenty-first and twenty-third Louisiana regiments. His desire not being granted, the hill was left to the enemy, who quickly perceived the advantageous position they had gained, and put it to good use accordingly.

From this point the enemy kept up a constant and concentrated fire on the works, and from the vigor with which he bombarded them; it became apparent that this position would be the principal point of attack. It was at first thought that the concentration of their fire on this particular point, was an endeavor to destroy the works, but it was afterwards discovered as only intended to cover their mining operations, under the fort comprising a portion of our defenses on the left of the road, which from the advantages possessed by the enemy, progressed rapidly, and was soon in a state of completion.

As soon as this was discovered, General Hebert, who had shown considerable skill and valor during the siege, set to work and endeavored to foil them in their efforts. He first had a number of hand grenades manufactured, which he directed to be thrown at the enemy's working parties, and in a measure stopped the prosecution of their work for a time, but this even failed, as the enemy worked perseveringly in the night, and succeeded in making an excavation under the fort of sufficient size to protect them from the hand grenades, while our men were unable to throw them in the hollow formed, in consequence of the slanting construction of the parapet.

Having failed in his endeavor to prevent the enemy from mining the fort, General Hebert immediately set to work, and had a new line, of some length, built in the rear of the threatened point. The work under his superintendence was pushed forward with as much alacrity as the number of laborers he could command could push it forward.

The work having been at last completed, by the twenty-fifth of June the majority of the third Louisiana were removed from the mined fort and positioned in the new line, which was very close to its rear. Previous to this, the enemy must have completed their mine, and made preparations to blow up the fort, for between four and five o'clock on the evening of this same day, their train was fired, and a terrific explosion took place. Huge masses of earth were thrown up in the air, and those who experienced it, state that the ground was shook as if from an earthquake or a volcanic eruption. As soon as the earth was rent, a bright glare of fire issued from the burning powder, but quickly died away, as there was nothing of a combustible nature in the fort to ignite. In consequence of the men having been previously removed from the work, but few of them were injured, but all of them were considerably jarred by the shock.

Perceiving the fort partially destroyed, a column of the enemy's infantry, which had laid concealed in the hollow beneath the fort all day for the purpose, rushed forward with loud cheers for the purpose of gaining possession of the ruins. They were gallantly met, and a desperate struggle ensued. The third Louisiana, which is without doubt one of the best fighting regiments in the service, stood up manfully against overwhelming numbers, and despite every exertion on their part to storm the line, held them in check, until the sixth Missouri, another gallant regiment, under Col. Eugene Erwin, had arrived and reinforced them. As soon as they arrived, Col. Erwin, who was ahead of his men, immediately ascended the parapet of the ruined fort, when a Minie ball, from one of the sharpshooters, pierced his heart and he fell dead. He was a grandson of Henry Clay, and from the commencement of the war an ardent supporter of the South.

The Missourians, enraged at the death of their Colonel, fought like demons, and, aided by the third Louisiana, sprang into the ruined fort, and after a severe contest of two or three hours duration, succeeded in repulsing the enemy with great slaughter.

From our men being very much exposed to the enemy in this engagement, our loss was not less than eighty-six in killed and wounded; a very heavy list of casualties, for the small number of men engaged on our side. So close were the enemy to our men during the fight, that they could have conversed in a low tone with one another. Brigadier General Hebert was himself present during this engagement, and acted with his usual coolness and intrepidity.

The loss of the enemy could not have been less than four hundred in killed and wounded, as they lay in large numbers before our works after the fight, and a large number of wounded men were taken from the field as they fell. So severely punished were they in this attack, that in the second attempt they made to blow up the remainder of this fort, they did not try to storm the line.

While this struggle was going on, no demonstrations were made on any other portion of the line, beyond the accustomed amount of shelling and sharpshooting. Rumors of a speedy relief to the garrison were still spread among the troops, but from all the past reports proving false, the soldiers had begun to doubt everything they heard, leaving it for time to decide whether they should be relieved or not.

CHAPTER XXV.
DEATH OF GEN. GREEN, OF MISSOURI.
RUMORS OF GEN. JOHNSTON'S ADVANCE.

Two or three days after the destruction of our works by the explosion of the enemy's mine, an event of a most melancholy nature transpired. Brigadier General Green, commanding a brigade of Missourians and Arkansians, in Bowen's division was shot in the neck by a Minie ball, while in conversation with his staff. Although medical aid was promptly given to him, it was of no avail; his wound was mortal, and after lingering for about an hour he expired.

Gen. Green was an aged man, esteemed by all who knew him for his unswerving devotion to the great cause for which he fell fighting, his intrepid valor, and his genial and amiable qualities. He was a quiet and unassuming man; all the unnecessary pomp and dignity of the high position he occupied were laid aside, and the meanest private in his command had free and uninterrupted access to his presence. So endeared was he to his men, that they looked upon him more in the light of a friend than that of a General. Many noble sons of Missouri have fallen in this struggle for independence, bravely fighting for their homes and firesides, now in possession of the foe, but none of her martyrs in this holy cause will be deserving of greater praise, or spoken of in more glowing terms, than the aged and patriotic Brigadier General Green. We were told that he wished, previous to his death, that he would not live to see the city surrendered. If such was his wish, he was gratified, for the fatal ball, that ended his career on earth, came just four days before the offer was to yield Vicksburg to the enemy.

No event of any importance transpired from this day to the twenty-ninth of June. The army and the citizens had almost despaired of ever seeing Johnston arrive. The couriers who ran the gauntlet through the enemy's lines, and arrived safely in Vicksburg, brought the most exaggerated reports possible of the strength and position of the army soon to march to our relief. They stated that Gen. Johnston's force was not less than from fifty to sixty thousand strong, and were stretched from Jackson to Canton, Mississippi. With these reports, the people and garrison in general were surprised at his not making an advance on the enemy, as they felt certain that if his force was as strong as represented, there would be no difficulty in defeating any army the enemy could possibly send against him.

At this period, some unprincipled persons, actuated no doubt by animosity against General Johnston, spread a report in our lines, that it was not his intention to relieve the garrison, as he bad given Lieutenant General Pemberton orders to evacuate the city, which order not being obeyed, if he (Johnston) came to the relief of the beleaguered army and succeeded in raising the siege, it would compromise his reputation as a commander and an officer. Such being the case, the garrison would not be relieved, and Vicksburg would be left to her fate.

These reports, coming to the ears of the soldiers, caused some feeling of anger against General Johnston for a short time. All doubts of his desire or intention to aid them were soon laid aside, however, by the reports given to the men by the enemy's pickets, and they determined to patiently await his arrival, being certain that as soon as he had organized a sufficiently large force, he would march to Vicksburg and raise the siege.

Among the many false reports brought into our line, was one which stated that Major General Loring had crossed the Big Black at Hankerson's Ferry, and was advancing towards Vicksburg, when he was met by an overwhelming force of the enemy. A severe engagement was then said to have ensued, in which General Loring was repulsed and compelled to fall back. After retreating for some distance, he was reinforced by Major General Breckinridge's division, and, making a stand the next day, fought a severe battle, routing the enemy and inflicting great slaughter on him, and capturing six thousand prisoners.

We make mention of these reports to show the deceptions practised on the men, although the statement narrated above was given by the enemy, so far as it relates to the repulse of Loring, but they said nothing about the subsequent defeat of their army. As may be supposed, these reports, cheering the men as they did, when contradicted, did not tend to lighten the sufferings of the men, or relieve the anxiety which all felt for the advent of succor.

The brave men, nevertheless, still continued to bear up cheerfully against the hardships and sufferings they were then enduring, and there were but few who expressed any fear of our ability to hold the city, or who grew doubtful of final success.

CHAPTER XXVI.
SECOND EXPLOSION OF THE ENEMY'S MINE, AND OCCUPATION OF A PORTION OF THE FORT - THE GARRISON REDUCED TO MULE MEAT.

After the explosion of their mine, on the 25th of June, and the partial destruction of the fort, the enemy set vigorously to work on a new mine, for the purpose of completing its destruction; and, having gotten everything in readiness, on the 29th of June, at about 4 o'clock in the afternoon, a second explosion took place, from which the enemy succeeded in destroying the remnant left standing. No effort was made to storm the works in the rear of the ruins, although several of our men were killed and wounded, either by the fragments of dirt, or by the explosion.

The third Louisiana regiment, which occupied this line throughout the siege, suffered more than any other body of men in the garrison. Several times their position was charged in the most desperate manner, and twice was it blown up by the enemy. The loss they sustained during the siege, was not far from two hundred out of about four hundred and fifty contained in the regiment when the siege commenced. This was a fearful loss, when we consider it with that of the other commands.

In spite of the exposed position they occupied, these men, heroes of Belmont, Oak Hill, Elk Horn and Corinth, stood up manfully to their posts, and held their position against every effort of the enemy to force their line. We make particular mention of this regiment without disparagement to any other of the commands, as all fought with a valor unsurpassed in the annals of war, but merely as an act of justice to a gallant body of men, the survivors of what was once a regiment nearly twelve hundred strong; and in giving them this praise, we but echo the opinion of every soldier in the Confederate army, who has seen them in battle.

The firing from the peninsula, with mortars and siege guns on Vicksburg, had meanwhile continued with violence. Additional guns were brought to bear upon the devoted city, making it almost untenable. Starvation, in its worst forms, now confronted the unfortunate inhabitants, and, had the siege lasted two weeks longer, the consequences would have been terrible. All the beef in the city was exhausted by this time, and mules were soon brought in requisition, and their meat sold readily at one dollar per pound, the citizens being as anxious to get it, as they were before the investment, to purchase the delicacies of the season. It was also distributed among the soldiers, to those who desired it, although it was not given out under the name of rations. A great many of them, however, accepted it in preference to doing without any meat, and the flesh of the mules was found equal to the best venison. The author of this work partook of mule meat for three or four days, and found the flesh tender and nutritious, and, under the *peculiar circumstances*, a most desirable description of food.

CHAPTER XXVII.
SHELLING OF OUR HOSPITALS - CASUALTIES AMONG OUR OFFICERS.

During the siege, the enemy, forgetful of, or disregarding all rules of civilized warfare, exhibited a refinement of cruelty in firing at our hospitals. There were between four and five thousand sick and wounded soldiers in the different hospitals in Vicksburg, over each of which the usual yellow flag floated to designate that they were hospitals. Without appearing to care whether they were or not, the enemy deliberately fired into them, killing and wounding several of the unfortunate beings, whose ill-luck it was to be quartered there for medical treatment. That this barbarous act was committed intendedly, was apparent when the Washington Hotel, which had been converted into one of the hospitals, in fall view of the enemy, on the banks of the river, was struck by a twelve-inch mortar. Humanity would scarcely feel inclined to believe that an act so fiendish could be perpetrated by men calling themselves civilized beings, but such was the case, and this conduct must forever remain a reproach upon the nation or people who could sanction such brutal behavior.

We have not been able to learn whether Lieutenant General Pemberton ever protested against the shelling of our hospitals, or remonstrated with General Grant at permitting it; if he did, no regard was paid to his complaint, as they continued their barbarity until the end of the siege. After the surrender of the city, the Federal officers, in explanation, and as an apology for their conduct, stated that the guns on the peninsula were manned by raw troops, and served the double purpose of annoying the city and practising the men, but that General Grant never countenanced, or gave his consent to the hospitals being shelled.

From the commencement of the siege to the time we write of, many noble and gallant officers had yielded their life in defense of their country. Among those killed were Colonel Herrick, of the 21st Louisiana; Lieutenant Colonel Rogers, of the 17th Louisiana; Major Hoadley, of the heavy Artillery; Colonel Garrett, of the 20th Alabama; Major Martin, of the 26th Louisiana; Brigadier General Green, of Missouri; Colonel Eugene Erwin, of the 6th Missouri, and others. Among the wounded were Colonel W. Hall, of the 26th Louisiana; Colonel Patton, of the 23rd Louisiana; Colonel Marks, of the 27th Louisiana, (since dead); and Brigadier General Baldwin, of Smith's division. There were, unfortunately, many others killed and wounded during the siege, who belonged to the field and staff, but their names, with those of the many hundreds of gallant spirits who fell in defense of the "Gibraltar of the South," could not be obtained; but though the world may never know their names, the silent voice of Freedom, more eloquent than all the praise we can bestow, will bless the memory of those who fell bravely fighting in a just cause, and a grateful nation will long mourn her unknown defenders who fell at their post of duty with their face to their foe, fighting heroically.

CHAPTER XXVIII.
SEALING OF THE FATE OF VICKSBURG - OFFER TO SURRENDER - INDIGNATION OF THE GARRISON.

No attempt was made to storm our works, or no demonstration made by the enemy, with their mines, from the twenty-ninth of June to the surrender of the city, although the same heavy cannonading and sharpshooting was kept up, until an armistice was requested by Lieutenant General Pemberton.

Several nights prior to the surrender of the city, the enemy's pickets told our men that preparations were being made to storm our works on the fourth of July, as Grant had determined to sup in Vicksburg on that night, or sup in h-l, to which remark one of our pickets replied, that as there was no chance of Grant's supping in Vicksburg on the fourth of July, it was very likely he would sup in the latter place. Not a man had the least idea that the city would be yielded up to the enemy on that day, all of them thinking that when the worse came we would cut our way out of the city. To cut our way out, however, was utterly impracticable. Our men were so weak and exhausted from the want of a sufficiency of food, that such an attempt would have resulted in the annihilation of the entire army, as we do not believe that out of the eighteen thousand men reported for duty, three thousand could have succeeded in reaching Big Black safely. This was evidently the opinion of Lieutenant General Pemberton and his subordinate Generals, and the surrender of the city was made. That surrendering was the best course to be adopted we will acknowledge, but that we should have surrendered *then* is what we do not believe, if the statements made in defense of General Pemberton be true. We will, however, refer to this in another chapter.

On Friday, the third of July, at about ten o'clock in the morning, a flag of truce was hoisted on the Jackson road and hostilities ceased. A short time afterwards General Bowen and Col. Montgomery, aid to General Pemberton, were seen leaving the works for the enemy's lines. As soon as they left the men conjectured that the object of their visit was to treat for a surrender of the city. The excitement among the men soon became alarming, until it was allayed by a statement that General Pemberton had sent to General Grant for the purpose of getting his consent to our removing the sick and wounded and the women and children from the city.

After remaining in the enemy's line for some time, General Bowen and Colonel Montgomery returned, when official correspondence in the next chapter took place.

CHAPTER XXIX.
OFFICIAL CORRESPONDENCE BETWEEN GENS. PEMBERTON AND GRANT. SURRENDER OF VICKSBURG MADE.

This chapter contains the official correspondence of Generals Pemberton and Grant, which we copy from the United States papers. We give it so as to complete as much as possible this work.

General Pemberton's Letter proposing the Surrender of Vicksburg.
HEADQUARTERS, VICKSBURG, July 3, 1863.
Maj. Gen. U. S. GRANT, Commanding United States forces.

General: I have the honor to present to you an armistice for – hours, with the view to arranging terms for the capitulation Vicksburg. To this end, if agreeable to you, I will appoint three commissioners, to meet a like number to be named by yourself, at such place and hour to-day as you may find convenient. I make this proposition to save the further effusion of blood, which must otherwise be shed to a frightful extent, feeling myself fully able to maintain my position for a yet indefinite period.

This communication will be handed you under a flag of truce, by Major General James Bowen.

Very respectfully, your obedient servant,
J. C. PEMBERTON.

To this General Grant replied as follows:

General Grants Reply.

HEADQUARTERS DEP'T OF TENNESSEE,
In the Field, near Vicksburg, July 3, 1863.

Lieut. Gen. J. C. PEMBERTON, commanding Confederate forces, etc

General: Your note of this date, just received, proposes an armistice of several hours, for the purpose of arranging terms of capitulation, through commissioners to be appointed, etc. The effusion of blood you propose stopping by this source can be ended at any time you may choose, by an unconditional surrender of the garrison. Men who have shown so much endurance and courage as those now in Vicksburg, will always challenge the respect of an adversary, and I can assure you will be treated with all the respect due them as prisoners of war. I do not favor the proposition of appointing commissioners to arrange terms of capitulation, because I have no other terms than those indicated above.

I am, General, very respectfully, your obedient servant,

U. S. GRANT, Major General.

Gen. Bowen, the bearer of Gen. Pemberton's letter, was received by Gen. A. J. Smith. He expressed a strong desire to converse with Gen. Grant, and accordingly, while declining this, Gen. Grant requested Gen. Smith to say, that if Gen. Pemberton desired to see him, an interview would be granted between the lines, in McPherson's front, at any hour in the afternoon which Gen. Pemberton might appoint.

A message was sent back to Gen. Smith appointing three o'clock as the hour. General Grant was there with his staff, and Gens. Ord, McPherson, Logan and A. J. Smith. Gen. Pemberton came late, attended by Gen. Bowen and Col. Montgomery. He was much excited and impertinent in his answers to General Grant. The conversation was held apart, between Gen. Pemberton and his officers, and Gens. Grant, McPherson and A. J. Smith. The rebels insisted on being paroled, and allowed to march beyond our lines; officers and men all with eight days' rations, drawn from their own stores, the officers to retain their private property and body servants.

Gen. Grant heard what they had to say, and left them at the end of an hour and a half, saying he would send in his ultimatum in writing, to which Gen. Pemberton promised to reply before night, hostilities to cease in the meantime.

Gen. Grant then conferred at his headquarters with his corps and division commanders, and sent the following letter to Gen. Pemberton by the hand of General Logan and Lieutenant Colonel Wilson:

General Grant's offer for the Surrender.

103

HEADQUARTERS, DEPARTMENT OF TENNESSEE,
Near Vicksburg, July 3, 1863.

Lieut. Gen. J. C. PEMBERTON, Commanding Confederate forces, Vicksburg, Miss.

General: In conformity with the agreement of this afternoon, I will submit the following proposition for the surrender of the City of Vicksburg, public stores, etc. On your accepting the terms proposed, I will march in one division, as a guard, and take possession at eight o'clock to-morrow morning. As soon as paroles can be made out and signed by the officers and men, you will be allowed to march out of our lines, the officers taking with them their regimental clothing, and staff, field and cavalry officers one horse each. The rank and file will be allowed all their clothing, but no other property.

If these conditions are accepted, any amount of rations you may deem necessary can be taken from the stores you now have, and also the necessary cooking utensils for preparing them; thirty wagons also, counting two two-horse or mule teams as one. You will be allowed to transport such articles as cannot be carried along. The same conditions will be allowed to all sick and wounded officers and privates, as fast as they become able to travel. The paroles of these latter must be signed, however, whilst officers are present, authorized to sign the roll of prisoners. I am, General, very respectfully,

Your obedient servant,

U. S. GRANT, Major General.

The officers who received this letter stated that it would be impossible to answer it by night, and it was not till a little before peep-of-day that the proposed reply was furnished:

Reply of Gen. Pemberton, accepting all the terms offered by General Grant.

HEADQUARTERS, VICKSBURG, July

Maj. Gen. U. S. GRANT, Commanding United States Forces.

General: I have the honor to acknowledge the receipt of your communication of this date, proposing terms for the surrender of this garrison and post. In the main your terms are accepted; but in justice both to the honor and spirit of my troops, manifested in the defense of Vicksburg, I have the honor to submit the following amendments, which, if acceded to by you, will perfect the agreement between us: At ten o'clock to-morrow I propose to evacuate the works in and around Vicksburg, and to surrender the city and garrison under my command by marching out with my colors and arms and stacking them in front of my present limits, after which you will take possession; officers to retain their side arms and personal property, and the rights and property of citizens to be respected.

I am, General, yours, very respectfully,

J. C. PEMBERTON, Lieutenant General.

To this General Grant immediately replied as follows:

HEADQUARTERS DEPARTMENT OF TENNESSEE,
Before Vicksburg, July 4, 1863.

Lieutenant General PEMBERTON, commanding forces in Vicksburg:

General: I have the honor to acknowledge your communication of the 3rd of July. The amendments proposed by you cannot be acceded to in full. It will be necessary to furnish every officer and man with a parole signed by myself, which, with the completion of the rolls of prisoners, will necessarily take some time. Again: I can make no stipulation with regard to the treatment of citizens and their private property. While I do not propose to cause any of them any undue annoyance or loss, I cannot consent to leave myself under restraint by stipulations. The property which officers can be allowed to take with them, will be as stated in the proposition of last evening - that is, that officers will be allowed their private baggage and side arms, and mounted officers one horse each. If you mean by your propositions for each brigade to march to the front of the lines now occupied by it, and stack their arms at ten o'clock, A. M., and then return to the inside and remain as prisoners until properly paroled, I will make no objections to it. Should no modification be made of your acceptance of my terms by nine o'clock, A. M., I shall regard them as having been rejected, and act accordingly. Should these terms be accepted, white flags will be displayed along your lines to prevent such of my troops as may not have been notified from firing on your men.

I am, General, very respectfully, your obedient servant,

U. S. GRANT,
Major General United States Army.

To this the subjoined answer has this moment been received:

Unconditional Acceptance by General Pemberton of the terms Proposed by General Grant.

HEADQUARTERS, Vicksburg,
July 4, 1863.
Major General U. S. GRANT, commanding United States forces, etc.

General: I have the honor to acknowledge the receipt of your communication of this date, and in reply, to say that the terms proposed by you are accepted. Very respectfully,

J. C. PEMBERTON, Lieutenant General.

CHAPTER XXX.
SURRENDER OF VICKSBURG AND GARRISON - TERMS OF CAPITULATION - LAYING DOWN OF THE ARMS.

At about three o'clock in the afternoon of the third of July, Lieutenant General Pemberton, accompanied by Major General Bowen, left our lines and proceeded to the neutral ground, previously designated, and had an interview with General Grant. The result of their conference we have already given in the correspondence. After an absence of about two hours' duration, Lieutenant General Pemberton and Major General Bowen returned into our lines. As an armistice had been declared until ten o'clock that evening, the firing ceased, and the shades of night descended upon the two opposing armies in quietude, unbroken, save by the voices of the soldiers in low but angry and indignant conversation, at what they deemed a disgrace upon their country in surrendering the city they had so long and nobly fought, and endured the pangs of hunger to defend.

At dark, on the evening of this day, a council of all the Generals was held at General Pemberton's headquarters, which lasted for several hours. Although we could not learn what transpired in an official way, we received information, from good authority, that it was decided, by a majority of the general officers, that the troops were entirely too weak from the want of food to cut their way through, and that if the position had to be yielded, it was useless to sacrifice the lives of the men in a fruitless endeavor; so that the only course left was to surrender the garrison on General Grant's terms of capitulation. Of the Major Generals present, we understand that Major General M. L. Smith was the only one who absolutely opposed surrendering on any condition, preferring to remain behind the breastworks and starve rather than give up the city. A majority of the council, being of a contrary opinion to him, however; he was, of course, necessitated to abide by their decision, and about three o'clock a messenger was sent into General Grant's lines with dispatches from Lieutenant General Pemberton.

On Saturday morning, a circular was issued from headquarters, announcing the surrender of Vicksburg and garrison, and stating the terms of capitulation to be as follows:

1st. The entire garrison of Confederate troops was to be surrendered to Major General Grant, commanding the United States forces.

2nd. The prisoners of war were to be paroled and sent out of the city as soon as blank paroles were printed.

3rd. All mounted officers to have the privilege of retaining their horses.

4th. All officers of every grade and rank were to retain their side arms, &c.

5th. All citizens desiring to leave the city with the Confederate forces, could do so on being paroled.

6th. All ammunition, stores, field artillery and siege guns, were to be surrendered to the United States forces, as also all small arms in our possession.

These are about the substance of the terms of capitulation. Although we made no copy of Lieutenant General Pemberton's circular, this will be found as correct a statement as could be desired.

When it was officially announced to our men that Vicksburg was surrendered to the enemy, their indignation knew no bounds. Having been among the troops, we can truthfully speak what we heard and saw of the expressions of sentiment on their part relative to the surrender. With almost a unanimous voice the soldiers declared that General Pemberton had yielded the city without their will, and against any desire on their part. All expressed a determination never to serve under him again, many stating that rather than be under the command of such a man, they would desert from the army, if they were afterwards shot for it. It is not to be denied that the feeling among the men amounted almost to a mutinous one - to such a degree, indeed, was it, that many threats were made, which only the argument and supplication of the officers prevented the men from putting into execution.

All the statements we have made above in reference to the feelings of the soldiers are truth - every word truth, and in substantiation of them, we call upon the soldiers and officers composing the garrison of Vicksburg, to vouch for all we have said.

On Saturday morning, the fourth of July, and the anniversary of American Independence, the troops composing the army of Lieutenant General Pemberton marched from the line of intrenchments they had defended and held for nearly two months, amid hardships and privations unsurpassed in the annals of modern warfare, and after stacking the arms they had so well and nobly used, and lowering the standards which had proudly floated on many a bloody battle-field, returned inside the works, prisoners of war to their bitterest foe.

CHAPTER XXXI.
OCCUPATION OF VICKSBURG BY THE ENEMY. CONDUCT OF YANKEE SOLDIERS. IMPUDENCE OF NEGROES.

On Saturday, at twelve o'clock, M. Logan's division of McPherson's corps, of the Federal army, commenced entering the city, and in a quarter of an hour Vicksburg was crammed with them. Their first act was to take possession of the court house, on the spire of which they hoisted the United States flag, amid the exultant shouts of their comrades, and a deep feeling of humiliation on the part of the Confederate soldiers who witnessed the hauling up of the flag which they had hoped never to see floating over the city they had so long and proudly boasted impregnable, and never to be taken by the enemy of the South.

After the enemy's forces had stacked their arms, they scattered over the city, and then commenced a scene of pillage and destruction which beggars all description. Houses and stores were broken open, and their contents appropriated by the plunderers. The amount of money and property stolen in this way was enormous, and the Yankee soldiers appeared to glory in their vandalism. One merchant, by the name of G. C. Kress, had his safe broken open, and twenty thousand dollars in money, with a large supply of clothing, taken away. Another merchant, and well-known citizen of Mississippi, by the name of W. H. Stephens, had his store broken open and nearly all the contents taken away. In fact, every place that they could possibly enter without fear of resistance, was broken open and robbed of what was contained in them. The enemy appeared to glory in their course, and on one occasion, in reply to a remonstrance on the part of a gentleman whose residence they had broken open, they said, "we have fought hard enough to capture Vicksburg, and now we have got it, we intend to plunder every house in the d-d rebel city."

As soon as Gen. Grant heard of the wholesale pillage of the city that his followers had commenced, he ordered guards to be stationed over the town, and issued an order prohibiting any of his men from entering any other residence than that in which they were quartered, and threatening to punish any soldier who might be caught in the act of robbing citizens; at the same time, he gave no satisfaction whatever, to those parties who had already suffered at the hands of his army. Several applications were made to him for redress, but he told the applicants he was unable to assist them, or give any permission to have the camps of the men searched; although, if any of his soldiers were discovered with stolen property in their possession, he would have it returned to their owners, on their proving it belonged to them. This was, of course, but poor consolation to the losers who were necessitated to be satisfied with this answer, and submit to their loss.

With that enterprise and greed for gain which characterizes the universal Yankee nation, on the same day that the Federal army entered Vicksburg, several places of business were opened, and signs informing the public that metalic coffins were on hand to remove the dead bodies of friends, and that express offices, book and fruit stores were "within," were to be seen upon several establishments on Washington street.

Soon after the enemy entered the city, Mr. William Lum, a well-known citizen of Vicksburg, took the oath of allegiance, and General

Grant made his headquarters at the residence of this gentleman. The Jewish portion of the population, composed principally of Germans, with but one honorable exception, went forward and received the oath of allegiance to the United States. The one honorable exception sacrificed a store of goods, which cost him between thirty-five and forty thousand dollars, rather than remain under the control of the enemy.

The conduct of the negroes, after the entrance of their "liberators," was beyond all expression. While the Yankee army was marching through the streets, crowds of them congregated on the sidewalks, with a broad grin of satisfaction on their ebony countenances. The next day, which was Sunday, witnessed a sight, which would have been ludicrous had it not galled our soldiers by the reflection that they were compelled to submit to it. There was a great turn out of the "contrabands," dressed up in the most extravagant style imaginable, and promenading through the streets, as if Vicksburg had been confiscated and turned over them. In familiar conversation with the negro wenches, the soldiers of the Federal army were seen, arm-in-arm, marching through the streets, while the "bucks" congregated on the corners and discussed the happy event that had brought them freedom.

So arrogant did the negroes become after the entrance of the Federal forces, that no white Confederate citizen or soldier dared to speak to them, for fear of being called a rebel, or some other abusive epithet. One of the Confederate soldiers, happening to enter the garden of the house that the author of this work resided in, for the purpose of picking a peach, a negro, belonging to a gentleman of Vicksburg, who had charge of the garden, brought out a gun, and, taking deliberate aim at the soldier, was about to fire. We immediately threw up the gun, and, drawing a knife, threatened the negro if he fired at the man; no sooner was the threat made, than the negro, with an oath, levelled the gun at us and drew the trigger; luckily the cap snapped without exploding, and we succeeded in getting the gun away and discharging it.

While making these observations about the negroes, we would say that it was confined to the city negroes alone. The slaves brought in by planters, and servants of soldiers and officers, did not appear the least gratified at their freedom. The majority of those connected with our army were very desirous of leaving with their masters, and

General Grant at first consented that those who desired it should leave; but as soon as a few passes were made out, he revoked the order, and compelled the balance to remain. These differences in the conduct of city and country negroes, should not be a matter of surprise, when we consider the privileges given to the negroes in the cities of the South, and demands a change of policy on the part of slaveowners residing in densely populated places. Many of the negroes, who were compelled to remain in Vicksburg when their masters in the army left, afterwards made their escape, and returned to the Confederate lines.

CHAPTER XXXII.
LOSS DURING THE SIEGE. NUMBER OF CONFEDERATE CAPTURED. ARMS AND AMMUNITION SURRENDERED. OPINIONS OF THE ENEMY.

The loss of the Confederate forces during the siege, is estimated by good judges at a number not exceeding 4,000 in killed and wounded. A number of our casualties resulted from the indiscretion of the soldiers in exposing themselves to the enemy's sharpshooters. The loss of the enemy we would estimate as follows:

Attack on Shoup's line, 19th of May, 600 killed and wounded.
General assault on the 22nd May……9,000 "
Attack on Hebert's line, 25th June…….600 "
Prisoners captured……………………. 500
Other casualties during the siege……2,000

 Making a total of……………… 12,700

This estimate we believe to be much beneath what it really was, as in our opinion the enemy lost nearly as much as the total, on the twenty-second of May, for, taking the ratio of six men wounded for one killed, we find that as many as two thousand dead bodies were buried by the enemy on the Monday following. This would make their loss on that day alone 14,000, or more than the grand total we give above. The assertion of Grant, in his official report, that he lost only 8,000 men during the campaign, is a glaring falsehood, as we feel certain that on the day mentioned above, he lost more than he states his casualties to be from the landing at Bruinsburg to the surrender of the city.

The total amount of prisoners captured at Vicksburg by the enemy did not exceed twenty-four thousand, of which, nearly six thousand were either sick or wounded. The following general officers were captured: Lieutenant General Pemberton; Major Generals M. L. Smith, J. H. Forney, J. Bowen, and C. L. Stephenson. The names of the Brigadier Generals captured were: Hebert, Moore, Barton, Lee, Buford, Shoup, Baldwin, Vaughn and Taylor; the latter being Inspector General of the army.

Our loss in small arms and artillery was about as follows:

      Small Arms…. 35,000
      Siege Guns………..27
      Field Artillery…… 70

A great many pieces of the artillery were unfit for use, and could have been of no use to the enemy.

The amount of ammunition delivered over to the Yankee officers was large, and as near as we could find out, was as follows:

      Musket Cartridges………..600,000 rounds.
      Field Artillery Cartridges.....15,000   "
      Heavy Artillery Cartridges...15,000   "
      Percussion Caps…………..350,000

This estimate we believe very moderate, as it only gives for each man thirty-five rounds of musket cartridges, and about twenty percussion caps each. We are quite certain that a considerably larger amount of ammunition was surrendered to the enemy. This estimate, however, is made to avoid all charges of exaggeration.

Our line of work was pronounced by the enemy's engineer officers to be the most contemptible they had seen erected during the war. All expressed great astonishment that, with fifteen months of time before us, we had not converted Vicksburg into an impregnable fortress. They expressed themselves very much deceived in the strength of our works, as the representations of the Northern press, and our own boasting, had made them believe that Vicksburg was defended by well made works and had between two and three hundred guns mounted.

Our works were, indeed, the most outrageous ever made during the war. The supervisors of their construction could have known no more about erecting fortifications than we do; in fact, there was not one engineer in the army of Vicksburg who understood his profession thoroughly - they existed but in name, and the position they held in the Confederate service. The ground on which the works were erected was naturally a strong one, and to that advantage alone were we enabled to hold the city for so long a time, otherwise they would have offered but little or no impediment to the overwhelming numbers of the enemy which were thrown on the line in their attack on the twenty-second of May.

After the enemy had taken possession of Vicksburg, Major General McPherson rode over the entire length of the line, and was so impressed with the defective manner in which they were constructed, that he is reported to have exclaimed: "Good Heavens! are these the long-boasted fortifications of Vicksburg? It was the rebels, and not their works, that kept us out of the city." While this was a great compliment to the valor of the "rebels," it certainly expressed the greatest contempt possible for the fortifications surrounding Vicksburg.

The Federal officers candidly gave the Confederate garrison the credit of being as brave troops as they ever saw, and more than one compliment to the heroism of our soldiers was paid, coupled with a regret on the part of the officers of rank, that such men should be in arms against the United States. Not a word was said by the Yankees claiming superiority in fighting qualities; they all acknowledged that starvation had conquered us, and not the prowess of their arms, and during the stay of the garrison in Vicksburg, the greatest courtesy and consideration was shown to our soldiers by the Federal officers; their privates alone manifesting any desire to gloat over our reverse.

CHAPTER XXXIII.
A WEEK IN THE ENEMY'S LINES. PAROLING THE GARRISON. DEPARTURE FROM VICKSBURG.

The Confederate army remained in Vicksburg, as prisoners of war, for one week after the surrender, that time being taken to prepare the rolls of the different commands, and parole the men. During this period many severe street fights took place between the Federal and Confederate soldiers, in consequence of the taunts and abuse of the victorious army. Several of the Federal soldiers were severely beaten, and one or two killed. In one of these street brawls, a young man, a citizen of Vicksburg, and volunteer aid on Gen. Baldwin's staff, shot a Federal soldier dead for using insulting language. He was taken to General Grant's headquarters, and after a hearing released.

During the week spent in the enemy's lines, we had several opportunities of hearing the sentiments of both the officers and soldiers of the Federal army. Among the officers, it was the same everlasting cant about the Union, and their determination that it should be restored; but among the privates the greed for gain, and the object with which they fight was not concealed in the slightest degree. They spoke in raptures of the capacity of Mississippi's soil for white labor, and declared their intention to get a grant of land from the United States, and settle there after the war is over. This unblushing declaration was accompanied by the assertion that, as the South had rebelled against their government, it was only just that the property of the people should be divided among their troops. Such remarks were the principal causes of the street fights between the two armies, as the high spirit of our soldiers could ill brook this style of apportioning their homes and property by the enemy.

By Friday, the 10th of July, the prisoners having been paroled, orders were issued to the different brigade commanders to make preparations for marching the next morning, and accordingly the troops were got in readiness for their departure.

On Saturday morning, at half-past eleven o'clock, the Confederate soldiers took up their line of march. It was a mournful and harrowing sight. The soldiers felt their disgrace, and there was not one gallant heart in the mass of men, that did not feel half bursting with sorrow and humiliation at being compelled to march through the enemy's guards who were stationed on both sides of the road to some distance beyond the entrenchments. But nothing could avert the degradation; so, with downcast looks, and countenances on which a knowledge of the bitterness of their defeat could be seen plainly stamped, they filed past the enemy, who gathered in large numbers to witness their departure.

It was a day never to be forgotten by those who assisted in the defense of Vicksburg. So filled with emotion were many of our men, that large tear drops could be seen on their weather-beaten countenances, and ever and anon they would pause in their march, and, turning back, take one last sad look at the city they had fought and bled for. All felt that, serious as the disaster was to the Confederate cause, it was nothing to their humiliation. Amid the storm of shot and shell that poured upon them, they had remained cheerful and confident; but at this moment their hopefulness had departed; the yell of defiance that had so often struck terror in the hearts of their foe, was not to be heard; their willing hands no longer grasped the weapons of a good cause; their standards trailed in the dust, and they were prisoners of war. Silently and sadly, they marched on, and in a few minutes, Vicksburg was lost to their view.

Thus fell the city of Vicksburg after a defense of over twelve months, and a siege which lasted for forty-seven days, forty-two of which a garrison of not more than twenty-five thousand effective men had subsisted on less than one-quarter rations. The Confederate army fought with a valor that not even the defenders of Saragossa and Mantua ever surpassed. Subject to a bombardment of a nature so terrific that its equal has never been known in civilized warfare; through rain and sunshine, storm and calm, writhing under the pangs of starvation, these gallant Southern troops, whose deeds will form one of history's brightest pages when the annals of this siege shall become known, stood up to their post, and, with almost superhuman valor, repulsed every attack made by their enemy, and inflicting tremendous loss on him, until surrendered by the General whose want of ability and confidence in himself had entailed these sufferings and hardships on them.

It is estimated that the number of missiles thrown in the entrenchments, exceeded thirty thousand daily; and by the official report of General Grant's Chief of Artillery, it would appear that twenty millions three hundred and seventy thousand one hundred and twenty-two missiles of all kinds were thrown in the works, which would make it, by calculation, over four hundred thousand missiles, including small arm ammunition, daily thrown. This, however, must be an exaggeration, unless Grant's Chief of Artillery included the number of rounds of small arms used in the different battles prior to the investment of Vicksburg, which lasted only forty-seven days. He, however, gives the number as having been fired *into the city*, which, if correct, would only show the gigantic nature of the bombardment. The number of shots from artillery are averaged by the Chief of Artillery for Grant's army, at 32,617 per day; but then he only gives 142,912 rounds as having been fired during the entire siege. It is very likely that an error exists in the last estimate as more than that number was fired. We are rather inclined to think the number should have been 1,420,912, as that would bring it nearer to his daily estimate.

We cannot close this chapter without passing a just compliment to the Surgeons attached to the garrison of Vicksburg. Although they were from morning to night engaged in their duties to the soldiers, they were always found administering to the sick and wounded non-combatants of the city. Among the many, we must mention Dr. E. McD. Coffey, Chief Surgeon of Bowen's division, who was unremitting in his attentions to this class of sufferers, and always had several sick and wounded women and children under his charge. To this gentleman we were indebted for an introduction to Major General McPherson, who is, without doubt, the only real gentleman among the Federal Generals to whom we were introduced. He was very polite, never using the epithet "rebel" in the presence of our officers or soldiers, and avoided, as much as possible, any expression of exultation at the fall of Vicksburg when in our company.

Before bringing this chapter to a close, we would endeavor to remove the false idea among our people, that Vicksburg was surrendered after a feeble defense. The city was defended as desperately as could be required. The only thing to be said is, that had proper generalship been displayed, there would have been no necessity to use the works surrounding Vicksburg. *After* we were invested, the defense of Vicksburg *commenced*, and though the city is now in the hands of the enemy, it has brought him no honor in its capture, nor added a single laurel to his wreath of victory. *Starvation* succeeded in doing what the prowess of their arms could never have performed. The result was a reverse to the Confederate arms; but when future generations shall speak of this war, the deeds of the gallant men who defended the city, will be extolled among the most heroic feats of the war, and the descendants of those who fought behind the entrenchments of Vicksburg, will be proud of the knowledge that their fathers aided in its defense. All honor to their unswerving patriots! Nobly did they sustain the honor of their country, and the glory of their past deeds; and, falling as they did, the historian of this war will declare that, in their fall as much honor was gained as if they had triumphed in their defense.

CHAPTER XXXIV.
REVIEW OF THE CAMPAIGN, FROM THE LANDING OF THE ENEMY TO THE SURRENDER OF VICKSBURG.

When writers far away from the scene of military operations attempt to censure the actions of military men, particularly if not well acquainted with the facts attending such operations, the voice of censure should be raised in condemnation of such a course; but when the case is reversed, and the writer is present, and witnesses the short-comings and errors of a General, it is a great folly to charge him with giving to the public opinions of the incompetency of Generals, because he happens not to be a military-educated man, or to hold no position in the army. It does not require military talent to decide whether or not a General is competent; common sense and a sound judgment, seasoned or strengthened by the opinions of other and better informed men, are all that is needed to make those ideas not only able, but in reality truthful and correct.

It is with these opinions that we venture to publish this review of General Pemberton's campaign, from the landing of the enemy at Bruinsburg to the surrender of Vicksburg. Many of the comments and criticisms made in these pages, are the result of strict observation before the investment; and fears of what we deemed errors and signs of incompetency on the part of Lieutenant General Pemberton, were expressed by us in private conversation, some weeks before the enemy had landed. We had, however, determined not to make them public, until they could be confirmed by men of well known military talent, and high position in the Confederate army. Circumstances having favored our wishes, special pains were taken to observe and note down all the sentiments expressed by those who, from their standing in the army, are quite capable of judging and of forming correct ideas.

We were not present in every engagement which we relate; but all the accounts given in this work were received from *General* officers who were present, and to whose information we attach importance, as they emanate from soldiers of great ability and valor. We found, in conversation with many distinguished officers, that their ideas were identical to ours, and, strengthened by their sentiments, we give to the public the criticisms and comments to be found in the following chapters.

CHAPTER XXXV.
THE ERROR IN NOT MASSING OUR ARMY AT GRAND GULF.

As soon as the enemy's fleet had passed our batteries at Vicksburg, it became apparent that the first point attacked would be Grand Gulf. The garrison at that place consisted of two small brigades of Missouri and Arkansas troops under Gen. Bowen, with the brigades of Col. Reynolds, of Stephenson's division, and Brigadier General Baldwin's, of Smith's, *in Vicksburg* as a reinforcing column. The total number of men in this force, when combined, could not have been seven thousand effective men. On the 30th of April, the enemy landed at Bruinsburg unopposed, and was allowed, from want of troops to oppose him, to march to Port Gibson, where he met General Bowen.

Here it was, in the opinion of military men, that Lieutenant General Pemberton committed an error in not massing his entire army at Grand Gulf, as soon as the enemy's fleet had passed our batteries. From the nature of the country around Bruinsburg, artillery and sharpshooters posted along the banks of the river would have effectually prevented the Federal army from landing at that point, and had they ventured to land lower down in the vicinity of Rodney, and marched through the country by way of Tabor's Creek to Bayou Pierre for the purpose of getting in our rear, the forces under General Johnston, at Jackson, Mississippi, could have been thrown rapidly from Clinton to Utica, Mississippi, and, crossing below where Bayou Pierre branches off in two bodies, have hemmed in the enemy between them, and our forces' at Grand Gulf. There would then have been but two alternatives left for the enemy: either to fall back in haste to Rodney, or fight a battle under such disadvantages that victory would almost have been a certain result to the Confederate army.

The enemy's entire force at that point did not number more than forty or fifty thousand men, while our army, under Lieutenant General Pemberton, was about twenty-five thousand, which, with an addition of ten thousand men, the estimated strength of General Johnston's army, from Jackson would have reduced the disparity of numbers sufficiently to give us strong hopes of victory. We comment, in this way, from the fact, that if General Bowen, with only seven thousand men, could have held in check the enemy's entire force for over twenty-four hours, we think it but reasonable to suppose that our army, when five times as strong, could have defeated him.

These, however, are but speculations, and granting, from our limited military experience, that the ideas given above are not feasible, what prevented Lieut. Gen. Pemberton from throwing his entire force on the enemy at Port Gibson, and crushing him before any more troops could have been brought across the river? The enemy had but a limited number of transports, and the time it would have required to convey troops across the river to reinforce their army, would have been amply sufficient for our forces to have inflicted a severe defeat upon the enemy, from which he could not have recovered.

The defenders and apologists of General Pemberton's movements, while acknowledging that the best course would have been to mass our army at Grand Gulf, assert that he was prevented from so doing by the conflicting opinions of his Major Generals. It is said by them that General Pemberton's desire was to fight the battle of Vicksburg at Grand Gulf, but that Major General Stephenson gave it as his opinion, that the enemy would attack the city in front; Major General Forney had an idea that Snyder's Bluff would be the point of attack, and Major General Smith expected the enemy to land and attempt the storming of the works at Chickasaw Bayou. Lieutenant General Pemberton, it is said, did not share these opinions, but from an apprehension, if disaster should follow his removing the troops from Vicksburg, by an attack of the enemy on the points above named, it would be said that he disregarded the opinions of his subordinates and brought on the evil, he yielded to them, and suffered General Bowen to be overpowered at Port Gibson, and through weakness in numbers, and fears of being surrounded, to destroy the works at Grand Gulf and evacuate the place, thus leaving a path open to the enemy through the State of Mississippi.

Whether this defense be a truthful statement of facts, we cannot tell, and will not venture to vouch for it, but we give it so that Lieutenant General Pemberton shall have the benefit of all the argument and assertions brought forward in his favor. If, however, this defense is true, we see no way in which it can aid in removing the responsibility off Gen. Pemberton's shoulders; on the contrary, it shows a weakness and want of confidence in himself, which would alone be proof enough of his incompetency to command a department of such magnitude and importance as the one he was in control of.

The statement is, that General Pemberton was in favor of reinforcing Gen. Bowen, but was overruled in so doing by the representations of his Major Generals, who entertained opinions which he did not share. The question is then natural, when we ask: who was the commander of the army at Vicksburg? If General Pemberton had ordered either of his subordinate Generals to march their divisions, or part of their divisions, to Grand Gulf, they could not have disobeyed the command, but would have reinforced Bowen according to the orders received. But granting that this story is not true, and we have grave doubts of its reliability, it would seem that some one was at fault in allowing the other divisions of our army to remain in idleness at Vicksburg, while Bowen, with only seven thousand men, was giving battle at Port Gibson to a Yankee army forty thousand strong.

It has been also said, in defense of Lieutenant General Pemberton, that the enemy were making feints upon his position at Chickasaw Bayou and Snyder's Bluff, and had he reduced his forces they would have known it, from the numerous spies they had in Vicksburg. Granting all this argument, we see no reason why General Pemberton could not have learned by the same source as they derived their information of the strength of our army, that the movements made by the enemy, were mere feints, which amounted to nothing, as they had not sufficient men to make an attack.

In addition to all this mass of argument, it was well known that the whole Federal army was massing near St. Joseph, Louisiana. Gen. Pemberton had, then, but one of two courses to pursue: either to prevent their landing at Bruinsburg, or massing his army at Grand Gulf, and giving battle as soon as they landed. It is absurd to suppose that General Grant, after landing his army, would have avoided a battle, and marched on Jackson or Clinton, with the knowledge that a Confederate force of nearly thirty thousand of the finest fighting men in the world, could, as soon as he attempted such a move, have been hurled upon his left flank and rear. We therefore concur in the opinion of not less than *seven* of Gen. Pemberton's subordinate Generals, that a grave error was committed in not massing our army at Grand Gulf, and fighting the battle of Vicksburg at that point.

CHAPTER XXXVI.
THE ERROR IN REMAINING ON THE
WEST BANK OF THE BIG BLACK.

After the battle of Port Gibson, and evacuation of Grand Gulf by General Bowen, the Confederate army fell back to the West bank of the Big Black, in the vicinity of Bovina, Mississippi, while detachments from it were engaged in watching the different fords on the river. All the troops on the east bank of the Big Black were posted on the railroad, as far as Edward's Depot, about twenty miles from Vicksburg. The strength of our army at that time could not have been less than from twenty-three to twenty-six thousand men, well-armed and equipped, and supported by at least sixty pieces of light artillery.

While our army was remaining on the west bank of the Big Black, the Federal forces were marching through the State by way of Cayuga, Raymond and Clinton, with the intention of driving Johnston across Pearl river, and thus removing the chance of his rear being exposed when he marched on Vicksburg. In making this movement, he detached a small portion of his troops for the purpose of making a feint on General Pemberton' s forces, and keeping him on the west bank of the Big Black. Here it was, that Lieutenant General Pemberton again allowed himself to be deceived, and no measures were taken to follow the enemy, whose rear and flank were now exposed to our forces. The question at issue is, whether General Pemberton was aware of Grant's marching on Jackson, Mississippi, or was he ignorant of the fact. If he was aware of it, we see no way in which he can defend himself from the charge of displaying a want of generalship in not pursuing the advantage opened to him, and attacking the enemy. It is said, in defense of this apathy displayed by the Lieutenant General, that he was opposed to crossing the river, his plan being to wait until the enemy had penetrated the State, when he would march forward and cut him off from the river, and thus either compel them to fight under great disadvantage, or starve from want of provisions. This idea is not feasible, for two reasons: First, because, as soon as Grand Gulf fell, Vicksburg became our base of operations, which required that the rear of our army should always be directed to the city. By making the move his defenders claim he contemplated, General Pemberton would have had the rear of his army to the Mississippi river, and liable to attack at any moment by reinforcements crossing to succor Grant, besides which Vicksburg would have been left exposed, and the enemy by rapidly marching would have been able to reach the city before we could, our army not being large enough to be divided so as to defend Vicksburg at the same time that this move was being made; and secondly, the idea of starving out the enemy was not feasible, as we have General Grant's official report to certify that his entire army subsisted on the country for eight days, and found a plenty of food wherever they went.

It is our opinion that General Pemberton was not aware of the enemy's marching toward Jackson, and this opinion is shared with us by officers of high rank. If this opinion is correct, we are at a loss to understand how a General commanding an army can remain ignorant of the movements of his adversary, unless he is incompetent. Did not General Pemberton have his spies? Or, why did he not have them? The country through which the enemy marched is the most patriotic portion of the Confederacy, and the citizens would have gladly given all the information they had of the whereabouts of the enemy.

What excuse can General Pemberton give for permitting Grant to march unmolested from Grand Gulf to Clinton? We see none. This alone would be sufficient to prove him incompetent to command an army like the one he had control of at Vicksburg. In no other instance, during this war, has such short-sighted Generalship been displayed, and we cannot but attribute it to a want of military talent. Common sense - common reason, should convince those desirous of shielding Gen. Pemberton from censure, that he was out-generaled, not by General Grant's military superiority, but by his own lack of ability.

It is an acknowledged fact, that the division and brigade commanders almost unanimously favored an advance of our forces on the enemy, but that General Pemberton opposed it, until ordered to do so by General J. E. Johnston. This statement is brought forward in defense of General Pemberton, and as an apology for the loss of the battle of Baker's Creek. We then see, in this assertion, the whole facts of the case laid bare. The Lieutenant General opposed marching on the enemy. Why did he oppose it? Because he was not aware that the enemy's rear was exposed to him, must be the natural inference drawn from his action.

Had our army followed Grant toward Clinton, we would have compelled him to turn back and give battle, which movement would have exposed his rear to Johnston, and no one imagines for a moment that Gen. Jos. E. Johnston would have failed to avail himself of the opportunity offered, and attacked with what force he had. But this was not done; our army remained on the Big Black in idleness, while the enemy were marching on Johnston, and General Pemberton failed to do his duty, until ordered by General Johnston, in an official dispatch, which was intercepted by the enemy, who availed themselves of its contents, and succeeded in defeating General Pemberton, after a battle long and gallantly contested, not through any Generalship on his part, but through the indomitable valor of our soldiers.

CHAPTER XXXVII.
THE BATTLE OF BAKER'S CREEK - MAJOR GENERAL LORING'S ACTION IN IT - FALSE CHARGES AGAINST HIM.

It has been charged by the friends of General Pemberton, that but for the unaccountable absence of General Loring's division, the battle of Baker's Creek would have been won. We shall now see in what way this charge is true. Major General Loring's division came into action after Stephenson's division had lost nearly all its artillery, and as soon as it became engaged was subject to the same terrible fire as Stephenson's had been; at the same time Stephenson's division, after fighting gallantly for some time without any artillery, was compelled to fall back from the overpowering numbers of the enemy, thus leaving Loring's flank exposed. What was then to be done? If Gen. Loring had made a stand and continued fighting, it would have been to have his division cut to pieces and captured, while to retreat to Vicksburg he knew full well would only hasten the downfall of the city.

With the capture of his artillery, and the breaking of Stephenson's division, the battle of Baker's Creek was irrevocably lost. This is the opinion of nearly all the officers who were in that battle, and from them have we derived ours. Nothing but the most desperate fighting on the part of General Bowen's division, and what of Stephenson's division remained together, saved our entire army from being captured. The enemy had already flanked us, and were marching rapidly upon our rear when he was checked by Bowen, and the army saved.

It was with the knowledge of this fact, that General Loring decided upon cutting his way through, knowing that he could better serve the country by so doing, than by being penned up in Vicksburg, where his division would be only so much more to feed. Accordingly, his men were all safely drawn off the battle-field, by one of the most brilliant movements of this war, and marched to Jackson.

Not the slightest responsibility can be made to rest on Major General Loring for the loss of the battle of Baker's Creek. So little was he blamed by the remainder of the Generals and the other officers, that it was universally believed that if he had been in command of our army, the enemy would have been defeated, and a victory instead of a disaster, been chronicled for the South in the history of this war. We see nothing that General Loring performed on that battle-field, which should make him responsible for its loss, and we believe the same opinion is held by the officers and men of the garrison of Vicksburg. Those parties who are now safe in the Confederate lines, trying to cast the blame on a gallant and tried veteran, should recollect that by General Loring's foresight and ability, his division of several thousand men, instead of being prisoners of war, is now in Mississippi, standing as a barrier to the advance of the enemy, and ready, under their leader, to fight as well as they have always done before.

CHAPTER XXXVIII.
OUR WORKS ON THE BIG BLACK RIVER.

After our defeat at Baker's Creek, the Confederate army fell back to a series of works erected on the east of the Big Black river, and were afterwards driven from them on the day following. It is said that the object of these works was to defend the bridges across the river, and to prevent Snyder's Bluff from being flanked. We do not believe that such was the idea, but rather think the intention was to make it a line of defense in the event of defeat. Before making any comments on what is generally deemed an error in our choosing this side of the river as a line of defense, we will endeavor to give a description of the country, and its surrounding features, on both sides of the Big Black.

The *east* bank of the river is a level and almost open country, extending for miles. It is true that it is cut up by creeks, and a portion of the land is swampy, but these offered but little impediment for an army to attack the line of works, which was thrown up on this side of the river, as was illustrated by the easy march of the enemy on the intrenchments, and their capture by them.

The *west* bank of the river rises to an almost precipitate height, overlooking the east shore, and forming a succession of lofty cliffs. The natural strength of this side offered the greatest inducements and the best advantages for a line of defense, as we will endeavor to show in our comments on the works that were erected on the opposite shore.

As soon as our army was defeated at Baker's Creek, instead of falling back to the intrenchments on the east shore of the river, had they crossed the bridge and burned it after them, they would then have placed the river between the Confederate army and the enemy. After crossing, the bluffs could have been lined with what artillery remained uncaptured, and the enemy could never have crossed under the raking fire which would have been kept up on the opposite shore below them.

By holding this position for two or three days, we would have been enabled to remove all the provisions from the adjacent plantations, and taken them into Vicksburg, thus supplying the garrison with sufficient food to last them at least three months full rations. It may be said that the enemy could have crossed the river, either above or below our position, and thus flanked us; but it must be apparent that for them to have made such a move would have taken at least three days, by which time the object with which the position was held would have been gained, and our army could then have fallen back to Vicksburg. Had we succeeded in holding the works erected on the east bank of the Big Black, our position would have been much worse, as the enemy could have, with greater ease, crossed the river from the east to the west than otherwise, and thus have cut us off from Vicksburg, and also capturing the city without any resistance whatever.

It has been said by parties desirous of defending Lieutenant General Pemberton, that it was never his intention to make the works on the east bank of the Big Black a line of defense; his object in attempting to hold the works being only for the purpose of gaining time to make a safe retreat into Vicksburg. If such is the case, we quote the opinion of a prominent officer of the garrison in saying, that the idea was a most absurd one, as common sense should show that to gain time for our men to fall back to Vicksburg, a river between them and the enemy would have been an aid instead of an obstacle.

With what object then were the works on Big Black erected? We have seen no official report of General Pemberton, but must certainly say, that to our limited military experience, the idea of making a line of defense at that point, or using the works for the purpose of gaining time for our army to fall back in the event of defeat, is something new in the annals of this war, and a species of generalship that no other commander in the service has yet displayed.

CHAPTER XXXIX.
THE NEGLECT TO PROVISION VICKSBURG.

The neglect to provision Vicksburg with a supply of food large enough to supply the garrison for a siege of six months, is too glaring an error to need much comment on. Suffice it to say that provisions could easily have been obtained, had those officials, whose duty it was to procure subsistence, attended to their business, and not depended solely on what could be found on the railroads, or impressed from the farmers, who chanced to be at convenient distances from Vicksburg or Jackson.

While censuring these subordinate officers, we insist that equal blame must be attached to the Commanding General of the department. It is said that Lieutenant General Pemberton always believed a large supply of food was stored away in Vicksburg. Believed! Let us quote what the Army Regulations say in relation to the duties of Generals commanding fortified places. Section 818 is worded as follows:

* * * * * * * * "He (referring to the general commanding) studies the works, and the exterior within the radius of attack and investment the strength of the garrison, the artillery, the munitions of war, *subsistence and supplies of all kinds*, and takes *immediate* measures to *procure whatever* is deficient."

We shall now ask: in what manner did the Lieutenant General commanding the department of Mississippi and East Louisiana perform the duties, not left for his judgment to find out, but actually laid down in the Army Regulations? All assertions that provisions could not be obtained are utterly false; it is well known, by all who were in Vicksburg, that numerous offers were made by the planters on the Mississippi river above the city, in the Fall of 1862, when boats were running up the Yazoo river, to give the Government all their crops, which were lying exposed to the enemy, if the officials would send for them. It is also well known that the planters of the Yazoo district offered their crops *free of charge*, and yet no step was made to accept the gift so patriotically tendered.

A correspondent of the Richmond *Sentinel*, in an article defending Lieutenant General Pemberton, claims that it never was intended to stand a siege of an indefinite length of time. We see no reason for this assertion. Sieges have been known to last for years, and in the same way could Vicksburg have been held. It is further claimed, that the garrison did not surrender from want of food, but from weakness. We now ask: what caused their weakness? Was it not the want of food? Had the men been well supplied with rations, they would have been almost as strong on the forty-seventh day as they were on the first. It was, therefore, from starvation, and nothing else, that they surrendered.

CHAPTER XL. CONCLUSION.

In concluding this work, we must disclaim having censured General Pemberton from any feeling of prejudice against that officer. Had the Court of Inquiry been held, as it was intended, this book would never have been published, as the true account of the operations in the Department of Mississippi and East Louisiana would have been given to the people, and a book of this nature would not have been necessary.

Our opinions of General Pemberton's inability to meet successfully the great movements, which resulted in the downfall of Vicksburg, were formed some time before the investment, on seeing the want of proper energy in transacting the military operations around Vicksburg. This war has developed two classes of Generals. One class is of opinion that positions on the water, even if well fortified, must always be taken, where the enemy possess a fleet and control such waters; while the other class, looking back to the history of past warfare, are of an opposite opinion. Of the former class belong Lieutenant General Pemberton, as his recommendation to evacuate Charleston and dismantle the fortifications would show; while in the second class we would place General G. T. Beauregard, who has for over three months been successfully defending the very city that General Pemberton advised evacuating. In making these remarks, we will not say that General Pemberton believed attempting the defense of Vicksburg hopeless. We are certain he did all in his *ability* for its defense, but that he was incompetent to hold the position in which he had been placed. To use the words of a distinguished General in the Confederate army, "General Pemberton tried to do his best, but was always busy doing nothing."

We must beg to disclaim any desire to make this work a portion of the *history* of this war, in the strict sense of the word. Our idea has only been to furnish the reader with a narrative of all that transpired during the two sieges of Vicksburg, and to do justice to the gallant men who fought, bled, and suffered in its defense. Many errors and misstatements *may* be found in it, but wherever they occur it has been from information obtained from parties whose high standing in the Confederate army warrants their publication. If there are any such found, we shall, with pleasure, after the error is shown and proved to us, make the necessary *amende honorable*.

In conclusion, we would say that our censure of General Pemberton has not been influenced by public opinion, as a proof of which we would state, that for months past, amid the storm of charges brought against General Bragg for incompetency, we have defended him through the columns of the press, because, with the lights before us he appeared an able and competent officer. None but the purest motives of *conscience* and *opinion* have induced us to chronicle the censure contained within, and though General Pemberton may, before long, regain the confidence of the people, and distinguish himself as an officer, while we would with pleasure record his achievements, we should always remain of the same opinion - that he exhibited a great want of competency in his control of the department of Mississippi and East Louisiana, and particularly in the defense of VICKSBURG.

THE END.

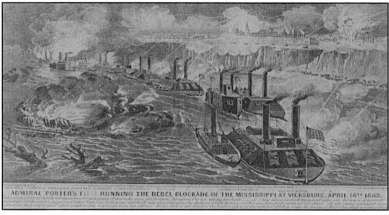

ADMIRAL PORTER'S FLEET RUNNING THE REBEL BLOCKADE OF THE MISSISSIPPI AT VICKSBURG, APRIL 16th 1863.

SIEGE OF VICKSBURG

TWO

Heralded In New York

Frederic Hudson, the managing editor for the *New York Herald*, was well-known throughout the journalistic profession as a man who was extremely persistent in obtaining the most accurate and detailed account of the news. In 1836, Hudson, at seventeen years of age, had traveled to New York from Massachusetts. He went to work for his brothers' news outlet, and soon after, met publishing innovator, James Gordon Bennett, who had started the *New York Herald* the prior year. Bennett hired Hudson, and they blended well. Bennett placed full trust in him. His confidence paid off, as the two men took the *New York Herald* to new heights of circulation and prominence.

When the war broke out in 1861, Hudson hired several army correspondents; and eventually, as the war continued, had over sixty on the newspaper's staff. Among them were Thomas W. Knox, who was instructed to cover the war in the west. Knox was told by Hudson that "every point of interest was to be covered, so that the operations of our armies would be fully covered from day to day." Knox added, after being told by Hudson that he expected a long and bloody war, "I was instructed to watch the military movement in Missouri, and hastened to St. Louis as fast as a team could bear me."

Hudson also hired Henry Villard, who had sent the *Herald* dispatches from Springfield regarding Abraham Lincoln, prior to his election as president. Villard had pro-Republican leanings but Hudson and Bennett, both hard Democrats, paid him well - $35 a week - to work for the *Herald*. Villard was on personal terms with Lincoln. After a short period of time assigned to camps around Washington, he moved to camps in Louisville, Kentucky, where he gained access to Southern newspapers. Villard wrote, "With clippings from them, which I accompanied by proper comments, made up regular budgets of Southern news, which became a highly-prized feature of the *New York Herald*.

The *New York Herald* wanted correspondents and a headquarters in every camp during the war. These photographs were taken in Virginia in 1863.

Bennett offered high pay to recruit good reporters. Horses and equipment were not spared. The pay and rewards appealed to *Philadelphia Press* reporter, George A. Townsend, who hired on. Townsend was on good terms with Major General George Brinton McClellan in Washington, as well as in the battlefields and encampments. Bennett and Hudson hoped to have correspondents in every camp – though that proved impossible. They expected in return from their reporters, fine writing and in-depth coverage. They wanted their correspondents to furnish maps, casualty lists, biographical sketches of the generals, military secrets, and Southern newspapers. Over time, in receipt of these Southern newspapers, is how St. Clair-Abrams became noticed by Hudson and Bennett. The *Herald* had a department that gathered and reviewed war coverage and editorials from Southern newspapers. So much information was collected from various sources that the *Herald* was able to publish almost complete rosters of the Confederate forces. But also, they were able to analyze and editorialize on the perspective of the Southern newspaper correspondents.

Bennett had an unusual, but invaluable confidential source, who lived in the residence of the president. It was Mary Todd Lincoln - President Lincoln's wife. Mary Lincoln appreciated the positive press stories the *New York Herald* wrote about her. She invited the Bennett's to the Grand Union Ball at the White House on New Year's Day 1862.

With their "you are there" sensationalistic style of reporting, which heavily favored the Federal Army, the *New York Herald's* popularity surged and they began to distribute their *penny paper,* which actually cost two cents at the start of the war, beyond the city by railroads and waterways.

Following the war, Bennett expressed his pride in "the large corps of trained and able men," who had covered the war for the *Herald*. He wished to keep many of them employed. His thought was to send correspondents around the globe as "Ambassadors to all the great capitals of the world." Bennet expanded their large staff and brought in *select* former war correspondents from struggling or defunct Southern newspapers. One such reporter and author that had been closely observed was Alexander St. Clair-Abrams.

Meanwhile, in late-autumn 1865, in Atlanta, St. Clair-Abrams continued to work on the reconstruction of the city. The need to support his young family, which now included a son, Alfred, born in September 1865, was desperate. He was a writer who needed to write. When an offer came from the *New York Herald*, he knew it would be a great opportunity to build a career and to acquire national name recognition. In December 1865, twenty-year-old St. Clair-Abrams, now a former Confederate soldier and veteran journalist, was officially hired by the *New York Herald* as a reporter and news editor, and moved with Joanna and their three-month-old son to Manhattan, New York City.

Soon after St. Clair-Abrams's arrival at the *New York Herald*, Frederic Hudson, due to his wife's ill health, took a year's leave of absence and moved to Concord, Massachusetts. Hudson never returned and tendered his resignation in July of 1867. Bennett had been contemplating retirement as well. He and Hudson had been training his son, James Gordon Bennett Jr. to take over the business, but Bennett continued running the *Herald* during Hudson's leave. Upon arrival at the *Herald* building, St. Clair-Abrams was highly regarded by Bennett; and the elder Bennett became a trusted mentor.

JAMES GORDON BENNETT, SR.

James Gordon Bennett was born in the small town of Keith in north east Scotland, on September 1, 1795. He was Catholic, studied in a seminary, and thought of entering the priesthood. At the age of twenty-four, Bennett traveled to Nova Scotia where he stayed for a short period of time before he moved on to Boston, Massachusetts. In Boston he worked for a book publisher. Then, after a brief stay in New York, he worked for Aaron Smith

James G. Bennett Sr.

Wellington in Charleston, South Carolina, as a translator for the *Charleston Courier.*

Bennett returned to New York and worked for the *New York Enquirer* newspaper as the first Washington correspondent. He then tried to launch a couple newspapers, but his attempts were unsuccessful due to of his lack of political support. He thought obtaining political support was wrong anyway, and innovated editorial ideas and techniques that would appeal to readers, without the backing of the special interest groups. In 1835, at the age of 40, he had saved $500, which he used to start a new publication where he could utilize his skills. He named his newspaper the *New York Herald.* And with this new adventure, he began his brilliant, extremely arrogant, and highly controversial career.

His first big story was the 1836 murder of prostitute Helen Jewett by accused killer Richard Robinson. Bennett was deeply focused on this case. His dramatization of the lurid crime and Robinson trial, as well as the exclusive stories on the people involved, sent the sales of the upstart *Herald* soaring. When Robinson was acquitted, the sordid news coverage continued and gave birth to a new brand of crime media reporting.

With this story, Bennett became the father of "sensationalism" news reporting. Author and historian, Professor James L. Crouthamel wrote about Bennett in his 1989 book *Bennett's New York Herald and the Rise of the Popular Press*, "Sensational journalism had its origins much earlier than is generally believed. James Gordon Bennett, a pioneer sensationalist, utilized the art to create a truly popular press and to underwrite new journalistic techniques." Crouthamel added, "Bennett did more than anyone else to establish an important American institution, the popular, cheap, mass circulation newspaper. A subsequent generation of more famous yellow journalists, most notably Joseph Pulitzer and William Randolph Hearst, taking advantage of technical innovations in format (especially headlines) and in pictorial reproduction simply carried Bennett's techniques of sensationalism and popular appeal to new heights – or depths. But Bennett was the pioneer."

Bennett had a compulsion for being ahead of his competitors, whether they were the rival penny papers or the so-called legitimate press, such as Horace Greeley's *New York Tribune.* He began daily Wall Street reports and printed high society events. He went directly to possible news sources before the people bearing the news arrived in New York. Bennett was one of the first publishers to use the telegraph when it first appeared in the 1840s. More and more businesses advertised in the *Herald* due to high consumer sales.

Over the following decades, Bennett would be competing and succeeding against heavyweights in the field of journalism, including the aforementioned New York publishers Pulitzer and Hearst, as well as Henry Jarvis Raymond. Bennett's contentious stories and his relentless sensationalism did get him into some rough spots. Physical attacks and threats plagued him every day, which drove his wife and children to live in France.

On June 1, 1872, James Gordon Bennett Sr. died in his sleep. The funeral was held at his home on Fifth Avenue and Thirty-Eighth Street after his wife, Henrietta Agnes Crean, and family arrived from Europe. And though for many years he had turned away from his Catholic Faith, in later years, he had reconciled with the church. Archbishop John McClosky had administered the last rites. His pallbearers were a who's who of publishing – Horace Greely of the *Tribune*, Charles A. Dana of the *Sun*, George W. Jones of the *Times*, William L. Stone of the *Journal of Commerce*, Erastus Brooks of the *Express*, Hugh J. Hastings of the *Commercial Advertiser*, Richard Bonner of the *Ledger*, J. M. Bundy of the *Evening Mail*, George A. Childs of the *Philadelphia Public Ledger*, and his old friend and managing editor, Frederic Hudson. Attendees included high ranking military officers, elected officials, Constitutional officers, and business leaders.

Lawyer, musician and diarist, George Templeton Strong, who carried a lifetime of critical criticism for Bennett wrote in his diary, "During about thirty-seven years, he has done more than any living man to debase American journalism." Strong was furious at all the respect and attention given in eulogies and resolutions and the flags flown at half-staff.

Greely's *Tribune* wrote, "He knew how to pick out the events of the day the subject which engrossed the interests of the greatest number of people, and to give them about that subject all they could read. The quality might be bad, and generally was; but it suited the multitude." A week after the funeral, the *Herald* published nine columns on their former leader, and six months later, Frederic

Hudson published his book, *Journalism in the United States from 1690 to 1872*. In Hudson's book, Bennett is the hero.

HEAR YE, HEAR YE, READ ALL ABOUT IT!

James Gordon Bennett Sr. shared some common similarities with his new young reporter from the South - St. Clair-Abrams. They were Catholics, Democrats, and had strong pro-Southern views. They also shared an especially long list of mixed personality traits; self-esteem, opinionated, and persuasive, but also compassionate, generous, and loyal. They drove to be the first and the best. They shared similar skills and talents with the styling and crafting of the written word - and they knew the power of the *printed* word.

In 1866, St. Clair-Abrams started as a news editor and reported on the heartbeat of New York City - government, crime, and high society. He was also the musical and dramatic critic – an enjoyable role he maintained throughout his employ with the *New York Herald*. It was a function in which he could include Joanna.

St. Clair-Abrams was promoted rapidly from 1866 through 1870; from city editor to state editor to national editor; the latter position took him to Washington on many occasions. During this time, the price of the *Herald* went from two cents to four cents, with the majority of the newspapers sold by soprano-shouting street-corner newspaper boys as opposed to subscriptions.

Following the war, the *New York Herald*, as did many newspapers throughout the North, continued with post-war related headlines and editorials through 1869. Amongst those stories included the conspiracy theory that the Confederate government were involved in the assassination of President Lincoln in an alliance with the high-profile actor, John Wilkes Booth; the Impeachment Trial of President Andrew Johnson, accused of high crimes and misdemeanors by the House of Representatives in early 1868; the Pardon of Jefferson Davis by President Johnson on Christmas Day 1868; the rise to the presidency of Republican and Union Army victor, Ulysses S. Grant; and the death of former Secretary of War Edwin Stanton, who passed away four days after having been nominated as an Associate Justice of the Supreme Court by President Grant.

DEATH OF EDWIN M. STANTON.

Scenes Attendant on His Last Hours.

Announcement of the Event by President Grant.

ACTION OF THE CABINET SECRETARIES.

Sketches of the Life and Services of Mr. Stanton.

FEELING IN THIS CITY AND ELSEWHERE.

WASHINGTON, Dec. 24, 1869.

The community this morning was shocked by the report of the death of Hon. Edwin M. Stanton. As his friends only a few days ago had announced that he was slowly but surely recovering his health, the sad intelligence was the more startling. Many persons refused at first to believe that he had deceased, but were soon convinced of the truth of the report. Little more than a week ago he made an argument before Associate Justice Sprague, in Chambers, in the Whitney and Mowrey case, and it was admitted by those present that it was the ablest

WASHINGTON.

Amnesty Proclamation by the President.

Jeff Davis, Toombs, Breckinridge and Other Ex-Rebel Leaders Pardoned.

The Financial Schemes in Congress.

MAIL SERVICE ON THE PLAINS.

AMNESTY PROCLAMATION.

Full Pardon to All Rebels—Jeff Davis, Breckinridge, Toombs, Mason, Slidell and Other Leaders Included—The Last Chapter of the Civil War.

Whereas the President of the United States has heretofore set forth several proclamations which offered amnesty and pardon to persons who had been or were concerned in the late rebellion against the lawful authority of the government of the United States, which proclamations were severally issued on the 8th day of December, 1863; on the 26th day of March, 1864; on the 29th day of May, 1865; on the 7th day of September, 1867, and on the 4th day of July in the present year, and

IMPEACHMENT.

Trial of President Andrew Johnson for High Crimes and Misdemeanors.

Examination of Adjutant General Thomas and Lieutenant General Sherman.

General Thomas Corrects His Previous Testimony.

General Sherman's Conversations With the President Ruled Out.

Argument of Counsel on the Admissibility of the Evidence.

WASHINGTON, April 11, 1868.

General Thomas made his appearance first to-day, and desired to make some few explanations about his evidence yesterday. His explanations were not of any very great importance; but Mr. Butler caught hold of him, and by some sort of management in his questions so muddled the mind of Thomas that the latter blundered into the strangest answers; yet anybody could see poor Thomas meant to deliver an honest statement of his share in the transaction of the 22d of February; but by some confusion of ideas he stumbled by the way and gave Butler an apparent triumph.

When General Sherman came on the witness stand there was an immense flurry in the audience to see the hero of the Great March. Opera glasses were levelled upon him and heads protruded over the galleries to get a good look at the distinguished witness. General Sherman behaved himself in character with his reputation, cool as a cucumber.

In St. Clair-Abrams first four years with the *New York Herald*, he opined and scrutinized primarily on the political scene, which included elections on every level. He was personally known to New York City democratic mayors John Thompson Hoffman, Thomas Coman, and Abraham Oakey Hall. Coman was the president of the Board of Alderman and was acting-mayor for several weeks when Hoffman resigned to become the governor. Coman was a lawyer, who earlier in his career, was a reporter for the *New York Herald*. St. Clair-Abrams continued his coverage of John T. Hoffman for a brief period in 1869 when Hoffman replaced Governor Rueben Fenton.

St. Clair-Abrams had an extreme motivation to *express* his opinions on a wide range of subject matter that affected society; and he didn't limit himself to a certain geographical area. His talent for taking *any* subject or event or occurrence and dramatizing it, made him very popular with the *Herald* readers, which now amounted to over 60,000 copies sold each day. On many occasions, he was quite unpopular with those he wrote about, only to be praised later by those same people after he wrote a glowing article about them.

His broad scope of stories included the Suez Canal - *One of the Wonders of the Age*; the Roxbury Tragedy, which was the story of the brutal murder of a sister and brother, Isabella and John Joice that took place in June 1865 in the West Roxbury neighborhood of Boston; the War on the Plains between the United States and Native Americans; the 1866 Cholera epidemic that took 1,137 lives; the 1867 New York State's Constitutional Convention that included recommendations for Black suffrage and women's suffrage, which were defeated; the construction of a new state capitol building and the construction of new elevated "El" trains; the substantial political power and control of Tammany Hall; the Irish organization of the Fenian Brotherhood of America; as well as the "Black Friday" gold panic of 1869 caused by three New York investors, which included President Grant's brother-in-law.

St. Clair-Abrams prioritized and edited stories that arrived from the *Herald's* correspondents based in Southern cities. Usually, a full page was dedicated to stories from "The South." On occasion he wrote about the weather and the national pastime - baseball. He sustained a wide-ranging work load of which he most enjoyed his assignments as the *New York Herald's* music and drama critic.

St. Clair-Abrams combined both business and pleasure as the music and drama critic for what was referred to as *amusements*. The job provided the opportunity to spend quality time with Joanna as celebutante guests at splendid galas, extravagant premieres, and opening night productions of plays, symphonies, ballets, and operas. Opera, with its stunning costumes, lavish scenery, and remarkable classical vocalists, became the creative art form the young couple intensely enjoyed and would patronize throughout their lives. His assessments and critiques of restaurants, fashions, museums, literary works, and what soon would be called vaudeville that featured comedians, magicians, circus acts, and minstrels, had found their way into the columns of the *New York Herald*.

St. Clair-Abrams and Joanna became acquainted with theatrical entrepreneurs and showmen that included William Niblo of Niblo's Garden, Antonio "Tony" Pastor of Tony Pastor's Opera House, Richard Hooley of Hooley's Theatres, Edwin Booth of Booth's Theatre, and Phineas Taylor "P. T." Barnum of Barnum's American Museum. In 1865, when Barnum's first museum on Ann Street was burnt down, the *New York Herald* purchased the property. Another notable entrepreneur was whiskey distiller Samuel Napthali Pike, who, fascinated by the famous soprano Jenny Lind while attending an opera in Cincinnati, built that city's first opera house. In 1868, in the Chelsea neighborhood of Manhattan, Pike constructed Pike's Opera House. A year later, he sold it to Jim Fisk and Jay Gould, who changed the name to the Grand Opera House. Fisk and Gould were the men who instigated the "Black Friday" gold panic that same year. Fisk was murdered in 1872 at the Grand Central Hotel by his business partner Edward Stokes over some slanderous business dealings, but more accurately was killed

Grand Opera House in Manhattan
as it appeared in 1895

140

because of a relationship they both shared with Helen Josephine Mansfield. Following the death of Fisk, over three dozen of his letters to Mansfield were published in the *New York Herald*.

In May 1996, St. Clair-Abrams' historian Kenneth Sears gave an interview to legendary Lake County columnist Ormund Powers for his *Lake Reflections* feature. In that interview, Sears recounted how, many years later, while St. Clair-Abrams was living in Florida, a rumor had been spread by an antagonistic rival, who had stated that while St. Clair-Abrams lived in New York, he had fallen in love with one of the top opera stars of the day; and that he wanted to bring her to Florida so that the world's aficionados of opera would beat a path to the doors of the new opera house that he had built in Tavares. And furthermore, that the penthouse of the opera house, which overlooked Lake Dora, would provide a convenient trysting place. Sears concluded, "he doubts that the tale is true. Both Maj. And Mrs. St. Clair-Abrams were ardent patrons of the theatre and were fond of opera and of each other."

It was a rumor that St. Clair-Abrams and Joanna readily dismissed and gave no further credence.

Alex and Joanna St. Clair-Abrams were life-time devotees of the opera and attended performances throughout the United States.

In 1866, Bennett Sr. turned the operation of the *New York Herald* over to his twenty-five-year-old son, James Gordon Bennett Jr., who officially took over operations on January 1, 1867. Bennett, Jr. had grown up in France and was taught by private tutors, as well as attended the prestigious institution of higher education – Ecole Polytechnique in Paris. Upon his return to the United States in 1861, Bennett Jr. hired shipbuilder Henry Steers to design and build a yacht, which he called the *Henrietta*, named after his mother. That same year, Bennett Jr.

James G. Bennett Jr.

volunteered his new yacht to the United States Revenue Marine Service and he was commissioned a third lieutenant.

During the first year of the war, the *Henrietta* patrolled the east coast from Long Island to South Carolina and then to Fernandina, Florida, where she captured the city and raised the American flag. By 1862, the *Henrietta* and Bennett Jr. were decommissioned.

The Great Ocean Yacht Race

Henrietta

Vesta

Fleetwing

Bennett Jr. was a spoiled, unpredictable, hard-drinking young pleasure-seeker, except, he was a natural seafarer and skilled yachtsman. In October 1866, Bennett Jr, along with two equally wealthy yacht owners, Pierre Lorillard IV and George Osgood, after each had bragged about the speed of their schooners, agreed to a race across the treacherous north Atlantic. In December of 1866, with a $90,000 prize for the winner - each man contributing $30,0000 - the three yachts, the *Henrietta*, Lorillard's *Vesta* and Osgood's *Fleetwing* left Sandy Hook, New Jersey, destined for the Isle of Wight, an island in the English Channel. Bennett Jr. was the only one of the three sportsmen that made the trip aboard their respective yachts. The *Henrietta* won the race with a time of thirteen days, twenty-one hours, fifty-five minutes.

Bennett Jr. received guidance from his father and veteran *Herald* staff members. Guidance he would need due to his serious risk taking. He would successfully raise the *New York Herald's* reputation world-wide through his years managing the newspaper. He financially sponsored the 1869 expedition of journalist, author, politician, and explorer Henry Morton Stanley to Africa to find physician and Christian missionary David Livingstone. The *New York Herald* would retain exclusive rights to the story. In 1871, Stanley located Livingstone in the city of Ujiji on Lake Tanganyika. It was at this discovery that Stanley made his simple, but famous, statement, "Dr. Livingstone, I presume?"

For a period of time, Bennett Jr. moved back to Paris, where his mother and sister lived, and launched the *Paris Herald.* He also sponsored the voyage of George W. DeLong's disastrous journey to the North Pole on the USS *Jeannette* - a ship he named for his sister. The DeLong expedition ended with the deaths of all twenty crewmembers, including DeLong. The sensationalistic stories that followed in the *Herald* regarding this tragedy made sales soar. Bennett Jr. returned to the United States and continued his unpredictable management of the *New York Herald*.

Former Confederate soldier, St. Clair-Abrams, fared well with his new former Union sailor boss. He shared the same interest in the New York entertainment and social scene as young Bennett. In 1867, he, along with support from the senior Bennett, assisted Bennett Jr. in establishing an entertainment, society, and gossip newspaper called *The Evening Telegram.*

In July of 1870, with concern for his mother in Paris, Bennett Jr's attention was directed on the emerging war between the French and Germans. He assigned St. Clair-Abrams in the new position as foreign editor; with his main focus the Franco-Prussian War. Bennett Jr. provided St. Clair-Abrams with a couple rooms at the Astor House to use as a headquarters, where he received encrypted dispatches through the new and improved, high speed transatlantic telegraph cable. Only he and a couple trusted overseas correspondents held the key to their transcriptions and meanings.

The Astor House
1862

THE FRANCO ~ PRUSSIAN WAR

Following Prussia's defeat of Austria in 1866, France felt that their dominate position in mainland Europe was in jeopardy. In 1868, following the Spanish Revolution that overthrew Queen Isabella II, the Spanish Crown was offered to Prince Leopold of Holhenzollen, a powerful political leader in European affairs. This maneuver was supported by Otto von Bismarck, the Prussian Prime Minister. French Emperor Napoleon III strongly opposed this for fear the installation of Leopold would give the Prussians a positional stranglehold over France. Leopold had first declined the crown, then in June 1870, accepted it, only to again decline it on July 11, 1870.

Diplomatic conversations between Paris and Berlin met with no solutions. The *Ems Dispatch* of July 13, 1870, was a telegram King Wilhelm I dictated to Heinrich Abeken at Ems, who sent it to Bismarck. The telegram described the meeting between Wilhelm and the French ambassador to Prussia, Vincent Benedetti. Benedetti had presented, in a diplomatic and courteous manner, an order to relay a demand from French Foreign Minister, Agenor, duc de Gramont, that the Prussians do not permit Leopold to accept the Spanish throne.

Bismarck used this telegram by submitting it to the newspapers in a fashion that would make the French believe that Wilhelm insulted Benedetti, and at the same time, making the Germans feel Wilhelm was the one insulted. Bismarck's intention was to provoke France into war and he succeeded.

France began to organize their army on July 15, 1870, prompting the Prussians to do the same. On July 16, the French Parliament declared war on Prussia and two weeks later, on August 2, invaded German territory. The German Confederation consisting of Prussia and the allied southern German states of Baden, Württemberg, Bavaria and Hesse-Darmstadt, were more than ready to affect a defense, as well as begin a strong offensive strike against the Second French Empire. On August 4, they invaded northeastern France. The combined Prussian forces outnumbered the French and were more efficient in moving troops with their superior leadership.

The Prussians moved swiftly and decisively with victories in France. Francois Bazaine and his Army of the Rhine was defeated by the German Confederation at the Battle of Gravelotte on August 18, which prompted Bazaine to retreat to the border town of Metz in northeastern France. The following day, Prince Friedrich Karl's German troops surrounded the fortress at Metz. Though unable to take the French by force, the Germans patiently waited until the French food supplies ran out. Attempts by the Army of the Rhine to break out resulted in defeats at Noisseville and Bellevue. From October 20–27, Bazaine surrendered the fortress and his entire army of over 190,000 men.

The Battle of Sedan on September 1-2, came about when the French Army of Chalons under the command of Marshal Patrice de MacMahon was sent to relieve the Army of the Rhine, but were soon surrounded by the Prussian Third and Fourth Armies, who greatly outnumbered and out-gunned MacMahon's forces. Napoleon III, who accompanied MacMahon, ordered the commander to break out, but the repeated artillery bombardment paralyzed every attempt. By late afternoon on September 1, Napoleon III ceased the attacks and hoisted the white flag on the Sedan fortress. He then sent a letter of

ADVANCE OF THE PRUSSIAN ARMIES ON PARIS.

Position of the German Forces—Situations of Laon, Soissons and Epernay—The Fortresses Held by the French—The Defences of Paris.

THE WAR.

Rapid Advance of the German Armies on Paris.

Entire Retreat of General Vinoy's French Corps.

Vigorous Measures for the Defence of the Capital.

JULES FAVRE'S POSITION.

France Can Go On Without the Parliament.

The Duke de Grammont's Views on the Situation.

Force Plans of Great Britain to the Belligerents.

MILITARY OPERATIONS.

THE SIEGE OF PARIS.

THE SITUATION IN PARIS.

PRUSSIA.

surrender with a courier to the Prussian headquarters. After Wilhelm and Bismarck read through the letter, the surrender was accepted.

On September 2, Napoleon III was taken prisoner and sent to a palace in Cassel, where his imprisonment was known to be quite comfortable. Without Napoleon III, the French had no government to negotiate peace. When word reached Paris of his capture, angry protestors stormed the palace, overthrowing the French Second Empire. The Government of National Defense was created and the Third French Republic was initiated. The Franco-Prussian war continued for five more months with new French armies, but the dominate Prussian Army besieged Paris and then captured the city on January 28, 1871. The Battle of Sedan though was considered the deciding defeat of France.

At the close of the war, the German states became the German Empire under the rule of Wilhelm I and Chancellor Otto von Bismarck. the *Treaty of Frankfurt* was signed by France and Prussia on May 10, 1871.

REMEMBER ME TO HERALD SQUARE.

In the spring of 1872, St. Clair-Abrams recovered from a bout of pneumonia. Also, he had suffered from the severe cramps that he experienced ten years earlier during the war. He and Joanna had been contemplating a move south. A combination of circumstances could be cited for their decision to leave New York. St. Clair-Abrams' health and need for a warmer climate was a primary reason - one which prompted Bennett Jr. to offer him a job in Atlanta or California. And though his poor health is what St. Clair-Abrams told the press corps, there may have been other reasons for their choice to move to Atlanta. While it was certainly true that St. Clair-Abrams had the desire to be the boss of his own company, Joanna may have been homesick for the place of her birth and youth. Also, on June 1, 1872, his mentor James Gordon Bennett Sr. passed away.

In 1872, New York City had reached a milestone of one million residents. Atlanta, a city of only 35,000 people, was a city still under re-construction. St. Clair-Abrams, a native Southerner, viewed a move to the homeland as a great opportunity.

Following the funeral of Bennett Sr., New York City lost three of their one million citizens as Alex and Joanna St. Clair-Abrams, with their six-year-old son, Alfred, bid farewell to the *New York Herald* and journeyed home to a "new" South – unaware that having worked for the father of sensationalized journalism over the past seven years since the war, he would face incredibly tough challenges. And though he met those challenges with spirit, energy and high standards, those same challenges also brought about a decision for St. Clair-Abrams and Joanna to make another move.

THREE

Return to the Gate City of the South

THE CONSTITUTION, ATLANTA, GA.,
THURSDAY, JUNE 14, 1928

Atlanta's Early Newspaper
INTERESTING LETTER FROM COLONEL ABRAMS
Days Described by Writer

*Herewith is printed a most interesting letter from one of the very
virile and vivid men who engaged in the vital work of resurrecting
and reinvigorating devastated Atlanta in the decade following the
end of the war between the states.*

*Colonel Alexander St. Clair Abrams will be recalled by the
elders of the city as a courageous, chivalric and constructive citizen.
He used a pen that struck fire from the armor of our then alien
governors and employed the enginery of the press to place the new
foundations of our civic stability.*

*The story he recites will be read with revived respect for his
services in a parlous time and reverence for his long and honorable
private and public life!*

Editor Constitution: After serving four years in the Confederate
army, in December, 1865, I moved to New York with my wife and
then infant son. The following year I became connected with the
New York Herald and had the good fortune of being very rapidly
promoted to the editorial department. During the war between
Prussia and France in 1870, which culminated in the surrender of
Louis Napoleon and his army at Sedan, I was in charge of all the
war news and was jocularly known as "secretary of war" and our
special cable-grams came in cipher and I alone had the key to it. I
had taken a room at the Astor House diagonally across the street
from the Herald building. After the surrender of Sedan my health
became very bad and I tendered my resignation to the Herald. The
younger Bennett very kindly offered me the choice of going to

California or back to Georgia as a representative of the Herald. The reconstruction laws of congress were then in force and the New York Herald was bitterly hostile toward them. The paper had strenuously opposed the impeachment of President Johnson and by direction of the elder Bennett, I was assigned to work of writing all the editorials condemning and denouncing the impeachment proceedings.

Forsyth Street c.1877

I decided to return to Georgia as my health had broken down and soon after my arrival in Atlanta, I acquired possession of the newspaper machinery stored in a building on Forsyth street, in which my wife had one-third interest, it having been the property of her father; and I started the Atlanta Herald. I had very little capital but was greatly helped by General Gordon.

Later Henry Grady and Robert A. Alston purchased an interest in the Herald. I was managing editor; Grady was general editor and Alston business manager. My interest in the paper was valued at $5,000, Grady raised and put in $5,000 and Alston was to put in the same amount. He became financially involved and could not meet the payments. As a result, the Herald went "on the rocks."

General Gordon was a great friend of mine and was at that time at the head of a large insurance company, and he boosted the Herald by subscribing to 5,000 copies of the paper. At that time Mr. Hemphill controlled The Constitution.

I cannot recall the details on how we succeeded in getting the Associated Press dispatched but we finally did get them, and I think it safe to assert that for a while, at least, the Atlanta Herald had the largest circulation, of any paper in Georgia.

One evening Grady told me that he and Alston and I had to have a conference.

As managing editor, I had strongly opposed Governor Brown. When we met Grady said to me "Major, we have come to a crisis. We owe the bank $5,000; Governor Brown controls the bank and unless we change our policy and back Brown, they are going to call for a payment of the $5,000 and we can't meet it." After trying vainly for days to raise the $5,000 we had another conference, and I told my partners that I had decided to step down and out and proposed for them to buy me out. This they promptly agreed to and gave me their notes for the amount, and soon after I moved to Florida where I have resided ever since.

The struggle between the Constitution and the Herald was very bitter. The Constitution won out when the bank called the Alston notes. After I retired from the Herald it backed Governor Brown for quite a while but could not get outside aid to meet the notes that Alston had given and the upshot was that it had to suspend.

I think my retirement terminated the fight between the papers.

It is a humorous incident that years afterwards Brown met my daughter, who was then the wife of Captain W. Strother Smith, afterwards rear admiral, now deceased, and good-naturedly remarked that he would have given almost anything if he could have secured my support and friendship while I ran the Herald, and that I came very nearly bankrupting The Constitution. In comparatively a few months after I left Georgia the Herald in some way was sold to The Constitution and disappeared.

General Gordon, who was always a warm personal friend of mine but was always of very little means, told me at a Confederate reunion in New Orleans to which I was a delegate that he had tried his best to borrow $10,000 and turn it over to me but failed to do so.

Well, as the Turks say, "Kismet!" It was fated that I should not win out but I am certain that I gave Hemphill many a sleepless night just as he gave me many a one. What is to be will be, especially if it happens!

At 84 years of age, feeble and crippled, but with my mental faculties unimpaired, I can look back to the past philosophically.

I scared The Constitution nearly to death. It killed the Herald and it was not even a drawn battle. It had the money by it, and I had not.

If I had had the capital, I would have killed The Constitution.

As I did not have it, The Constitution killed the Herald.

Again Kismet! Kismet!

Alexander St. Clair Abrams,
Jacksonville, Fla., June 10, 1928.

St. Clair-Abrams had brought to his *Atlanta Herald* the sensationalized techniques he practiced at the *New York Herald*. The technique was known as "yellow journalism." It was a skill that wasn't immediately adopted by the editors and reporters from rival Atlanta newspapers, especially the powerful *Constitution*, who severely berated him. The readers of the *Atlanta Herald* however, responded well to the new format - and to St. Clair-Abrams. Later, after *The Constitution* bought out the *Herald*, they, in turn, would begin the practice of yellow journalism. St. Clair-Abrams partners, Grady and Alston, were quite wary of St. Clair-Abrams' flair for dramatization, too. Grady thought that this form of writing had a "coldness" that didn't work in small cities. Grady, five years St. Clair-Abrams junior, who worked at one point in his career as a Southern correspondent for the *New York Herald*, would eventually become a leader in sensationalized journalism when he went to work for *The Constitution.*

HENRY WOODFIN GRADY AND THE NEW SOUTH.

St. Clair-Abrams' general editor, Henry W. Grady, was known as the "Spokesman of the New South," after he wrote an editorial in the March 14, 1874, edition of the *Atlanta Herald* entitled "The New South." In the article, he advocated industrial development as a solution to the postwar South's economic and social troubles. An influential member of the Atlanta Ring of Democratic political leaders, Grady used his position to promote a "New South" program of northern investment to stimulate Atlanta's industrial growth.

Henry W. Grady

Grady promoted his "New South" throughout the country. He was a dynamic orator, who, referring to his speaking prowess to a large gathering in Boston, quipped "I am a talker by inheritance; My father was an Irishman and my mother was a woman."

Many of his speeches and editorials promoted Anglo-Saxon supremacy. On various occasions, he appeared to contradict himself. In an 1886 "New South" speech, Grady began his presentation with a quote from a Georgia senator who had opposed secession, Benjamin Harvey Hill. "There was a South of slavery and secession - that South is dead. There is a South of Union and freedom - that South, thank God, is living, breathing, growing every hour."

Henry W. Grady was born in Athens, Georgia, on May 24, 1850, and passed away from typhoid pneumonia on December 23, 1889. He was only 39 years old. His obituary and life story appeared in newspapers throughout the country and abroad. The *Chicago Tribune* wrote, "From the first his command of language was remarkable. His pen transferred his thoughts to the paper in graphic and glowing phrases with almost lightning rapidity. His ringing style of speaking soon won for him the name of the "silver tongued orator. Demands upon him for speeches came from Texas to Maine. Every word he wrote and every word he spoke but added to his fame."

SHOOTIN' IT OUT IN THE STATE CAPITOL.

Robert A. Alston

St. Clair-Abrams' business manager, Robert Augustus Alston, was a wealthy slave-owner prior to the War Between the States. He entered the war and served as an adjutant for Kentucky cavalry general, John Hunt Morgan, and later, commanded his own brigade with the rank of lieutenant colonel. Alston condemned the looting and malicious behavior of Morgan's men and had reported the lack of discipline and inaction of Morgan to Confederate authorities. Morgan, known as the "Thunderbolt of the Confederacy" went on to lead many successful raids that culminated on September 4, 1864, while encamped in Greenville,

Tennessee. Morgan was shot in the back and killed in a surprise attack by a Union cavalryman.

Following the war, Robert Alston's attitude toward slavery and white supremacy had changed - in contrast to his partner Henry Grady, who was eighteen years younger than Alston.

He became a cotton planter who employed freedmen, and, along with his partnership in the *Atlanta Herald*, was a lawyer and insurance salesman. Alston became very active in the political landscape as a member of the Democratic Party and served as a State Representative from DeKalb County. In 1878, he was chairman of the penitentiary committee and was the first to fight for reform of the inhuman conditions of privately leased convict camps. Joseph Brown, the former governor who had feuded with St. Clair-Abrams several years earlier, was one of the well-known investors in the convict camps. Governors Alfred Colquitt and John Gordon were also financially involved and the three Georgia giants gained substantial wealth from the convict system. Colquitt, Gordon, and Brown formed what was called the "Bourbon Triumvirate" – a trio of men who controlled much a Georgia's political power from 1870 to 1890

In March 1879, a business disagreement between Alston and an associate, Captain Edward Cox, had seriously escalated. Alston was well-aware his life was in danger from the unmistakable public threats made by Cox. A friend of Alston gave the former brigade commander a pistol for protection. On March 11, 1879, when Alston entered the State Capitol in Atlanta for a meeting, Cox drew his gun on Alston and a shoot-out erupted. Alston was hit and was mortally wounded. The subsequent trial of Edward Cox ended on May 7, 1879, with a jury verdict of murder in the first degree.

FEUDING WITH THE MOST POWERFUL MAN IN GEORGIA.

In 1872, St. Clair-Abrams, through his editorials in the *Atlanta Herald*, maintained a feud with former war governor and Chief Justice of the Georgia Supreme Court, Joseph Emerson Brown.

St. Clair-Abrams' disdain for Brown conceivably had its roots during the war when Brown was the governor and St. Clair-Abrams was writing for the *Intelligencer*. Though Brown believed in the "Cause" of Southern states' rights, he was an opponent of the policies of the Confederate government. He thought that Georgia men should solely provide for the home guard, and that the state's animals, food, supplies, and slaves to work in the camps, should not be forced into the overall Confederate army. Brown believed President Jefferson Davis to be on the verge of tyranny. Also, there was Brown's flip-flopping of political parties from Whig to Democrat to Republican after the war, and then back to Democrat.

Joseph E. Brown

Publicly, the 1872 feud with Brown commenced when St. Clair-Abrams researched into the operation of the Western and Atlantic Railroad after private investors took over operation from the state.

The construction of the Western and Atlantic Railroad was voted on and approved by the Georgia General Assembly in 1836. The initial route was to connect Fulton County with Chattanooga, Tennessee, and then continue to points in the Midwest, as well as to Savannah and South Georgia. The "zero milepost" was placed at Forsyth and Magnolia Streets, and later, in 1842, was moved to another location at a settlement that would be incorporated in 1843 as Marthasville - and two years later renamed Atlanta.

The Western and Atlantic Railroad's most famous locomotive was called *The General*. It was a 4-4-0 steam locomotive #3 built in 1855 by the Rogers, Ketchum & Grosvenor Company of New Jersey. On April 12, 1862, *The General* was commandeered near Big Shanty (now Kennesaw), Georgia, by Union soldiers, led by the Federal spy, James J. Andrews, in an attempt to thwart the Confederate railroad network. In what would be called the Great Locomotive Chase, *The General* was pursued by Western and Atlantic conductor, William Allen Fuller, on the *Texas*. *The General* eventually lost steam near Ringgold, Georgia, and Andrew and his raiders fled. Andrews was hung as a spy in Atlanta on June 7, 1862.

While Brown was governor, he wanted to divert a portion of the state-owned railroad's profits to help fund schools for poor white children. Resistance from affluent planters and insufficient income generated by the Western and Atlantic Railroad, due to mismanagement, prevented Brown's plans. In 1858, businessman John Woods Lewis was appointed by Brown to reverse the economic problems of the railroad, which, within three years, Lewis succeeded in doing. Once the railroad became profitable, Lewis resigned, causing a quarrel between the old friends, Brown and Lewis. Brown felt it was bad timing for Lewis to resign, as he was campaigning for re-election in 1861. They eventually reconciled.

Up until 1870, the "State Road" as the Western and Atlantic was called, was operated under the direction of a governor appointed superintendent. On December 27, 1870, operations were transferred to a group of investors, which included Joseph Brown, who had resigned as Chief Justice prior to the takeover. No surprise to St. Clair-Abrams, Brown was named president.

The feud was on when St. Clair-Abrams denounced the activities of the railroad under Brown's leadership, including the policy of the state's leasing of the railroad, as well as many other shady business deals he uncovered. Joseph Brown did not win the war of words, but won the feud, as he threatened St. Clair-Abrams and his partners, Grady and Alston, of foreclosure of the $5,000 the *Atlanta Herald* owed the bank, of which Brown also controlled.

MANUAL AND BIOGRAPHICAL REGISTER OF THE STATE OF GEORGIA FOR 1871-72.

In 1872, St. Clair-Abrams published the *Manual and Biographical Register of the State of Georgia, 1871-2*. The manual was printed and distributed by the prominent book publisher, Plantation Publishing Company's Press.

In the *Preface* of the manual, which he penned on December 14, 1871, he stated his reason for undertaking this work. At this time in his early life - twenty-six years old - St. Clair-Abrams, though never having been a slave-owner, still held lingering racial prejudice. It was an attitude that would change after his move to Florida.

PREFACE: "When the writer of this MANUAL formed the idea of its compilation, the session of the Legislature was near at hand, and as he desired, above all things, that the work should appear as early after the adjournment as possible, and before the close of the present year, he did not deceive himself with the expectation that the MANUAL would be as comprehensive and as perfect as it can be made. Nevertheless, he believed that, despite the limited period allotted himself for its preparation, he could place before the public a book not altogether devoid of interest, instruction and reference, which might prove the

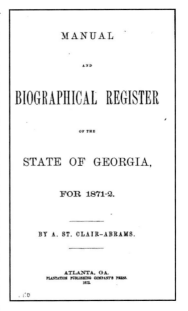

MANUAL

AND

BIOGRAPHICAL REGISTER

OF THE

STATE OF GEORGIA,

FOR 1871-2.

BY A. ST. CLAIR-ABRAMS.

ATLANTA, GA.
PLANTATION PUBLISHING COMPANY'S PRESS.
1872.

foundation of a really valuable historical record. Whether or not he erred in this impression, the reader must decide. His task was certainly a difficult one. Sources of information were not always accessible, either for the statistical matter required, or for the materials needed for the biographies. Besides, the anomalous character of the political situation rendered it no easy task to prepare a MANUAL strictly non-partisan and, consequently, historical.

As regards the Sketches themselves a few words are necessary. To prepare them, the Editor was compelled to obtain dates and facts from the Members. Accordingly, a circular was sent to each Member, setting forth the purpose of the work and asking the requisite information concerning his past career. Less than one-half the gentlemen addressed, replied. A mistaken idea of propriety restrained the majority, while not a few of those who did reply forwarded the most meagre material. The general reluctance seems to have arisen from an impression that each subject was desired to write his own Biography. Nothing was further from the Editor's mind. He simply required dates, places and incidents not attainable from any other sources than the parries immediately concerned. Another idea was, that there was little in the past lives of the Members worthy of publication. This idea was quite erroneous. It would be an insult to the intelligence of the entire white population of Georgia to suppose that they sent none other than obscure men to the Legislature men of little mental capacity. The fact is, that, taken as a whole, the present Legislature contains an unusually large number of able men. Many of them, it is true, are young men, but they are talented, patriotic and ambitious, and not a few of them possess a War Record of which their constituents, their children and they have every reason to be proud. Besides, the Editor has every reason to believe that the people of Georgia do feel an interest in the past careers of their representatives, and will read the Biographical Sketches herein published with pleasure and satisfaction. And just here it is proper to state that, whatever opinion concerning the abilities and capacity of any Member may be expressed, is the personal opinion of the writer, formed after acquaintance, or derived from information from friends of the subject, in whose unbiased judgment confidence could be reposed. This explanation is made because many Members and among them the ablest of both Houses were, and still are, sensitive on the subject, fearing lest the impression be left on the reader that they influenced what is written. Indeed, the Editor cannot write more flatteringly of all the Members than by recording the fact that, in not a single instance was he approached by any gentleman on the-subject of his own biography something which Congressional Biographers can scarcely say.

It is pleasant to the Editor to state that, but five members of the Legislature declined positively to furnish the materials requested. Of the others, four promised to furnish them, but failed to do so; while the remainder neither promised nor refused. One hundred and seventy-nine sketches appear, out of about one hundred and ninety-four; so that the Biographical Record may be justly claimed as full and complete. It will be observed that some of the sketches of prominent members are very brief. This is not the fault of the Editor; but is due solely to the meagreness of the materials furnished him.

The reader will perceive that no biographical sketches of the Colored Members appear. Aside from the manifest absurdity it would have been to have written the lives of men who were but yesterday our slaves, and whose past careers, probably, embraced such menial occupations as boot-blacking, shaving, table-waiting and the like, there was, perhaps, another motive prompting the Editor to exclude them from biographical notice. It may have been that he felt a secret exultation over the fact that, though Congress could compel him to associate with negroes in a deliberative body, sit beside them in railroad cars, etc., neither Congress, Military Government, a triple Reconstruction, nor even anorher [sic] Amendment to that national patch-work, the United States Constitution, could compel him to publish their biographies in this book. Hence, it may be that, more in assertion of at least one right left, than in any spirit of partisan ship, he decided upon keeping them out. Of course, it was necessary to publish their names in the list of members; and this has been done but this only.

Two causes have prevented the Statistical and Historical information being written as full or as satisfactory as the Editor desired, and, probably, as the public would justly expect. The first has been the inaccessibility of nearly all sources of information in the brief period in which the MANUAL has been compiled. The next reason has been the expense. After the greater part of the MANUAL had been put in type it was found that if all the Statistics compiled were published, they would swell the number of pages considerably beyond what had been contracted for, and involve an additional expense far greater than the price at which the book is sold will permit. Such Statistics as are given will, the Editor believes, be found interesting. It will be perceived that the sketch of Mr. COXLEY appears under the heading of Governor. This is owing to the fact that it was printed before the election of Governor SMITH, and before it was known that Mr. COXLEY would retire. In the next Edition, Colonel SMITH'S sketch will appear in lieu thereof. The next volume of the MANUAL will be published in 1873, and as the Editor will have had one entire year in which to compile the work, he promises that it will be, in every respect, full and comprehensive."

St. Clair-Abrams did not publish another edition of the biographical register in 1873.

THE CASE OF THE BOGUS BELLE.

In an August 20, 1881, a front-page story in the *Silver Reef Miner* of Washington County, Utah, re-printed from an article in the *Philadelphia Record*, told a tale of spy Belle Boyd. It was titled "A

Noted Lady Spy – Story of an Ex-Confederate Agent Corresponding with Lincoln." The feature article read - "During her residence in Washington "Belle Boyd" formed an intimate acquaintance with President Lincoln, and a friendly correspondence was kept up between the two during a greater portion of the war. On one occasion her letter-paper was adorned with the Confederate motto, a snake entwined around a Confederate flag, and the inscription, "Don't tread on us, or we will bite."

Broken down in health and bereaved by the death of her father, who had died in the endeavor to release her from captivity, Belle Boyd determined to leave for foreign shores, and in May, 1864, she embarked on the Greyhound at North Carolina as the bearer of important dispatches from Jefferson Davis and Judah P. Benjamin to friends of the cause in London. In endeavoring to run the blockade, however, the Greyhound was captured by a United States steamer. Belle Boyd was taken to Boston, kept a prisoner for some time, and finally banished to Canada. From there she went to England, where she passed the second epoch of her life. She was married at the aristocratic Church of St. James, Piccadilly, received with open arms in titled society, became a widow, and finally, having a talent for the theatrical profession, took to the stage. Probably no person in the country has been afflicted with so many "doubles" as this lady. Since her return to America and marriage to Colonel J. S. Hammond, an English gentleman, once a member of the "Louisiana Tigers," she has completely sunk her history with that of her husband, and with the exception of a few occasions, when she appeared upon the reader and elocutionist, "Maria Isabella Hammond," her mind has been engrossed with domestic affairs. Yet every few months she is vexed and annoyed by coming across an announcement that "Belle Boyd, the Ex-Confederate spy," has turned up in some part of the country. Now the pretender is being entertained by some prominent Southerner; again, she is in distress soliciting aid. Several years ago, one of the bogus Belles visited Atlanta on a lecturing tour, and was denounced by Captain St. Clair Abrams, of the News, as an imposter. Next morning, she proceeded to the office and demanded satisfaction, which being refused she proceeded to draw a couple of derringers, but was seized before the weapons could be pointed. Since that time, she has not turned up in Georgia."

THE CASE OF BAD BLOOD AND
THE DOUBLE-BARRELED SHOT-GUN.

In late May, 1873, a story circulated in every newspaper across the country regarding a struggle that escalated between two Atlanta editors - St. Clair-Abrams and Colonel Cary W. Styles. The Daily Memphis Avalanche titled the story: *A Question of Blood: Why an Atlanta Editor Sought a Brother Quill Driver with a Double-Barreled Shot-Gun.* The following is the story as it appeared in the *Missouri Republican* on Tuesday, May 27, 1873 -

"Two Atlanta, Ga., editors have had an unpleasantness, which just escaped furnishing a subject for the coroner, and a trial for a killing. Mr. St. Clair-Abrams and Col. Cary W. Stiles [sic] are the principals. They had not been on speaking terms for years, and thus got along very harmoniously. Mr. St. Clair-Abrams had been several years in Atlanta, and was captain of artillery in the southern cause during the rebellion. Col. Styles was also well known in the community, and it was also well known that the two had a political dispute, and newspaper vengeance, and afterwards did not speak.

A short time ago St. Clair-Abrams first heard Col. Styles had been long circulating a report that he (St. Clair-Abrams) had negro blood in his veins, and that his mother was a negro woman of bad character. It made St. Clair-Abrams very angry when he heard this and the extent to which the report had been circulated. It had become so common that his best friends deemed it their duty to tell him of it. He immediately addressed a note to Col. Styles, and sent it by a friend, simply asking if he had circulated such reports, and demanding an unequivocal answer.

Styles refused to have any communication with St. Clair-Abrams, and told the friend that his principal was no gentleman. The friend told Styles to prepare to be killed or kill Mr. St. Clair-Abrams. The latter, when he received the verbal answer, loaded a shot-gun and went hunting for Styles. He saw him near the post office in Atlanta and was levelling the gun at him, when he was seized by two policemen, and a third one took the gun away. St. Clair-Abrams was taken to jail. The next day his case was examined and he was placed under ten thousand dollars bonds to keep the peace in the state of Georgia.

Col. Styles reconsidered his resolution and wrote a letter to St. Clair-Abrams' friend, stating that he was mistaken in his adversary's ancestry and parentage, and particularly in his mother, and took it all back, saying it was not the St. Clair-Abrams family he meant. St. Clair-Abrams refused to be satisfied unless an apology was made full and directly to him. That note has not been written, and so the matter stands.

Col. Styles appears to have wakened up the wrong passenger. Mr. Alex. St. Clair-Abrams is said, by those who know him, to be of good Spanish blood. His mother is a native of the West Indies, and now lives in Kingston, Jamaica, and he is an honorable gentleman, who, for the past fifteen years, has been connected with the press in Mobile, Macon, Atlanta and New York."

THE ATLANTA NEWS AND RETIREMENT FROM WRITING.

After his buy-out from Grady and Alston, St. Clair-Abrams tried again to establish a newspaper in Atlanta. He began publication of the *Atlanta News* in 1874. He persevered for nearly a year, facing plenty of obstacles that included rising costs of materials and printers.

The *Wheeling Daily Intelligencer* of West Virginia wrote: "Daily journalism in Atlanta is not without its trials. Having been somewhat annoyed by strikes, Mr. Alexander St. Clair-Abrams, of the *News*, unburdens the story of his struggles in a four-column paragraph. 'Every time I yielded to the despotism of the printers, he says, 'the despotism increased in severity. One day the office was 'struck' for four dollars and fifty cents. There was neither legal nor moral claim on me to pay it. I am not ashamed to state that as we were unusually pushed for money, rather than have a scandal about so small a sum, I went home, took from my wife all the money she had, and paid the demand.' Mr. Abrams announced that he intends to stick."

Even with the notoriety of his name, he could not compete. In late May 1875, he prepared a card for distribution that appeared in newspapers throughout the country. Prior to his announcement of retirement, St. Clair-Abrams had made a couple trips to the "Eastern Frontier" of Florida in late 1874 and early 1875 to scout for land and a new homestead. While there, he had met with old acquaintances and former war veterans who had previously moved to, in what at that time was referred to as South Florida – today's Central Florida.

On June 3, 1875, The *Daily Times* in Atlanta reported: "Alex. St. Clair-Abrams, in a card to the public, announces a permanent suspension of the Atlanta *News*. He says: "I have been disheartened by the indifference of men whose interests I advocated. The influence of those whom I opposed was active and prompt; while those who applauded my cause (excepting a handful), fed me with approbation and nothing more."

He intimates that this will be his permanent retirement from journalism, but so brilliant a journalist with such enthusiasm in his work will find it impossible to adhere to this resolution. When a man once gets the stain of printer's ink on his fingers, he can never get it off. The fascination with newspaper work is wonderful. It holds men on through all imaginable reverses and hardships, leading them to sacrifice all, even life itself, that the paper may live.

The pay of journalists is very poor, not one fifth what the same talent, energy and applications would command in other avocations, but in journalism more than any other profession the work itself is its own reward. It is fortunate that this fascination exists, for without it, newspapers would be rare."

Comments upon his retirement and his move to Florida from his *nemeses* and *antagonists* included such remarks as -

"Alexander St. Clair-Abrams, having failed as editor of a paper, is going to Florida to raise oranges. He has been raising Cain some time, but it was not sugar cane." - June 11, 1875, the *Public Ledger* of Memphis, Tennessee.

"Alexander St. Clair-Abrams who started the Atlanta, Ga., *Herald* several years ago, and made it to one of the best newspapers in the United States, worked himself out of it somehow and started the *News*. We now have the intelligence that the *News* has been forced to the wall and has been suspended. Abrams will be remembered as the rip roaring little rebel, who couldn't find words sufficiently treasonable to express his hatred for the United States, or those who gave their adhesion to it." - June 2, 1875, the *Topeka State Journal*, Topeka, Kansas.

"Alex. St. Clair-Abrams has again lost his occupation - the Atlanta *News*, of which he was the head and front, having forced to suspend publication. We always feel a deep sympathy for genius, especially newspaper genius, in distress. One of the Atlanta papers ought to be magnanimous and tender Mr. Abrams a situation. He is a writer of extraordinary powers and only needs a cool level head to advise him and give general direction to his pen." - June 15, 1875, the *Charlotte Observer*, Charlotte, North Carolina.

"Having permanently retired from journalism, Alexander St. Clair Vesuvius Abrams, late of the Atlanta News, has gone to Florida to edit an orange grove." - June 16, 1875, *Memphis Daily Appeal*, Memphis, Tennessee.

FOUR

Gone to Florida to Edit an Orange Grove

Central Florida's prehistoric landscape of the mid-1800s was a long way from the hustle and bustle of the metropolis of New York, and even Atlanta. Most settlers to Florida prior to the War Between the States did not travel further south than Gainesville. Some courageous families, mainly from the Carolinas and Georgia, utilized the Armed Occupational Act of 1842 or the Homestead Act of 1862, to venture deeper south into the wilderness.

These pioneering families carved their way through extremely treacherous backwoods and thickets, swamps and bogs that were home to every imaginable, and unimageable, creature that bit, slithered, clawed and crawled.

In the heat and humidity that played a remorseless tug of war on their senses, these new Floridians laid the foundations for a new life. With saws and shovels, adzes and axes, they built their cracker-style houses, barns, smokehouses, and corrals from the hard pine of the meadow woods and the cypress trees that lined the crooked creeks and sun-beamed lakes. Their nearest neighbor may have been five miles away, but the animals that preyed on their livestock and chewed up their gardens lived right in their own backyard.

But also, within this wilderness, settlement towns, large and small, began to emerge with the influx of wealthy men with money to invest. Some of these towns would prosper into the future, while others were destined to become ghost towns. Surrounding these growing communities, cattle ranches, along with cotton and sugar cane plantations, developed and thrived. But more and more acreage of land began to fill with seemingly endless rows of what would become Florida's commodity crop - oranges! With railroads inching deeper into the region, the packaging and shipping of oranges to the north became a huge business bonanza.

Federal land agent, surveyor, orange grower, and master real estate promoter and salesman, John A. MacDonald, was paid $10 a day to guide investors from Jacksonville to his home and office in

Mellonville, a town located on the south shore of Lake Monroe near Sanford. The trip up the St. Johns took three days and two nights. From there, he would take them on an adventure through the overgrown trails to the relatively unknown inner region of Florida. Investors satisfied with what they saw, purchased 160 acres at $1.25 an acre. Much of the area in West Orange County that MacDonald brought his speculators to was called the Highlands, then in 1876, the name was changed to Pendryville, and then Lake Eustis and finally Eustis. Pendryville was named for A. S. Pendry, because it was on his land that the town began to build.

In 1875, St. Clair-Abrams arrived in Mellonville and met with MacDonald, who had expected his arrival through their recent correspondences. Joining St. Clair-Abrams on the trip was Confederate veteran Florence J. Titcomb of Savannah, Georgia.

Having described some land in West Orange County to the expected buyers, MacDonald hitched the carriage and took the two veterans to the pre-described area. St. Clair-Abrams had commented that he now understood why Florida soldiers were often tasked to lead their battalions through the unknown, untamed countryside.

St. Clair-Abrams and Titcomb approved of the well-described land and purchased and settled there. On September 24, St. Clair-Abrams purchased sixty-plus acres on the southeast corner of the "beautiful lake," as described by MacDonald. Titcomb bought land on the northwest corner. Titcomb would later move to Dunnellon in Marion County.

St. Clair-Abrams filed for an additional 190 acres from the Federal Land Office in Gainesville. With that purchase, he owned the entire west shore of the lake that would be named for his wife, Joanna. Two other lakes, which were named for his daughter, Irma, and his son, Alfred, were encompassed on his property. Today, Lake Alfred is now part of a ninety-acre conservation preserve located between Eustis and Mount Dora known as Hidden Waters Preserve.

St. Clair-Abrams would continue to add acreage to his property over the six-year period of 1875 to 1881, which included land along Loch Leven. The Lake Region, as first described in 1845, included West Orange and parts of Sumter and Marion Counties. By the late-1870s, when St. Clair-Abrams became one of the largest orange growers in the area, the region was referred to as the Great Lake Region.

Alex and Joanna received their mail at the Fort Mason post office located on Lake Eustis. The post office was established exactly three years earlier by Colonel John M. Bryan. The Fort Mason settlement was named after the military fort that was located on the east side of Smith Lake and built during the Second Seminole War. The fort, built in 1836, was named for Lieutenant Colonel Pierce Mason Butler, whom Fort Butler on the St. Johns River at Astor, was also named. After the war ended in 1842, Fort Mason was used to support settlement in the Lake Region.

ORANGE COUNTY COURTHOUSE ~
MELLONVILLE OR ORLANDO?

Orange County, having been renamed in 1845 from the equally appropriate designation of Mosquito County, would soon have a decision to make as to where to locate the permanent seat of government. Since 1845, when Mosquito County was broken apart to establish new counties, as well as received its new name, Mellonville, the port town on Lake Monroe, served the majority of the early period as the seat of government of the new Orange County.

In 1857, the village of Orlando was laid out. The town grew from the remnants of Fort Gatlin; a military outpost that was built in 1838. Fort Gatlin was named for Army Assistant Surgeon John S. Gatlin, one of the casualties of the Dade Massacre that took place at the opening of the Second Seminole War on December 28, 1835, near present day Bushnell in Sumter County. Then, in 1843, two brothers, Aaron and Isaac Jernigan, homesteaded near the fort. For a period of time, the settlement was known as Jernigan before it received the name Orlando; arguably named for militiaman Orlando Reeves.

On July 31, 1875, Orlando was incorporated. Eighty-five residents - and rapidly increasing - inhabited the four-square mile town. The twenty-two registered voters elected William Jackson Brack as its first mayor. Railroad operators had begun to survey and build tracks toward the flourishing town. With that reason, and the citizens belief that the town was the most centrally located in Orange County, prompted Orlando town leaders to request of the county commissioners that a new courthouse be built there and to establish Orlando as the official county seat.

Mellonville contended that they should be the county seat on the strength that their location on Lake Monroe, with entry into the St. Johns River, made them a more appropriate location for the county seat and to build the new courthouse there. People and supplies could easily be transported to any destination in Florida and beyond.

The battle lines were drawn, and the region's most wealthy prepared their cases for the county commission. In 1871, former American Consul to Belgium under President Lincoln, Henry Shelton Sanford, purchased 12,000 acres of land at Mellonville. Besides planting oranges, Sanford built the infrastructure for a large town, which included a hotel, shipping wharf, general store, restaurant, lumber mill, a stern-wheeler service, and roads. He was one of the wealthiest men in the entire state of Florida. He offered to build a courthouse if the people of Orange County located the county seat in Mellonville. Sanford's northern friends who invested in the region sided with him.

Henry S. Sanford

On the other side was cattle baron, Jacob "Jake" Summerlin. In 1873, Summerlin moved his family to Orlando. He soon purchased two hundred acres of land from W. R. Lovell. The land included, within its boundaries, Lake Eola, a landmark that is still a popular gathering and event site today. Summerlin was intent on Orlando remaining the county seat. And so, the two heavyweight contenders faced off in the latter half of 1875 at the existing 1869 courthouse in Orlando.

Sanford, in his eloquence as an orator and diplomat, described the beauty and potential of Mellonville to the county commissioners, of which

Jacob "Jake" Summerlin

St. Clair-Abrams served. He offered land and money if Mellonville were chosen as the county seat.

So too, Summerlin, with quite the opposite personality and with a mellower voice, made an offer. He explained that Orlando already had the land by the large city well and to "leave the place the county seat and I will build a $10,000 courthouse, and if the county is ever able to pay for it, all right, and if not, I won't ask to be repaid."

The county commissioners accepted Summerlin's offer with St. Clair-Abrams' promise to Summerlin that he would be repaid if it took "all the land in the county." The three-story frame courthouse was built at a final cost of $7,800 of Summerlin's loan, which took the county ten years to repay.

1875 Orange County Courthouse and town well in Orlando

ALEX. ST. CLAIR-ABRAMS ~ ATTORNEY AT LAW.

In 1876, St. Clair-Abrams opened a law practice in Orlando. By 1878, he had partnered with Jacob Summerlin's son, Robert Lee Summerlin. They maintained an office in Orlando, where Summerlin lived with his wife and children on property owned by his father at Lake Eola. The post office address used for the business was at Fort Mason, near St. Clair-Abrams' home.

The talented and highly sought-after attorneys had a strong partnership for several years, and their partnership accumulated much wealth for the two well-known men. Summerlin, who served as Orlando mayor in 1880, would become a considerable, but

Robert Lee Summerlin

possibly a reluctant, investor in the aspired dreams and grand vision of St. Clair-Abrams.

St. Clair-Abrams, too, remained extremely active in the political arena during this partnership. In 1877, he successfully organized Orange, Volusia, Polk, Brevard, and Manatee Counties into a strong Democratic alliance. It was through St. Clair-Abrams' efforts that Florida elected its first Democratic governor since David Shelby Walker left office in 1868. Since that time, Republicans Harrison Reed, Ossian Bingley Hart (died in office), and Marcellus Stearns served as Florida governors. As a reward, Governor George Franklin Drew appointed St. Clair-Abrams State Attorney for the Seventh Judicial Circuit.

In 1880, St. Clair-Abrams, a prominent figure in political campaigns on all levels, supported Confederate veteran and Florida native, William Dunnington Bloxham, for governor over the incumbent, Governor Drew. Bloxham was a leading voice among the Democrats at that time and served as the Secretary of State - a position he resigned to run for governor. Bloxham won the election to become Florida's thirteenth governor.

St. Clair-Abrams accepted re-appointment as State Attorney; a post in which he distinguished himself and built his reputation.

DRAIN THE SWAMP ~ THE DISSTON LAND PURCHASE.

By 1877, Florida's Internal Improvement Fund, more commonly referred to in modern times as Public Works, was nearly one million dollars in debt. This trust fund, managed by the governor and four state officials, had pledged land, mostly swamp land, to the railroad companies with guaranteed bonds on the land. With the high cost of the "late war," as well as the cost of the subsequent reconstruction, though not nearly as costly as Florida's sister Southern states, had prompted the railroad companies to default on the bonds. When the St. Clair-Abrams' supported governor, George Franklin Drew, took

170

office in 1877, no major rail lines had pierced the interior of the state, along the coasts, and into the far southern region.

When an application to foreclose on the Internal Improvement Fund was filed in federal court in 1880, several investors negotiated to relieve the enormous debt. St. Clair-Abrams was one of those investors, as well as Henry S. Sanford; but the negotiations had fallen through.

Going back three years to 1877, Sanford had invited Industrialist and Real Estate Magnate, Hamilton Disston of Philadelphia, to Florida for a leisurely fishing excursion. This first-time trek through the waterways and swamps had the land developer imagining the great agricultural possibilities of the millions of acres of marshy terrain.

George Franklin Drew

Disston had a contract to drain the Everglades, which included an area of up to twelve million acres. Over the next few years, the contract still was unable to cut into the Internal Improvement Fund debt, and as a result, an order from the court was about to cancel the contract.

William D. Bloxham

In 1881, one month into newly elected governor, William Bloxham's, term, he traveled to Philadelphia to meet with Disston. A persuasive Bloxham was able to convince Disston to purchase four million acres of land from The Internal Improvement Fund at a cost of twenty-five cents an acre. The agreement between the two gentlemen became an official contract on June 1, 1881. This sale was said to be the largest sale of land to an individual person in the world. Six months later, Disston sold two million of those acres to Sir Edmund James Reed, a member of the English Parliament for six hundred thousand dollars.

And though there were detractors of Bloxham's sale to Disston, especially for such a low sales price, the development of the land led to the first in a series of land booms into the state. The towns of Kissimmee, where Disston had his office, and St. Cloud, where he had a huge sugar mill, as well as Tarpon Springs, known for their sponge harvesting, grew from the drainage efforts of Disston's company.

Hamilton Disston

He spent ten years on the drainage operation, but eventually was unable to complete his great plan around Lake Okeechobee and the Kissimmee River, and sold much of the land. Disston's accomplishments led several other distinguished figures in Florida, such as Henry Flagler and James Ingraham, as well as prominent politicians, to take over where Disston left off – to bring farmers and planters and railroads full of tourists southward.

THE CASE FOR ANNIE DONNELLY.

Annie Donnelly

In 1879, St. Clair-Abrams was hired by Mrs. Annie Stone to file for divorce from her estranged husband, who had deserted her and their child two years earlier. In the petition, St. Clair-Abrams described Annie's plight, asserting that William Stone left her "in the woods, in a strange country." On August 5, 1879, Annie was granted a divorce from Stone.

Annie had married Stone at the age of sixteen in Ohio. The unhappy marriage led to several separations. Her parents, Clark and Helen McDonald, were planning a move to Florida, and urged their daughter and son-in-law to join them in hopes the marriage would revive.

McDonald and Stone purchased, at 80 cents an acre, two parcels of, what they believed to be, worthless swampland; but inherently it was beautiful lakefront property.

Stone deserted his family in 1877 and disappeared from Florida. Not long after Stone left, Pennsylvanian John Phillip Donnelly arrived in Mount Dora and purchased 160 acres next to Annie's property. Donnelly and Annie became a couple over time and in the summer of 1881, they married.

Annie had paid Stone's *owed balance* of four dollars on her land. With her property, and that of her parents, they owned two miles of waterfront property on Lake Dora. The new Mr. and Mrs. Donnelly went into the hotel business and built, along with James Alexander and John MacDonald, a two-story, ten room building called the Alexander House, and later in 1893, after they sold it to Emma Boone of Boston, the name was changed to the Lake House, and finally, as it is still called today, the Lakeside Inn. The author of this book installed the air-conditioning equipment in 1985-86 when the hotel was saved from demolition and refurbished. The Lakeside Inn remains a fabulous tourist destination today and is listed on the National Register of Historic Places.

Annie Donnelly passed away in 1908.

A GOOD CARRIAGE RIDE.

In the spring of 1875, on a visit from Atlanta to search for property, St. Clair-Abrams was accompanied by his wife Joanna. They took what he described as "a good carriage ride" north of Orlando. It was on this journey that he first caught a glimpse of a bridge of land well located between Lake Dora and Lake Eustis. He knew immediately that this area would be the site where he would carve out a city that someday would be the *hub* of Florida.

After he purchased land to homestead three miles from this location in West Orange County (today's Eustis-Mount Dora area), and then began his law practice and citrus operation, he planned his most adventurous enterprise to date.

A Good Carriage Ride
Spring 1875

FIVE

Building Florida's New Capital

ALEX. ST. CLAIR-ABRAMS
ATTORNEY AT LAW
615-619 DYAL-UPCHURCH BUILDING

Jacksonville, Fla. March 18, 1925.

Miss Elizabeth Burleigh,
℅ E. H. Burleigh,
Tavares, Florida.

My dear Miss Burleigh,

Pursuant to my promise I enclose a memoranda concerning Tavares. You will understand that this is not to be publicized as I have written it as it is hastily written and is intended only to furnish you with data for you to get up an article you may see fit under your own name.

I have hesitated to prepare this. As I was practically the only factor and actor in the town it is necessarily very personal and puts me too much in the position of "blowing my own trumpet", although it necessarily couldn't be helped. I trust however that the data will enable you to prepare an article such as you desire. I could have written much more as to Mr. Frank Jones' repudiation of his contract with me and some day if I ever get time to write my reminiscences of my life in Florida will do so.

Trusting that this memoranda is what you want, I am

Very truly yours,
/s/ Alex. St. Clair-Abrams

MEMORANDA ON TAVARES PART I.

"The name "TAVARES" given by me to the town being that of a remote Spanish Ancestor of mine who was an officer in command of Spanish Soldiers, which helped to conquer Mexico or Peru, I am not certain which. He remained on this side of the Atlantic and his

175

descendants are scattered all over the United States, Central and South America.

I was first on what is now Tavares in 1875. The Lake Dora Section of the town was occupied at that time by a man named Steely, who had preempted the land, one of the forties being on the other side of the canal or creek running into Lake Eustis. The balance of the land to Lake Eustis was occupied by a man named Hull, who entered it as a homestead from the United States Government. He lived in a log cabin in a little orange grove of some 28 or 30 trees. He told me that his wife planted the sweet orange seeds and as they grew up he set them out for shade trees. They were among the largest seedlings in the state of Florida and when the double freezes of 1894 and '95 took place there was not one of them less than three feet in diameter and 50 feet in height. Hull was a hunter and trapper and traded with the Indians. When he homesteaded the land there was a United States Military Company stationed near Lake Dora right on the canal. The station was called "Eustis Station."

At the time Lake Eustis was called "Lake Helen Hawkins". He got his patent to the homestead and sold it to State Senator Brantley of Orange County. After Brantley's death the property was sold to Mr. L. P. Westcott of Orlando and my partner and I subsequently bought out Westcott and also bought out Steeley and later I acquired title to all of the property. In the early eighties I had the land laid out into a town and immediately set to work to put railroads into it. At first, I intended to make it a tourist resort and educational center and platted Ridge Park and River Park to put a 200 room tourist hotel in Ridge Park and a school house on about the same plan as they now have in Monteverde, in River Park. I also intended to place an ornamental park fronting on Lake Dora. Later I had to abandon this plan for two reasons:

One was because I could not get any railroad to come into Tavares without running along the shore of Lake Dora, and in carrying out my railroad plans we had to cut obliquely through River Park.

The other and most important reason was because a very careful study of this situation by me satisfied me that if Tavares ever became a big town it would have to be an industrial and railroad center and not an exclusive tourist resort."

The "my partner" mentioned in the Memoranda on Tavares is Robert Summerlin, whom I wrote about in the previous chapter.

The "St. Clair-Abrams ~ Summerlin" law partnership, as well as their business collaboration in the establishment of Tavares, dissolved on November 15, 1882. The new town was well underway by the time Summerlin left. Though the reason is relatively unknown as to why the successful partnership ended, there could have been several reasons, ranging from financial stress with loans and commitments in undertaking a project of such magnitude, to Summerlin not sharing the lofty vision of St. Clair-Abrams' dream, to political and personality conflicts, to Summerlin having private personal problems in his life that prompted him to move on and start a new life elsewhere. Summerlin and his wife, Texas, had divorced. She relocated with their children, Ruby and Maude, to Polk County, while the cattle baron's son turned up in San Antonio, Texas, where he practiced law, remarried, and then relocated to Los Angeles, California. Robert Summerlin passed away there in 1926.

When St. Clair-Abrams laid out his town, the partners named streets for family and investors. After the split of the partners, St. Clair-Abrams changed the name of Summerlin Avenue to Park Avenue, for Ridge Park that borders the street, and then changed it again to Rockingham Avenue. He did not change the name of the street named for Summerlin's former wife, as Texas Avenue remains today.

Memoranda on Tavares Part II.

"At the time I laid out the town the only railroad down there was one from Ft. Butler (now called Astor) to Ft. Mason but its only connection was with the St. Johns River and that did not satisfy me. When the Florida Railway and Navigation Company, later the F. C. & P, and now the Seaboard was built to Leesburg I took the contract to build from Leesburg to Tavares for freight certificates.

We built it and in this I sunk some $30,000 of my money. About the same time, I planned the railroad from Tavares to Orlando and we built this road. In this I sunk over $30,000 more. I then persuaded

The Lane Park train station was the terminus of the
St. Johns & Lake Eustis Railroad

Col. Lane who owned the road from Astor to Mason to run the road through Tavares to Lane Park, instead of going to Leesburg, as he had at first intended. I also got a charter to build a road from Tavares to Sanford, but later when Dr. Bishop of Sanford took the matter up, I abandoned that and persuaded him to run it to Tavares, instead of going to Eustis and that cost me about $6,000. I then obtained a charter for the Tavares Apopka & Gulf Railroad and unaided by anyone built it to Clermont. Sinking $35,000 of my money in it. Still later I obtained a charter from the Legislature to build a railroad from Jacksonville to Tampa with numerous branches. The other railroad owners of Florida railroads successfully fought my efforts to place my bonds within the United States so I got Mr. Washington Conner, the well-known banker of New York, to take the matter up in England and I made a tentative contract with the English Syndicate to sell $4,000,000.00 of the bonds just before the double freeze took place in the early nineties. Your father was a stockholder to a small extent in that Company. I had the entire road surveyed from Palatka to Tampa with a branch to Bartow graded several miles to Little Lake Harris and through the Drake Grove on the other side and had prepared a contract for the English Syndicate to sign when the double freeze took place and the English Syndicate declined to complete the contract. In the work of surveying and platting the line of road and grading I sunk about $50,000 of my own money."

DOCTOR, DOES TAVARES GET YOUR RAILROAD?

The story of Dr. Bishop, who was mentioned in Part II of St. Clair-Abrams' Memoranda on Tavares, appeared in the *Lake County Citizen* on June 1, 1923.

"One day Dr. Bishop, who then lived in Sanford, was driving up the street by Major St. Clair-Abrams' office. The Major asked Mr. Butler, who was sitting in his office in Tavares, to go invite Dr. Bishop up to his office for a few minutes, which he did.

The Major asked, "Doctor, does Tavares get your railroad from Sanford?"

The doctor looked puzzled stating, "Abrams, I'm afraid not. We are making a cut-off to Eustis. I'm on my way to Eustis to a meeting to get their decision whether they will come on my terms."

The Major responded, "How long do you propose to give them to decide?"

The doctor replied, "I will give them one hour."

"If they do not decide in that hour does Tavares get the road?"

But the reply was evaded, so the Major shot again, "If they do not decide within that hour will you stop up in my office here as you go back?"

The doctor promised he would. When the doctor had gone on to Eustis, Mr. Butler was asked to write up a contract, stating that for certain reasons the railroad was routed through Tavares.

Promptly a little later, Dr. Bishop appeared in his office, reporting that Eustis had not accepted, and asked the Major, "Why do you suppose those people would not accept my offer?"

But Major St. Clair-Abrams had already handed him the contract, which the doctor read, and then walked to a table and signed without further argument or comment. The Major then signed it, and Butler witnessed the signatures.

Dr. Bishop asked the reason why the Major had expected and prepared for the results. The Major could not state the reasons, but knew they would not sign, and then asked the doctor for the story of what had occurred in Eustis.

From the office window, Dr. Bishop smiled as he looked down in the street and saw some buggies hurriedly driving up. Members from the Eustis delegation were following him, wanting to finish the contract at the doctor's money figure. Back in Eustis, they wanted to give a thousand or two less, with a couple of the men asking for an extension beyond the hour to find another investor that might help. Dr. Bishop told the men the contract was already signed and the matter closed.

"I wonder how the Major knew?"

TROPICAL CONSTRUCTION COMPANY.

St. Clair-Abrams is not remembered today on a national, or even on a state-wide level, unlike his extremely famous contemporary, Henry Bradley Plant, for his contributions to bring railroads and steamboat service into the heart of Florida. With much less of a financial foundation than Plant, but possessing formidable salesmanship skills in securing investors, enabled him to succeed amidst tough conditions and set-backs.

In 1880, upon acquiring the first section of land to build Tavares, St. Clair-Abrams incorporated the Tropical Construction Company, along with J. L. "Letcher" Bryan and W. H. Latimer. The Tropical Construction Company, with its place of business listed as Tavares, Orange County, Florida, commenced operation on October 1, 1880, with St. Clair-Abrams as president and George Butler as Secretary. According to the Articles of Incorporation, the business of the company was the "construction of railroads, steamboats, canals, bridges and buildings of every description."

Railroad historian, Clayton Bishop, in an interview with this author in 2006, spoke of St. Clair-Abrams and the railroads around Tavares: "The *Florida Railway & Navigation Company* was incorporated on February 28, 1884, and consisted of many small roads, one of which was the *Leesburg and Indian River Railroad*. Soon after the organization of the company, they undertook the construction of a ten-mile line extension from Leesburg to Tavares. This was completed by June 1885 and ran from Leesburg through Sunnyside along the north shore of Lake Harris and south of the present-day Leesburg International Airport, and then paralleled present day U. S. Highway 441 to Dead River, where a swing bridge, known as the Eustis Transfer, was built, along with a freight house and a steamer dock with a ramp up to the tracks. From there, it was on to Tavares where it joined the *St. Johns & Lake Eustis,* the *Sanford & Lake Eustis,* and the *Tavares & Gulf.*

Shortly after the *Florida Central & Peninsular Railroad* was organized, the company purchased, at foreclosure, the property and franchise of the *Tavares, Orlando & Atlantic Railroad*. The T. O. & A. had built a thirty-two-mile line from Tavares to Orlando. The railroad had been projected and built by Major Alexander St. Clair-Abrams during the spring of 1885. The Charter called for the track to be laid into Orlando by May 15, 1885. The crews worked day and night, and Sundays, laying track at the rate of better than a mile a day. They were in such a hurry to get the track finished before the contractor's agreement expired that trains were running with the rails being spiked at the ends, quarters, and centers. This meant that there were spikes about every ten feet. Around 1900, the T. O. & A. and the *Leesburg & Indian River* were merged with other lines in Orange County and became the *Orange County Branch*."

Clayton continued his interview, "I've saved the best for last. The one and only! Our very own! 'Taters and Grits'! 'Tug and Grunt'! Best known in corporate circles as the *Tavares & Gulf.*

This famous railroad was incorporated as the *Tavares, Apopka & Gulf Railway Company* with a capital stock of $660,000. The company set about the ambitious project of building a railroad from Tavares to Punta Rassa, down to the mouth of the Caloosahatchee River. Work began on the road from Tavares to Kissimmee on July 15, 1885, with twelve miles graded south that year as far as Double Run Swamp. In 1886, the construction continued on into Minneola and two more miles to Clermont in 1887. This was the end of the line to Punta Rassa. The T & G never built any further west. In 1890, the railroad was sold under foreclosure and reorganized as the T & G Railroad. The T & G operated until 1926 when the Seaboard Air Line bought all the stock from the estate of A. H. Jackson. By then the railroad was in horrible shape, but repairs by the Seaboard through the 1930s, 40s, and 50s enabled the company to continue making a profit, despite the handwriting on the wall. In 1968, the T & G was closed by the Seaboard Coast Line. The track was removed by 1972-1973, and the T & G was but a fond memory."

After St. Clair-Abrams announced his retirement from the newspaper business when he moved from Atlanta to Florida in 1875, his fellow journalists across the nation knew it wasn't the end for the sensationalistic reporter. In 1881, St. Clair-Abrams established the *Tavares Herald*, a bi-monthly publication that promoted his new town, as well as undo the myths of Florida living to northern citizens. On the strength of his name recognition and his style of writing, the newspaper became widely popular.

St. Clair-Abrams turned over editorship of the paper to his twenty-year-old son Alfred in the mid-1880s. T. W. Greenslit, another northern friend of St. Clair-Abrams from Lowell, Massachusetts, was the editor. The *Tavares Herald* office on West Ruby Street was one of the casualties of the Tavares fire of 1888.

The newspaper was sold to J. W. Bell and then, in 1922, was purchased by A. P. Vaughn, who changed the name to the *Lake County Citizen*. One year later, Vaughn sold it to R. K. Gore.

FAITH AND EDUCATION.

Tavares grew with a steady stream of transplants of various cultures and creeds. St. Clair-Abrams, a devout Catholic, recognized the need for churches to be an important aspect of the new town.

The Union Congregational Church was organized in 1885 by Reverend W. W. Winchester of Mount Dora. In May 1886, with plans submitted by John G. Sinclair, church construction began. Jabez H. Sears of Boston was the architect who modeled the church after the Trinity Church built in 1846 in New York City.

The estimated cost of the church sanctuary, located at St. Clair-Abrams Avenue and Alfred Street, was $3,000. St. Clair-Abrams donated the land and the lumber. After construction was completed in 1888, the Union Congregational Church was also used by other Christian denominations. The church was not affected by the Tavares fire of 1888.

St. Clair-Abrams built a schoolhouse in 1886. It was located at New Hampshire Avenue and Ianthe Street. The school was a two-story, wood frame building with a belfry. There was an auditorium on the second floor and two classrooms on the first floor. The auditorium was used for town meetings, and for club and lodge meetings. The first floor was also used as a Sunday school. Students from all grade levels attended the school. Gertrude "Miss Gertie" Gates was the teacher for many years. Kate Lacey, Maud Wakelin, and Lucille Tally were some of the teachers who taught at the school and who would become quite influential in the town's development.

The original schoolhouse was used until 1916, when a new elementary school was built. The old structure was moved and made into the Buck-eye Flats.

MEMORANDA ON TAVARES PART III.

"After laying out the town of Tavares I built a small hotel fronting on Lake Dora, calling it the Peninsular Hotel. It was a two-story building and had about 30 rooms. Later I enlarged it to a four-story building with 100 rooms and in 1888 the last year it was run it had over 4,000 arrivals during the winter season, including such men as the Duke of Sutherland and some other English Noblemen. Just as the season was closing the old town of Tavares was destroyed by fire and the subsequent freeze practically depopulated the town and so impoverished me that I had to leave Tavares and move to Jacksonville in 1895."

The Peninsular Hotel

The Duke of Sutherland

The Duke of Sutherland, mentioned in St. Clair-Abrams' Memoranda on Tavares Part III, is George Granville William Sutherland-Leveson-Gower, the 3rd Duke of Sutherland. He was a former member of Parliament, a colonel of the Sutherland Regiment of Highland Volunteers and the 20th Middlesex Rifle Volunteer Corps, and, similar to St. Clair-Abrams, a leader in the railroad industry in England. The Duke was married to Anne Hay-Mackenzie, the Countess of Cromartie. They had five children. He had been estranged from Anne when he began an affair with the *married* Mary Caroline Blair. Anne passed away in November 1888 while the Duke and Mary Caroline were in Florida. The couple had been on tour around the world and to Florida following an illness the Duke had suffered, in which Mary Caroline was at his bedside and not his wife.

Mary Caroline had been married to Captain Arthur Kindersley Blair, an officer in the Highlander Regiment, who had resigned to work for the Duke as a land agent and business manager for his railroad enterprises. Mary Caroline soon became involved with the Duke, which prompted the mysterious death of her husband. Captain Blair's death was reported as accidental, but many believed it was suicide from grief, or murder by a subordinate of the Duke to free Mary.

While the Duke and Mary Caroline travelled the world in Sutherland's yacht the *Sans Peur*, she was addressed as *Lady Clare*. After their arrival in Florida, the Duke had purchased a large section of land where he built the Sutherland Manor Estate. On March 4, 1889, less than four months after Anne's passing, the Duke of Sutherland married Mary Caroline Blair despite the urging of Queen Victoria to wait a year. At this period of time, it was considered appropriate to mourn for a year following the death of a spouse before remarriage. Officiating in the marriage was the Episcopalian Church's third Bishop of Florida, Edwin Garner Weed, who married the couple in a small church called the Church of the Good Shepard on the Gulf Coast in Dunedin, Florida. The marriage caused a scandal in England and Scotland; however, the Duke was too well known to be affected by the negative press. He died in September 1892 at the age of sixty-three at the Dunrobin Castle in Scotland. He left his entire property and fortune to the new Duchess, which prompted a contest from the Duke's children, and an

Mary Caroline Blair

additional scandal, which had no negative affect on her future as she remarried again, followed by another scandal, and then her passing from a short illness in 1892. She is buried with her second husband, the Duke of Sutherland.

MEMORANDA ON TAVARES PART IV.

"Immediately on laying out the town I established a saw and planing mill on the shores of Lake Dora, as finally completed, at an investment of over $40,000 which was a double deck saw mill on the second floor, with machinery on the first floor for manufacturing shingles, orange and vegetable crates, laths and machinery for other products. North of the saw mill was a planing mill and kiln drying building for drying and seasoning lumber.

The saw mill had a nest of three 50 H. P. boilers and an engine of 100 H. P. while the planing mill was operated by a 50 H. P. engine and 75 H. P. boiler. And also purchased a very large amount of timber and timbered land, bought the little Steamer Wekiwa in Jacksonville, brought it up the Ocklawaha River to Lake Eustis and through the canal into Lake Dora. These mills were the largest in the State south of Cedar Keys and in a very short time were doing an immense business with an average profit of $1,000 to $1,200 a month. So large was its business that for weeks at the time it was run 24 hours a day with two crews and gave employment to over

200 hands. As we had neither gas nor electricity it was lighted at night by a number of big locomotive headlights. As the mill had been several times set on fire by sparks from the J. T. and K. W. Railroad locomotives, I had an expensive fire apparatus attached to the rear of the big nest of boilers with an ample supply of hose. In this summer of 1886, it was closed down for overhauling at an expense of $3,000 or $4,000. In order to clean out the boilers the fire apparatus was disconnected from the boilers. On the Saturday before starting it again I left Tavares for Pensacola to attend the Democratic State Convention as a delegate. Before leaving I warned the manager not to start the mill again without first re-attaching the fire machinery to it. In disobedience to my orders, he started the mill to work without doing this and at noon that day fire broke out in the planing mill and the entire plant was destroyed together between $65,000 and $75,000 worth of lumber stocked on the yard. So demoralized was the manager that he made no effort to put out the flames. I learned afterwards that he walked up and down wringing his hands and saying "What will Major Abrams say?" and disappeared from Tavares that night and I have never seen him since.

The mill was supplied with timber by a logging outfit which consisted of over 60 mules, 15 log carts and a crew of over 30 men under a foreman. The payroll of the mill varied from $2,000 to $3,000 a week. The little Steamer I had brought into Lake Dora I had remodeled and renamed The Lake Dora. It towed rafts of logs from Lake Beauclair and along the shores of Lake Dora to Tavares and also made one trip daily to and from Mt. Dora, carrying freight and passengers.

As soon as I started constructing the big mill, I established a commissary to supply the hands. Later when my big store was constructed, I put in a stock of goods and at one time had a $50,000 stock in it. At my insistence prices were made very reasonable and very soon people from surrounding Tavares would come in and purchase, and on Saturdays I have seen as many as 15 wagons in front of the store coming from the country to buy goods. On a single day this store did a business of $4,000.

Discovering that outsiders would not start any business in the town and come into competition with me, I offered to withdraw from the stock of the store any line of goods to anyone who would come in and start a business. So, when Mr. Vontano proposed to start a hardware store, I turned over all my hardware to him. Later when Freeland proposed to start a grain and feed business, I withdrew everything of the kind from my store, and as others offered to engage in business, I gradually took the company out of mercantile business, so that when the big fire destroyed the town there were between 35 and 40 business houses in it. Financially this Company's store was quite a success, but as I didn't want to make a one-man town thought it best to close up the store.

Annie Burleigh and the Great Tavares Fire.

As we have read thus far in St. Clair-Abrams' Memoranda on Tavares, he had mentioned on a couple occasions, the fire that destroyed the business district of Tavares, as well as his world-renowned hotel, the Peninsular. The following are excerpts from Mrs. Annie Burleigh's memoirs written in 1941. She was 81 years old and wished to leave a written history of her life to family and friends. A newspaper article paid tribute to her and included excerpts of her memoir in the paper.

The reporter wrote, "She has a most colorful and interesting background and it is hoped that she will share her "memoirs" so that her children, grandchildren, neighbors and friends may share in the richness of her experiences.

Because everyone who meets Mrs. Burleigh is impressed with the feeling that she has learned the secret of successful and happy living."

Annie wrote: "Major St. Clair-Abrams had started a town and prospects seemed good. The town was well located between lovely Lake Dora and beautiful Lake Eustis, with railroads on the way, a fortune for machinists. Gov. Sinclair drove my husband to Tavares, quite a trip, with a span of horses and a wagon, going by way of Apopka. It was a beautiful moonlit night, and the moon, the lake and Major Abrams won. Ed decided to move to Tavares, and the next day he went out and bought seven lots for a beginning. They started the machine shop on the Lake Dora shore, and on the line of the little railroad which was just being built from Astor to Lane Park, three miles from Tavares and on Lake Harris. That was in the fall of 1885.

Annie Burleigh Circa 1900
Seated Second Row Center

The machine shop was not a success, and soon Ed had another idea. He and Mr. N. B. Whitley started the Lake Abstract Company. They got some records from Sumterville in Sumter County and had to have records in Orange County copied from books in Orlando.

In April, 1888, the business portion of the town was devastated by fire. The business houses had been built along Tavares Boulevard, facing the railroad and Ruby Street, the abstract offices being located about where the Lake Region Packing office now stands. When the train started out of the station at nine o'clock on that April morning, sparks from the engine ignited papers that had blown under the stores. Someone saw them and thought he had extinguished the fire, but more papers had blown in under the store, and soon there was a big blaze. A stiff breeze was blowing and in less than an hour the three-story hotel, two boarding houses, drug store, grocery, meat market, as well as the saloon, the abstract office and hardware store were a mess of smoldering ruins. I was out in the barn harnessing Dolly when I saw the smoke. I was worried about Ed in the smoke on account of his lungs, and drove down as fast as I could. I drove to where the courthouse now stands and came up to the abstract office from the west. Mr. Whitley and Ed were taking out the papers and books and putting them in a new, fire-proof safe. When they saw me, Ed said, "let's put them into the buggy." Mr. Whitley finally agreed, although he thought the safe was alright. The safe blew open and all that was in it burned. Ed drove Dolly down the lake shore beyond any buildings and into the lake, and so kept our abstract books safe. Afterwards he brought them to our house and put them in my parlor."

Legend has it that it was actually Annie herself that drove Dolly and the abstract books into Lake Dora.

MEMORANDA ON TAVARES PART V.

"I also constructed eight cottages, six of which are still in existence, two large stores, two warehouses and a tramway from Lake Dora to Lake Eustis and later built a steamboat on Lake Eustis called the SPEER, which for many months connected with the railroad at Ft. Mason and carried freight and passengers to all points on Lake Eustis and Lake Harris.

Just before the destruction of the town by fire in 1888, Frank Jones of New Hampshire entered into a contract with me whereby he agreed to invest approximately $1,000,000 in the town in building a 200-room hotel in the middle of Ridge Park, also a saw and planing mill, a packing house, a canning factory, a Machine Works, a cigar factory and two or three other industries that I cannot recall. The plan for a big hotel was prepared and a picture of it sent to me at Tavares. Two or three weeks after this contract was made the town was destroyed by fire.

At Jones' suggestion I started a Cigar Factory, a few citizens of the town taking stock with me in it and Mr. Charles Sinclair, the husband of his step-daughter, taking some stock but after the fire, notwithstanding my repeated calls on him Jones kept putting me off and in 1893 the great commercial panic forced the closing of the factory although it had built up a business and was employing over 30 hands. We paid every dollar of its indebtedness. The books show that I lost more than all the other stockholders combined.

Although I repeatedly wrote and urged Mr. Jones to carry out the contract, he kept insisting on delay alleging that he was in a big fight to keep control of the Boston and Maine Railroad and until he had settled that he could do nothing and this delay continued until the double freeze of 1894 and '95 when he repudiated the whole contract claiming that the town, having been destroyed by fire, the consideration for which he had signed it had failed.

From first to last I spent over half a million dollars in building up the town constructing in addition to the hotel three stores and building eight cottages in it as well as railroads, nearly every dollar of which expenditure I made in the practice of my profession and in speculations in land and in Wall Street."

MR. JONES OF NEW HAMPSHIRE.

Frank Jones

Frank Jones of New Hampshire was yet another wealthy northern businessman that the staunch southern visionary, St. Clair-Abrams, befriended and convinced to invest in his construction of Florida's new state capital.

Born on September 15, 1832, in Barrington, New Hampshire, Jones became a successful merchant and one of the largest brewers in the country. He also became a prominent politician in his home state. He served as mayor of Portsmouth and as a congressman for his district. He lost an attempt for the New Hampshire governorship in 1880. He was a democrat who had crossed paths with St. Clair-Abrams prior to their business collaboration.

And though there were stressful episodes in their relationship, and a likely bitterness within St. Clair-Abrams that lasted for many years, Jones did contribute a large sum of money into Tavares before and after the fire of 1888. St. Clair-Abrams named two of the town's streets in courtesy for Jones - New Hampshire for the distinguished gentleman's home state and Rockingham after the county in which Portsmouth is located, and where Frank Jones built his fortune. Rockingham Avenue, as mentioned previously, had been named for St. Clair-Abrams' former partner, Robert Summerlin.

"Mr. Hull told me some very fascinating stories of his trading and association with the Indians. Not far from the canal and creek on Lake Dora we dug up part of the skeleton of an Indian.

Not the least interesting is the fact that the big hammock fronting on Lake Eustis was originally an immense wild orange grove. Hull told me that he dug up and destroyed nearly all these orange trees clearing up the hammock so as to plant long staple cotton on it. When I purchased the property there were some wild orange trees still left in so much of the hammock which had not been cleared, which I removed and set them out in enlarging the Hull grove.

Perhaps it might interest you to know that when I laid out the town in opening it Governor Bloxham and a party by invitation came down and in a speech I made at a banquet I gave them, I announced that I intended to make Tavares the seat of a new County and that I ultimately expected the town to become the capital of the State. I still believe that if the people of Tavares will display a broad and liberal spirit, they will some day get the capital although I do not expect to live to see that day.

Of course, there are numerous other very interesting incidents which it would take too long to narrate.

The streets and avenues were named for relatives of mine and friends including Hamilton Disston of Philadelphia and Mr. Pulsifer of Boston, from whom I had received large fees for legal services and who were warm personal friends of mine. Rockingham and New Hampshire were given those names at the suggestion of Mr. Frank Jones after he had agreed to spend a large amount of money to help build the town up. It is well known that he went back on me and did nothing except to put up the building now known as a hotel.

The story of the three County Seat fights is well known. These three conflicts cost me $40,000 more with money borrowed from Frank Jones, which I subsequently paid him back and finally deeded him everything my Company had.

You will perceive from this recital that I have never benefited one cent from this enterprise but the town is there, the railroads are there and there to stay, and some day Tavares ought to be the capital of Florida.

AN OLD ACQUAINTANCE NOT FORGOTTEN.

The Atlanta Constitution: Tuesday, June 27, 1882.
Alexander St. Clair-Abrams
His Arrival in the City-What He Says of Florida

Yesterday Major Alexander St. Clair-Abrams, accompanied by
Mrs. Abrams and their two children, reached the city on their return
to Florida from a tour of the northern states, and as far east as
Boston. Major Abrams and family took quarters at the Kimball,
where they met many of their old friends. At every turn Major
Abrams encountered an old acquaintance, whom had known him in
the old days when he was one of the proprietors of the Atlanta
Herald, and later, when he was the editor and proprietor of the News.
He was much improved in appearance having increased in weight
from 123 to 174 pounds. He was as plump as a butter ball and as
rosy as the most hardy inhabitant of the mountain districts. He wore
a black mustache and moved with that elastic step with which he
used to get over the streets of Atlanta. Last night a CONSTITUTION
reporter sat beside him in the arcade of the Kimball and asked him
numerous questions concerning what has happened to him since he
left Atlanta in 1875. Major Abrams said:

"I will go on to Florida to-night but my family will remain in
Atlanta for about three months."

"What are you doing in Florida, and at what place do you live?"

"I live in Orange County and am solicitor general. I have held
the office for about five and a half years, under appointment by the
governor. I have three orange groves also. You people all have a
very wrong idea of Florida. You seem to have an idea that the state
is filled up with northern people. Really the greater part of the
population not native Floridians may be counted as Georgians,
Alabamians, Carolinians and Virginians. Georgia people form a
greater part of the population of Florida than all the others put
together."

"It is very unhealthy down there, is it not?"

"On the contrary I have about 75 men who have been since
October working on a canal between Eustis and Dora lakes in a
cypress swamp up to their waists in water, and out of this 75 and a

population in a town of 400 there have been but two cases of malarial fever. I give you this as an illustration."

"Do you have any chills?"

"I have not had a chill since I went there. The people are full of energy, as they are anywhere, and lose none of it by remaining in the state. Few people who visit Florida ever see anything characteristic of the state. They all go down the St. Johns and on the Indian river. They never get among what we call the clear water lakes and among the high hammock lands. They are charmed with what they see but they don't see Florida. They should go into the interior where they can see bluffs a hundred feet high. The entire state is, however, one of the most beautiful in the whole country, and no man who ever stays there for a while will go away and stay away."

"Don't people fear that they will overstock the orange market?"

"Not at all. There is plenty of room for all the oranges that Florida can ever raise."

"How is the Disston land?"

"It is doing well. I think it was a good move when the state sold it. There is a considerable amount of it that is poor of course, but other portions are good, and all of it can be used in some way; some for grazing, some for timber and other parts for cultivation."

"There was of the Disston land a track of 4,000,000 acres," continued Mr. Abrams. "I think it was a wise policy in Governor Bloxham to sell it when he did. It brought a million dollars, and that sum was added to the taxable property of the state. The company owning the land can make money only by having it settled and thus a powerful agent is set at work to stimulate immigration. Disston sold Sir Edward Reed half of it; on the other half, which cost him, say, $600,000, he will be able to make considerable money. It will take time, but it is bound to come at last."

"Florida has a remarkable population," continued Major Abrams. "They are not farmers, and yet they farm. They are professional men and merchants. They go to work with energy, however, and all are satisfied. They are good people – above the common average, and thus we have good society – men who are educated and refined."

Mr. Abrams left last night for Florida. He says if he ever starts another paper it will be a weekly county paper. He says they pay enough, and the work is easy. He has settled in Florida.

DREDGING THE ELFIN RIVER
AND UNCOVERING A SUBMERGED CITY.

The Atlanta Constitution: Friday, March 24, 1882.
Tavares Boom.
The Lake Dora and Eustis Canal Completed – Florida Union

PENDRYVILLE, Fla., March 18 – About 8 o'clock last evening St. Clair-Abrams and Summerlin's steamer Wekiva steamed up to the landing on Lake Dora in front of Tavares. Mr. St. Clair-Abrams arrived in town about noon, and the passage of the steamer up the canal which he has been cutting for the past four months to connect lakes Eustis and Dora was determined upon. The canal has been practically complete since the 25th of February, but the taking out of dams thrown up to keep back the water while the work was being done delayed somewhat and the passage of the boat was deferred until Mr. Abrams could reach here from Volusia County. The canal is a complete success. As the boat rounded in to the lake the steam whistles on the two large mills were turned loose, and the shouts of over a hundred mechanics, laborers and residents of the town attested their joy in the success of the enterprise. Mr. Abrams was loudly cheered and responded in a short, pithy speech, which was applauded to the echo. The steamer made the tour of the lake this morning, and left for her regular trip to Lake Harris at 3 o'clock, going out of the canal in fine style, a large number of excursionists being on board.

The new three-story hotel is nearly done; the plasterers and painters are putting on their finishing touches and the carpeting and furnishing will commence at once. The formal opening of the upper Ocklawaha and the Tavares hotel will take place early next month.

The Pamlico Enterprise: Friday, July 14, 1882.
A SUBMERGED CITY
Curious Discoveries Made in Florida

The following very interesting story of a submerged city or town belonging to centuries long past, we find in the Tavares Herald of this week:

For the past six months the work of digging the canal to connect Lakes Eustis and Dora, in order to open up the more southern lakes of the "Great Lake region of Florida," has been prosecuted by St. Clair-Abrams and Summerlin, near Tavares. The work was undertaken and prosecuted in the interests of commerce and the development of this portion of the peninsula of Florida.

The work, which was undertaken, however, with the view of only opening the channel between two of the larger lakes in the great chain of lakes which form the headwaters of the Ocklawaha River, has, in the completion of the work, opened up to science a chapter in the history of Florida as yet unthought of and unwritten.

At the outlet of Lake Dora, the sand bar had already been cut to the depth of nearly or quite three feet on the previous digging, and was dug about two feet deeper than last week. At a distance of over four feet below the old level of Lake Dora a mound was discovered. The first excavations revealed the existence of a clearly defined wall, lying in a line tending toward the southwest from where it was first struck. This wall was composed of a dark sandstone, very much crumbled in places, but more distinct, more clearly defined, and the stone more solid as the digging increased in depth. The wall was evidently the eastern side of an ancient house or fortification, as the slope of the outer wall was to the west. About eight feet from the slope of the eastern wall a mound of sand was struck, imbedded in the muck formation above and around it. This sand mound was dug into only a few inches, as depth of the water demanded but a slight increased depth of the channel at that point, but enough was discovered to warrant the belief that here, on the northwest shore of Lake Dora, is submerged a city or town or fortification older by centuries than anything yet discovered in this portion of Florida. Small, curiously shaped blocks of sandstone, some of them showing traces of fire, pieces of pottery and utensils made of a mottled flint were thrown out by the men while working waist deep in the water.

The finest of these specimens was presented to the Herald on Monday by Mr. Sprott (foreman), who promised to use his best endeavors to secure, if possible, more of these submerged curiosities.

FUNERAL FOR A "SOUTHERN" FRIEND.

When he first visited the area around Lake Dora and Lake Eustis in West Orange County in 1875, St. Clair-Abrams met a family who lived at the Woodlea groves, three miles to the southwest, just across the border into Sumter County. Woodlea, a peninsula of land that jutted into Lake Harris, was the home of Captain Melton Haynes and his wife Sarah Isabella, who had homesteaded the property in 1868.

Haynes served as a militia officer in the Seminole Uprising of 1849, as well as a Confederate captain of the Fifth Battalion, Company H, Second Florida Cavalry, attached to the command of Captain John Jackson Dickison. Haynes served as a State Representative from Duval County prior to the war and State Senator from Sumter County following the war.

Haynes is credited with introducing the sweet orange into the Lake Region in 1845. That sweet orange would famously be known as the Parson Brown orange. In the July 1951 issue of the *Florida Historical Quarterly*, published by the Florida Historical Society, Mercer W. Brown, who was the grandson of Rev. Nathan L. "Parson" Brown wrote - "Early orange growing in Sumter County is described in a booklet "Our American Italy" published in 1882 by the Agricultural and Fruit Growers Association of Sumter County: About 1847 Mr. Melton Haynes, then a young man reared in North Carolina, brought into Sumter County some orange seeds taken from

the best imported fruit he could find in Charleston. These he planted on his farm on the south side of Lake Harris and cultivated them with moderate success for two years. From this planting young orange trees were carried into various sections scattered all about this great lake region, some finding their way into adjoining counties, and it is believed that from it have grown all the oldest sweet seedling trees of the region."

The date of Haynes' arrival and planting was actually in the early summer of 1845. Brown said his grandfather Parson Brown arrived into Sumter County from Alabama in 1847. Brown continued, "The orange tree from that time became a door yard ornament but few families taking trouble to have one. The business of the sparse settlements was the culture of cotton, sugar cane, etc. and hundreds of acres of wild orange groves were cut down. Something of an awakening on the subject of orange culture was noticed about 1851, which resulted in the planting of the grove at Yalaha, now owned by Captain Phares, the trees being obtained from Mr. Haynes."

In 1913, when Haynes' wife Sarah Isabella passed away, the newspapers wrote, "In 1849, she was united in marriage to Melton Haynes, who was the first person to introduce sweet oranges in the Lake Region."

Mr. John Jackson, retired Extension Agent for the University of Florida and former president of the Florida Citrus Hall of Fame, as well as a 2021 inductee into the hall of fame, wrote, "In 1847, seven years after the first settlement at Leesburg, the citrus industry began. According to the 1923 "soil survey" Melton Haynes started the first seedling nursery on the north shore of Lake Harris."

On February 16, 1923, the *Lake County Citizen* interviewed Isabella May Haynes Keeling, the eldest of the Haynes' six children, about her family first settling in the Lake Region. The interview provides a great description of the Lake Region that St. Clair-Abrams scouted in 1875.

"Away before the war, and before the last of the Indian wars and scares, when all the settlers through this section "forted up" in the army posts and left their plantations to the ravages of the hostiles, Melton Haynes scouted all through Marion and Sumter counties. He built his cabin first in 1845 or '46 at Sunnyside, the high bluff looking across Lake Harris to the Harris settlements on the south -

Captain Melton Haynes

the only human habitation in the region, before Leesburg was even dreamed of. The place was known for a generation as Haynes Point.

Even after taking the Woodlea homestead, they were isolated. M. V. Hull the first settler on Lake Eustis being four miles distant, but their nearest neighbor. On the east was no settler between Lake Harris and Apopka. In 1875, Col. Blackman came and settled a mile from the Haynes homestead, and Col. Troy of Alabama came and developed Oxmoor, spending part of each year.

At that time travel was by sailboat about the lakes, and steamers came twice a week from Jacksonville and Palatka, up the Ocklawaha, until the lowering of water and clogging streams made passage impracticable, and the coming of the railroads offered other means of access to the settlements.

Capt. Haynes held the office of county surveyor of Sumter County until his death in 1883, knowing the county as probably no other man in the section. Mrs. Keeling returned from Alabama in March 1884, living for a short time in the cottage now occupied by Mr. and Mrs. Amos Wakelin, until it was purchased by the latter owners."

On Wednesday January 10, 1883, while returning home from a surveying job, Captain Haynes accidentally drowned in the Little Ocklawaha (Elfin River, Dora Canal).

On Sunday, January 14, 1883, The St. Clair-Abrams family, along with many of the local residents and dignitaries from all over the state of Florida, boarded the *Tuskawilla* steamer on the Dora Canal. After having picked up friends from various points, the steamer picked up Melton's remains and family at Woodlea and went across Lake Harris and docked at Yalaha. Upon arrival at the cemetery, as reported by the *Altoona Argus*, "At Yalaha, a procession, the largest ever seen in south Florida, formed. Nearly a mile distant!"

The reporter described the mood of the ceremony, "The muffled whispers of the crowd was sufficient evidence of the love and respect which alike pervaded all the hearts of the two hundred and twenty persons present. And when the casket was lowered, the people joined in singing, *Jesus Lover of My Soul*."

The Woodlea homestead would become part of a settlement called Lane Park, named for Colonel Lane, whom St. Clair-Abrams collaborated with on one of his railroad projects. St. Clair-Abrams owned property on nearby Lake Melton, named for the beloved Lake Region pioneer.

1871 Woodlea House ~ Home of Capt. Melton and Sarah Haynes
Preservation Photograph 2007

LOPEZ PARA Y TAVARES.

ALEX ST. CLAIR-ABRAMS
ATTORNEY AT LAW
615-619 DYAL-UPCHURCH BUILDING
                              Jacksonville, Fla. March 23, 1925.

Miss Elizabeth D. Burleigh,
Tavares, Fla.

My dear Miss Burleigh,

I have received your letter of the 21st and glad to know that my memoranda of Tavares will be of service to you. I forgot to mention one fact, which I now do:

The name of my ancestor was Lopez Para y Tavares. He is said to have been a grandee of Spain and the prefix "y Tavares" meant Lopez Para of Tavares but the prefix was always inseparable from the actual family name. And as in other cases of this prefix the family was always known as The Tavares family.

The meaning of the word "Tavares" I have been told is "the center", "the middle"; "The gut" - a rather vulgar meaning.

It might also amuse you to know that I saw a photograph of this reputed ancestor of mine in the possession of one of my aunts when I was a boy eight years old and when asked what I thought of it promptly replied that he looked like a murderer, as he certainly had what appeared to my childish mind of a most villainous countenance. I don't think my rather aristocratic aunt ever forgave me for my American democratic plebeianism.

Of course, all this is not written for publication but I thought possibly it might afford you some merriment.

I trust that you will have a pleasant entertainment on the 3rd and that you might live to celebrate the first 100 years of the founding of Tavares with the City the capital of the State and a population of a half a million. When I read of the many towns in Florida that will have this half million population in 15 or 20 years, I don't see why we can't claim the same for Tavares in 75 years.

With regard to your father and mother and other members of your family, I am

Very truly yours,
(signed) Alex St. Clair-Abrams

Through the decades that followed, and even as of this book's publication, it has been written that Tavares is the Spanish word for the center, middle, or gut. Local historians and the general public throughout the twentieth century assumed that, because the Major said that's what it meant, so indeed, that's the translation. But this letter by St. Clair-Abrams to Elizabeth Burleigh shows that he did not say it meant the center, but that he had *been told* it meant that. His little *suggestion* of the meaning worked well as Tavares is in the geographical center of the state, and that meaning served in the promotion of Tavares as the appropriate location for the capital of Florida. Later, the city of Tavares would use a variation of the word center as it promoted the city as the "Hub of Lake County."

From the earliest times of the Portuguese monarchy the lineage of Tavares (Tabares) has played a part among those of the highest Portuguese nobility. The family history dates back to the end of the Twelfth Century when Pedro Viegas Tabares was a great servant to Portuguese king, Sancho I, a grandee and feudal lord of the state of

LaGuardia. The family distinguished through the ages in politics, military careers and as ambassadors. A grandee is a nobleman of Spanish or Portuguese heritage.

During the fifteenth century some members of the Tabares nobility participated in the conquest of the Canary Islands in the service of Spain. The Island of Tenerife has a valley that is still called the valley of Tabares or Tavares, which dates back to the family's settling of that area. Alonzo Hernandez de Tabares from Portugal went to the Canaries Archipelago soon after its incorporation with the Crown of Spain and became a citizen of Tenerife in the 1530s.

Another branch of the Tavares family went to Galicia, Spain, where the family flourished until the end of the 18th century. Then another branch of this lineage became established in Andalusia, Spain, and was decorated by King Phillip V with the title of Marquis of Casa Tabares April 16, 1720.

The transferred origin or meaning of the Spanish and Portuguese surname of Tavares (Tabares) was originally the name for someone from Tabara in northern Spain near the Portugal border or from the Portuguese places named Tavares in northern Portugal. The slang meaning of the families from those regions may be "descendant of the hermit" or "descendant of the retired man."

Another history that describes the meaning and origin of the name Tavares says that the suffix of "es" at the end of Portuguese names means "son", which would translate Tavares to mean "son of Taveiro." The suffix "eiro" means occupation. "Tav" may be short for Tavola, a Latin name for timber board. The name Taveiro may have had its origin as a timber worker.

Research has shown that the family history as described by St. Clair-Abrams' aristocratic aunt to her young nephew may be the most accurate.

CAN'T TAKE COUNTY SEAT AWAY FROM ORLANDO.

"In a speech I made at a banquet…I announced that I intended to make Tavares the seat of a new County and that I ultimately expected the town to become the capital of the State."

Maj. Alexander St. Clair-Abrams

In 1882, during the ground-breaking ceremony of his new town, and with a large contingent of dignitaries in attendance that included the Florida governor, St. Clair-Abrams declared his momentous intention to make Tavares the state capital.

However, he knew that Tavares must first be the county seat. With Tavares located in Orange County at that time, he knew it would be quite impossible to have the county seat taken away from Orlando. Afterall, he was an Orange County commissioner that voted in favor of Orlando as the county seat.

No sooner did he plan, develop, and lay out his new town, he began his formulation for a new county.

"In this serenity, Major Alexander St. Clair-Abrams loomed up, in his greatest adventure, as a developer and soon became the acknowledged leader, on a platform of more expansive and progressive future."

Kenneth Sears, 2009

Rand McNally & Company 1888 Map of Lake County, Florida

SIX

Land of 1400 Lakes

In the spring of 1887, following many months of surveying, mapping, documenting, planning, meetings, and preparation, St. Clair-Abrams and his team were ready to travel to the state capital in Tallahassee to discuss their conception of a new county with Representative H. H. Duncan and Senator George Marion Lee. Both men represented Sumter County in the Florida Legislature. The towns of Yalaha, where Duncan resided, and Leesburg, where Lee resided, fell within the boundary lines of the proposed new county.

After the funeral for Emily Roberts, Joanna's mother, who passed away from bronchial consumption on February 20, 1887, at the age of fifty-eight in Tavares, St. Clair-Abrams' entourage travelled to the state capital and met with Duncan and Lee to introduce the bill. At the meeting, it was suggested by Duncan to name the new county *Lake* because there were over 1400 lakes within the proposed borders.

How Many Named Lakes Are There in Lake County?

In his 1995 book *About Some Lakes and More In Lake County*, Lake County historian Walter Sime wrote, "We all know that we took the name "Lake County" because of the many lakes within its boundaries, the number most frequently stated has been "1400." Depending upon the source document you use, you can come up with just about any number you want, except the magic "1400". The Lake County Soil and Water Conservation District, undated report, lists 257 named lakes. "Florida Place Names" states, "when lakes were counted in 1969 by the State, Lake County had 505 lakes either named or unnamed, and of 10 acres or more." The "Gazetteer of Florida Lakes," by Florida Water Resources Research Center, Dec. 1986, lists 292 named lakes and 258 unnamed lakes of 10 acres or more, for a total of 550 lakes. We have gained 45 lakes between these two reports. However, we lost a lot of ground. "Eustis Lake Region," Nov. 30, 1934, stated "2293 lakes of which 1400 are named." Whatever happened to those 1593 (2293-1400=1593) lakes? Did we lose lakes or gain them?"

Walter Sime continued, "During my study I was able to identify 642 named lakes, of which there are at least 143 variant names (two or more names for the same lake). Of all these names, I could only conclusively confirm the source of the lake name for 185 of the lakes. There are 310 more bodies of water located, but not named, for a total of 952 "Lakes." Where are the other 448 to make up the 1400?"

The boundaries of the new proposed county - and Lake County today - is a region filled to the brim with many bodies of water that includes lakes, ponds, sink holes, brooks, streams, creeks, rivers, and canals. The number of named lakes have changed through the decades and continue to change - with the current number as of this publication being that of 362.

GEORGE MARION LEE.

George Marion Lee

Since the founding of Lake County, one figure has not received the recognition due him for his role in the creation of Lake County – George Marion Lee.

Lee was born on August 18, 1839, in Alabama. In 1849, he came with his parents, Evander and Susannah Lee, to Leesburg, Florida. Leesburg was named for his family. He married Margarite Gamble in Wildwood, Sumter County, and the couple had seven children. By trade, Lee was a fruit and vegetable grower.

In 1863, Lee began a long career in local politics. He was elected Tax Collector of Sumter County, and later, the County Treasurer. Politics took a pause during the midway point of the War Between the States while he served in Company C, Second Florida Cavalry, of the Confederate Army. Lee was elected State Senator from Sumter County from 1884 to 1888, and was elected as a Lake County Senator in 1905; but died on August 1, 1905, while in office. Other offices he held were Lake County Commissioner and member of the Leesburg City Council.

CHAPTER 3771 (NO. 91).

On May 27, 1887, fifteen days after its southern border neighbor, Osceola County, was created, Lake County was established from portions of Orange and Sumter Counties.

The *Act* to create Lake County contained twelve sections. *Section 1* described the boundary lines and description of Lake, while *Section 2* states: Be it further enacted, That the new county so created and bounded and described shall be known and designated as Lake County; that it shall form part of the Second Congressional District of this State, and shall constitute the Twenty-third Senatorial District of this State, and shall be included in the Seventh Judicial Circuit of Florida.

In accordance with *Section 3* of the *Act*, Governor Edward Aylesworth Perry appointed prominent men from various locations in the county to the constitutional offices. D. H. Yancy of Umatilla as the County Judge; H. H. Duncan of Yalaha as Clerk of the Circuit Court – a position he held until his passing in 1920; J. P. Galloway of Leesburg as the Sheriff; J. C. Compton of Clermont as the Superintendent of Public Instruction; A. J. Cassaday of Lisbon as the Tax Collector; F. S. Woodward of Okahumpka as the Tax Assessor (today known as the Property Appraiser); Bogue Dyches of Lady Lake as the County Treasurer; and J. C. Terry of Yalaha as the Supervisor of Registration (Elections).

On August 2, 1887, the county commissioners met for the first time in Bloomfield, near Yalaha. Lake County's first commissioners included W. B. Denham of Eustis; H. J. M. Porter of Montverde; J. S. Mahoney of Bloomfield; P. B. Weaver of Leesburg; and Jas. M. Owens, Sr. of Umatilla. The new board appointed J. B. Gaines, Esq. as the County Attorney.

Section 5, Be it further enacted, that it shall be the duty of the Board of County Commissioners of said county at their first meeting to provide for an election to be held within ninety days thereafter for the location of a permanent county seat for said Lake County, and the place obtaining a majority of all the votes cast shall be the county seat of said county, as provided by the general laws of this State. If, at said election, no place voted for shall obtain a majority of all votes cast it shall be the duty of the Board of County Commissioners to order another election within ninety days thereafter, and if such second election no place shall obtain a majority of all votes cast, to hold succeeding election until a permanent county seat is established according to law.

St. Clair-Abrams had no intentions in having his goal of Tavares as the County Seat be de-railed after all the time and money invested in the evolution of Lake County. He soon learned that other men from nearby towns eyed the coveted designation - among them were Fort Mason, Bloomfield, Clermont, Mount Dora, Eustis, and Lane Park, with the largest town of the time period, Leesburg, prepared to compete in a no-holds-barred contest.

As the intense battlelines commenced between St. Clair-Abrams and Leesburg, the residents of the pineapple-growing community of Lane Park knew they had no chance to claim the County Seat, but a committee penned a letter of eloquence and common-sense determination to the citizens of Lake County, which they submitted to the local publications. The following excerpts are from that letter.

"Lane Park does not enter the race to antagonize any other place, but in hope that patriotic, sensible men throughout the county, and especially in localities where antagonisms have become so intense, will see in her great natural advantages the way to secure the most desirable county seat, and at the same time secure public harmony, a matter of far more consequence than the selection of any particular locality."

The letter continued, "We are assured that if the court house is located here, the Florida Southern Railway Company will run trains from Lane Park to Tavares to connect with all trains to and from Tavares on other roads, and if this assurance should not be made good, a line of horse carts will be established from Lane Park to Tavares. This will secure to Lane Park practically all the railway facilities for transportation enjoyed by Tavares; and our location on Lake Harris gives direct communication by steamboats with Astatula, Yalaha, Bloomfield, Leesburg, and all points on Lake Harris and Eustis. A large proportion of the people of Lake County can conveniently reach Lane Park by public conveyance than any other place in the county. It is the center of railway and steamboat transportation."

The letter from the committee concluded, "It is not the purpose to resort to the ordinary means used to carry elections. Without intending to criticize the action of others, we feel constrained to say that we doubt the propriety of doing so in a matter of this kind. Even if successful, such means tend to divide and disrupt a people who ought to be united. We appeal to the patriotism, good sense, and public spirit of the people of Lake County, and all the citizens of Lane Park will cheerfully acquiesce in their decision whether it be for or against their quiet little town which now enters the race for county seat."

While Lane Park competed as a clear underdog, Bloomfield took another approach.

THE RECORDS WERE LOADED FOR TAVARES.

Bloomfield served as a temporary meeting place for the county commissioners - and the county records were kept there. If the records were locked away in Bloomfield, then possession of those records should determine the location of the County Seat. At least that's what the town's founder thought.

In his biography of his brother-in-law, E. H. Peet wrote the story of how H. H. Duncan outwitted W. D. Mendenhall.

Peet wrote: "W. D. Mendenhall, founder of Bloomfield, in his over-weening ambition, thinking he saw a chance to hold the seat of government of the county in his town, went before Circuit Judge

Broome at Deland, and obtained a Writ of Mandamus to forestall the removal of the records for the time being, at least. The quickest and only way for Mr. Mendenhall was to go by rowboat to Lane Park and there catch the morning train to connect at Tavares for Sanford and Deland.

Mr. Duncan, assuming full responsibility and custody of all various records, had put out a runner to keep tabs on Mr. Mendenhall's movements, and the moment he was well started across the lake for Lane Park that quiet August morning, all the record books and papers were hurriedly packed in boxes, conveyed to waiting rowboats at the lakeshore. As the train bore the eager Mendenhall to his destination, the small boats, propelled by stalwart oarsmen, in due time were landed and hidden in Gaskin's store at Lane Park, there to await further safe conveyance in their destination. There must be no slip up. At the close of the day, Mr. Mendenhall returned from Deland with a perfectly good writ in his pocket, and met Mr. Duncan in the store, where the records were temporarily secreted. The latter afterwards laughingly told how the former walked into the store and they both leaned up against the counter beneath which the records lay hidden within easy reach. The ambitious Mendenhall was no match for this cool-headed, easy, affable, unconcerned man who faced him, as they stood and conversed with the books and writ close together. Friend Gaskins, of course, knew the situation and said nothing.

At last, the unsuspecting Mendenhall went to his rowboat where his oarsman, who knew nothing, met him. As the splash and rattle of the oars and locks told they were well out upon the lake, a signal was given, and out of the darkness came a horse and wagon; the records were loaded in and started for Tavares, where they were deposited in an unoccupied dwelling, selected for that purpose. The writ, in the meantime, reached Bloomfield only to find a deserted building and nothing to be served upon."

The heroism of the young Confederate soldier, H. H. Duncan, on the battlefield was a sample of the great strength of character that he possessed. In over forty years as a public servant, his generosity to all who needed his assistance, no matter what race or heritage, never ceased, for he was known to dip into his own pocket for those who could not afford to pay county fees. Duncan assisted local Black Union and Confederate soldiers with their applications to receive a military pension.

E. A. Peet wrote about Duncan, "One notable feature, inspired, not by policy, but by his culture and courtliness, and the innate breadth of mind that recognizes the fact that: A man's a man for that, every person who come into his office, be he rich or poor, learned or illiterate, black or white, received the same deferential attention and consideration."

E. A. Peet added, "It was the decree of fate that here in Tavares there was a man of the most singular loftiness of character and Christian purity; combined with the rarest intellectual power."

In a letter dated January 16, 1920, St. Clair-Abrams wrote to Duncan's widow, Marian, "Need I say to you how much I thought of him and how I highly regarded him? Our relations were always most friendly and harmonious during our acquaintance of over a third of a century. In common with all who knew him I greatly admired him for his sterling integrity of character, his devotion to public interests, and his exceptionally fine private life. The record he left behind will be a source of the greatest comfort and consolation to you in your bereavement."

L to R: Haynes, Duncan, St. Clair-Abrams

In a 1924 dedication ceremony of the installation of a bronze plaque dedicated to Duncan in the new Lake

County courthouse (today known as the historic courthouse), keynote speaker, Major General Charles Summerall said, "These characteristics which Mr. Duncan possessed, are the characteristics which make the true man, the true soldier, the good citizen and the best nation. A man can be as great a man in Tavares as a man in Washington can be, for it is ideals that count."

THREE ELECTION GIVE TAVARES COUNTY SEAT.

On October 14, 1887, the first contentious election was held for the County Seat. St. Clair-Abrams was well-liked by the black population, especially by the laborers that he employed in the construction of the railroads. He loaded them onto boats at Tavares and transported them to Bloomfield to get registered to vote. Black voters were key and their votes were bought by St. Clair-Abrams and Leesburg. St. Clair-Abrams and Leesburg officials had offered substantial cash incentives to several influential Black leaders.

St. Clair-Abrams hosted an extravagant barbeque in Tavares, with people attending from all over the county. Many came for the lavish menu of ham, chicken, and roast beef, while others attended for the promise of their vote. An incredible amount of money was spent on the first election by both St. Clair-Abrams and the representatives from Leesburg. The highly publicized battle, which made national headlines, drew over three thousand citizens of the sparsely populated new county to the polls. The election ended in a draw between Leesburg and Tavares.

The same behavior continued that lead up to a second election, which resulted in yet another tie.

The campaign for a third election motivated St. Clair-Abrams to use every means at his disposal to complete his vision for Tavares to be the power seat of Lake County - and Florida - government.

On July 17, 1888, fourteen months after the creation of Lake County, the third election finally yielded a winner - Tavares. The vote was 1162 votes for Tavares and 927 votes for Leesburg. Leesburg protested and publicly stated that Tavares received the majority of votes by fraudulent means. Tempers flared and turmoil ensued. But Tavares, and St. Clair-Abrams, prevailed. The pandemonium from the elections spilled over into the Convention to elect County Officers. Rumors of Yellow Fever, heated episodes of shouting and fighting, as well as other various interruptions, delayed the Convention delegation from creating a ballot of candidates. The ballot was finally established, and the officers voted upon two months after the County Seat election.

Of special note, Lake County was the first county in the nation to have its own flag. A contest was held in 1936 to select the official flag. Eighteen designs were submitted, with Mrs. E. G. Owens of Leesburg being awarded the winning design. The flag featured white lettering and white Florida image on a blue background, with Lake County also highlighted in blue. The flag was raised for the first time on March 5, 1937, at Lake County's semi-centennial celebration at the 1924 Lake County Courthouse.

THE PIONEER BUILDING.

During the campaign for County Seat, it was well publicized that Tavares already had the funds to build a new courthouse. St. Clair-Abrams had secured a loan of $10,000 from New Hampshire investor, Frank Jones. A loan of which St. Clair-Abrams paid back in full at 15% interest.

Soon after the 1888 fire that destroyed the business section of Tavares, St. Clair-Abrams immediately invested funds to rebuild. In 1890, construction of Lake County's first official courthouse was

completed. The home of Judge Milam had been temporarily used. The new two-story building was called the Pioneer Building and served as the courthouse for thirty-four years until 1924.

When construction of a new courthouse began in 1923, the Pioneer Building was moved across the street. After the new courthouse was opened, the Pioneer Building became home to the Civil Defense, Veterans Services, driver's license offices, the county agricultural agents, and the Lake County School Board.

In 1975, Tavares's citizens, county employees, and the media watched as the Fort Lauderdale Wrecking Company began to raze the Pioneer Building. The building did not succumb easily to the bulldozer and battering rams. The effort to demolish the building continued into the night when finally, the building appeared to self-destruct as one of its support beams suddenly gave way and the building began to tumble.

HAPPY NUPTIALS ~ PRELUDE TO A KILLING.

In c1886, St. Clair-Abrams' son Alfred was married in Lancaster, Ohio. The following excerpts are from the local newspaper in the bride's home state of Ohio.

The Nuptials of Miss Rose Helen McNeill
and Mr. Alfred St. Clair Abrams.

"The handsome and hospitable home of Mr. and Mrs. J. B. McNeill, on Wheeling Street, was the scene of a brilliant and pleasant event on Tuesday, July 10, the occasion being the marriage of their charming daughter, Rose Helen, to Mr. Alfred St. Clair Abrams, a popular and rising young attorney of Florida.

Long before the hour announced for the ceremony…reception rooms were filled with invited guests. Floral displays were quite profuse and the dwelling was handsomely embellished with rare plants and foreign flowers, making the air fragrant with their perfume. There were also clusters of oranges but recently plucked from the grove of the groom's father in Florida, green palms and Florida moss displayed in many parts of the house.

Helen and Alfred married in Lancaster, Ohio

The bride and groom entered the parlor at the appointed hour...and took their places beneath the roses. Rev. J. N. Pilger of St. Mary's Catholic church officiated, and the ceremony was brief and appropriate.

The bride looked charming in a dress of marvelous beauty. The garment was of rich white faille and moire en traine, trimmed with seeds of pearl. The customary bridal veil and pearl jewelry was also worn by the bride. The groom wore the customary black.

The groom resides in Tabares, Florida, is a gentleman of excellent character and fine legal attainments, and is in every way worthy of the prize he has won. The bride is a fascinating and intelligent young lady, of many charms and accomplishments, and was a great favorite in Lancaster circles.

At the conclusion of the ceremony many sincere congratulations were showered upon the happy pair, and they were the recipients of many elegant and valuable presents.

The reception was from two until five o'clock, during which hours the very best and most cultured of our people called to congratulate the happy couple. The elegant refreshments were served by C. G. Ziegfeld a Columbus caterer.

The bridal party left on the 9 o'clock train for Magnolia Beach...before taking up permanent residence in Florida."

MR. ABRAMS WILD RIDE ~ 1891-1895.

The years between 1891 and 1895 were challenging, stressful, and at many times quite dangerous for St. Clair-Abrams, who served as a state senator from Lake County during that time period. While he continued to rebuild Tavares following the fire of 1888, his life was deeply entrenched in Lake County and State politics, where name-calling and gun-toting threats became an almost day-to-day occurrence. At the 1892 Lake County convention held at the Pioneer Building, the sheriff's office assigned three deputies to preserve order. Unruliness had erupted early at that convention anyway, with St. Clair-Abrams at the forefront. The deputies were able to intervene and cooler heads prevailed - somewhat.

At the state level, in-fighting at the conventions regarding the direction, policies, and views of Florida's Democratic party made national headlines. St. Clair-Abrams was again front and center.

St. Clair-Abrams' mastery in utilizing the press enabled him to succeed in many of his ventures. There was no shortage of newspapers who wrote opinion pieces and editorials severely opposing anything St. Clair-Abrams did. The *Pensacola News* made it their mission to destroy both his accomplishments and his reputation.

His law practice had prospered to yet another level of success, and his case schedule became extremely hectic. Political and business relationships with friends at times became heavily strained, though many of those relationships, not all, eventually recovered and survived into the future.

A deep Florida freeze at the end of 1894 and early in 1895 would cap off a *wild ride* for the soon to be fifty-year-old Florida advocate that prompted another change in his life and career.

FLORIDA FRIENDS FIGHT FOR FUNDS.

Long after Jacob Summerlin's son Robert departed Florida, St. Clair-Abrams, Robert's former law partner, was retained by the land and cattle baron for legal services. By the spring of 1892, the

Orlando icon owed St. Clair-Abrams' and his new law partner and future judge, Frederick C. Bryan, a large sum of money for legal services. The *Weekly Tribune* of Tampa reported on Monday, April 18, 1892: "An important case is set to be tried at Orlando next Tuesday. Senator Alexander St. Clair-Abrams has brought suit against Uncle Jacob Summerlin for the sum of $20,000 as fees in certain cases in which Mr. St. Clair-Abrams has acted as his attorney. Judge G. A. Hanson will go up there on Monday to act as counsel for Mr. Summerlin."

SENATOR MARKS ATTACKS VIA THE NEWSPAPERS.

In June of 1894, following a speech St. Clair-Abrams gave in Ocala, former Orlando mayor and now senator, Matthew R. Marks, wrote a blistering letter against St. Clair-Abrams, which he sent to the newspapers for publication. In the Friday, June 15, afternoon edition, the *Pensacola News*, a newspaper devoted to taking down St. Clair-Abrams, Frank Clark of Polk County, General Bullock of Ocala, Dr. Jackson of Liberty, Colonel Cockrell, and other leaders of the democratic party who wanted to reform the party instead of the party reforming them, was eager to print the nearly three-column letter by Marks. St. Clair-Abrams, though making minor rebuttal statements, didn't over-react to Marks' challenging defensive tirade.

MARKS TO ABRAMS. ORLANDO, June 10, 1894.
Editor Reporter: Whereas, the numerous readers of your valuable paper are largely my constituents, and do not read the metropolitan journals, it would be a great injustice to myself and to them as their senator to allow this man Abrams in an adjoining county to openly attack the character of your representative in a public speech at Ocala on Saturday last by insinuating that my vote on the railroad bill, introduced by my friend Williamson was influenced or bought by lobbyist. The Times-Union (his organ) of 10th instant, says: "Let Major Marks answer," in bold type. Answer what? Why the charge that I was full of enthusiasm for the bill; that I had written a speech, part of which I read to him, but when it came to a vote I recorded,

no! He could only surmise what caused a change of heart. "Railroad lobbyist had swarmed at Tallahassee, etc." Personally, I feel a supreme contempt for this man Abrams, and but for the fact that I am a senator from Orange and Osceola counties, and that it is a duty I owe my constituency, whom I consider the noblest, truest and wealthiest people represented in Tallahassee, I would allow this vile calumniator of myself and my people to pass by "as the idle wind which I respect not."

Mr. Williamson, who introduced this commission bill, is a warm hearted enthusiastic young man who has the good of his people and his state at heart, and he is manly enough and honest enough to state if he will, that although repeatedly urged by him to support his bill, I invariably said to him, "Williamson, I will study your bill closely and if I can be convinced that it is for the good of the whole people and the state, I will support it." He will also have the candor to say that I never promised to support the bill, and that I, two weeks before the bill was put on its passage, said to him I could not support it. Senators, Baya, Summers, Genovar, Whidden and Perrinot, with whom I was more closely associated than any other senators, will bear me out that this was my position on the Williamson bill. Now for this man Abrams, who is afflicted with gas, to address my friends and your friends in a distant part of the state, and try to heap calumny and disgrace upon me, your senator, and upon the proud old county of Orange and her progressive sister, Osceola, is so mean, so low, so cunning, so unwarranted from any standpoint, that it is with little patience that I can think of it. The cunning in the man's attack on me at Ocala is worthy of notice. He well knows that I have as many personal friends in South Florida as many men in it, and if he can discredit my character, he makes a long stride in his reformation.

There are many differences between Abrams and me. He represents Lake County by a very scant majority, and many good men of Lake County think it doubtful he was elected at all. I represent Orange and Osceola by a large and flattering majority. He was born a major, I won that honorable title from the ranks of the Confederate army. He was born smart; I was born honest. He is trying to reform the democratic party; I am willing to let the democratic party reform me. He attacks the democratic party from Mr. Cleveland down to Major Marks; he is an incendiary in the ranks; hires opera houses and makes speeches against the nominees of the party. I go through the woods to school houses and cross roads and sustain the actions of my party; I go to Tallahassee and vote on bills as I think for interest of my constituency and my state. He goes to Tallahassee to make eloquent speeches, to introduce dozens of bills and pass none. I go to Tallahassee to introduce a few bills and pass three-fourths of them. He goes to Tallahassee to attack every man, woman or child as dishonest, treacherous and influenced by lobbyists, if they don't think and act as he desires. I go to Tallahassee to watch the interests of my counties and state and to find all those gentlemen square, fair and honest.

I don't wish to "throw any more bouquets at myself" but finally answering his uncalled for, unjust, unmanly attack on me at Ocala on Saturday, will say to you that no lobbyist or any other person attempted in any manner to influence my vote upon any bill, except by argument. No bribery or offer of rewards or emoluments by any person to me or any other senator, came to my knowledge. And all this attempts by Abrams to do your senator such gross injustice will rebound, and the men who put him forward to disrupt the party, and to traduce the characters of life-long democrats, will, when brought before the people, call upon the rocks to hide then from an outraged public. I am willing to borrow $10 and contribute it to build a large auditorium at some central location and give it to Abrams for the campaign. I am willing to introduce a bill in the next senate allowing the gentleman fourteen days, fourteen hours and fourteen minutes to make speeches in, and that the senate adjourn at that time. I am willing to do almost anything that is honorable in the interest of the democratic party to keep this man before the people; a pretended democrat, he would disrupt the party; a pretended senator, he would traduce the character of the senate; a pretended anti-railroad man, he has had as much to do with railroads in his mind; miles of cross ties are rotting in the woods under his administration.

Talk about tyranny, consummate scoundrels, tyrannical corporations. In the last few years this man has filched more money from the people of my district than forty railroads have ever done in the same length of time; and at a time when every nerve was stretched to resume a bank in the interest of a whole people! Thousands for a few days' legal service! Great God, what would he do if he had the power? A professed catholic, he would disrupt the church; a professed patriot, he would impoverish the country; and would "grasp without remorse and wear without shame," the character of a patriot; and carry out his ambitious designs, would rob the poor - impoverish the rich, and bankrupt the state! I have no patience with the man or his methods. His forte is his pen and he is never more delighted than when he has a chance to show through the press an intellect that "God created for nobler purposes," but which he has transformed to purposes so egotistical, so base, so untrue, so unmanly, that I throw back in his teeth the insinuations thrown at me as vile, untrue and totally uncalled for! To show that I have Abrams down right, after his speech at Ocala and after the report of both correspondents of the city papers, he telegraphed the following to me:

"TAVARES, Fla., June 10, 1894

To M. R. Marks: "The statement made in to-day's Citizen that I claimed your vote was obtained by improper influences is an absolute falsehood and I have telegraphed a demand for correction.

ALEX. ST. CLAIR-ABRAMS."

He gives no inference that he telegraphed the Times-Union, which makes a distinction without a difference. This fight is not of my choosing. I have an interesting scrapbook of twenty-five years filled with good things about this great reformer, some of them quite interesting reading.

My main object in this article is to say to my constituency that any man who says that any vote of mine was influenced as insinuated in Abrams' Ocala speech, lies, maliciously, vindictively, unnecessarily, and that I am responsible to my constituency and individually for this statement." M. R. MARKS.

Publications that opposed St. Clair-Abrams, especially in the tempestuous year of 1894 when the Florida reform-movement of the democratic party was high, continued to discredit and impugn Senator St. Clair-Abrams. Newspapers, such as the *Florida Times-Union* based in Jacksonville, supported the reformists. *The Florida Times-Union* was a Northern owned newspaper that supported the Republican party and the conservative Democrats.

An op-ed in the *Pensacola News* on Tuesday July 10, 1894, read:

"A few years ago, when St. Clair-Abrams was a railroad man and in charge of a road which, under his able management grew to be almost as long as his name before it went into the hands of a receiver, he was travelling with several other railroad officials. In discussing the professional matters of interest to all the party, Abrams said in his characteristically modest manner:

"Well, Plant has done much for Florida and he stands deservedly high in the estimation of *our* profession, and of the public, but he is now old, and when we both come to die, if I am permitted to live anywhere as long as he has, I will far outstrip him as a developer."

Just at this time I would like to ask if "our profession" quit the major or did he do the leaving act?

Or, when he comes to die will he rest his reputation "as a developer" on his opera house in the pine woods about Tavares or on the mortgage he succeeded in placing on certain lands in the same section?

Or on the pavement built elsewhere by his "good resolutions" will he offset Mr. Plant's Tampa Bay Hotel, his town at Port Tampa, his Seminole Hotel, his line of steamships, his hundred miles of railroad through a wilderness and the civilization and industry these made possible?

Or when Abrams comes to die will he plead his support of the lottery in bar of judgment? Let us know.   CROSS-TIE.

SUFFRAGE EASY AND BIG MONEY PAID FOR VOTES.

In a special correspondence published in the *Delaware Gazette and State Journal* in Wilmington, Delaware, on Thursday October 11, 1894, the Delaware correspondent wrote:

"LEESBURG, FLA., Oct. 2. – This is election day in Florida and I have just been around the polls. I wanted to see for myself whether the colored man was being intimidated, and if so to what extent. I found him fraternizing with the whites to a degree I never witnessed in Delaware – and voting the Democratic ticket as a rule. I applied to a gentleman seated in a carriage for information, stating that I was just from a city where people were still to be found who really believed negroes in the South were accorded no political rights.

'I, myself, am a Northern man and a Republican,' he answered, 'and I tell you there is no hindrance here to any man voting his real sentiments.' To-day, however, the issue is not Democrats versus Republicans, but commission versus railroads - in this town, Alex. St. Clair-Abrams versus the Leesburg ring. My Republican informant told me he was an Abrams man and that the negroes were generally for Abrams, where they had not been bought. He pointed out one colored man who, after wobbling for several days, had, he said, accepted $150 - a pretty steep bribe seemingly - to work and vote for the ring ticket. Abrams has gotten out a dodger in which he asserts that he and his son, both being unarmed, were menaced yesterday by drawn revolvers in the hands of the sheriff of Lake County and his deputy."

FREEZES PRACTICALLY DEPOPULATED THE TOWN.

In the 1890s, citrus groves covered nearly 150,000 acres of Florida land that extended as far north as Jacksonville. The industry provided a substantial financial income to the grove owners and employment for local and migrant workers.

Through many generations of Florida citrus growing, Northern, winter-like temperatures, were rarely experienced. But on

Alex and Joanna walk through their orange grove during the
Great Freeze of 1894-1895

December 29th and 30th of 1894, a devastating freeze, with temperatures that plummeted to 10 degrees, overtook the trees. Leaves on a great percentage of the vulnerable trees were killed, but, with some great fortune, the damage to the trees was not severe enough to cause major alarm amongst the growers.

A warming trend, with a more than fair amount of rainfall, followed in January of 1895. Unprepared, the growers were hit by an equally powerful freeze on February 8th and 9th that devastated a vast amount of the orange and grapefruit trees. After the damage had been calculated, the acreage of operating Florida citrus groves was reduced to well under 50,000 acres.

Many growers in the northern and central regions of Florida had sold their groves and moved further south into the Florida peninsula; with some growers transplanted to Cuba and the Caribbean. Lake County would experience this exodus; one-day to regain its status as a major citrus-growing county after another double freeze occurrence in 1897 and 1898. But in 1895, many overwhelmed family growers pulled up stakes and re-located.

For the extreme wealthy, re-growth of the citrus industry was a vital investment in the Florida economy. Men like Henry Flagler provided seeds, tools, crates, and financial loans to encourage planters.

For St. Clair-Abrams, rebuilding Tavares after the fire, planning the new county of Lake, and securing Tavares as the County Seat, cut deep into his bank account. After the double freeze of 1894-1895, it was near impossible to finance further expansion. Tavares still had a great core of citizens that included men like H. H. Duncan, Edward Burleigh, and his son Alfred, as well as the railroads, industry, waterways, recreation, and being the County Seat, which St. Clair-Abrams believed would transform Tavares into one of Florida's major metropolitan areas.

The five years that preceded the February 1895 freeze were quite arduous and contentious for St. Clair-Abrams. His exploits in the Florida senate were now over. For Alex and Joanna, it was time for a change. The double freeze sealed their decision. As he stated in his "Memoranda on Tavares" written for Elizabeth Burleigh thirty years later, "…the subsequent freeze practically depopulated the town and so impoverished me that I had to leave Tavares and move to Jacksonville in 1895."

IT CAME FROM THE SWAMP ~ RIOTING RATTLERS!

In late June of 1895, as Alex and Joanna St. Clair-Abrams prepared for their move to Jacksonville, a weeklong reign of terror plagued the town of Tavares. National headlines featured the story of Lake County's capital city being overrun by an army of rattlesnakes.

The Tavares correspondent of the *St. Louis Globe Democrat* wired the story, saying, "the reptiles are of all ages and sizes, and have practically taken over the town. No woman or child dares venture out of doors, and when the men go out their legs are encased in stout leather leggings which reach to the thighs, and they armed with clubs with which to dispatch the serpents. The advance guard of the army of rattlers appeared just a week ago, and since then the snakes have come in such numbers that it is estimated that there are now 1,000 within the corporate limits of the town.

Last Sunday as Mayor Yorke and his family were going to church, they met the advance guard. It consisted of two old rattlers about five feet long, each with 12 rattles and a button, and a dozen smaller reptiles. The mayor and his family beat a retreat, and the city magistrate called for the neighbors to assist him in dispatching the reptiles. This brood was killed, but before it was done shouts from different quarters of the town announced the approach of more snakes. Since then, the men have been busy killing the reptiles. It is said 400 snakes have been killed, and still the town is full of them. Their warning rattle is heard at all hours and at all sides. The dogs made a gallant fight against the reptilian army, but nearly all have been bitten and are dead. Several horses have also died of snake bites. So far, no person has been bitten, though there have been several narrow escapes. Mrs. Sallie Jacobs had the most remarkable escape. While washing linen in the yard she put her 2-year-old baby in a dry goods box nearby. Soon Mrs. Jacobs heard the baby laughing, and looking around, was horrified to see an immense rattler coiled behind the box. The mother rushed for the baby, and the snake struck at her, fastening its fangs in her clothing. Her screams brought her husband, who killed the rattler.

The snakes came from a hammock at the foot of St. Clair-Abrams Avenue. The council has voted an appropriation, and this week the hammock will be cleared and the homes of the snakes destroyed."

Joanna and Alexander St. Clair-Abrams
bid farewell to Ye Towne of Tavares in 1895

SEVEN

Fury, Fire, and Farewell

Arriving in Jacksonville, St. Clair-Abrams set up his law practice and, with his widespread reputation and business and political connections, established an impressive clientele list. His bank account reversed its course, and all past debts were paid.

SON ALFRED SHOOTS RIVAL FOR ROSE.

At 8:30 in the evening of July 26, 1896, thirty-year-old Alfred St. Clair-Abrams, armed with a double-barreled shotgun loaded with buckshot, entered the residence of Captain W. Baily Tucker in Tavares. Alfred found Tucker sitting in a bedroom, and from across the room, discharged one barrel of the gun. One fatal bullet struck Tucker in the head.

Tucker was the general manager of the Tavares, Atlantic and Gulf Railroad and local manager of Florida Central and Peninsular Railroad. He opposed Alfred for the state legislature and claimed Alfred was anti-railroad. Tucker defeated Alfred, which prompted speculation that the reason for the ambush was the unethical manner in which Tucker campaigned against Alfred and that Alfred suspected Tucker of illegally using railroad money for his campaign.

It was revealed that Tucker was having an affair with Alfred's wife, Rose Helen, who was visiting her family in Ohio at the time of the shooting. Alfred had sworn vengeance and justice. He was told that his wife had been seeking advice from Tucker regarding the marital problems she was having with Alfred. The couple had three young children at this time. Alfred was arrested soon after he shot Tucker.

Rose Helen was asked by reporters why she had returned to Ohio at this time just prior to the shooting. She responded, "I have for years spent the summer with my mother in Lancaster, Ohio, and my visit this year was no exception to the rule."

When asked if she left her home in Orlando without her husband's knowledge, Rose Helen responded, "My husband, of course, knew that I was going to visit my mother. He accompanied me to Jacksonville and purchased my tickets and checked my baggage for me. We had no trouble whatsoever, except for the trouble which I have had for years. Mr. Abrams has time and again treated me in a heartless, cruel manner, and has been in a fiendish mood of late. A long-standing enmity existed between my husband and Captain Tucker's father on account of railroad business matters, and for some time this has been directed toward Captain Tucker. My husband's defeat for the legislature on an independent ticket, no doubt, further infuriated him, as he believed Captain Tucker used his influence to defeat him."

Rose Helen was then asked what were her relations with Captain Tucker. She replied, "I have known Captain Tucker for years; long before I was married, and frequently met him while his wife was living. Since her death I have occasionally met him at our hotel, but as my husband disliked him, owing, as I said, to the old feud, but he rarely called to see me." Rose Helen said she had never consulted Tucker regarding her marital problems with Alfred and that Tucker had absolutely nothing to do with her coming north. She told the reporters that her husband wished for her to live in Tavares, but she considered it an undesirable place to live, and that he had spent all her inheritance from her father.

Alfred gave his accounting of the events in which he was able to provide testimony that proved the affair and that he was threatened. He also provided detailed proof of Tucker's corrupted business handling of the railroad funds. Alfred was not convicted.

THE CASE OF THE HYPNOTIZED GIRL.

In June 1897, the newspapers reported the on-going, nationally publicized story that was quite strange if it were true. It was the case of Grace Darnell, who claimed she was under a hypnotic influence.

The story read, "Another phase of the Grace Darnell case developed Thursday. The case has attracted a great deal of attention from the fact that a hypnotic influence is said to possess the girl. The case started in Sumter County two years ago, where the Armstrong family, who now reside in Jacksonville, now live. Grace Darnell claimed to have been kidnapped, taken to the woods, stripped of part of her clothing, and tied to a tree, where she was found the next morning. Four young men were charged with the crime, arrested and convicted, but a new trial was granted. The young men were afterwards arrested and tried here in the United States court, charged with sending obscene letters to Miss Darnell.

Numerous letters were submitted in evidence, and the case was sensational in the extreme. The prisoners were convicted, but again the court set aside the decision. Recently Miss Darnell made a sworn confession to Major St. Clair-Abrams, counsel for the defense, saying that her testimony was false, and that the letters were written by James Armstrong, her guardian, and others, for the purpose of convicting the young men. When the fact that she had made this confession became known she was taken to the newspaper offices by Armstrong and there denied ever having made it.

Thursday she was brought into court again and denied having made the confession, despite the fact that it was witnessed by four prominent and reliable citizens. Armstrong was present when these denials were made. Thursday night Miss Darnell escaped from the Armstrong residence and declared that the confessions were absolutely true. She says that Armstrong has a Svengali-like influence over her and that she is powerless to do otherwise than as he tells her to do. She is at present in the care of Major St. Clair-Abrams, and will be kept away from the influence of Armstrong."

THE CASE OF MARIE LOUISE GATO.

St. Clair-Abrams, as a newspaper reporter, wrote with a nationally-known sensational flair. As an attorney at law, his cases, and his handling of those cases, exuded the same sensationalistic capacity. One such case was the murder of the beautiful nineteen-year-old Marie Louise Gato, in which St. Clair-Abrams defended the accused murderer, Edward George Pitzer.

Miss Marie Louise Gato, who was the daughter of wealthy Jacksonville cigar merchant Gabriel Hidalgo Gato, was shot five times as she entered the gate of her father's home at Laura and West Eleventh Streets in the North Springfield neighborhood in Jacksonville shortly after 7:00 p.m. on April 20, 1897. She died the following day.

After she was shot, Marie was brought inside her home. She regained consciousness for a while and, knowing she was about to die, stated to her father, and later to Judge A. O Wright, that it was Eddie Pitzer who shot her, and that she looked right at him and saw his face. The judge questioned her, only to have Marie respond with answers formulated on the questions he asked. The written dying-declaration was signed with a cross by Marie due to her inability to hold a pen. According to an article in the *Florida Times-Union*, the excitement caused by her deathbed declaration was indescribable.

The spectacular trial lasted nearly two weeks. The lawyers in the case were State Attorney A. G. Hartridge, assisted by D. U. Fletcher and A. W. Cockrell. And for Edward Pitzer's defense, Major Alexander St. Clair-Abrams, with D. C. Campbell and F. W. Pope as associates. The trial judge was R. M. Call and D. Plummer was foreman of the jury.

Pitzer was reported as having stepped out from behind a bush when he opened fire. Marie had been carrying a bag of candy, which fell to the ground. Georgia Gato, Marie's sister, who had fainted on the witness stand, said she saw Pitzer run through the gate after the shooting, while a neighbor boy, who had walked Marie to the home's gate, said he saw a large man, but didn't think it was Pitzer.

During the trial, there were several witnesses who said they saw Pitzer at or near the scene and even some witnesses said they saw the flash from the pistol. Still others said they recognized his shadow or his way of moving in the dark.

St. Clair-Abrams questioned Marie's state of mind after having been shot five times and having been medicated with opium as she gave her deathbed declaration. The judge sustained St. Clair-

Abrams' objections to admit the dying-declaration into evidence, and instructed the jury that the declaration should not be considered.

The trial, billed by the media as a "battle royal," made national headlines. The good-looking young defendant, Edward Pitzer, had mesmerized the young ladies of Jacksonville, who would faint when he would look at them. The courtroom was packed with women, who brought picnic baskets with food to the trial as to not lose their seats during a recess. His jail cell was full of flowers from his female admirers. Pitzer's attitude gave the impression of being unconcerned. He would whistle a cheerful tune as he was brought to the courtroom. He believed that either St. Clair-Abrams would have no problem getting him acquitted, or that his popularity in Jacksonville society would prevail. Pitzer had hundreds of friends who believed him innocent.

Love letters between Marie and Pitzer, which were read aloud in court, revealed that Pitzer had fought a duel for Marie's affections. The rival was Domingo Herrera. A couple hours after Pitzer had taken a letter from Herrera to Marie, he received a note from a stranger, which originated from Herrera that requested Pitzer give him the satisfaction of meeting on Bridge Street (now Broad Street) late at night. Pitzer accepted Herrera's request and met that night at the designated place in the black neighborhood of LaVilla. Herrera was a no-show, but several of his friends were there with their faces covered with burnt cork. One of Herrera's friends said he was paid to fight in his place. The stage for the traditional duel was set. Herrera's surrogate shot first and hit Pitzer in the arm. Pitzer then shot, hitting the man who he described as falling quick as a flash.

St. Clair-Abrams introduced no witnesses during the trial except for Pitzer himself. Pitzer had testified that he and Marie were engaged and they had gone steady for three years.

When it came time for summation, St. Clair-Abrams gave the "performance" of his life. He felt he needed to convince the jury that, though he defended a man accused of murder, he himself despised murder. And that fact should prove his client's innocence. St. Clair-Abrams exclaimed that he who did that deed may never enjoy a woman's love! And referring to Pitzer, St. Clair-Abrams

demanded, "Do you mean to tell me that the hand of love fired that weapon?" When he reached his crescendo after a *six-hour* summation, he cried to the jury that he prayed for Pitzer's mother as they reached their verdict. He then collapsed into the arms of the sheriff's deputy. St. Clair-Abrams was taken to the judge's chambers and revived. As he awoke delirious, he continued his dramatic summation, believing he was still in front of the jury. When he regained his composure, he cried out, "Where is that boy? They can't hang him! They haven't hung that boy, have they? Did I finish my speech?"

The jury deliberated for 22 hours following the nine-day trial that lasted from May 26 to June 5. After the audience was warned by the judge not to make a sound after the verdict was read, friends, family, and the large contingent of women, cheered with approval after hearing the *not guilty* verdict.

Marie Louise Gato was buried at the Old City Cemetery. In 1898, her father died. In 1899, the Gato cigar factory in North Springfield burned. Edward Pitzer left Jacksonville for Pittsburgh and was never heard from again.

HETEROGENEOUS MASS OF HUMANITY.

In September 1898, St. Clair-Abrams voiced his opinions to the media regarding American colonization and annexation. In a September 21, 1898, edition of the *Herald* of Union Springs, Alabama, the newspaper printed a letter St. Clair-Abrams wrote to the *Atlanta Constitution's* editors.

"In the batch of mail which daily finds its way into the Constitution office is a letter signed by a name well remembered in Atlanta, that of Alex St. Clair-Abrams, in which he urges upon the democratic party a broad national stand upon the subject of territorial expansion. 'As more than half the territory of the United States,' he writes, 'has been acquired, either by conquest or purchase, under democratic administrations, and as the democratic party years ago advocated the annexation of the West Indies and of Hawaii, it is certainly humiliating to find the party at this late date forced by a few leaders into a position diametrically opposite to that which it has always historically occupied.' From this Mr. Abrams goes on to notice that, 'as for the talk that our government unfits us for holding colonies, those who indulge in it seem to forget that we have the greatest colonizing people of modern days. Our territories have been practically colonial possessions. Into them have poured a motley and heterogeneous mass of humanity, representing every nation and clime, and these diverse, and in many instances, conflicting elements have had to be governed and welded together until they form that homogenous entity which ultimately rendered safe the admission of these territories as states.' - Atlanta Constitution."

THE CASE OF THE ONE-EYED FIREMAN.

In March 1899, St. Clair-Abrams secured for his client, J. A. Moon, who was a former fireman for the Plant Railway System, a verdict of $12,500 against the huge railroad and steamboat operator in the circuit court of Orange County. Moon had lost an eye in a wreck while he was employed by Henry Plant's company.

FLORIDA'S "INSANE" DIVORCE LAW.

On April 22, 1901, St. Clair-Abrams became vocal regarding a new divorce law that was passed by the Florida Legislature, and had sent out a press release that, with his national reputation, was printed in publications throughout the United States.

The *New York Times* reprinted an article out of Jacksonville which read, "A bill that has just been passed by the Florida Legislature now in session at Tallahassee is attracting considerable attention from its particular wording, and also because Major St. Clair-Abrams of this city, a lawyer, well-known throughout the State, has written a long open letter in one of the local newspapers strongly denouncing it. The bill adds one more to the causes for divorce in this State, namely, 'incurable insanity.'

It is a lengthy bill, and, according to lawyers who have seen it, is very strongly drawn. It provides that where insanity has existed, in either the husband or wife, for four successive years, divorce may be granted. It provides that in the court where the suit shall be brought, a lawyer shall be appointed as guardian of the defendant, to defend the suit. But, according to lawyers, the guardian can only bring up as a defense the issue whether or not incurable insanity exists, and cannot go outside of this to ascertain for himself the truth of the matter. Some lawyers say that there are other matters in the bill that seem out of place in a measure of this kind.

Mr. Abrams in his letter denounces the bill as a blot upon Florida and says it was carried through not because the public demanded it, but because one person required it. He further adds: 'The alleged reason for this bill is that the person's property is imperiled by the claims of an insane wife and that he cannot dispose of his property as he wishes under the Florida dower laws.' He calls the law a monstrous outrage upon the rights of an insane person."

JOANNA'S THIRD AND FINAL FIRE ~
THE GREAT JACKSONVILLE FIRE OF 1901.

Around 12:00 noon of May 3, 1901, a spark from a wood-burning stove sparked some Spanish moss that was laid out to dry at the Cleveland Fiber Factory, located at the intersection of Beaver and Davis Streets in downtown Jacksonville. Factory workers attempted to put out the blaze but the stiff breeze fanned the fire, which began to ignite houses in the black neighborhood around the factory. From that point, the fire jumped across hundreds of wood-shingled, wood-framed houses, and eventually spread into an influential area of the city, burning the residences of prominent Jacksonville citizens, including United States senator, James Piper Taliferro. The Windsor Hotel and the St. James Hotel fell victim to the fire. The black churches, Ebenezer Methodist and Bethel Baptist, were also lost, as well as the Catholic church of the Immaculate Conception, St. Joseph's orphanage and convent.

Other public buildings that fell were the Emory Auditorium, the Board of Trade, the Baldwin House, the Hubbard Building, and Jacksonville City Hall.

The Confederate monument in Hemming Plaza on West Monroe Street was one of the few surviving structures, where witnesses stated the base of the monument glowed red. The fire continued east toward Hogan's Creek, where a neighborhood bucket brigade held back the flames. The fire turned southward toward Bay Street's riverfront docks. The Furchgott Building and the six-story Gardner Building were a mass of flames.

The fire department had fought valiantly against the great conflagration. In just over eight hours, around 8:30 in the evening, the devastating fire, the worst in Florida history, had torched 146 blocks and destroyed over 2,300 buildings. Reports read that the glow of the fire could be seen in Savannah, Georgia, and the smoke was visible as far away as Raleigh, North Carolina – over 450 miles away.

Florida Governor William S. Jennings had declared martial law in Jacksonville and ordered the state militia to assist. The city was returned to civil authority on May 17. The initial estimate of the total loss of property was ten to fifteen million dollars. Reconstruction began immediately, with renowned architect, Henry John Klutho, as a significant figure in the rebuilding of Jacksonville. Within five months, over a thousand building permits were issued, and homes began to resurrect from the devastation.

Nearly 10,000 people were left homeless from the fire, with seven lives lost. Joanna was trapped at home in the fire, but was rescued. The effects from Joanna's third tragic fire - Atlanta, Tavares, and Jacksonville – left her in a state a shock. St. Clair-Abrams traveled to Atlanta with his beloved wife to convalesce with her family – in hope for her rapid recovery.

HENRY JOHN KLUTHO.

Henry John Klutho

After he read about the Jacksonville fire in the New York newspapers, twenty-eight-year-old architect, Henry John Klutho, was captivated by the opportunity of a clear new canvas to rebuild the city utilizing his personal design techniques and his attraction to the new "Prairie" style architecture.

In the summer following the fire, Klutho moved to Jacksonville from his home in New York. He wasted no time introducing himself to prominent citizens, and by August, 1901, was designing the city's largest building on Bay Street – The Dyal-Upchurch Building, where St. Clair-Abrams would relocate his law offices. Two months later, Klutho designed the new Jacksonville City Hall and the home of one of the governors of the Jacksonville Board of Trade.

He had completed Jacksonville's first skyscraper in 1909 – the ten-story Bisbee Building, which survived hurricane force winds during its construction. The building was the first reinforced concrete frame high-rise built in the South. Klutho had become Jacksonville's leading architect and had more structures built than any other architect.

When Klutho made a trip to New York, he met world-famous architect, Frank Lloyd Wright, from Oak Park, Illinois, a city bordering Chicago's west side. Klutho was intrigued by Wright and various Chicago architects' "Prairie" style design. The new style blended nature using strong horizontal lines, picture windows, and natural materials. He began to utilize the "Prairie" style in Jacksonville, and by the end of World War I, the city had more of the style structures than any city outside Wright's Midwest domain. Klutho was a master salesman and convinced much of his clientele to go with a "Prairie" design.

On October 21, 1921, Klutho completed the four-story St. James Building - a department store for Jacob and Morris Cohen that covered a city block that overlooked Hemming Park. The "Prairie" style St. James was the largest building in Jacksonville at that time and was the ninth-largest department store in the United States. The building would serve as Jacksonville's City Hall in December 1997.

Klutho had a remarkable career that involved not only his artistic and design skills, but as an urban planner, inventor, philosopher, and was hugely involved in Jacksonville's movie industry. He died in 1964 at the age of 91. He was near poverty at his passing and his contributions were seemingly lost to future Jacksonville generations. Many of his buildings were demolished or in a heavy state of dereliction. Klutho's legacy has had a rebirth in Jacksonville and his home on West 9th Street (originally located on Main Street) was placed on the National Register of Historic Places in 1978. Many Klutho homes and buildings have been restored.

St. Clair-Abrams Home at 1649 Osceola Street in Jacksonville

St. Clair-Abrams became friends with Klutho, who designed the St. Clair-Abrams' mausoleum at Evergreen Cemetery in 1901. The mausoleum was the first private commission designed by Klutho. In 1914, Klutho design St. Clair-Abrams' "Prairie" style home at 1649 Osceola Street in Jacksonville. The two-story stucco house features seventeen "Tree of Life" stained glass windows. The tree-of-life motif followed the "Prairie" style theme that brought earth and nature indoors. The house also had French doors, coffered ceilings, wood floors, a wraparound porch, tile roof, and four wood-burning brick fireplaces. St. Clair-Abrams had a large library-parlor and office within the home.

THE CASE OF "THAT CATTLE CASE".

On August 20, 1901, St. Clair-Abrams penned a letter to the *Tampa Tribune* in regards to a false statement the newspaper had printed about the suit against the estate of the late Ziba King.

"Editor Tribune: My attention has been called to an article in the Tribune relative to the King estate cattle suit, which I desire to correct.

The late Judge, sometime in 1887 or 1888 purchased from the agent of Mrs. Johnson, the cattle which belonged to her, and the marks and brands of which were on record in Osceola County, in her name.

At the same time there was another stock of cattle the marks and brands of which were on record as belonging to the child, who was then an infant. This cattle was carried off by the judge along with Mrs. Johnson's cattle, and restitution of this property, or the value thereof was sought. So far, our side of the question is concerned, we do not feel the slightest uncertainty as to the result, so that you are in error as to this. The sole reason for negotiating a compromise is to prevent a delay, which seems inevitable in all Florida litigation.

As we have refused to accept less than a specified sum, this would not indicate that we feel an uncertainty as to the ultimate issue."

Ziba King was an early settler at Fort Ogden in DeSoto County, located on the east side of the Peace River. King was a Confederate veteran who moved to Florida from Georgia after the war. When he arrived in Florida, he had only five dollars. After he worked several jobs, he earned enough to open a dry goods store in Tampa in 1868. After a short period of time, he moved to Fort Ogden and homesteaded a 160-acre parcel and opened a general store. He began to acquire cattle and was appointed a judge. He eventually became president of the First National Bank of Arcadia.

King was a big man who stood six foot six inches tall and weighed 225 pounds. He was highly respected and known for his soft heart. He was a master poker player and at times, after he won all the opponent's money (and sometimes all their possessions) he would then give them some money back.

He owned a local newspaper, and was elected to the Florida Senate, as well as served on the local school board, when at one point, he bank-rolled the entire school system. When King passed away in 1901, he was reported to own over 50,000 head of cattle worth $500,000, which represented ten percent of the cattle in the state. Some of the cattle in his possession were in question as to King's ownership as herds occasionally blended.

The Passing of Alex's Beloved Joanna.

While Joanna was in Atlanta, the trauma from the Jacksonville fire overtook her. On October 7, 1901, Joanna passed away. The *Atlanta Constitution* wrote of her passing, "Mrs. Joanna Immel Abrams, of Jacksonville Fla., died here at 7:30 o'clock yesterday morning after a critical illness of several weeks. She was 54 years of age. She was the wife of Hon. St. Clair-Abrams of Jacksonville, Fla., one of the most prominent lawyers of that state and a former Atlantan. She was the daughter of Philip Lewis Immel, who was well known in Atlanta before the war. She had several relatives and a large number of friends in the city.

The body was taken to Jacksonville for burial last night, and the funeral will take place this afternoon.

Mrs. Abrams was distinguished for her many personal attractions and was a woman of that strength and nobility of character that made her beloved wherever she was known. She was one of the social leaders of Jacksonville and one of the most philanthropic women in that city.

She had many friends here among the oldest and best-known people."

Hiring Florida's First Woman Lawyer
Louise Rebecca Pinnell.

Louise Rebecca Pinnell

In 1901, St. Clair-Abrams hired twenty-four-year-old Louise Rebecca Pinnell to his law firm. Louise was the daughter of Ethan Allen Pinnell, who practiced law in Illinois and Missouri. In 1882, Pinnell was elected probate judge, a position he held for four years. In the 1890s, the judge moved his family to Bronson, Florida, where he practiced law for many years. Her family, that included her father, encouraged Louise to become a lawyer. Florida had no law schools prior to the turn of the century, so Louise studied the law as an apprentice in her father's office for two years.

Florida law required a person to be twenty-one to take the oral examination, which Louise did in May 1898. The four-hour examination in front of the Supreme Court justices was difficult, and most likely was made more difficult because she was a woman. After she waited five months for the results of her examination, the justices approved her admission to the bar in October 1898, which made Louise the first woman lawyer in the State of Florida.

For three years she practiced law in her father's office, but needed an opportunity to prove her skill outside the confines of Judge Pinnell's office. One of her father's clients was the Florida Central & Peninsular Railroad, of which Louise worked closely. Her work associated with the railroads was noticed by St. Clair-Abrams, who offered her a position. Much of St. Clair-Abrams law business was related to railroad activities - regulations and personal injury cases. He represented many railroad companies. Louise became a major asset in his firm and would work for St. Clair-Abrams for nineteen years, when she, with a recommendation from St. Clair-Abrams, went to work in 1920 for the Florida East Coast Railway Company in St. Augustine. After a sixty-year career, Louise passed away on May 22, 1966, at the age of 89 in Jacksonville.

Author, Historian, Rollins College Educator, and Winter Park, Florida, Community Activist, Lucy Worthington Blackman said of Louise, "Louise Rebecca Pinnell should...be cited for bravery, for it took no small degree of courage to fly in the face of tradition in a conservative Southern society, and to open up a masculine field of activity to a woman, proving that women may be successful and useful in that sacrosanct profession of law. To all such pioneers among women, honor and glory."

And so too should Major Alexander St. Clair-Abrams be given credit for his confidence and belief in Louise Rebecca Pinnell's ability and skill to hire her, and for his courage to give her major responsibility in his law firm, which gave Louise the opportunity to build a long and successful career.

DAISY.

At 1:00 in the afternoon on Monday, November 10, 1901, St. Clair-Abrams married Daisy Sligh in St. Augustine - two weeks prior to her twentieth birthday. St. Clair-Abrams was fifty-six.

Daisy, the daughter of Melvin and Lillie Lee Flanagan Sligh of Miami, was described as a charming young lady, blonde, and very attractive both in person and in manner. She attended St. Joseph's Academy in St. Augustine. St. Joseph's is the oldest Catholic high school in Florida. Originally founded by the Sisters of St. Joseph in 1866, the school is still in operation today.

As much of a public figure as St. Clair-Abrams was, the marriage was not publicized. Friends of the Sligh family and that of St. Clair-Abrams were quite surprised when they heard the news.

No record as to the reason for the marriage, but the marriage lasted almost twenty years, ending on June 8, 1921. St. Clair-Abrams provided for her financially until her marriage to John Cecil

Hickson of Miami on April 14, 1930. Hickson was one of three men that held a *trust* set up by St. Clair-Abrams for Daisy.

ABRAMS ON DRAINAGE.

In a letter to the media in September 1906, St. Clair-Abrams pushed back against Governor Napoleon Broward regarding the Constitutional Amendment to drain the Everglades.

The following is from his letter.

"In his harangue throughout the State in support of the outrageous constitutional amendment now before the people, Governor Broward is acting with characteristic political trickery and dishonesty. Practically the entire burden of his talk is his denunciation of the land grants given to the railroad corporations and his singling out the East Coast Railway Company and Mr. Flagler for denunciation and in holding them up to public obloquy.

The only issue before the people of the State is whether or not the Constitutional Amendment shall be adopted.

Whether or not it was wise or unwise to give land grants to railroad companies in Florida is not and cannot be an issue of this campaign.

Whether or not the Everglades should be drained is not an issue involved in the Constitutional Amendment.

No one knows better than Governor Broward that the real and only issue before the people involved in this Constitutional Amendment is whether or not five irresponsible executive officers of the State shall be vested with the autocratic and sovereign power to impose a tax aggregating $25,000,000 annually upon the people of Florida.

Another issue which Governor Broward seeks to shirk is whether or not several hundred land owners in the drainage district recently formed shall be taxed to drain lands for the benefit of the Louisville and Nashville Railroad and other railroad corporations of the State.

Governor Broward knows that there is pending before the United States Court one single law suit brought by the Louisville &

Nashville Railroad Company which, if decided in favor of that corporation, will turn over to it almost every acre of land claimed by the State of Florida. He knows that there are other claims on these lands also in suit which decided in contrary to his contention will wipe out the title of the State to every acre of land now claimed by it and leave a deficit of several million acres.

In answer to the argument in forcing this drainage scheme on the people until these suits are decided, he coolly replies that if his views prevail the railroads will not get the land.

Now, if the Louisville and Nashville Railroad Company wins, by what right will he and his clique have to force hundreds of persons to pay for the drainage of the Everglades for the benefit of the Louisville and Nashville Railroad Company. He does not and cannot answer this question. By appeals to the passions and cupidity of the designing, the credulous, the vicious and ignorant, he endeavors to put into the background the real issue involved in this Constitutional Amendment and to lead the masses of the people to vote for it regardless of the consequences that will follow, except to those who may get the contract to do the drainage.

In all his speeches he seeks to impress his hearers with the idea that the Florida East Coast Railway Company and Mr. Flagler are the chief would be grabbers of these lands.

Nothing more despicable and more infamously dishonest has ever been attempted in the politics of this State. Governor Broward knows perfectly well that the Florida East Coast Railway Company has never obtained a single acre of land from the State under and land grant. He knows very well that the special land grant to the Florida East Coast Railway Company is the youngest grant in the State, and he further knows that if the United States Supreme Court should confirm the validity of these grants the older grants (principally that of the Louisville and Nashville Railway Company) will absorb every acre now claimed by the State, and that the Florida East Coast Railway Company will not get a single acre!

In his harangues before the people Governor Broward bases his claim on behalf of the State under the act of 1855, putting the title to these lands in the Trustees of the Internal Improvement Fund. He conceals from the people the fact that sections 28 and 29 of the act (which was passed on the 6th of January, 1855) distinctly reserved to the Legislature the power to grant the alternative sections of these lands for six miles on each side to such railroad companies thereafter chartered as they may deem proper; and that by a later act passed in 1881 it was distinctly provided that these alternative sections should not even be subject to the rights of creditors of the Internal Improvement Fund.

There is not a lawyer with professional standing above the grade of shyster who will question the right of this road (Florida East Coast Railway Company) to the grant of these alternate sections under the act of 1855 and the subsequent acts of the Legislature.

How many acres of these alternate sections has the Florida East Coast Company received?

Not a single acre.

And yet, in the face of this fact, Governor Broward is going before the people of the State of Florida criticizing the Florida East Coast Railroad Company and Henry M. Flagler.

The law ignored and nullified alike by Governor Jennings and his board, and by Governor Broward and his board; the faith of the State violated, its honor smirched, its implied and expressed contract with the men who have built hundreds of miles of railroad repudiated and nullified, this man Broward nevertheless has the temerity to go before the people of Florida and denounce as thieves and land-grabbers men who have simply asked the State to carry out its contracts and agreements with them, on the faith of which they have expended millions of dollars!

To violate the law, to put upon the State the seal of dishonesty, were enough; to add to this infamy the reckless denunciations indulged in by Napoleon B. Broward are evidence of his utter unfitness for the position he holds, and cannot fail to impress upon the minds of thoughtful, intelligent and honorable men the strongest doubt of his individual integrity, as well as of the sincerity and honesty of his public utterances."

GRANDDAUGHTER MARRIES.

On Wednesday evening November 18, 1908, St. Clair-Abrams gave away her granddaughter, Clara, at her wedding to Judge Grambling. St. Clair-Abrams acted for his son Alfred, Clara's father, due to an illness that kept him from having taken an active role. Alfred would be plagued by illness over the next few years. He had recently sold his home in Tavares, and in August of 1907, sold the *Tavares Herald* newspaper to Dr. F. A. Reed of Eustis, and moved to Jacksonville.

The wedding took place at Alfred's home, where Rev. Father Maher of the Church of the Immaculate Conception officiated. Till's orchestra with Professor Wenzel Joseph Schubert and his wife, Catherine, rendered several beautiful numbers before the wedding march that announced the bridal party. St. Clair-Abrams' wife, Daisy, described as wearing an exquisite gown of pale blue hand-embroidered chiffon, carrying an armful of chrysanthemums, was the matron of honor. Lilian Sligh was Clara's maid of honor.

OVERWORKED CIRCUIT COURTS.

In July 1910, St. Clair-Abrams weighed-in on the Constitutional Amendment, which would be voted on in November of that year that would give the Florida Legislature authority to increase the number of judges.

St. Clair-Abrams, in an interview, stated, "It is to be hoped that the prohibition question will not cause the voters to ignore the constitutional amendment to be voted upon in November vesting in the Legislature the power to increase the number of circuit courts in this State at its discretion. This has become an absolute necessity. In some of the circuits it has become impossible for the judges to try and decide promptly because of the large number of cases brought before them. In this circuit Judge Call has probably five or six times as many cases presented to him during the year as the supreme court with six judges has to consider and determine. In many instances, in some of the circuits, cases are presented and important legal questions raised without briefs, and the judge is compelled to investigate the authorities himself before deciding them.

We have only one more circuit court in this State now than we had in 1868, when the population was less than one-third what it is. It seems to me that the press and members of the bar throughout the State should make it their duty to impress upon the public mind the necessity for the adoption of this amendment, so that the much-desired relief might be obtained.

The people of the State cannot expect, with our population nearing the million mark and the volume of litigation keeping ahead of such increase, that the same number of judges we had in 1868, can properly handle the great number of cases brought daily before them.

The amendment should be adopted unanimously, as there is absolutely not one reasonable or plausible ground for opposing it."

POET OF PINE CASTLE.

In 1909, newspaper writer, editor, correspondent and well-known poet, William "Will" Wallace Harney, moved to Jacksonville from Orlando to live with his son, William Randolph Harney, who was a vegetable and fruit dealer.

In 1868, Harney, born in Bloomington, Indiana, had moved from his home in Louisville, Kentucky, where he worked for the *Louisville Democrat*, to the southside of Orlando, on the western shore of Lake Conway. He hoped that the warm Florida climate would improve his wife, Mary St. Mayer Randolph's health. But unfortunately, twenty-five-year-old Mary passed away shortly after their arrival in 1869. Their son was only six months old at the time.

After he built up his homestead with a small grove, vegetable garden, and cow pen, the heart-broken Harney began to send the influential *Cincinnati Commercial* newspaper letters that described life in the developing Florida frontier. His feature stories earned him an extra income, as well as some national popularity.

In 1874, Harney built a storybook-type house of pine he called "Pine Castle." As a house-warming celebration, he invited many of

Will Wallace Harney's home he called Pine Castle

Orange County's leading residents to a Christmas gala. He began to use *Pine Castle* as his byline for his feature stories and correspondents. He assisted homesteaders in the area, many from Kentucky and Ohio, with the construction of a school, church, and post office - and soon after, the community that grew around his homestead was called by that moniker - Pine Castle.

Harney, like many newspaper correspondents, was quite opinionated regarding people, places, and politics. He operated a weekly publication called the *Kissimmee Bitter-Sweet* from September 1883 to February 1885. Much of his focus was on the Orange County commissioners. His reporting of county politics became filled with animosity. In 1884, another Orlando legend, Mahlon Gore, editor of the *Orange County Reporter*, wrote that Harney was looking for any reason to attack the county commissioners. Harney and Gore thus began a war of words. Gore charged Harney with insulting the Florida Newspaper Exchange.

St. Clair-Abrams was not immune to Harney's pen. He was a veteran newspaper man who did not mind verbal warfare. While he was state and county prosecutor, Harney accused St. Clair-Abrams of earning over $1,000 as a public attorney. St. Clair-Abrams responded with the quip by calling Harney the "little creature" who publishes a "little paper." After the sarcastic insult, St. Clair-Abrams said that he spent more on prosecutions than he earned in fees.

And through Harney was ruffling a few other high-ranking feathers, he again attacked St. Clair-Abrams when the latter's lumber mill burned down in Tavares. Harney claimed the mill was owned by an assignee and not by St. Clair-Abrams. He also reported that St. Clair-Abrams was receiving fees from liquor dealers for processing licenses for them under the local option law. Mahlon Gore came to St. Clair-Abrams' defense when he replied, "For months Harney has given free rein to his venom, and has made assaults upon and charges against the honor and integrity of men whose reputations have never before been assailed."

St. Clair-Abrams filed a criminal libel suit against Harney, which prompted the arrest of Harney twice within a two-week period. Harney defended himself in his newspaper. The grand jury found sufficient evidence for the remarks made by Harney, but Gore felt justice was not served and cited the county commissioners' refusal to grant St. Clair-Abrams $500 to apprehend the perpetrator of a murder.

By early 1885, the operational cost of Harney's newspaper was more than he could afford. He had lost many subscribers and advertisers. He had lost possession of his Pine Castle property in 1892 and his beloved home was demolished two years later. Harney continued to write, and through the years, his stories and poems, many of which were inspired by the memory of his wife, appeared in the pages of *Harper's Weekly*, the *Atlantic Monthly, Lippincott's*, and many other prominent publications.

When Harney moved to Jacksonville, he published books, which included a collection of poems he titled, "The Spirit of the South." Harney's grandfather, William Ross Wallace (1819-1881), was a world-renown poet. Will Wallace Harney passed away in Jacksonville in 1912 at the age of 79. He is buried at Greenwood Cemetery in Orlando.

THE CASE OF THE GREEN ORANGES.

In October 1911, St. Clair-Abrams wrote a letter to the *Florida Times-Union* that circulated throughout the state. The *Miami Metropolis* reported, "Major Alex St. Clair-Abrams has furnished the public another of his most thoughtful articles in condemnation of the tactics pursued by the Citrus Fruit Exchange of Florida. The provocation for his second article is the information that E. B. Peters of Leesburg has been convicted of shipping green fruit, and coincident reports also show the indictment, at Fort Pierce, of J. S. Stratton and Representative Fred Fee, on the same charges.

In his argument of the general proposition that an owner of oranges, for instance, would be a positive fool to ship the fruit so green that's its quality was impaired if he expected to continue in the business for other seasons. The shipper and dealer receiving the fruit, he contends, are the logical and rightful judges of the condition of the consignment. His argument is aimed at the system, which undertakes to permit the exchange to fix the time at which shipments from the state may be made, resulting in a detriment to the owners of groves in which fruit ripens earlier than others."

St. Clair-Abrams wrote, "I cannot imagine any monopoly more odious than that which the citrus exchange is attempting to secure. While many of its aims and purposes are admirable and I heartily endorse them, its attempt to dragoon growers into joining it, the penalties it seeks to exact from men who do not join it and the close corporation it is attempting to establish are all utterly indefensible from any reasonable standpoint. It is no wonder that a great deal of excitement and indignation has been aroused by its present course.

I repeat that the claim that an immature orange is poisonous as fruit is the veriest rot and nonsense. It is simply not a sweet orange, it contains a great deal of citric acid and but very little sugar, so, for that matter, with lemons and limes; and we pick lemons and limes when they are green and let them turn yellow afterwards.

It must not be forgotten that when an orange or that matter any fruit, becomes fully ripe the process of decay begins. This is a law of nature. And this decay is either accelerated or retarded by circumstances; it can be arrested by refrigeration or exposure to cold; it can be hastened by heat or other conditions. If we wait until all the oranges are fully ripe on the trees, this very process of nature results in a heavy loss and the rotting of a large percentage before consumption. Our Florida oranges do not keep as well as California oranges because we have more juice and a larger percentage of sugar in them than there is in the California fruit.

If to ship an orange that is turning yellow in the latter part of September or in early October be injurious to public health, then one-third of the California fruit should be confiscated and destroyed.

The very men of the citrus exchange who are seeking the establishment of a monopoly in Florida are the most vociferous in denouncing railroad and other corporations and in assailing monopolies, and yet this citrus exchange corporation is seeking to establish in Florida a monopoly in restraint of trade; although for doing less than it is attempting we find the Standard Oil Company forced to disintegrate, the American Tobacco Company under the ban and other corporations ordered to dissolve by federal courts. I suppose that the gentlemen who are attempting to fasten this monopoly upon Florida will claim that they are protected by the "light of reason" rule of the supreme court of the United States, but I can see no "light of reason" in a proposition which compels a man to refuse 75 cents per box for his fruit on the trees under the penalty of having to pay 50 cents per box to the monopoly for daring to sell his fruit at a satisfactory price and afterwards sells this man's fruit and returns him an average of 10 cents per box.

Because of the tendency to impugn the motives of individuals, I repeat that I hold no brief for anybody, but as a citrus grower I am affected and, as much, I have been placed under the ban of this attempted monopoly and feel it my duty to all other growers to aid in the termination of the existing condition. Nor any howl or denunciation that I am endeavoring to authorize the shipping of immature fruit affect me in the slightest degree. I will not permit denunciation as to motives to deter me from resisting this palpable and undisguised attempt to monopolize the handling and sale of the entire crop of citrus fruits of the state.

If the citrus exchange can be reasonable and successful management secure such a monopoly, I have no objection, but attempt to secure it by penalizing men, subjecting them to criminal prosecutions and fine and imprisonment, or by confiscation of their property involve methods to which Russians and Turks may be accustomed but Americans will not tolerate."

The editors of the *Palatka News*, a newspaper that strongly opposed anything St. Clair-Abrams represented, distributed an editorial the following month, November 1911, in opposition to St. Clair-Abrams letter that stated, "The citrus exchange is an organization which four-fifths of the growers of the state not members will admit is doing excellent work throughout the entire country in the interests of the Florida orange. That organization, largely instrumental in securing the Florida green fruit law has taken upon itself the duty of seeing that the law is enforced. That is all. No, that isn't all. The men who are making the most vigorous "kick" against the enforcement of this law probably know most concerning the temporary profits to be derived from the sale of green fruit. Thousands of boxes of absolutely unripe oranges were shipped from Florida last year in September and the early days of October, misbranded "Parson Brown" and other varieties of oranges. What was the result? The Florida orange got a black eye to its original beauty and standing. No wonder these shippers of unripe, misbranded fruit wince. The Florida law does not prohibit the shipment of the earliest varieties of oranges – fruit that everyone knows is ripe within while still green without. It simply prohibits the shipment of unripe and misbranded fruit. The Federal pure food ruling simply stops artificially colored fruit. These are the righteous laws the Florida Citrus exchange is invoking and no Alexander St. Clair-Abrams or other writers will be able to convince the growers of the state that this organization is not doing them a real service."

Two years later, in September 1913, St. Clair-Abrams commented on the recent passing of a new green fruit law. He writes, "Of this nature is that delectable statute known as the immature citrus fruit law, which will be found on page 375 of the Acts of 1913. I had been invited to attend the meeting held in

Gainesville by the learned theorists who evolved this remarkable piece of legislation from their inner consciences, but declined to do so because I utterly disagreed with the proposed legislation. I well know, however, that its very absurdity would secure its enactment. Hence it did not surprise me when it was passed. Curious enough, it became a law without the approval of the Governor, a circumstance which surprised me, since, after signing the act which provided for a minimum length and width of bed sheets and towels in hotels, I do not understand why his excellency balked at this immature citrus fruit law.

If the law is to be strictly construed, as it will be, being in derogation of the common law, then it is perfectly safe to ship oranges and grapefruits during the month of August…since it is only between September 1 and November 5 that they are immature under the laws of this state. From November 6 until August 31 all citrus fruits are mature and can be shipped with impunity. Can anything in the shape of legislation be imagined more asinine or unreasonable? Of course, nobody in Florida thinks of shipping citrus fruits before September, yet the law, as it stands, allows them to do so.

Another curious provision of the law is…it is perfectly right and proper to ship them between September 1 and November 5 if they show an average on the trees of 'one half color indicating ripeness.' It follows then that it is not the amount of citric acid which determines the maturity or immaturity of citrus fruits but the color of the rind. Now what is meant by "half-color" is not stated. An orange or grapefruit in its early stage is a dark lustrous green and gradually becomes a light green before it turns yellow. Now, is the "half-color" the light green? Mind you, the statute doesn't say it shall become half yellow, but "half color." Now, people don't eat the rind either of oranges or grapefruit unless it is crystalized. The part consumed is the pulp. Under our wise legislation it is not the pulp that is the real test, but the color of the skin. Hence, an orange or grapefruit that is of a pale yellowish green is mature even if one has 5 per cent, and the other has 10 per cent, of citric acid.

Now what has been the results so far of this law? A friend of mine, who has a large grapefruit grove in Dade County, was in New

253

Orleans the middle of last month and there saw hundreds of crates of grapefruit imported from Cuba and Jamaica. Most of them were still green, while others had either turned yellow or were turning yellow, but all had been picked and shipped when green. As fast as the fruit turned yellow it was put on the market and was being sold at from $6.50 to $7.50 per crate. I learned that the same islands and also Porto Rico have been shipping grapefruit to New York for weeks, also picked green and held until they turned yellow, then put on the market and sold at high prices, and I noticed on the day previous this fruit was selling in New York at from $10.50 to $12 per crate. In the meantime, because of the law of this state, grapefruit in the same condition of maturity as the West Indies fruit, were permitted to hang upon the trees unpicked and unsold, through apprehension of seizure or criminal prosecution, If this law had not been passed the extreme southern end of the state could have commenced shipping of its grapefruit last month and have gotten large prices for it as the season advances the grapefruit in the more northern sections of the state would have commanded higher prices than they are now likely to. Cuba, Jamaica and Porto Rico have thus gotten the cream of prices for their grapefruit, while Florida will begin shipping and receiving largely reduced prices as a result of the unspeakable folly of this legislation. I have protested against it all along. I again most energetically protest against it."

TAKE IT TO THE UNITED STATES SUPREME COURT.

On January 15, 1913, St. Clair-Abrams and Frederick Bryan represented the Florida East Coast Railway Company in the United States Supreme Court regarding the appellant's appeal of the Interstate Commerce Commission's decision in favor of the Florida Fruit and Vegetable Shippers' Protective Agency rates as to pineapples, citrus fruits, and vegetables from places of production in Florida to exterior points of distribution or consumption. The Interstate Commerce Commission promulgated an order requiring the railway company to establish certain reduced rates.

The Florida East Coast Railway Company complied but made an appeal to the Commerce Court in June 1912. The Commerce Court upheld the decision of the Interstate Commerce Commission. The railway company then appealed to the United States Supreme Court. On June 8, 1914, the Supreme Court made their decision, with Chief Justice Edward Douglass White Jr. delivering the opinion of the court.

The Supreme Court reversed the findings of the lower court, which the shippers believed was due to some technicalities. The Florida East Coast Railroad Company advanced the rates on August 5, 1914, to the old basis.

The Florida East Coast Railroad Company was developed by Henry Morrison Flagler, who was partners with John D. Rockefeller in the Standard Oil Company. In 1912, Flagler arrived aboard the first train into Key West. That milestone marked the completion of the Over-Sea Railroad along the entire east coast of Florida. Flagler had first become acquainted with St. Clair-Abrams in 1878.

THE SOCIAL SIDE OF MIAMI.

THE MIAMI METROPOLIS MONDAY MARCH 15, 1915
MIAMI IN PARAGRAPH.

"Friends of Major Alexander St. Clair-Abrams, of Jacksonville, will be glad to learn that the threatened attack of pneumonia, is no longer dreaded. Major St. Clair-Abrams has been confined to his bed with a heavy cold, but is improving now. The major recently returned to Jacksonville from a business trip to Miami."

"Mrs. Strother Smith of Philadelphia, is expected in Jacksonville shortly after an absence of some time spent in the southern part of the state."

Mrs. Strother Smith is St. Clair-Abrams' only daughter, Irma, who was married to Rear Admiral William Strother Smith.

The Passing of Alfred.

Alfred, the only one of Joanna and Alex's three sons that lived to adulthood passed away after a long illness at his home in Tavares on May 5, 1915. He was forty-nine years old. He is buried in the St. Clair-Abrams' family mausoleum in the St. Mary's Cemetery at Evergreen Cemetery in Jacksonville.

Demoralization of the Democratic Party.

In September 1916, St. Clair-Abrams, a life-long democrat asserted that the new primary law in the State of Florida opens the way to demoralization of the democratic party.

He writes, "Our troubles have all arisen as a result of the factional legislation that has been enacted during the past fifteen to twenty years by the dominant party, calling itself democracy, in possession of the legislature and government of Florida. The very worst of this legislation was and is the primary laws which are now in the statute books. They affected no reform; they made no improvement of the old system of nomination by convention; they have opened the door to the worst wide-spread corruption and fraud; they have enabled republicans, socialists, populists and prohibitionists to control the majority of the democrats in the state; they have driven from office-seeking the ablest and best fitted men in the state."

Alex Prepares for Retirement.

In early February 1923, St. Clair-Abrams sold a 100-acre tract of a full bearing grove, located on the shores of Lake Eustis, between Tavares and Eustis, to Orlando grower George S. Marsh Jr.

This sale began St. Clair-Abrams in disposing of his Lake County properties and interests, as he prepared for retirement. His dream of Tavares, Eustis, Mount Dora, and a greater portion of the surrounding land becoming one city would not come to pass.

Marsh, a progressive citizen in Orange County, was confident that the new boulevard from Mount Dora to Tavares and through the grove to Eustis will add untold thousands in value to the property.

In March, 1923, the newspapers reported of St. Clair-Abrams' disposal of his Lake County properties, "Major St. Clair-Abrams of Jacksonville, the founder of Tavares, and whose memory will always be revered by the people of Lake County, has disposed of every parcel and tract of land he owns in Lake County, and can retire for life with a most comfortable income. Huntley and Burleigh of Tavares, has turned over $50,000 in property for the major during the year, and other realty concerns in the county have figured in other transactions.

A TRIBUTE TO GEORGE A. BUTLER.

LONG TIME RESIDENT OF TAVARES WHO DIED JULY 16, 1923
BY ALEXANDER ST. CLAIR-ABRAMS.

Permit me to pay tribute to the memory of my dear friend, George A. Butler. Excepting myself he was the last survivor of the few I brought to Tavares over forty years ago when I started to lay out and found the town.

He was, I think, a native of Tallahassee, his parents being natives of Nassau. I first made his acquaintance more than forty years ago when he was employed as a clerk in a store in Orlando. Subsequently, I employed him as a clerk in my law office in that town. From that time until the dreadful freezes of 1883 and 1894, which compelled me to leave Tavares and move to Jacksonville, he was not only an employee, but the most cherished, devoted and affectionate friend I ever had.

Our relations were more those of brothers than employer and employee. His integrity was absolute. The greater part of the more than half million dollars I expended in building the town and railroads passed through his hands. Necessarily I was absent a great deal of the time. I would sign blank checks and leave them with him to fill up so as to defray the expenses of the work while I was absent and he never failed on my return to present me with a tabulated statement of every dollar he had spent. Blunt in speech and at times rather eccentric in his views, he was nevertheless always the very soul of honor. He was absolutely incorruptible; neither flattery nor compensation could swerve him from what he thought was right. As a husband and father, he was devoted and affectionate; as a citizen he was absolutely without reproach.

Few men have lived with less in their lives for censure or blame than he; and still fewer whose lives were as stainless and without reproach as his was. The few faults he had were forgotten in his many virtues.

I cannot without emotion, and a heart suffering with grief at his passing away, dictate this little tribute in his memory, feeling that words cannot express the thoughts that crowd into my mind of the many years of our warm and devoted friendship, and of my regard and affection for him, which I know was fully reciprocated. And I feel that when he died Tavares lost one of its very best citizens and that as the years pass by his memory will be more and more revered and honored.

I am now the only survivor of the few men I carried to Tavares when I started to build the town. In the years that are to come when the history of Tavares shall be written I trust that the name of George A. Butler will appear in it as one of its most devoted workers who did more than his duty as a pioneer of the town in helping to build it up, and who labored night and day to promote its prosperity and the welfare and happiness of its people.

Personally, I cherish the hope that our parting is only temporary and that in the great Hereafter we will meet again holding the same affection and regard for each other that held us bound together on this earth as with bands of steel for more than forty years.

Letcher Bryan, W. H. Latimer, S. B. Harrington and Musto Givens - all gone, and now George A. Butler. The ghosts of these men stand around me beckoning me to join them in the world "where the wicked cease from troubling and the weary are at rest" and enjoy an eternity of peace and happiness. At least I hope so. And as on earth George A. Butler will continue to be my closest and dearest friend.

BADLY BEATEN BY CALVIN COOLIDGE.

After the presidential election of 1924, St. Clair-Abrams expressed his opinion to the press as to why his candidate John W. Davis was pummeled at the polls by Mr. Coolidge.

On November 15, 1924, the *Tampa Times* wrote, "One of the diversions in perusing literature growing out of the recent quadrennial election is in observing the various reasons assigned for the triumph of Calvin Coolidge and the failure of the other aspirants to the presidency to win the coveted plum. Here, for example, is an old Confederate soldier, a citizen whose home is in Jacksonville, Fla., who voted for Mr. Davis, and greatly admired the West Virginia-New York lawyer, who writes interestingly. His name is A. St. Clair-Abrams. He begins by saying the expected has happened. 'John W. Davis, decidedly the best qualified of the three aspirants,' he affirms, 'has been badly beaten by Calvin Coolidge, notwithstanding his many advantages in point of statesmanship and mental ability.'

'The result of the election,' Mr. Abrams continues, 'shows that Davis was and is not a vote-getter; it further demonstrates that Mr. Davis is not a politician. His selecting Governor Bryan of Nebraska as his running-mate was the poorest piece of political strategy imaginable. It drove thousands of democrats all over the country into voting for Coolidge. Even in the rock-bound Democratic Southern states the nomination of Bryan alienated thousands of Democrats. But I believe in common with many other Democrats that the responsibility for the Democratic defeat rest upon Southern Democratic delegations to the National convention. Defeating Governor Alfred Smith made certain the election of Coolidge.'

Mr. Abrams in summing up the cause for the defeat of the Democratic ticket, says: 1. The reaction against the excessive demands of the labor unions and the astounding assumptions of the radical elements. 2. A revolt by thousands of Democrats in the East and West against the truculent spirit displayed by the Southern delegates to the National convention. 3. The utter failure of the Teapot Dome investigation as a political factor in the aid of Democracy. 4. The determination of the American people to destroy radicalism which has become rampant.

Meanwhile, Back in Tavares.

In November 1925, Mayor Jesse Hunter of Tavares indicated that residents of outlying districts wanted to become part of the city of Tavares. The *Orlando Evening Star* wrote, "Extension of limits of this city was decided as immediately as necessary by a representative gathering of citizens at the Biltavern Hotel recently. Mayor Hunter, who presided, placed the question before the meeting, stating that he was of the opinion that considerable territory lying just outside the present limits was benefitting directly from the progress made by Tavares, and that the property holders in the territory affected were both willing and ready to be taken into the city.

Tavares, at present, has a very restricted area for its population as compared with other towns and cities in Florida. The original town laid out by Major St. Clair-Abrams has grown to considerable extent; in fact, while the original plat remains much the same as when drawn. The last undeveloped section of the city, that lying along Lake Eustis, has been recently opened for residences and streets, water and electric lighting, in conformance with plans and specifications governing the rest of the city, are being installed.

This additional territory will afford some relief, but present indications are such as to show need of more space within the city limits."

The Men Who Wore Gray.

In March 1929, eighty-four-year-old St. Clair-Abrams was still actively involved with the Florida Division, United Confederate Veterans. On March 14, 1929, in Tallahassee, appointments to the general staff were made by Major-General T. J. Appleyard, commander of the organization. St. Clair-Abrams was appointed judge advocate-general with the rank of lieutenant-colonel.

The United Confederate Veterans was organized in St. Clair-Abrams' hometown of New Orleans on June 10, 1889. St. Clair-Abrams close friend from Georgia, General John B. Gordon, was elected the organization's first commander in chief - a position he held until he passed away in 1904.

St. Clair-Abrams never forgot the War Between the States and reminisced with his compatriots throughout his lifetime. As the years passed, he became equally proud to be an American citizen and loyal to the United States flag. The United Confederate Veterans and the Grand Army of the Republic (the fraternal organization of Union veterans) would assist each other in the planning of events, parades, social functions, reunions, fund raising, and much more.

FAREWELL MAJOR.

Major Alexander St. Clair-Abrams, long a resident of Jacksonville and once a powerful figure in the state, died here yesterday, June 5, 1931, noon at his home, 566 May Street.

Death came to Major St. Clair-Abrams in his 86th year and after a brilliant career as a soldier, lawyer, editor, and public servant.

Surviving him are his daughter, Mrs. William Strother Smith, Washington D. C., a grandson, Alex St. Clair-Abrams Jr., two granddaughters, Mrs. Clara Gramling, New York City, and Mrs. George H. Kennedy, Jr., Worcester, Massachusetts, and four great-grandchildren, John Carrington Gramling, Jr., Claire Ellen Gramling, Madelin Gramling, and Douglas Kennedy.

Funeral services for the Major were held at 3:00 o'clock yesterday afternoon from St. Paul's Catholic Church. The Reverend Father D. A. Lyons, pastor of the church, officiated.

Pallbearers were: Honorary, Thomas P. Denham, Judge W. H. Baker, Judge George Couper Gibbs, J. C. Cooper Sr., Judge A. G. Hartridge, Colonel W. E. Kay, Judge DeWitt T. Gray, E. J. L'Engle, F. C. Russell Sr., C. D. Rinehart, and E. P. Axtell. Active, Charles

P. Cooper, R. P. Daniel, Miles W. Lewis, W. A. Hallowes Jr., Raleigh O. Dowling, and Lorenzo Baldwin.

The interment was in the family mausoleum in St. Mary's Cemetery with Moulton & Kyle in charge of arrangements.

Scores of friends and acquaintances attended the funeral services yesterday afternoon to pay last respects to one of Florida's most able barristers. The services were among the most impressive services held in Jacksonville.

RESOLUTION FROM THE FLORIDA BAR.

MAJOR ALEXANDER ST. CLAIR-ABRAMS, a distinguished member of this bar, recently died at a ripe age, full of years and honors, and it is fitting that this Bar should honor his memory in an appropriate manner.

Major Abrams during his long public and professional life, notably contributed, to the upbuilding of the State of Florida, to the making of its laws, and to their enforcement in its Courts. In his early career he served with distinction in the Confederate Army, and his services and valor were, at that time, appropriately remembered by his friends. His versatility and ability exhibited themselves in distinguished work in the newspaper field, abroad, as well as in his own country. His talents as a lawyer were recognized by a large clientele over a long period of years. He was a kind and generous friend. His fidelity, ability and industry as an advocate and counselor rendered his services notable and outstanding.

BE IT RESOLVED That this Bench and Bar express their keen sense of loss in the death of their distinguished brother Alexander St. Clair-Abrams, and that a copy of this preamble and resolution be recorded in the Minutes of this Court and that a copy be furnished the Press of the City.

Jacksonville, Florida, July 3rd, 1931.

William H. Baker   Miles W. Lewis
Richard P. Daniel
Committee.

Epilogue

It is impossible to fit the amazing life and career of Major Alexander St. Clair-Abrams into one single body of work. A volume could be written for each of his careers - Soldier-correspondent during the War Between the States, Newspaper Editor and Reporter, Attorney at Law, and his political career - as an elected and appointed official and as a delegate.

During the War Between the States, St. Clair-Abrams was cited twice for bravery - at the Siege of Vicksburg and at Oostanaula River during the Battle of Resaca, Georgia. At the beginning of his service in the Confederate Army, he served as an aide to two Louisiana commanders.

St. Clair-Abrams and Joanna's only daughter, Irma, passed away on May 8, 1934, at the age of sixty. The press initially wrote that she had committed suicide based on the certificate of suicide issued by the District Coroner in Washington D. C. She was found unconscious in her bedroom at the historic Wyoming Apartments. They transported her to the Emergency Hospital, where she died.

The suicide conclusion was based on a note Irma left for her daughter, Mrs. George Kennedy that read, "I died in my sleep." Her daughter had been on her way to Washington to be with her mother during Irma's illness. Irma may have felt that she wouldn't last the night, and therefore left the note to assure her daughter that there was no foul-play involved.

Irma was married to Rear Admiral William Strother Smith, who passed

William Strother Smith

away on September 6, 1927, a few days prior to his seventieth birthday. Smith had been a cadet at the Naval Academy and graduated in 1880. During the Spanish-American War he served aboard the *Columbia* and the *Yankee*. He was the Chairman of the Naval Advisory Board and led a team to construct the Naval Research Laboratory in Washington D. C. He retired from the Navy after forty-five years of service. Admiral Smith and Irma are buried at Arlington National Cemetery.

St. Clair-Abrams had named the main thoroughfare through old Tavares in honor of Irma, but later, the city changed the name to Main Street. Lake Irma and Irma Road near the St. Clair-Abrams' original 1875 homestead, were named for her.

St. Clair-Abrams and Joanna had two sons who passed away in infancy. One son, named Alexander St. Clair-Abrams Jr., was born on February 25, 1884, and passed on April 10, 1884. Junior is buried in the family mausoleum in Jacksonville.

St. Clair-Abrams signed his name with a hyphen. St. Clair was his mother's maiden name. St. Clair is a French-Latin surname, with its origins in Normandy, France. The name moved into the British Isles, primarily in Scotland, in 1066 A. D.

His father's name, Abrams, was derived from the name Abraham, which means the chief or father of the multitude. The Abrams surname has an early history in the British Isles.

His colleagues, friends, and foes had many nicknames for him through the years that included the monikers - the Volcanic Creole and Vesuvius. In 1875, a rival newspaper reporter in Memphis quipped about St. Clair-Abrams using a hyphen in his name when he wrote, "A. St. Clair Abrams, of the Atlanta *News*, uses a hyphen in his name, and he is therefore called a 'hyphen-nuten' editor." St. Clair-Abrams went through most of his life with the title Major. There were

Hyphen-nuten!

many newspaper accounts that used the military titles of captain and colonel as well. The honorary titles were most likely derived from his involvement with the United Confederate Veterans organization.

There was an incident during the War Between the States when he went to pick up a new uniform and was given a captain's uniform. There are some documents and newspaper articles that refer to him as Major soon after the war.

St. Clair-Abrams spoke fluent French and classical Latin. He belonged to several community and civic organizations throughout his life that included membership in the National Rifle Association soon after the organization formed in 1871. In later years, he visited Clifton Springs, New York, for the Sulphur water springs. The springs - combined with a strong religious faith - were believed to restore the vigor of youth.

In 1887, the Dickson Manufacturing Company named a 4-4-0 locomotive after St. Clair-Abrams.

St. Clair-Abrams has two homes currently standing today. His home at 1649 Osceola Street in Jacksonville was listed on the National Register of Historic Places in 1985 as part of the Riverside Historic District. His home on New Hampshire Avenue, one of his original eight cottages in Tavares, has a plaque mounted on the front of the home that designates his induction into the "Great Floridians 2000" program. Abrams Road in Eustis and St. Clair-Abrams Avenue in Tavares are named for him.

Though Tavares continued to grow through the decades that followed St. Clair-Abrams' departure, the city went through many highs and lows. The citizens, at times, struggled to maintain the characteristic identity of its small-town charm. Much of their role as the County Seat was as the *place to go* for court or jail or to file official documents.

A series of "town hall" meetings began in 2006 to establish a plan for Tavares. The meetings resulted in the creation of a vision statement that begins, "Tavares, the Capital Waterfront City of Lake County, building on a historic foundation..." In 2007, Tavares began implementing its plan. The city reached back in time to the dawn of aviation when, in 1914, Tony Jannus, the first licensed airline pilot, landed his Benoit XIV airboat onto Lake Eustis and Clara Adams, known as the "maiden of maiden voyages" landed as a passenger in a Thomas Flying Boat, also on Lake Eustis. With that history, Tavares branded itself *America's Seaplane City.*

In April 2010, Tavares held a ribbon-cutting ceremony of its new Seaplane Base located at Wooton Park on Lake Dora that included (at that time) Governor Charlie Crist, Senator Alan Hayes, Tavares Mayor Robert Wolfe, Vice-Mayor Lori Pfister, Councilmembers Sandy Gamble, Kirby Smith, and the author, Bob Grenier, as well as former mayor, Nancy Clutts, Historical Society of Tavares board member, Brenda Smith, and City Administrator, John Drury, who had conceived the idea.

In a magazine interview, Drury stated, "We didn't just develop a plan and let it sit on the shelf. After all, a vision without implementation is just a hallucination." This sentiment by Drury resonates an attitude reminiscent of St. Clair-Abrams.

In a 2010 interview, this author was asked what St. Clair-Abrams would have thought about the new Seaplane brand. I responded, "St. Clair-Abrams would have been absolutely delighted and proud to see what Tavares has become. I believe he would have been front and center if he were here."

The success of the Seaplane Base has been phenomenal and Tavares continues to prosper as it builds on a historic foundation and the inspiration of its founder.

In 1864, nineteen-year-old soldier-correspondent, Alex St. Clair-Abrams wrote and published the novel, "The Trials of the Soldier's Wife." The novel was based on true stories he witnessed from several different soldiers. He wrote the book while in the camps and battlefields during the War Between the States.

The story, as read today, is a period piece, but when St. Clair-Abrams wrote it, the story was current, and unfolded around him as a young Southerner. Though there are many grammatical errors and misspellings, it was a well-crafted story. St. Clair-Abrams did his best to phonetically spell the words of the characters' accents, as well as the vernacular of the time. I, as the author of this biography, kept his self-admitted errors in the text.

As the modern-day reader will encounter, "The Trials of a Soldier's Wife" and the 1864 book review, *will* place you in the perspective of Southern patriots of the Nineteenth Century.

In a December 1, 1864, issue of the *Greensboro Patriot*, the book reviewer wrote, "This revolution has produced only a few books which bear the impress of brilliant genius and splendid fancy. Especially is this remarkable, when there have been so many and such startling and thrilling incidents as the foundation for the most interesting and captivating novels and novelettes. This can be accounted for only on the supposition, that all the best talent of the country, is occupied in the prosecution of the war and in the achievement of Southern independence.

A few days ago, Alex St. Clair-Abrams, the Author of the siege of Vicksburg, laid upon our table "The Trials of the Soldier's Wife." We have read his little book. In it there is a good moral, one which should be impressed upon our people in every conceivable way. Though the work is full of typographical errors and the style is not altogether accurate and far from elegant; yet some of the characters, that are, new cursing our land and in a good measure destroying our cause, are depicted with such graphicness and truthfulness, that we humbly conceive the work will be highly useful to the reading public.

He draws the character of a libertine in such colors as to make one shudder, that such men are dishonoring God and their own sex and race. None can read what is said of Horace Antry [sic] without his blood boiling and the quiet of the most placid nature being disturbed. He paints a speculator in such style as would enrage the most cool and indifferent heart - and he draws, in the liveliest manner, the flint-hearted speculator and follows him through the crooked windings of his black and diabolical mind. He, also, gives the history of Eva Wentworth in the most touching manner, and in that character illustrates most forcibly the condition, troubles, hardships and oppressions of a refugee. Here a sublime moral lesson can be learned, our duty to these true and patriotic men and women, who have been compelled to flee their homes and forego the pleasures of a quiet life on the spot where their affections centre. We do not think the plot is well conceived, or that the characters are, as a general thing, well sustained. Still, it is a readable book, and whoever runs through it will feel that he has learned much that he can carry with him out into the great battles of life.

We saw several copies of Mr. Abrams' new book in the book store of Messrs. Sterling, Campbell & Co., of this place, a few days ago. There all, who wish to read this book, can procure it at a reasonable Confederate price. Mr. Abrams has received a severe wound, from which he may never altogether recover. This itself ought to bespeak for his work a liberal encouragement. Buy it, and you give some money to a gallant and patriotic soldier, one who has bared his breast to the death-blows of the enemy, who acted nobly and intrepidity on some of our bloodiest fields. Go, purchase it, encourage this hero, learn the invaluable lessons taught in it, and you will never regret the outlay of money made in its purchase."

THE TRIALS
OF
THE SOLDIER'S WIFE:

A TALE OF THE
SECOND AMERICAN REVOLUTION.

BY ALEX. ST. CLAIR ABRAMS.

ATLANTA, GEORGIA:
1864.

Entered according to act of Congress, in the year 1864,
BY THE AUTHOR,
In the Clerk's Office of the District Court of the Confederate States
for the Northern District of Georgia.

DEDICATION

TO
COLONEL JOHN H. JOSSEY.
Of Macon, Georgia.

MY DEAR SIR --

Accept from me the dedication of this little work as a token of appreciation for the kind friendship you have ever displayed towards me. Wishing you all the happiness and prosperity that can fall to mortal man, believe me.

Your Friend,

THE AUTHOR.

PREFACE.

The plot of this little work was first thought of by the writer in the month of December, 1862, on hearing the story of a soldier from New Orleans, who arrived from Camp Douglas just in time to see his wife die at Jackson, Mississippi. Although the Press of that city made no notice of it, the case presented itself as a fit subject for a literary work. If the picture drawn in the following pages appears exaggerated to our readers, they will at least recognize the moral it contains as truthful.

Trusting that the public will overlook its many defects, the Author yet hopes there will be found in this little book, matter of sufficient interest to while away the idle hour of the reader.

ATLANTA, April 20th, 1864.

CHAPTER FIRST.
THE "CRESCENT CITY" -- THE HUSBAND'S DEPARTURE.

Kind reader, have you ever been to New Orleans? If not, we will attempt to describe the metropolis of the Confederate States of America.

New Orleans is situated on the Mississippi river, and is built in the shape of a crescent, from which it derives the appellation of "Crescent City." The inhabitants -- that is, the educated class - are universally considered as the most refined and aristocratic members of society on the continent. When we say aristocratic, we do not mean a pretension of superiority above others, but that elegance and etiquette which distinguish the 'parvenu' of society, and the vulgar, but wealthy class of citizens with which this country is infested. The ladies of New Orleans are noted for their beauty and refinement, and are certainly, as a general thing, the most accomplished class of females in the South, except the fair reader into whose hands this work may fall.

It was in the month of May, 1861, that our story commences. Secession had been resorted to as the last chance left the South for a preservation of her rights. Fort Sumter, had fallen, and from all parts of the land troops were pouring to meet the threatened invasion of their homes. As history will record, New Orleans was not idle in those days of excitement. Thousands of her sons came forward at the first call, and offered their services for the good of the common cause, and for weeks the city was one scene of excitement from the departure of the different companies to Virginia.

Among the thousands who replied to the first call of their country, was Alfred Wentworth, the confidential clerk of one of the largest commission houses in the city. He was of respectable family, and held a high position in society, both on account of his respectability and the elevated talent he had displayed during his career in the world. He had been married for about five years, and two little children - one a light-eyed girl of four summers, and the other an infant of two years -- were the small family with which heaven had blessed him.

After joining a company of infantry, and signing the muster roll, Alfred returned home to his wife and informed her of what he had done, expecting that she would regret it. But the patriotic heart of his wife would not reproach him for having performed his duty; so, heaving a sigh as she looked at the child in her arms, and the little girl on her father's knee, a tear trickled down her flushed cheek as she bade him God-speed. The time that elapsed between his enlistment and departure for the seat of war, was spent by Alfred Wentworth in providing a home for his family, so that in the event of his being killed in battle, they should not want. Purchasing a small residence on Prytania street, he removed his family into it and concluded his business in time for his departure.

The morning of the twenty-second of May broke brightly over the far-famed "Crescent City." Crowds of citizens were seen congregating on Canal Street to witness the departure of two more regiments of Orleanians. The two regiments were drawn up in line between Camp and Carondelet streets, and their fine uniforms, glistening muskets and soldierly appearance created a feeling of pride among the people. They were composed principally of Creoles and Americans, proper. The handsome, though dark complexions of the Creoles could be seen lit up with enthusiasm, in conversation with the dark-eyed Creole beauties of the city, while the light-haired and fair-faced sons of the Crescent City were seen mingling among the crowd of anxious relatives who thronged to bid them farewell.

Apart from the mass of volunteers -- who had previously stacked their arms -- Alfred Wentworth and his wife were bidding that agonizing farewell, which only those who have parted from loved one can feel. His little bright-eyed daughter was clasped in his arms, and every minute he would stoop over his infant and kiss its tiny cheeks. Marks of tears were on the eyelids of his wife, but she strove to hide them, and smiled at every remark made by her daughter. They were alone from the eyes of a curious crowd. Each person present had too much of his own acquaintances to bid farewell, to notice the speechless farewell which the soldier gave his wife. With one arm clasped around her, and the other holding his daughter, Alfred Wentworth gazed long and earnestly at the features of his wife and children, as if to impress the features of those loved ones still firmer in his mind.

"Attention, battalion!" rang along the line in stentorian tones, and the voices of the company officers calling "fall in, boys, fall in!" were heard in the streets. Clasping his wife to his heart, and imprinting a fond, fond kiss of love upon her cheeks, and embracing his children, the soldier took his place in the ranks, and after the necessary commands, the volunteers moved forward. A crowd of their relatives followed them to the depot of the New Orleans, Jackson and Great Northern Railroad, and remained until the cars were out of sight. After the troops had entered, and the train was slowly moving off, one of the soldiers jumped from the platform, and, embracing a lady who stood near, exclaimed: *"Farewell, dearest Eva! God bless you and the children -- we shall meet again."* As soon as he spoke, Alfred Wentworth sprang into the cars again and was soon swiftly borne from the city.

Mrs. Wentworth remained standing where her husband had left her, until the vast crowd had dispersed, and nothing could be seen of the train but a thin wreath of smoke emerging from the tree-tops in the distance. Calling the colored nurse, who had followed with the children, she bade her return home, and accompanied her back to her now lonely residence.

CHAPTER SECOND.
THE WIFE AND CHILDREN -- A VISITOR

The weeks passed slowly to Mrs. Wentworth from the departure of her husband; but her consciousness that he was performing his duty to his country, and the letters he wrote from Virginia, cheered her spirits, and, in a measure, made her forget his absence.

She was alone one evening with her children, who had become the sole treasures of her heart, and on whom she lavished every attention possible, when the ringing of the bell notified her of the presence of a visitor. Calling the servant, she bade her admit the person at the door. The negro left the room to do her mistress' bidding, and shortly after, a handsome gentleman of about thirty-five years of age entered.

"Good morning, Mrs. Wentworth," he said, on entering the room. "I trust yourself and children are in good health."

Mrs. Wentworth rose from her chair, and, slightly inclining her head, replied: "To what circumstance am I indebted for the honor of this visit, Mr. Awtry?"

"Nothing very particular, madam," he replied; "but hearing of your husband's departure, I thought I should take the liberty of paying a visit to an old acquaintance, and of offering my services, if you should ever need them."

"I thank you for your kindness; and should I 'ever' need your services, you may depend upon my availing myself of your offer; although," she added, "I do not think it likely I shall stand in need of any assistance."

"I rejoice to hear it, my dear madam," he replied; "but I trust," he continued, on noticing the look of surprise which covered her features, "that you will not think my offer in the least insulting; for I can assure you, it was only prompted by the most friendly motives, and the recollections of past days."

Mrs. Wentworth made no reply, and he continued: "I hope that, after an absence of five years, the memory of the past has been banished from you. With me things have changed materially. The follies of my youth have, I trust, been expiated, and I am a different man now to what I was when I last saw you."

"Mr. Awtry," replied Mrs. Wentworth, "I feel rather surprised that, after your presence in New Orleans for so many months, you should not have thought proper to renew our acquaintance until after the departure of my husband."

"Pardon me," he quickly answered. "I was introduced to your husband by a mutual friend; and as he never thought proper to extend an invitation to me, I did not think myself authorized to call here. Learning of his departure this morning, and knowing that his circumstances were not of so favorable a character as he could wish, I thought you might pardon my presumption in calling on you when you learned the motive which actuated this visit -- believe me, I am sincere; and now," he continued, "will you accept my proffered hand of friendship, and believe that my desire is only to aid the relatives of one of the gallant men who have gone to struggle for their rights?"

Mrs. Wentworth paused a moment before she accepted the extended hand, while her brow appeared clouded. At length, holding out her hand to him, she said: "I accept your offered friendship, Mr. Awtry, in the same spirit, as I hope, it is given; but, at the same time, trust you shall never be troubled with any importunities from me."

"Thank you -- thank you," he replied eagerly; "I shall not prove otherwise than worthy of your friendship. These are your children?" he continued, changing the conversation.

"Yes," she replied, with a look of pride upon her little daughter and the sleeping infant on the sofa; "these are my little family."

Mr. Awtry took the little girl upon his knees and commenced caressing it, and, after remaining for a few moments in unimportant conversation, took his departure with the promise to call at some future time.

As soon as he left Mrs. Wentworth sat down, and resting her hands on the table, spoke to herself on the visit she had received. "What could have induced him to pay me this visit?" she said, musingly; "it is strange -- very strange that he should choose this particular time to renew our acquaintance! He spoke honestly, however, and may be sincere in his offers of assistance, should I ever need anything. He is wealthy, and can certainly aid me." She sat there musing, until the little girl, coming up to her, twined her tiny arms round her mother's neck, and asked if it was not time to light the gas.

"Yes, darling," said Mrs. Wentworth, kissing her fondly; "call Betsy and let her get a light."

After the negro had lit the gas, Mrs. Wentworth said to her, "Should that gentleman, who was here to-day, call at any time again, let me know before you admit him."

"Yes, mistis," replied the negro with a curtsey.

CHAPTER THIRD.
MR. HORACE AWTRY.

Mr. Horace Awtry was a native of the State of New York, and was, at the time of writing, about thirty-live years of age. He was a tall and well-formed man, with light hair clustering in curls on a broad and noble looking forehead; his features were well chiselled, and his upper lip was ornamented with a mustache of the same color as his hair. Notwithstanding his handsome features and extravagant display of dress, there was an expression in his dark blue eyes, which, though likely to captivate the young and innocent portion of the fair sex, was not deemed elegant by those who are accustomed to read the features of man. He was very wealthy, but was a perfect type of the 'roue', although a good education and remarkable control of himself rendered it difficult for his acquaintances to charge him with dissipation, or any conduct unworthy of ft gentleman. As this gentleman will occupy a somewhat conspicuous position in our tale, we deem it necessary to go into these particulars.

Some seven years previous to her marriage, and while yet a child, Mrs. Wentworth, with her father, the only surviving relative she had, spent the summer at Saratoga Springs in the State of New York, and there met Mr. Awtry, who was then a handsome and dashing young man. Struck by her beauty, and various accomplishments, he lost no time in making her acquaintance, and before her departure from the Springs, offered her his hand. To his utter astonishment, the proposal was rejected, with the statement that she was already engaged to a gentleman of New Orleans. This refusal would have satisfied any other person, but Horace Awtry was not a man to yield so easily; he, therefore, followed her to New Orleans on her return, and endeavored, by every means in his power, to supplant Alfred Wentworth in the affections of Eva Seymour -- Mrs. Wentworth's maiden name -- and in the confidence of her father. Failing in this, and having the mortification of seeing them married, he set to work and succeeded in ruining Mr. Seymour in business, which accounts for the moderate circumstances in which we find Mrs. Wentworth and her husband at the commencement of this book. Worn out by his failure in business and loss of fortune, Mr. Seymour died shortly after his daughter's marriage, without knowing who caused his misfortunes, and Horace Awtry returned to the North. After being absent for several years, he came back to New Orleans some months before the departure of Mrs. Wentworth's husband, but never called upon her until after he had left, when she was surprised at the visit narrated in the foregoing chapter.

This gentleman was seated in the portico of the St. Charles Hotel a few mornings after his visit to Mrs. Wentworth, and by his movements of impatience was evidently awaiting the arrival of someone. At last, a young man ran down the steps leading from the apartments, and he rose hurriedly to meet him.

"You are the very man I have been waiting to see," said Horace Awtry; "you must excuse my apparent neglect in not calling on you before."

"Certainly, my dear fellow," replied the gentleman. "I am certain your reasons are good for not attending to your arrangement punctually - by the way," he continued, "who the deuce was that lady I saw you escorting to church last Sunday?"

"An acquaintance of mine that I had not seen for years, until a few days ago chance threw me in her path and I paid her a visit."

"Ha, ha, ha," laughed his companion. "I understand; but who is she, and her name? She is very pretty," he continued, gravely.

"Hush, Charlie!" replied Horace; "come to my room in the St. Louis Hotel, and I will tell you all about it."

"Wait a moment, my friend, and let me get some breakfast," he replied.

"Pooh!" said Horace, "we can have breakfast at Galpin's after I have conversed with you at my room; or," he continued, "I will order a breakfast and champagne to be brought up to my room."

"As you like," said the other, taking a couple of cigars from his pocket and offering one to his companion.

After lighting their cigars, the two men left the hotel, and purchasing the New York 'Herald' and 'News' from the news-dealer below, proceeded to the St. Louis Hotel, where Horace ordered a breakfast and champagne for himself and guest.

Throwing himself on one of the richly-covered couches that ornamented the apartment, Charles Bell -- for that was the name of the gentleman -- requested his friend to inform him who the lady was that he escorted to church.

"Well, my dear friend," said Horace, "as you appear so desirous to know I will tell you. I met that lady some seven years ago at Saratoga Springs. If she is now beautiful, she was ten times so then, and I endeavored to gain her affections. She was, however, engaged to another young man of this city, and on my offering her my hand in marriage, declined it on that ground. I followed her here with the intention of supplanting her lover in her affections, but it was of no avail; they were married, and the only satisfaction I could find was to ruin her father, which I did, and he died shortly after without a dollar to his name."

"So, she is married?" interrupted his companion.

"Yes, and has two children," replied Horace.

"Where is her husband?"

"He left for Virginia some time ago, where I sincerely trust he will get a bullet through his heart," was the very charitable rejoinder.

"What! do you desire to marry his widow?" asked his friend.

"No, indeed," he replied; "but you see they are not in very good circumstances, and if he were once dead, she would be compelled to work for a living, as they have no relatives in this State, and only a few in Baltimore. To gain my object, I should pretend that I desired to befriend her -- send the two children to some nurse, and then have her all to myself. This," continued the villain, "is the object with which I have called upon her" –

"And paid a visit to church for the first time in your life," said Bell, laughing; "but," he resumed, "it is not necessary for you to wish the husband dead -- why not proceed to work at once?"

"Well, so I would, but she is so very particular, that on the slightest suspicion she would take the alarm and communicate to her husband the fact of my having renewed my acquaintance with her, which would, perhaps, bring him home on furlough."

"Nonsense," replied his friend, "the secessionists need every man to assist them in driving back McDowell, and there is no chance of any furloughs being granted; besides which, we are on the eve of a great battle, and for any of the men to ask for a furlough would lay him open to the charge of cowardice."

"That may be all true," said Horace, "but I shall not venture on anything more as yet. As far as I have gone, she believes me actuated by no other motives than the remembrance of my former affection for her, and, with that belief, places implicit trust in me."

The conversation was here interrupted by the appearance of two waiters, one carrying a waiter filled with different descriptions of food, and the other a small basket containing six bottles of champagne. After setting them on a table, Horace inquired what the charges were.

"Twelve dollars, sah," was the reply.

Horace took out his pocket book, and throwing the man a

twenty-dollar gold piece, told him to pay for the breakfast and champagne, and purchase cigars with the remainder.

The negroes having left, Horace Awtry and his friend proceeded to discuss their breakfast and champagne. After eating for a few minutes in silence, Horace suddenly said:

"Charlie, what do you think of this war?"

"My opinion is, that the South has got in a pretty bad dilemma," replied that gentleman.

"That is identically my impression, but for heaven's sake do not let anyone hear you say so. The people are half crazed with excitement, and the slightest word in favor of the North may lay you at the mercy of an infuriated mob."

"What do you intend doing, now the ports are blockaded, and no one can leave the country?" asked his friend.

"Why, remain here and pretend all the friendship possible for the South. Maybe I will get a contract or two, which will further the design of covering my opinions on this contest."

"Such was my idea, but I am afraid that the secesh government will issue their cotton bonds until all the gold is driven from the States, and then we will have nothing but their worthless paper money," replied Bell.

"I have thought of that, and made up my mind to convert all the property I have here into gold at once, which will give me between sixty and seventy thousand dollars, and as fast as I make any of the bonds from contracts, I will sell them for whatever gold they will bring."

"That's a capital idea, my dear follow," said Bell, rising from his chair and slapping Awtry on the shoulder; "I think I shall follow your plan."

The cigars having been brought in, after a few minutes of unimportant conversation, Charles Bell left his friend, with the arrangement to meet at the Varieties theatre in the evening, and Horace Awtry, divesting himself of his clothing, retired to sleep until the evening should come.

CHAPTER FOURTH.
A POLITIC STROKE -- THE TELEGRAPHIC DISPATCH.

June and half of July had sped swiftly away. The great battle, which everybody daily expected, had been fought, and the Yankee army ignominiously defeated. As every one of our readers are well acquainted with this battle, I shall not go into any details; enough; as history will tell, to know that it resulted in a glorious victory to the Confederate army, and covered the gallant Southerners with honor.

On the arrival of dispatches giving an account of this victory, to use a vulgar phrase, New Orleans "ran wild." The excitement and exultation of the people were beyond description, and during the same night that the news was received, one scene of gayety was observed in the city. There was one heart, however, that did not share the joy and merriment so universal among the people. In the privacy of her dwelling, with her two children nearby, Mrs. Wentworth spent a night of prayer and anxiety, and next morning rose from her bed with the same feeling of anxiety to know whether her husband had escaped unhurt. At about ten o'clock in the morning, a knock was heard at the door, and soon after Mr. Awtry entered.

"How are you this morning, Mrs. Wentworth?" he said, taking her little daughter in his arms and kissing her; "so we have gained a great victory in Virginia."

"Yes," she replied; "but I do feel so anxious to know if my husband is safe."

"Do not think for a moment otherwise," he answered; "why a soldier's wife should not show half as much solicitude as you do."

"I am, indeed, very desirous of knowing his fate and I am sure the fact of being a soldier's wife does not prevent my feeling a desire to ascertain if he is unhurt, or if he is" -- she paused at the thought which seemed so horrid in her imagination, and lowering her face in her hands, burst into tears.

"Mother, what are you crying for?" asked her little daughter, who was sitting on Mr. Awtry's knees.

"My dear madam," said Mr. Awtry, "why do you give way to tears? If you desire," he continued, "I will telegraph to Virginia and learn if your husband is safe."

"Thank you -- thank you!" she answered eagerly; "I shall feel deeply obligated if you will."

"I shall go down to the telegraph office at once," he said, rising from his seat and placing the child down; "and now, my little darling," he continued, speaking to the child, "you must tell your ma not to cry so much." With these words he shook Mrs. Wentworth's hand and left the house.

The day passed wearily for Mrs. Wentworth; every hour she would open one of the windows leading to the street and look out, as if expecting to see Mr. Awtry with a telegraphic dispatch in his hand, and each disappointment she met with on these visits would only add to her intense anxiety. The shades of evening had overshadowed the earth, and Mrs. Wentworth sat at the window of her dwelling waiting the arrival of the news, which would either remove her fears or plunge her in sorrow. Long hours passed, and she had almost despaired of Mr. Awtry's coming that evening, when he walked up the street, and in a few minutes was in the house.

"What news?" gasped Mrs. Wentworth, starting from her seat and meeting him at the door of the apartment.

"Read it, my dear madam. I shall leave that pleasure to you," he replied, handing her a telegraphic dispatch he held in his hand.

Taking the dispatch, Mrs. Wentworth, with trembling fingers, unfolded it and read these words: "Mrs. Eva Wentworth, New Orleans, Louisiana: Yours received. I am safe. Alfred Wentworth." As soon as she had read the dispatch, her pent-up anxiety for his safety was allayed, and throwing herself on her knees before a couch, regardless of the presence of Mr. Awtry, who stood looking on, Mrs. Wentworth poured forth a prayer of thanks at the safety of her husband, while tears of joy trickled down her cheeks.

"Allow me to congratulate you, Mrs. Wentworth, on the safety of your husband," said Horace Awtry, after she had become sufficiently composed. "I assure you," he continued, "I feel happy at the knowledge of being the medium through which this welcome intelligence has reached you."

"You have, indeed, proved a friend," she said, extending her hand, which he shook warmly, "and one that I feel I can trust."

"Do not speak of it," he answered; "it is only a natural act of kindness towards one whom I desire to befriend."

"And one I will never cease to forget. Oh! if you had but known how I felt during these past hours of agonizing suspense, you would not have thought lightly of your kind attention; and I am sure when I write Alfred of it, he will not have words sufficient to express his gratitude."

"In my haste to impart the good news to you," said Mr. Awtry, rising, "I almost forgot an engagement I made this evening. It is now getting late, and I must leave. Good evening."

"Good evening," she replied. "I trust you will call to see me soon again."

"With 'your' permission I will," he answered, laying particular emphasis on the word "your."

"Certainly," she said. "I shall be most happy to see you at anytime."

"I will call soon, then," he replied. "Good night," and he stepped from the threshold of the house.

"Good night," she said, closing the door.

Horace Awtry stood for a moment near the house; then walking on he muttered: "A politic stroke, that telegraphic dispatch."

CHAPTER FIFTH.
JACKSON, MISSISSIPPI -- A HAPPY HOME.

We will now change the scene of our story, and, using the license of all writers, transport the reader to Jackson, the Capital of the great State of Mississippi, and there introduce him or her to other characters who will bear a prominent part in this book.

In the parlor of an elegant resident on Main Street, a beautiful girl was sitting with an open book in her hand. She was not, however, reading, as her bright blue eyes rested not on the pages, but were gazing at the half-opened door, as if expecting the arrival of someone. While she is thus musing, we will endeavour to give a description of the fair maiden. Fancy a slight and elegant figure, richly dressed in a robe of 'moiré antique', from under the folds of which the daintiest little feet imaginable could be seen. Her features, though not regularly carved, made her, at the same time, very beautiful, while her bright blue eyes and rich golden hair, braided smooth to her forehead, and ornamented with a jewelled tiara, then much worn, lent additional charm to her appearance. Her hands were small, and as Byron, we think, has it, was an undoubted mark of gentle birth.

She remained in this reverie for some time, but was at last aroused by the entrance, unannounced, of a handsome young man dressed in the uniform of a lieutenant, when she started up, and meeting him, said in a half-vexed, half-playful tone:

"Oh, Harry! why did you not come earlier? I have been waiting for your arrival over an hour!"

"Excuse me, dearest," he answered. "I was just on the point of starting from my office when I received a mass of orders from regimental headquarters, which detained me until a few minutes ago. You must, therefore," he continued, "excuse me for this once, and I shall not offend again," and as he spoke, he parted the hair from her forehead and pressed a kiss upon her lips.

"I forgive you for this time," she answered, playfully tapping him on the shoulder with her fan; "but the next offence I will not be so likely to excuse."

"I will take good care not to offend again, then," he laughingly said.

The conversation continued for some time in this light way, which lovers will sometimes indulge in, when, assuming a serious countenance, she spoke to him:

"When does your regiment leave for Virginia?"

"I hardly know," he replied, "if it will go to Virginia at all. The Colonel informs me that it is likely the regiment will be sent to Tennessee; so, if it is sent there, I will be nearer than you thought."

"What a horrid thing war is!" she said, without appearing to notice his last remarks.

"You are not inclined to show the white feather now, are you?" he said, laughing.

Her bright blue eyes sparkled for a moment, as if repudiating the question; then lowering them she answered: "No, indeed. I would not have a single one that I love remain at home while the Abolitionists are invading our homes."

"Spoken like a brave girl and a true Southern woman," he replied, "and I shall remember your words when I go into battle. It will nerve and inspire me to fight with redoubled courage, when I recollect that I am battling for you." As he spoke, he gazed at her with mingled pride and affection, and for some minutes they remained gazing at each other with that affection which springs from

"Two souls with but a single thought --
Two hearts that beat as one."

Oh, Love! ye goddess of all that is blissful and elevating in man! How thy devotees bow down to thy shrine and offer all that they possess to purchase but a smile from thee! And when you have cast your favors on some happy mortal, and the pure feeling of affection becomes centered on woman, the fairest flower from Eden, how should not mankind cherish the gift you have bestowed upon him, and look upon it as the first and priceless object on earth, and but second to one above in heaven!

The lovers remained in this silence, which spoke more than words could have done, until the entrance of a tall and venerable looking gentleman of about fifty years of age. As soon as he entered, they rose up together, the young lady addressing him as "father," and the young man as "doctor."

"How are you, Harry, my boy? give me a kiss, Em'," he said, in one breath, as he shook the young man warmly by the hand and pressed a parental kiss on the brow of his daughter. "Pretty warm weather, this," he continued, speaking to the young man; "it is almost stifling."

"Suppose we step out on the balcony, pa," said the young lady; "it is much cooler there."

"Ha, ha, ha," he laughed; "you had not found that out until I entered. However," he went on, "do you both go out there. I am certain you will do better without than with me."

His daughter blushed, but made no reply, and the young man removing two chairs to the balcony, they both left the old gentleman, who, turning up the gas, proceeded to read his evening 'Mississippian'.

Dr. James Humphries was one of the oldest and most respectable citizens of Jackson, and was looked upon with great esteem by all who knew him. He had been a medical practitioner in that city from the time it was nothing more than a little village, until railroad connections had raised it to be a place of some consequence, and the capital of the State. He had married when a young man, but of all his children, none remained but his daughter Emma, in gaining whom he lost a much-loved wife, she having died in child-birth.

At the time we write, Emma Humphries was betrothed to Henry Shackleford, a young lawyer of fine ability, but who was, like many of his countrymen, a soldier in the service of his country, and been elected first lieutenant of the "Mississippi Rifles."

We will now leave them for the present, and in the next chapter introduce the reader to two other characters.

CHAPTER SIXTH.
THE SPECTATOR AND EXTORTIONER.

Mr. Jacob Swartz was sitting in the back room of his store on Main Street counting a heap of gold and silver coins which lay on a table before him. He was a small, thin-bodied man, with little gray eyes, light hair and aquiline nose. He was of that nationality generally known in this country as "Dutch;" but having been there for over twenty years, he had become naturalized, and was now a citizen of the chivalrous States of Mississippi, a fact of which he prided himself considerably.

Mr. Swartz was busily engaged counting his money, when a little boy, who seemed, from a similarity of features, to be his son appeared at the door, and mentioned that Mr. Elder desired to see him.

"Vot can he vant?" said Mr. Swartz. Then as if recollecting, he continued: "I suppose it is apout that little shtore he vants to rent me. Tell him to come in."

The boy withdrew, and a few seconds after a tall and scrupulously dressed gentleman, with his coat buttoned up to the throat, and wearing a broad rimmed hat, entered the room. This was Mr. James Elder, a citizen of Jackson, but not a native of the State. He came from Kentucky several years before, and was a man with "Southern principles." To do him justice, we will say that he was really true friend to the South, which fact may have been not only from principle, but from his being a large slaveholder. He was also the possessor of a considerable amount of landed property and real estate, among which were several buildings in Jackson. He was also looked upon by the 'world', as very charitable man, being always busy collecting money from the people in aid of some benevolent object, and occasionally his name would appear in the newspapers, accompanied by a flattering compliment to his generosity, as the donor of a liberal amount of money to some charitable institution or society. There were people, however, who said that the poor families, who hired a series of tenement buildings he possessed in the lower part of the city, were very often hard pressed for their rent, and more than once turned out for non-payment. These reports were considered as slanders, for being a member, and one of the pillars of the Methodist Church, no one, for a moment, believed that he would be guilty of so unfeeling an action.

On entering the room, Mr. James Elder made a stiff bow to Mr. Swartz, and declining the hand offered to him, as if it were contamination to touch the person of one of God's likeness, dusted a chair and sat down opposite his host.

"Vell, Mr. Elder, have you decided whether I can get the shtore or not? Tis place of mine is in very pad orter, and I tinks yours vill shust suit me," began Mr. Swartz, after a silence of about three minutes.

"Yes, Mr. Swartz, I think you can have the place, if you and I can come to terms about the price of the rent, which must be payable always in advance," replied Mr. Elder.

"I tont care," answered Mr. Swartz. "I would as soon pay you in advance as not. But vot price to you charge?"

"I charge fifty dollars per month," was the short answer.

"Vell, dat vill do; and I suppose you vill give me the shtore for von year certain?"

"I am not decided about that," replied Mr. Elder, "as I do not like to bind myself for any given time; for," he continued, "there is no telling what may be the worth of a store in six months."

"I vould not take it unless I could get a lease by the year," replied Mr. Swartz; "for the fact is, I have made a large contract with the government, and vill have to extend by pisness."

Mr. Elder remained thoughtful for a few moments; then he replied: "As you won't take it unless I give a lease for twelve months, I will do so on one condition: that on your failure to pay the rent monthly in advance, you forfeit the lease, and I am at liberty to demand your removal without any notice."

"Shust as you like," he replied, "for I know te monish vill always pe ready in advance."

"Well, I shall have the lease drawn out to-day and bring it to you to sign," said Mr. Elder, rising and putting on his gloves. "Good morning; be here at three o'clock, as I shall call round at that hour," and with those words he left the room, and the Dutchman resumed the counting of his money.

CHAPTER SEVENTH.
THE HUSBAND A PRISONER –
EXILE OF THE SOLDIER'S WIFE.

Months rolled on, during which time Mrs. Wentworth was cheered by many kind and affectionate letters from her husband, who had not been sick a day since his departure from home. One of the letters received from him stated that he had been detailed from his regiment to act as clerk in Brigadier General Floyd's adjutant general's office, his superior intelligence fitting him admirably for such an office; and the next letter from him was dated at Fort Donelson, whence General Floyd had been ordered with his brigade.

Fort Donelson fell. We need not record here the heroic defense and stubborn fighting of the Confederate forces, and their unfortunate capture afterwards. These are matters of history, and should be recorded by the historian, and not the novelist. Sufficient to say, that in the last day's fight Alfred Wentworth, having received a severe wound in the arm, was marching to the rear, when an officer, dressed in the garb of a lieutenant, who was lying on the field, called faintly to him, and on his going up, he observed that the lieutenant's left leg was fearfully mangled by a fragment of shell, and was bleeding so profusely, that, unless medical aid was quickly procured, he would die. Forgetting his own wound, which was very painful, he lifted the officer on his shoulder and bore him to the hospital, where his leg was immediately attended to, and his life saved. The severity of his own wound, and the length of time which elapsed before any attention was paid to it, brought on a severe fever, and on the escape of General Floyd, he was delirious and unable to accompany him. He was, therefore, sent to Chicago, and placed in the same hospital with the lieutenant whose life he had saved.

On their recovery, which was about the same time, Lieutenant Shackleford -- for it was he -- and Alfred Wentworth were both sent to "Camp Douglas," the military prison near Chicago.

On the receipt of the news in New Orleans, that Fort Donelson and nearly its entire garrison had surrendered, Mrs. Wentworth underwent another long suspense of excitement and anxiety, which was, however, partially allayed by the intelligence that General Floyd and staff had escaped. But as the weeks rolled on, and she received no letter from her husband, the old fear that he may have been killed came over her again, until relieved by seeing his name as being among the wounded at the Chicago hospital in one of the city papers.

In mentioning these hours of grief and suspense on the part of Mrs. Wentworth, it must not be understood that we are representing a weak-minded and cowardly woman. On the contrary, Mrs. Wentworth would have rather heard that her husband was killed than one word spoken derogatory to his courage, and would never have consented to his remaining at home, while so many of his countrymen were hurrying to protect their country from invasion. Her suspense and grief at the intelligence of a battle in which her husband was engaged, were only the natural feeling of an affectionate wife. At that moment she was no longer the patriot daughter of the South; she was the wife and mother, and none should blame her for her anxiety to know the fate of one so much loved as her husband, and the father of her children.

Soon after her husband was taken prisoner, Mrs. Wentworth observed that Horace Awtry became more assiduous in his attentions to her. Every day he would call with presents for her children, and several times small packages of bank-bills were found in the parlor, which, when presented to him, he would always disclaim being the owner of; and although Mrs. Wentworth truly believed that they had been left there by him, the kind and respectful tone he used to her, and the intense interest he appeared to take in the welfare of her children, were such that she never imagined, for a moment, he was using this means to cloak a vile and unmanly purpose. Once, and only once, was she made aware that the scandal tongues of her neighbors were being used detrimental to her honor; and then the information was given by her slave Elsy, who overheard a conversation between two of her neighbors not at all complimentary to her, and which the faithful negress lost no time in repeating to her mistress, with the very indignant remark that, "ef dem people nex' doh fancy dey can do anyting to take away your name, dey's much mistaken, as I will tell you ebery ting dey say 'bout you, an' you will know what to do." Mrs. Wentworth made no reply to the negro, but on the next visit of Mr. Awtry's, she candidly told him what had been said of her in consequence of his visits. He appeared very much surprised, but told her that such scandalous remarks, emanating as they did out of pure malice, should not be noticed, as all who were acquainted with her knew very well that her character and fair name were above suspicion. With that the subject was dropped, and he continued paying her his visits.

New Orleans fell into the hands of the enemy, and the whole Confederacy was convulsed, as if shaken by an earthquake. None anticipated such a thing, and its fall brought misery to thousands. The enemy had scarcely taken possession, then Horace Awtry and his bosom friend, Charles Bell, went to the provost marshal's office and took the oath of allegiance, after proving, entirely to the satisfaction of the Yankees, that they were Northern, and had always been Union men. Mr. Awtry immediately received a commission in the Federal army, and by his willingness to point out prominent "secession" men and women, soon ingratiated himself in the favor of "Beast Butler."

No sooner had he gained the favor of Butler, than his attentions to Mrs. Wentworth changed to that of unmanly presumption, and at last he had the baseness to make proposals at once dishonorable to her as a lady of virtue and position in society, and disgraceful to him as a man. These propositions were accompanied by a threat to have her turned out of the house and exiled from New Orleans. With a spirit worthy of a Southern woman, she indignantly spurned his base offers and ordered him never to place his feet across the threshold of her house, at the same time defying to do his worse. He left her, declaring that she should be turned out of the city, and a few days after, in proof of his threat, an order was presented to her, signed by General Butler, commanding her to leave the city.

Her faithful slave, Elsy, shed bitter tears on hearing that her kind mistress would have to leave New Orleans, and declared that she would not remain in the city, but would follow her.

"But they will not let you go with me, Elsy," said Mrs. Wentworth. "You are free now, they say, to do as you like -- you are no longer belonging to me."

"I ain't a gwine to stay here, missis," replied the negro, "for any money in dis world, and if dey won't let me go out wid you, I will come arter you by myself."

"Well, Elsy," said Mrs. Wentworth, "I do not force you to leave New Orleans, but should you get out, come to me at Jackson. You are a good girl, and I shall not forget your fidelity."

"I'll be dere, shure," said the negro, quite pleased at the permission to follow her mistress if she could.

Mrs. Wentworth immediately set to work packing up a few necessaries, and with the small amount of money she had left awaited the next morning, when she would start for Pass Manchac.

On the following morning she proceeded to the boat, amid the cries and lamentations of the faithful Elsy, and with throbbing heart and many sighs gazed on her loved city until it had receded from her view.

On arriving at the "Pass" she was about to step from the boat, when a hand was laid upon her shoulder, and looking round she observed Mr. Awtry, dressed in the full uniform of a Yankee captain, standing by her.

"Are you determined to leave home," he said, "and all its pleasures; and starve in the rebel lines? Why not accept my offer and lead a life of ease and affluence? Your husband shall never know of our connection, and thus you will be spared many a weary day and night working for bread to feed your children."

She looked at him for a moment with all that withering scorn and indignation which outraged virtue and innocence can assume, and then said: "Leave me! Go to the land from whence you came and make such offers to the women there, but remember now you are speaking to a Southern woman."

"But think a moment, and -" he began.

"Leave me this instant," she said excitedly, "or I shall call others with more the heart of men than you to my assistance. Accept your offer?" she continued with all the scorn she could use. "Accept such an offer from a 'Yankee'! Go, I would despise and hate were you not too despicable for either feeling of enmity."

Several persons approaching at that moment, he moved away hurriedly after hissing in her ear: "Take your choice. In either one way or the other I am revenged on you for the way you rejected my addresses in past years."

She landed on the shore, and a few minutes after the boat moved back on its way to New Orleans, when taking her small trunk in her hands the soldier's wife, with her two children, started on their long and lively march. For where? She knew not. There she was, an utter stranger with two tender children, far from her home, and with only two hundred dollars in money. Where could she go to for support. Her husband was in a foreign prison, and she a wanderer in a strange State. Her heart sank within her, and the soldier's wife wept. Aye, wept! Not tears of regret at what she had sacrificed, but tears of loneliness. Who would not weep if they were parted from those they love, and were cast in a strange land without a friend, and with scarcely any means?

We leave the soldier's wife for a brief while, and transport the reader to her husband. Her trials have commenced -- God help her!

CHAPTER EIGHTH.
THE PRISONERS -- THE HUSBAND AND THE LOVER.

We stated that on the recovery of Alfred Wentworth and Lieutenant Shackleford from their wounds, both were sent to Camp Douglas together, and as Alfred had no regiment of his own captured, the lieutenant promptly requested him to become one of his mess. The generous courage exhibited by Alfred Wentworth, and the fact that but for his chivalric attention, he should have died on the bloody field of Fort Donelson, had created a feeling of gratitude in Lieutenant Shackleford for his preserver, which, on closer acquaintance, had ripened into a warm friendship, and he soon made Alfred acquainted with the fact of his betrothal to Emma Humphries, and Alfred in turn would speak of his wife and children in such tones of affection as only those who love can use. They would sit down for hours and converse on the loved ones at home, thus wiling away the sad and lonely hours of a prison life, until the news was received in Chicago of the fall of New Orleans. Although he bitterly regretted his native city having fallen into the hands of the enemy, the opportunity which it presented of once more being able to correspond with his wife, made him feel happier, and as soon as mail communication was received with the city, he requested and obtained permission to write her.

Alfred Wentworth had not the slightest idea that Horace Awtry would ever dare to offend his wife, much less to offer infamous proposals, and on their being refused have her driven from the home he had placed her in. It is true that his wife had written to him that Mr. Awtry had renewed his acquaintance with her, but her statements of his kind attention to her and the children, and her mentioning the eager manner in which he had relieved her anxiety after the battle of the 21st of July, 1861, instead of raising any suspicion on his part of the honesty and purity of his motives, only made him return thanks in his heart for the previous kindness shown to his wife.

On obtaining permission to write her, he immediately penned a long and affectionate letter which was forwarded. For many days after he remained in a long suspense for the expected answer, as he never believed for a moment that she would delay answering him, but as days rolled into weeks, and no letter came, while the other prisoners from New Orleans received letters regularly, he became alarmed, and spoke his fears to Shackleford.

"Do not be afraid of any harm having occurred to her, Alf," said the lieutenant, after listening attentively to his friend's words. "You may depend that your letter never reached her, and she, in ignorance whether you escaped unhurt from the engagement, cannot write, not knowing where you are."

"It is not her silence which troubles me as much as the knowledge that she possess no other money than Confederate notes," replied Alfred. "How she will manage to support herself and the children God only knows."

"Have you not friends there?" enquired Harry.

"Yes, but I cannot depend on them for assistance, for two reasons: first, because from the disordered state of the money market in New Orleans, they are almost as badly off as she is; and second, I am quite certain that Eva would rather starve than ask for charity."

"Charity!" echoed his companion. "Do you call it charity to assist another situated as your wife is, particularly where her husband is far from her fighting for his country?"

"You do not know the people of New Orleans," replied Alfred. "No matter how kindly a favor may be bestowed on them, it is still considered charity, and though dire necessity may induce them to accept aid if proffered, the knowledge that they were eating the bread of charity, would embitter each mouthful."

"Pooh, pooh," said his friend, "all these fine notions would do very well before the war, but at the present time the least we think of them the better."

"It is all very well for you to speak that way," answered Alfred, "for you have no wife and children to cause uneasiness, but I cannot be otherwise than anxious to know what has become of her, that I receive no letters, while other prisoners have had theirs regularly by mail."

"An unfortunate fact, which you may depend has been caused by no other reason than the neglect of the Yankee officers to forward your letters," said Harry, then continuing: "Come, cheer up, and throw aside your dullness. Another battle like that of Shiloh, will give the South as many Yankee prisoners as they have of us, and then ho! For home and the "Sunny South!" As soon as we return, I will take you to Jackson, and then you can write your wife to come out, and she can live with my mother, if you are not too proud to accept my hospitality."

"Thank you," he replied, "but I must first wait until we are exchanged, and God knows when that will be."

"Why, man, I tell you there is no doubt of our whipping the Yanks and capturing a lot of them in the next battle; then adieu to Camp Douglas, and hurrah for the Confederacy once more!" replied Harry, taking his companion by the arm, and dragging him to their tent where dinner had been placed in readiness for them.

CHAPTER NINTH.
ROOM TO RENT.

We must now return to my heroine, who, with her two children, we left slowly travelling toward Jackson, Mississippi. On arriving at Ponchatula, she took the cars on the New Orleans, Jackson and Great Northern Railroad, and in a few hours was in Jackson. On arriving there she proceeded to the Bowman House, and purchasing a newspaper eagerly scanned the columns to find an advertisement of rooms to rent, knowing full well that, with her limited means, she would never be able to remain at the hotel, or live at a boarding house.

After looking for some time, without finding the desired advertisement, her eye at last lit upon the following notice under the heading of "To rent:"

"TO RENT,"

"Unfurnished rooms in the one-story tenement buildings on -- street. For particulars, apply to the undersigned at his office on Main Street, near the State House.   JAMIE ELDER."

After reading it she folded the paper, and remained musing for several minutes, when rising up she went to her children, and, kissing them, told them she was going out for a few minutes, and to play like good children until her return. She then left the hotel, and, after some little trouble, at last found out the office of Mr. Elder, which she entered.

"Is Mr. Elder in?" she inquired of a clerk.

"Yes, madam," he replied.

"Can I see him?" she asked.

He gave her no answer, but going to an adjoining door, half opened it, and announced, in a loud voice, that a lady desired to see Mr. Elder.

"Admit her," was the reply of that gentleman.

Mrs. Wentworth passed the desk, and, entering the room from whence the voice proceeded, found herself in the presence of Mr. Elder, who was seated in an arm chair reading a newspaper.

"Be seated, madam," he said, rising and handing her a chair. "What can I have the honor of doing for you this morning?"

"This is your advertisement, I believe," she replied, handing him the newspaper.

"Yes, madam," he answered, looking at her through his spectacles.

"Well, sir, it is my desire to rent one of the rooms."

"You, madam!" he replied, evidently surprised at her question.

"Yes, sir," she replied; "I am a refugee from New Orleans, having been driven from there by General Butler. My husband is now a prisoner of war in the hands of the enemy, and my means being limited, I am compelled to live economically."

"Ahem, ahem," said Mr. Elder, clearing his throat; "indeed, madam, I sympathise with you. This war has cast many people homeless and in need throughout the country. I sympathize with you, 'indeed' I do," and he looked on her in the most benevolent manner possible.

"Well, sir, what is the price charged for the rent of one of your rooms?" asked Mrs. Wentworth after a few moments' silence.

"Well, ah -- well, ah -- you see, my dear madam, the price of everything has gone up immensely," he replied.

"And what do you charge for the room?" she asked.

"Well, ah, I think sixteen dollars per month as cheap as I could possible rent it," he answered finally.

"I will take it, then, by the month," she answered, rising, "and will go into possession to-day."

"Well, ah, my dear madam, it is a rule I have always made, only to rent my houses for the money, paid in advance--not that I have the 'least' apprehension of your inability to pay me, but you see it never does any good to deviate from fixed rules."

"I am perfectly willing to pay you in advance," she replied, taking her port-moniæ from her pocket and handing him the advance pay for one month's rent.

Calling a clerk, Mr. Elder handed him the money, and ordered a receipt to be made out; then turning to Mrs. Wentworth, he said: "There is another thing, I desire to have you understand, madam, and agree to. The fall of New Orleans has occasioned the inflation of all kinds of real estate in price, and this, added to the rapid manner in which Confederate notes are depreciating in value, may compel me to raise the price of rent. I would, therefore, like you to agree, that in no way am I bound for any time longer than the month you have paid for, to take the present price; and another thing I desire is, that you agree not to take advantage of the stay law, in the event of non-payment, or refusal to pay any additional price I may charge. In making these conditions, madam," he continued, "I must not be understood to say that the contingencies mentioned are at all likely to occur, as I trust and hope they will not; but at the same time, I only desire to avoid all deviation from my usual course of doing business."

"Any terms you may desire I will agree to," she replied in an absent manner, "as I wish to remove from the hotel, the charges there being above my means."

"Very well, madam, very well," he responded.

After the clerk had brought the receipt for the month's rent, Mr. Elder rose from his chair, and, requesting Mrs. Wentworth to remain seated for a few minutes, left the apartment. He shortly after returned with a printed document in his hand, which he requested her to sign. Without reading the paper, she obeyed his request, and, receiving the key of the room she had just rented, requested that Mr. Elder would have her shown where it was situated. Calling a negro boy, who was lounging at the door, he directed him to accompany Mrs.

Wentworth to -- street and show her the rooms. With that he made a low bow, and she left following the boy.

"Humph!" said Mr. Elder, half aloud, as soon as she had left. "I do not care much about hiring my rooms to such tenants. Refugees are certainly becoming as thick as locusts in the State, and are nearly all as poor as Job. However, I have made myself secure against any excuse for pay on the ground of poverty, by the paper she signed," and with these reflections, that worthy gentleman re-entered his room, and was soon deeply interested in his newspaper.

CHAPTER TENTH.
THE NEW HOME.

Mrs. Wentworth followed the boy till he arrived in front of series of wretched looking rooms, situated on one of the miserable lanes with which Jackson abounds. Stopping in front of one of them, he pointed to it, and with no other words than "Dem is de room, ma'm," walked off. Taking the key, which Mr. Elder had previously given her, she opened the door and entered.

Mrs. Wentworth's heart sank within her as she viewed the wretched looking apartment. The interior of the room was exceedingly dirty, while the faded paper, which once gaudily adorned it, now hung in shreds from the walls. The fireplace was broken up, and disgusting words were written in every part of the room. It had been, in fact, the lodging of a woman of dissolute character, who had been accustomed to gather a crowd of debauched characters in her apartment nightly, but who, from a failure to pay her rent, had been turned out by Mr. Elder. The other apartments were still occupied by abandoned women; but of this fact Mrs. Wentworth was not aware.

As she looked at the room a feeling of indescribable sadness crept over her, and a sigh of bitterness burst from her throbbing bosom. It was, however, not to be helped; she had already paid the rent, and was compelled to keep it for the month. Sadly, she left the room, and locking it after her, repaired to a store to purchase a few necessary articles of furniture.

On entering a store, the first person she saw was Mr. Swartz, who had, by this time, risen from the lowly position of a grocer to that of a "General wholesale and retail merchant," as the sign over his door very pompously announced.

Mr. Swartz remained on his seat at her entrance, barely raising his eyes to see who had entered. She stood for a few moments, when, seeing that no one appeared to notice her presence, she walked up to him and informed him that she wished to purchase a few pieces of furniture.

"Vot kind do you vant?" he inquired, without moving from his seat.

"A small bedstead, three or four chairs, a table and a washstand," she answered.

"Look at them and see vich you like te best," he said, "and I vill tell you te brice."

After a little search, Mrs. Wentworth selected the plainest and most homely she could find of all the articles she desired, and, turning to him, inquired what the price would be.

"Te pedstead is forty tollars; te chairs is three tollars apiece; te taple is twenty tollars; and to washstand is fourteen," he replied.

"And how much will that amount to, altogether?" she asked.

"Eighty-six tollars," he responded.

"Can you take no less, sir?" she asked.

"No, ma'am," he answered. "I have put one brice, and if you don't vant to pay it you can leave it."

Taking out the desired amount, she paid him without making any further remark, and requested that they would be sent after her. Calling a drayman, Mr. Swartz told him to follow her with the furniture, and he returned to his seat, satisfied with having made sixty dollars on the eighty-six, received from Mrs. Wentworth, the furniture having been bought at sheriff's sale for a mere trifle.

Having purchased a few other household utensils, Mrs. Wentworth proceeded to the Bowman House, from which, after paying her bill, she removed her children, and, followed by the dray with her furniture, proceeded to the wretched hovel site had rented. Her stock of money had now been reduced to less than sixty dollars, and with this she embarked upon the world with two tender children.

After paying the drayman, who was a kind-hearted negro, and getting him to erect the bedstead, he departed, and a feeling of desolation and loneliness spread its dark shadows over the heart of Mrs. Wentworth. Seating herself on a chair, with her two children clinging to her knees, the long pent-up fountain of grief burst forth, and tears bedewed the cheeks of the Soldier's Wife; tears, such as only those who have felt the change of fortune, can shed; tears, which, like the last despairing cry of the desolate, can only be answered in heaven!

CHAPTER ELEVENTH.
THE ATTEMPTED ESCAPE.

We must now return to Alfred, whom we left in a disconsolate mood at Camp Douglas, with his friend trying to cheer his spirits. But he could think of nothing else but his absent wife, until at last he determined to attempt an escape. The idea once in his mind could not be dismissed. He, therefore, informed Harry of his intention, and asked if he thought it feasible, or likely to result in success.

"So far as the feasibility of the attempt is concerned," observed Harry, as soon as Alfred had concluded, "I think it could be attempted. But about the result, you will have to trust to luck."

"I am aware of that," he replied. "But I do not know how the attempt can possibly be made. The camp is so well guarded, that an attempt to escape is almost hopeless of success."

"Pshaw! If you are determined to go, I see nothing to prevent your making the attempt. If it even fails, the most that will be done to you by the Federals is closer confinement."

"I do not care much about that risk," he replied. "My desire is to form some plan of escape. Can you devise one by which I can get away?"

"That is a difficult task," said Harry. "But as we are of the same desire, I suppose something must be done. What do you say about digging a tunnel, and escaping by that route?"

"That is a very good idea; but it will take too long," replied Alfred. "Besides which, what are we to do with the dirt that is dug up?"

"I never thought of that," he answered. "But now that you have reminded me of it, I do not believe the plan will suit. Some other must be devised, but what it is to be, I cannot, for the life of me, imagine."

"What do you say to scaling the walls?" asked Alfred.

"A very good idea it would be, if we had anything to scale them with," he replied.

"Suppose we tear up our blankets and make a rope of them."

"How will you attach the rope to the wall?" asked Harry.

"We can easily get a hook of wire and throw it over. It will be certain to catch," he replied.

"Very likely," observed Harry, drily, "and make such confounded noise, that the first thing we heard after, it would be a Minie ball whistling past our ears; or should it catch without making any noise, the chances are that, when one of us ascends, it will be to meet the burly form of some Dutch sentinel traversing the walk. The idea is not feasible; so, we must think of something else."

"I do not know what to think," replied Alfred; "and the probability is, that if I even did, you would find some objection to its performance."

"That is true," answered Harry, laughing, "and I accept the reproach in the spirit it is given. It will never do for us to be raising objections to every plan offered, for that will not hasten our escape."

"Then think of something else, and I will acquiesce, no matter how extravagant it may be," said Alfred. "I am tired of this cursed prison, and intend to get away by some means or other."

"It is all very good to talk about getting away," said Harry. "For the matter of that, I am as anxious to leave as you are, but in the name of wonder, how are we going to manage it?"

"That is the very thing I desire to consult you about. We certainly will never escape, unless we make the attempt; but in what manner we are to attempt it, is exactly what I desire to know."

"What do you say to bribing one of the sentinels?" asked Harry.

"Where will we get the means from?" inquired Alfred. "I have some Confederate Treasury notes, but they will not be any temptation to a Yankee."

"Leave me to find the means," replied Harry. "I have a fine gold watch, and about seventy dollars in gold. These will be sufficient, I think, to attempt the cupidity of any Dutchman in the Yankee army."

"And how do you propose offering the bribe?" Alfred inquired.

"I shall look out for the first chance to speak to the sentinel at the gate, sometime during the day, and will make the necessary preparations to escape to-night, if the Yankee will accept my offer."

"That will do very well," observed Alfred, "There is one thing, however, I must remind you of. It will not do to offer the sentinel all your gold, for we will require money to pay our way into Tennessee."

"Do you never fear that," replied Harry. "I will be certain to reserve enough funds for our expenses. It does not cost much at any time to travel through these Northern States."

"Well, I trust to you to make all the necessary arrangements," replied Alfred. "I am determined not to remain in this place, with my mind so disturbed about my wife and children. If I can only reach the Confederate lines safely, I will have no difficulty in hearing from New Orleans."

"I will make every effort to facilitate an escape," remarked Harry; "and if my penetrating qualities do not deceive me, there is a sentinel at the gate to-day, who would not be averse to taking a bribe, even if it permits a "rebel" to escape. Cheer up, my friend," he continued. "I will guarantee that your wife and children are all well and happy, except a natural anxiety on your account."

Alfred made no reply, and the two friends shortly after separated.

Harry kept an assiduous watch for an opportunity to speak with the sentinel. The time for the man to remain on guard expired, however, without any favorable chance presenting itself. He was, therefore, compelled to wait until the evening, when the same sentinel would be again on guard, before he could attempt to bribe him. At four o'clock he was posted, and after some hesitation, Harry determined to address him. Walking up as soon as he perceived no one near the man, he called out to him.

"Vot to deuce do you vant? you rebel," asked the sentinel in a broad Dutch accent.

"Will you let me come a little nearer?" Harry inquired, perceiving that the distance between the guard and himself too great for a conversation.

"Vot do you vant to come a leetle nearer for?" asked the sentinel.

"I want to talk to you," he replied, making a motion of his hand to indicate that he wished to converse in secret.

The sentinel, looking carefully around to be certain that no one was near at hand who could perceive him, beckoned to Harry to approach. The young man went forward cautiously, as the numerous sentinels around the wall were likely to perceive him, and would not hesitate to fire if they imagined he was about to attempt an escape. As soon as he reached the sentinel, he made known his wishes, and ended by offering the man his watch and forty dollars in gold if he would permit himself and his friend to pass the gate at night. At the same time, he promised the man he would take all the responsibility in the event of detection or re-capture.

The sentinel listened attentively, and at first appeared unwilling to receive the bribe, but upon Harry representing to him that there was no chance of his agency in the escape being discovered, he finally consented to receive it. It was, therefore, arranged between them, that at twelve o'clock that night the two prisoners should start. The signal was to be a faint whistle, which would ultimate to the guard that they were there, if it was answered they should advance, but if not they should return, as his silence would either indicate that he was not alone, or that he was not on his post. Everything having been amicably arranged between them, Harry promised to pay the bribe as soon as they had reached the gate. This the fellow demurred to at first, but as Harry was determined, not to pay over the watch and forty dollars, until the hour of their departure, he was compelled to assent.

On Harry's return to his tent, he found Alfred reading a Yankee pictorial newspaper.

"Well," he remarked, looking up from his paper as soon as Harry entered.

"Everything progresses finely," replied Harry.

"Have you been able to speak to the sentinel?" he asked.

"I have seen him, and made all the necessary arrangements," Harry replied.

"And when will we leave," Alfred asked.

"To-night at twelve is the time fixed between us," he replied. "The fellow appeared unwilling at first, but a little persuasion with a sight at the watch and money, was too much for his nature, and he yielded to my wishes."

"Then everything goes on well, if the fellow does not play us false," Alfred remarked.

"That is a risk we are bound to run," replied Harry. "I think the fellow means to be honest, if a man can be honest who agrees to allow a prisoner to escape, who is placed under his charge."

"Did you inform him there were two of us who desired to leave," asked Alfred.

"Yes," was the reply; "I would never have bothered to escape and run the risk of re-capture and harsh treatment, did not you desire to leave this place, and the trip could as well be made with you as otherwise."

Alfred pressed his friend's hand warmly, as he replied. "Thank you, Harry, I trust I will be able to return the kindness you have shown me, at some future and more favorable time."

"Pooh, pooh!" he replied. "Don't speak of it. The kindness has been paid for long ago," pointing to his wound as he spoke.

"I expect we may as well make preparations to leave," remarked Alfred, after a moment's pause.

"Preparations!" echoed his friend, "What in the name of all that is glorious, do you require any preparations for?" And then, he added dryly, "there is one thing certain, my trunk (?) is already packed, although I don't know if yours is."

"A truce to joking about trunks," replied Alfred, "but seriously you must be aware that we cannot leave here without being dressed in citizens clothes."

"The thunder!" exclaimed Harry, "are you going to raise any more objections?"

"No," he replied, "but it is absolutely necessary that we shall be appareled in different clothes to those of a soldier."

"I think we can get a couple of suits to borrow from the officers, but how I will get them, without their knowing our intention to escape, is a matter of much difficulty. If they should once know it, the whole crowd will desire to leave with us."

"That would be unreasonable on their part," replied Alfred. "They must be aware that every man cannot get away at the same time, and to desire or attempt such a thing would be to ensure the re-capture of every man."

"Well, I will start now on the borrowing expedition, and by some subterfuge, be saved the necessity of informing any person of our intention."

Having moved off as he spoke, and proceeding to the tent of a brother officer, succeeded in borrowing a citizens' coat and pants without exciting any suspicion of his intended escape. At the next place he went to, a few remarks were made, but upon his informing the Captain to whom he applied, that he desired to have his uniform renovated, and had no change of clothing while that was being done. The citizens' clothes were cordially loaned, and he returned to Alfred with a joyous heart.

301

"What luck have you had?" enquired Alfred as soon as he returned.

"See for yourself," was the reply of Harry, as he threw down the coats and pants.

"Then everything needed is procured," he observed.

"Yes," replied Harry. "We must now mix with the other prisoners, as if nothing was transpiring in our minds, like an attempt to escape. It will be no use keeping away from them, as it is likely to excite suspicion."

The two friends left the tent and proceeded to where a group of prisoners were seated. Their appearance was greeted with cheers, as Harry was a universal favorite among both officers and men, on account of his lively and genial temper, combined with a fine voice for music -- an accomplishment that with soldiers endears, and makes a favorite of any person possessing it. He was soon called upon for a song, and in accordance with the request commenced a song, and soon the rich and clear voice of the young man rang out on the air of the soft twilight. He sang of home, and as each word fell with distinctness on the ears of the soldiers, who grouped around him, each heart throbbed with emotion, and each mind wandered back to the distant land, where, in the mansion, or in the little cottage, loved ones there dwelt, pining for those who were now prisoners in a foreign country.

The hour of nine having arrived, the soldiers dispersed to their respective quarters, and soon after the command "lights out" was uttered in stentorian notes. Long and anxiously the two friends remained lying on their bunks in the tent, awaiting the hour of twelve. Each moment seemed an hour to Alfred Wentworth, whose mind was wrought up to a pitch of excitement, almost unendurable. Several times he rose from his bed and paced the tent. At last, the long wished for hour arrived. Harry who had been smoking all the night, looked at his watch by the faint light the fire of his segar emitted, and perceived that it was only five minutes for twelve. Crossing over to the bunk on which Alfred was lying, he whispered: "It is time." Silently they put on the citizens clothes borrowed in the evening, and left the tent. The night had changed from the pleasant, starry evening to a black and dismal gloom. Heavy clouds covered the skies, giving every indication of rain. The night was just such a one for an escape, and although the darkness was so intense, that it was impossible for the eye to penetrate a distance of five paces, both felt that their chance of escape was accelerated.

"Give me your hand," whispered Harry, as soon as they had left the tent.

"Do you know the direct way to the gate," asked Alfred,

"Yes," he replied, "cease speaking now and follow me. The least whisper may be heard, and then our attempt will be foiled."

Grasping the hand of his friend, Alfred followed him, and they moved with noiseless tread toward the gate. As soon as he descried the faint light of the sentinel's lamp near him, Harry stopped, and stooping down gave a faint whistle. For some time, no answer was returned. The two friends remained in almost breathless suspense awaiting the signal. At last, it was returned, and moving forward, they reached the gate.

"Here," whispered Harry to the sentinel, as he handed him the watch and money.

The man raised the little lantern near him, and looked at the bribe to see that it was all right. "Pass on," he said.

As Harry and his friend passed the gate, the former perceived several forms flit across the darkness, and a suspicion of treachery instantly flashed through his mind.

"We are betrayed," he whispered to Alfred.

"No matter, let us push boldly forward," was the reply.

They had not moved ten paces before the command "Halt" given.

"Push on!" exclaimed Alfred, darting forward.

The two friends moved on at a rapid run, when a volley of musketry was fired at them. Harry escaped unhurt and continued running at the top of his speed, and not until he had gone a considerable distance, did he discover that his friend was not with him. It was, however, too late for him to turn back, and entering Chicago, he made his way through the city, and continued his journey.

At the fire of the Federals, Alfred received four wounds; and sunk without a word to the ground. The enemy shortly after coming up found him insensible, and conveyed his inanimate body to the hospital. He was dangerously wounded, and the physicians declared there was but little hope of his recovery.

Two weeks after this unfortunate occurrence, a cartel for the exchange of prisoners was agreed upon between the Federal and Confederate authorities, and the prisoners at Camp Douglas were transported to Vicksburg. The doctors declared that Alfred was not in a state to be removed, and was left at the hospital. His condition at that time was very precarious. One of the balls that had entered his body could not be found, and the wound was kept open with the view to discovering where it had lodged. His agony of mind at the failure of his attempt to escape had retarded his recovery in a great degree, and when the information came that the prisoners were about to be exchanged, and he was declared unable to be removed, it added further to his detriment. A fever seized him, and for many days he remained on his bed, hovering between life and death.

CHAPTER TWELFTH.
THE STARVING CHILDREN.

Long weeks rolled on, and the small sum possessed by Mrs. Wentworth, had been entirely exhausted. She had, however, by sewing, contrived to supply herself and children with food. It was the same old tale of sleepless nights of toil. Often the grey streak which heralds the morning, would find her still pouring over her work, while her two children were sleeping on the bed in one corner of the room. At times she would cease her work, and think for long hours on the loved husband, now a prisoner in the hands of the Federals. In those hours, tears would course her cheeks, as the stern reality of her position presented itself; to know that he was absent, while she was leading a life of penury and toil. Still, she struggled on. When at times despair rose up before her like a demon, and she felt herself about to succumb to it, the memory of her absent husband, and the sight of her loved children, would nerve the soldier's wife to bear with fortitude the misery to which she had been reduced.

And thus, she toiled on, until the last source of support had vanished.

The Quartermaster from whom she received work, having completed all the clothing he required, had no further use for her services, and she then saw nothing but a blank and dreary prospect, looming up before her. She had no means of purchasing food for her children. Piece by piece her furniture was sold to supply their wants, until nothing was left in the room but a solitary bedstead. Starvation in its worst form stared her in the face, until at last she sold what clothing she had brought out from New Orleans. This relieved her necessities but a short time, and then her last resource was gone.

If her present was dark, the future seemed but one black cloud of despair. Hope, that 'ignis fatuus', which deceives so many on earth, left the soldier's wife, and she was indeed wretched. The blooming woman had become a haggard and care-worn mother. She had no thought for herself. It was for her children alone she felt solicitous, and when the day arrived that saw her without the means of purchasing bread, her long filling cup of misery overflowed, and she wept. Yes, she wept. Wept as if her whole life had been changed in a moment, from one of joy and happiness, to that of sadness and misery.

Her children in that dark hour clustered around her. 'They' could not cry. A fast of over twenty-four hours had dried all tears within them. They only wondered for a while, until the sharp pangs of hunger reminded them of another and greater woe. They too had been changed. The bloom of youth had departed from their little cheeks, while in the eyes of the oldest an unnatural light burned. She was fast sinking to the grave, but the mother knew it not. Knew not that her darling child had contracted a disease, which would shortly take her to Heaven, for the little Eva spoke no word of complaint. Young, as she was, she saw her mother's agony of soul, and though the little lips were parched and dry, she told not her ailing.

The tears continued to flow from Mrs. Wentworth, and still the children gazed on in wonderment. They knew not what they meant.

"Mother," at last said her little infant, "why do you cry?"

She took her on her knees. "Nothing, my darling," she replied.

"Then stop crying," he said, pressing his little hand on Mrs. Wentworth's cheek. "It makes me feel bad."

"I will stop crying, darling," she replied, drying her tears and smiling.

Smiles are not always the reply of the heart. We have seen men smile whoso whole life was a scene of misfortune, and yet this emblem of happiness has lit their features. It is outward show -- a fruit, whose surface presents a tempting appearance to the eye, but which is blasted and withered within. Smiles are often like the fruit called the 'Guava'. It is a beautiful looking fruit which grows in the

West Indies, and to the taste is very luscious, but when examined through a microscope, it presents the appearance of a moving mass of worms. Its beauty is deceptive, nothing but a wretched view presents itself,

> *"Like dead sea fruit, that tempts the eye,*
> *And falls to ashes on the lips."*

The child saw her mother smile, and the little heart forgot its hunger, and for a moment beat with joy. The gleam of sunshine that spread itself over him, did not last, for soon after the face of the mother assumed the same sad and cheerless expression, it had worn for many weeks. The child saw it, and again felt his hunger.

"Mother," she said, "give me a piece of bread."

"I will get some for you to-morrow," she replied. "There is no bread in the house this evening."

"I am 'so' hungry," remarked the child. "Why is there no bread?"

"Mother has got no money to buy any," she replied.

The other child had remained quiet all the while. She still nestled to her mother's side and looked long and earnestly into her face. She was not thinking, for one of her years knew nothing of thought, but divined that all was not right with her mother.

"Eva, my child," the mother said, speaking to her for the first time, "go to the grocers, and ask him if he will let me have a loaf of bread on credit."

"I am so glad you have sent for bread," exclaimed the infant on her knees, as he clapped his hand joyfully together.

Eva left the room, and in a few minutes returned empty handed.

"Has he refused to let you have it?" asked Mrs. Wentworth.

"Yes, mother," replied the child sadly. "He says he will not give credit to anybody."

"I thought as much," Mrs. Wentworth remarked.

"Then I won't get any bread?" asked the child on her knees.

"No, my darling," Mrs. Wentworth answered, "you must wait until to-morrow."

"I haven't eaten so long, mother," he said. "Why ain't you got any bread?"

"Because mother is poor and without any money," she replied.

"But I feel so hungry," again the child remarked.

"I know it, my sweet boy," replied his mother, "but wait a little longer and I will give you something to eat."

Her heart was wrung with agony at the complaint of the child and his call for bread; but she knew not how to evade his questions or to procure food. The thought of asking charity had never once entered her mind, for those with whom she had daily intercourse, were too much engaged in self-interest to make her hope that any appeal for help would touch their sordid hearts; and yet food must be had, but how she knew not. Her promise to give her child food, on the next day, was made only to silence his call for bread. There was no prospect of receiving any money, and she could not see her children starve. But one recourse was left. She must sell the bed -- the last piece of furniture remaining in the room -- no matter that in so doing her wretchedness increased instead of diminished.

The child was not satisfied with her promise. The pangs he endured were too much for one of his age, and again he uttered his call for bread.

"There is no bread, Willy," said Eva, speaking for the first time. "Don't ask for any bread. It makes mamma sad."

The child opened his large blue eyes enquiringly upon his sister.

"My sweet, darling child," exclaimed Mrs. Wentworth, clasping the little Ella to her heart, and then bursting into tears at this proof of her child's fortitude, she continued: "Are you not hungry, too?"

"Yes, mother," she replied, "but" -- Here the little girl ceased to speak as if desirous of sparing her mother pain.

"But what?" asked Mrs. Wentworth.

"Mother," exclaimed the child, throwing her arms round her mother's neck, and evading the question, "father will come back to us, and then we will not want bread."

The word "father," brought to Mrs. Wentworth's mind her absent husband. She thought of the agony he would endure if he knew that his wife and children were suffering for food. A swelling of her bosom told of the emotion raging within her, and again the tears started to her eyes.

"Come, my sweet boy," she said, dashing away the tears, as they came like dewdrops from her eyelids, and speaking to the infant on her knee, "it is time to go to bed."

"Ain't I to get some bread before I go to bed?" he asked.

"There is none, darling," she answered hastily. "Wait until tomorrow and you will get some."

"But I am so hungry," again repeated the child, and again a pang of wretchedness shot through the mother's breast.

"Never mind," she observed, kissing him fondly, "if you love me, let me put you to bed like a good child."

"I love you!" he said, looking up into her eyes with all that deep love that instinct gives to children.

She undressed and put him to bed, where the little Ella followed him soon after. Mrs. Wentworth sat by the bedside until they had fallen asleep.

"I love you, mother, but I am so hungry," were the last words the infant murmured as he closed his eyes in sleep, and in that slumber forgot his agonizing pangs for a while.

As soon as they were asleep, Mrs. Wentworth removed from the bedside and seated herself at the window, which she opened. There she sat, looking at the clouds as they floated by, dark as her own prospects were. The morning dawned and saw her still there. It was a beautiful morning, but the warble of the bird in a tree nearby, as he poured forth his morning song, awoke no echo in the heart of the soldier's wife. All was cheerless within her. The brightness of the morning only acted like a gleam of light at the mouth of a cavern. It made the darkness of her thoughts more dismal.

CHAPTER THIRTEENTH.
THE APPEAL FOR CREDIT.

The first call of the little boy, when he awoke in the morning, was for bread. He was doubly hungry now. Thirty-six hours had passed since he had eaten the last mouthful of food that remained in the room. Mrs. Wentworth on that night of vigils, had determined to make an appeal for help to the man she had purchased the furniture from, on her arrival at Jackson, and in the event of his refusing to assist her, to sell the bed on which her children were wont to sleep. This determination had not been arrived at without a struggle in the heart of the soldier's wife. For the first time in her life, she was about to sue for help from a stranger, and the blood rushed to her cheeks, as she thought of the humiliation that poverty entails upon mortal. It is true, she was not about to ask for charity, as her object was only to procure credit for a small quantity of provisions to feed her children with. The debt would be paid, she knew well enough, but still it was asking a favor, and the idea of being obligated to a stranger, was galling to her proud and sensitive nature.

"Mother," exclaimed the child, as he rose from his bed, "it is morning now; ain't I going to get some bread?"

"Yes," she replied, "I will go out to the shop directly and get you some."

About an hour afterwards she left the room, and bidding Ella to take care of her brother, while she was absent, bending her steps towards the store of Mr. Swartz. This gentleman had become, in a few short weeks, possessed of three or four times the wealth he owned when we first introduced him to our readers. The spirit of speculation had seized him among the vast number of the southern people, who were drawn into its vortex, and created untold suffering among the poorer classes of the people. The difference with Mr. Swartz and the great majority of southern speculators, was the depth to which he descended for the purpose of making money. No article of trade, however petty, that he thought himself able to make a few dollars by, was passed aside unnoticed, while he would sell from the paltry amount of a pound of flour to the largest quantity of merchandize required. Like all persons who are suddenly elevated, from comparative dependence, to wealth, he had become purse proud and ostentatious, as he was humble and cringing before the war. In this display of the mushroom, could be easily discovered the vulgar and uneducated favorite of fickle fortune. Even these displays could have been overlooked and pardoned, had he shown any charity to the suffering poor. But his heart was as hard as the flinty rocks against which wash the billows of the Atlantic. The cry of hunger never reached the inside of his breast. It was guarded with a covering of iron, impenetrable to the voice of misery.

And it was to this man that Mrs. Wentworth, in her hour of bitter need applied. She entered his store and enquired of the clerk for Mr. Swartz.

"You, will find him in that room," he replied, pointing to a chamber in the rear of the store.

Mrs. Wentworth entered the room, and found Mr. Swartz seated before a desk. The office, for it was his private office, was most elegantly furnished, and exhibited marks of the proprietor's wealth.

Mr. Swartz elevated his brows with surprise, as he looked at the care-worn expression and needy attire of the woman before him.

"Vot can I do for you my coot voman," he enquired, without even extending the courtesy of offering her a seat.

Mrs. Wentworth remained for a moment without replying. She was embarrassed at the uncourteous reception Mr. Swartz gave her. She did not recollect her altered outward appearance, but thought only of the fact that she was a lady. Her intention to appeal to him for credit, wavered for a while, but the gaunt skeleton, WANT, rose up and held her two children before her, and she determined to subdue pride, and ask the obligation.

"I do not know if you recollect me," she replied at last, and then added, "I am the lady who purchased a lot of furniture from you a few weeks ago."

"I do not remember," Mr. Swartz observed, with a look of surprise. "But vot can I to for you dis morning?"

"I am a soldier's wife," Mrs. Wentworth commenced hesitatingly. "My husband is now a prisoner in the North, and I am here, a refugee from New Orleans, with two small children. Until a short time ago I had succeeded in supporting my little family by working on soldiers' clothing, but the Quartermaster's department having ceased to manufacture clothing, I have been for several days without work." Here she paused. It pained her to continue.

Mr. Swartz looked at her with surprise, and the idea came into his mind that she was an applicant for charity.

"Vell, vot has dat got to do vid your pisness," he observed in a cold tone of voice, determined that she should see no hope in his face.

"This much," she replied. "For over twenty-four hours my two little children and myself have been without food, and I have not a dollar to purchase it."

"I can't do anything for you," Mr. Swartz said with a frown.

"Dere is scarce a day but some peoples or anoder vants charity and I-"

"I do not come to ask for charity," she interrupted hastily. "I have only come to ask you a favor."

"Vat is it?" he enquired.

"As I told you before, my children and myself are nearly starving," she replied. "I have not the means of buying food at present, but think it more than likely I will procure work in a few days. I have called to ask if you would give me credit for a few articles of food until then, by which I will be able to sustain my family."

"I thought it vas something like charity you vanted," he observed, "but I cannot do vat you vish. It is te same ting every tay mit te sogers' families. Dey comes here and asks for charity and credit, shust as if a man vas made of monish -- Gootness gracious! I don't pelieve dat te peoples who comes here every tay is as pad off as tey vish to appear."

"You are mistaken, sir," Mrs. Wentworth replied, "if you think I have come here without being actually in want of the food, I ask you to let me have on credit. Necessity, and dire necessity alone, has prompted me to seek an obligation of you, and if you require it I am willing to pay double the amount you charge, so that my poor children are saved from starvation."

"I reckon you vill," Mr. Swartz said, "but ven you vill pay ish te question."

"I could not name any precise day to you," answered Mrs. Wentworth. "I can only promise that the debt will be paid. If I cannot even pay it myself, as soon as my husband is exchanged, he will pay whatever you charge."

"Dat ish a very doubtful vay of doing pisness," he remarked. "I cannot do as you ask."

"Consider, sir," she replied. "The amount I ask you to credit me for is but small, and even if you should not get paid, which I am certain you will, the loss cannot be felt by a man of your wealth."

"Dat makes no differenish. I can't give you credit. It ish against my rules, and if I proke tem for you I vill have to do so for everybody."

Mrs. Wentworth's heart sank within her at the determined manner in which he expressed his refusal. Without replying she moved towards the door, and was about to leave the room when she thought of the bedstead, on the sale of which she now depended. He may loan money on it she thought, and she returned to the side of his desk. He looked up at her impatiently.

"Vell," he remarked, frowning as he uttered the single word.

"As you won't give me credit," said Mrs. Wentworth, "I thought you may be willing to loan me some money if I gave a security for its payment."

"Vat kind of security?" he enquired.

"I have, at my room, a bedstead I purchased from you some time ago," she replied. "Will you lend a small sum of money on it?"

"No" he answered. "I am not a pawnbroker."

"But you might accommodate a destitute mother," remarked Mrs. Wentworth. "You have refused to give me credit, and now I ask you to loan me a small sum of money, for the payment of which I offer security."

"I cannot do it," he answered. "Ven I says a ting I means it."

"Will you buy the bedstead then?" asked Mrs. Wentworth in despair.

"Vat can I do mit it?" he enquired.

"Why you can sell again," replied Mrs. Wentworth. "It will always find a purchaser, particularly now that the price of everything has increased so largely."

"Veil, I vill puy te pedstead," he said, and then enquired: "How much monish do you vant for it?"

"What will you give me?" she asked.

"I vill give you forty tollars for it," he replied.

"It must be worth more than that," she remarked. "The price of everything is so increased that it appears to me as if the bedstead should command a higher price than that offered by you."

"Shust as you like, my goot voman," Mr. Swartz remarked, shrugging his shoulders. "If you vant at mine price, all veil and goot; if not, you can leave it alone. I only puy te piece of furniture to accommodate you, and you should pe tankful."

"I suppose I will be obliged to take your price," replied Mrs. Wentworth, "although I believe I could get more for it, did I know anyone in town who purchased such things."

He made no reply, but calling his clerk ordered him to bring forty dollars from the safe. The clerk having brought the money retired, and left them alone again.

"Vere is te pedstead?" asked Swartz.

"It is at home," Mrs. Wentworth replied.

"Den you must pring it round here before I can pay for it," he observed.

"I am in want of the money now to buy bread," she answered. "If you will pay me and let your clerk follow with a dray, I would return home immediately and have the bedstead taken down and sent to you."

Mr. Swartz called the clerk again, and ordered him to bring a dray to the front of the store. The clerk did as he was requested, and soon after returned with the intelligence that the dray was ready.

"Do you follow dis voman to her house, and she vill give you a pedstead. Bring it down here," and then he added, speaking to the clerk who had not yet left the room: "Vat does te trayman sharge."

"One dollar and a half," was the reply.

Taking up the forty dollars which had been previously brought to him, Mr. Swartz counted out thirty-eight and a half dollars, and handed them to Mrs. Wentworth.

"De von tollar and a half out ish to pay for te trayage," he remarked as she received the money.

She made no reply, but left the room followed by the clerk, when, with the drayman, they soon arrived at her room. The bedstead was soon taken down and removed to Mr. Swartz's store.

"Sharge one huntred tollars for dat pedstead," he remarked to his clerk as soon as it had arrived.

While he was rejoicing at the good speculation he had made, the soldier's wife sat on a box in her room feeding her half-famished children. The room was now utterly destitute of furniture, but the heart of the mother rejoiced at the knowledge that for a couple of weeks longer her children would have food.

CHAPTER FOURTEENTH.
DR. HUMPHRIES BUYS A SLAVE
AND BRINGS HOME NEWS.

A few days after Mrs. Wentworth had sold her last piece of furniture, Dr. Humphries was walking along one of the principal streets in Jackson when he was stopped by a crowd that had gathered in front of an auction mart. On walking up, he learned that it was a sheriff's sale of a "likely young negro girl." Remembering that Emma had requested him to purchase a girl as a waiting maid for her, he examined the slave and found her in all respects the kind of house servant he desired. Going up to the auctioneer who had just mounted a bench for the purpose of selling the slave, he enquired where she had come from. The auctioneer responded by handing the doctor a small hand bill setting forth the sale. After reading it he walked up to the slave and commenced to question her.

"What is your name?" he enquired.

"Elsy, sir," she replied.

"You say that you come from New Orleans," he continued.

"Yes, sir," she responded.

"What was your master's name?" asked the doctor.

"His name is Mr. Alfred Wentworth," the negro answered.

"Where is your master now?" he enquired, continuing his questions.

"Massa is a prisner in de Yankee army," she replied.

"And what made you leave New Orleans?" was the next question.

"My missis was turned away from de city, and I runaway from dem Yankees and come here to look for her."

"Have you not been able to find your mistress?" asked Dr. Humphries.

"No, sir. Jest as I came here de city police took me up and put me in jail."

"Excuse me," interrupted the auctioneer, "but I must sell this girl at once. Time is precious, so you must excuse me;" then turning to the crowd he continued: "Here is the slave, gentlemen. She is an intelligent looking negro; says she understands all that appertains to the duties of a house servant. What will you bid for her?"

"Seven hundred dollars," exclaimed a voice in the crowd.

"Thank you, sir; seven hundred dollars; going at seven hundred dollars. Look at the girl, gentlemen, going at seven hundred dollars. Can I get another bid?" exclaimed the auctioneer in the rapid voice peculiar to his class.

"Seven hundred and twenty-five," was the next bid.

"Seven hundred and fifty," Dr. Humphries cried out, having made up his mind to purchase her.

In a few minutes the slave was "knocked down" to the doctor for eleven hundred dollars, and after the proper form was gone through and the money paid, he ordered her to follow him, and retraced his steps homeward.

As our readers must have recognized already, Elsy was no other than the slave who was left at New Orleans by Mrs. Wentworth, and who declared that she would follow her mistress into the Confederate lines. After making several ineffectual attempts she had succeeded in reaching Baton Rouge, the capital of Louisiana, at which place she eluded the Federal pickets, and made her way to Jackson. The first part of her journey being through the country she passed unnoticed, until on her arrival at Jackson she was stopped by the police, who demanded her papers. Not having any she was confined in the county jail, and after due notice in the papers, calling for the owner to come and take her away, she was sold at auction according to law. The girl was very much grieved at her failure to find her mistress, but being of a good disposition soon became contented with her lot. Accordingly, when Dr. Humphries purchased her, she followed him home with a cheerful step.

On entering his house, the doctor presented the negro to Emma.

"Here, Emma," he observed, "is a girl I have bought for you to-day."

"Thank you," she answered, looking at Elsy. "This is really a nice-looking girl. Who did you buy her from?"

"She says she is from New Orleans. Her master is a prisoner in the hands of the Yankees, and her mistress being turned out of her home by Butler, is now somewhere in the Confederacy, but where, the girl cannot tell. When her mistress left New Orleans, the Yankees would not permit the slave to leave with her, but she succeeded in escaping from their lines, and came to Jackson, where she was arrested, and as no owner claimed her, she was sold to me at auction this morning according to law."

"Then we will not be doing justice to the owner of the girl, if we keep her constantly. Perhaps her mistress is some poor soldier's wife who would be glad to get the money you have expended, or may require her services."

"I have thought of that before I purchased her, but as she seems honest, I did not make the thought prevent me from getting her. I have also made up my mind to give her up should her owner at any time claim her, and he is a poor man."

"I am glad you have so decided," Emily replied, "for I should not have liked the idea of depriving any Confederate soldier of his slave, particularly if he is a poor man. And now," she continued, speaking to Elsy, "do you go in the next room and wait there until I come in."

Making a curtesy, Elsy left the parlor, and entered the room pointed out by Emily.

"I have some news for you, Emily," remarked the Doctor as soon as the negro had left the room.

"What is it about," she enquired.

"Something that will interest you considerably," he answered.

"If it will interest me, let me know what it is," she remarked

"I have received a telegraphic dispatch from Harry," Dr. Humphries replied.

"Why, how could he have arrived in our lines?" she enquired, as a smile of joy illumined her features.

"Here is what the dispatch says:" 'I arrived here this morning, having escaped from prison. Will be in Jackson on to-morrow's train. Show this to Emily.'

"I am so glad," exclaimed Emily joyfully, as soon as her father had concluded reading the dispatch, "for," she continued, "I was beginning to be afraid that our unfortunate prisoners in the hands of the Yankees, would never be exchanged."

"You need not have labored under any such fear," Dr. Humphries observed. "The papers of this morning announce that a cartel has been arranged, and the prisoners held on both sides will be shortly exchanged."

"Nevertheless, I am glad that Harry has made his escape, for it will bring him to us sooner than we anticipated. Besides which, it is gratifying to know that he had no occasion to wait for an exchange."

"That is very true" replied her father, "and as he has safely escaped, you can rejoice, but the dangers which must have, necessarily presented themselves in the attempt, were of such a nature, that you would not have desired him to make the effort had you known them."

"He is safe, and we can well afford to laugh at them," she answered, "all I hope is that he may never be taken prisoner again."

"I do not believe he will relish the idea, much less the reality of such a thing again occurring," observed Dr. Humphries. "However," he continued, "he will be here to-morrow, and the little cloud that his capture had sent over our happiness, will have been removed, and all will again be bright."

As he concluded speaking, a servant entered with a letter

containing a summons to attend a patient, and Dr. Humphries kissing his daughter once more, left the house.

CHAPTER FIFTEENTH.
ARRIVAL OF HARRY.

The next day Emily prepared herself to welcome the return of her lover, while Dr. Humphries proceeded to the railroad depot to meet him. In the meantime, we will give our readers a brief account of Harry's escape.

After leaving Chicago, Harry made his way through the country towards the Tennessee river. His journey was a dangerous one, for the people of Illinois where then highly elated at the successes which had attended the Yankee arms, and the few sympathizers that the South had in their midst, were afraid to express their sympathies. He, luckily, however, succeeded in finding out a worthy gentleman, who not only befriended him, but furnished the necessary means for his journey, and procured a passport for him to visit Nashville. Prepared for a continuation of his travel, Harry, who had been staying at the residence of his noble hearted host for three days, bade him adieu, and started on his way to Nashville. On arriving at Frankfort, Kentucky, he met with a man he had become acquainted with in Mississippi, but who, on account of his strong Union proclivities, was compelled to leave the South at the commencement of the war. This creature immediately recognized Harry, and knowing that he had always been an ardent Secessionist, conjectured that he was either a spy, or an escaped prisoner. Harry was accordingly arrested and carried before the military authorities, but his persistent denial of any knowledge of the man who had caused his arrest, and the passport he had received from the generous Illinoisan, induced the Yankee officer by whom he was examined, to release him, and permit his departure for Nashville.

Harry had many hair breadth escapes from detection and capture, but surmounting all the dangers which beset his path, he succeeded In reaching the Confederate lines in safety, and immediately started for Jackson. But one thing marred the joy he experienced at his daringly won freedom, and that was his ignorance of Alfred's fate. Had not the love of freedom been too strong in his breast, he would have returned and endeavored to find his friend, but the success of his escape, and the idea that Alfred may have pursued a different road, deterred him from so doing. He determined, however, to make enquiry on his return to Jackson, whether his friend had arrived there, he having promised Harry to call on Dr. Humphries after they should arrive in the Confederate lines. He was not aware of the wound his friend had received, for though the Chicago papers made a notice of the attempted escape, and wounding of one of the prisoners, the notice was never seen by him, as he had no opportunity of getting a newspaper.

On arriving at Jackson, the evening after he had forwarded his telegraphic dispatch, Harry found Dr. Humphries at the depot awaiting his arrival. After they had exchanged hearty expressions of delight at meeting each other again, they proceeded to the house where Emma was anxiously looking out for her lover.

The customary salutations between lovers who have been separated being over, Harry proceeded to give an account of his escape, which was listened to with great interest by his hearers.

"By the way," he remarked, as soon as he had concluded, "has a soldier giving his name as Wentworth, and claiming to be a friend of mine, called here within the last ten days."

"No one has called here of that name," replied Dr. Humphries.

"I am very anxious to receive some intelligence of him," remarked Harry, "He was the friend I mentioned, having made my escape with."

"He may have taken a different road to the one you pursued," Dr. Humphries observed.

"If I were satisfied in my mind that he did escape safely, my fears would be allayed," he answered, "but," he continued, "we left the gates of the prison together, and were not four yards apart when the treachery of the guard was discovered. We both started at a full run, and almost instantaneously the Yankees, who lay in ambush for us, fired, their muskets in the direction wc were going. The bullets whistled harmless by me, and I continued my flight at the top of my speed, nor did I discover the absence of my friend until some distance from the prison, when stopping to take breath, I called him by name, and receiving no answer found out that he was not with me. I am afraid he might have been shot."

"Did you hear no cry after the Yankees had fired," enquired Dr. Humphries.

"No, and that is the reason I feel anxious to learn his fate. Had he uttered any cry, I should be certain that he was wounded, but the silence on his part may have been caused from instant death."

"You would have heard him fall at any rate; had he been struck by the Yankee bullets," remarked Dr. Humphries.

"That is very doubtful," he replied. "I was running at such a rapid rate, and the uproar made by the Yankees was sufficient to drown the sound that a fall is likely to create."

"I really trust your friend is safe," said Dr. Humphries. "Perhaps, after all, he did not make any attempt to escape, but surrendered himself to the Yankees."

"There is not the slightest chance of his having done such a thing," Harry answered. "He was determined to escape, and had told me that he would rather be shot than be re-captured, after once leaving the prison. I shall never cease to regret the misfortune should he have fallen in our attempt to escape. His kindness to me at Fort Donelson had caused a warm friendship to spring up between us. Besides which, he has a wife and two small children in New Orleans, who were the sole cause of his attempting to escape. He informed me that they were not in very good circumstances, and should Alfred Wentworth have been killed at Camp Douglas, God help his poor widow and orphans!"

"Did you say his name was Alfred Wentworth," inquired Emma, for the first time joining in the conversation.

"Yes, and do you know anything about him?" he asked.

"No," she replied, "I know nothing of the gentleman, but father bought a slave on yesterday, who stated that she has belonged to a gentleman of New Orleans, of the name you mentioned just now."

"By what means did you purchase her?" asked Harry addressing himself to Dr. Humphries.

The Doctor related to him the circumstances which occasioned the purchase, as well as the statement of Elsy. Harry listened attentively, for the friendship he felt for his friend naturally made him interested in all that concerned Alfred, or his family.

"Is there no way by which I can discover where Mrs. Wentworth is residing at present?" he enquired, after a moment of thought.

"None that I could devise," answered Dr. Humphries. "I know nothing of the family personally, nor would I have known anything of their existence, had not chance carried me to the auction sale, at which I purchased Elsy."

"Call the girl here for me," Harry said: "I must learn something more of the departure of Mrs. Wentworth and her children from New Orleans, and endeavor to obtain a clue to her whereabouts. It is a duty I owe to the man who saved my life, that everything I can do for his family shall be performed."

Emma left the room as he was speaking, and shortly after returned, followed by Elsy.

"Here is the girl," she said, as she entered.

"So, you belonged to Mr. Wentworth of New Orleans, did you?" Harry commenced.

"I used to belong to him," replied Elsy.

"What made Mrs. Wentworth leave New Orleans?" he asked, continuing his questions.

Elsy gave a long account of the villainy of Awtry, in the usual style adopted by negroes, but sufficiently intelligible for Harry to understand the cause of Mrs. Wentworth being compelled to abandon her home, and take refuge in the Confederate lines.

"Did not your mistress state where she was going," he asked.

"No, sah," replied Elsy. "My mistis jest told me good bye when she left wid de children. I promised her I would get away from de Yankees, but she forgot to tell me whar she was gwine to lib."

"Did she bring out plenty of money with her?" he enquired.

"Yes, sah," Elsy answered. She had seen the sum of money possessed by Mrs. Wentworth, on her departure from New Orleans, and it being a much larger amount than she had ever beheld before, made the faithful girl believe that her mistress had left with quite a fortune.

"Very well, you can go now," remarked Harry. "It is a satisfaction," he continued as Elsy left the room, "o know that Wentworth's wife is well provided with money, although it does appear strange that she should have a plenty of funds, when her husband informed me, while in prison, that the money he left her with could not maintain his wife and children for any great length of time."

"She may have been furnished with money by some friend, who intending to remain in the city, had no use for Confederate Treasury notes," Dr. Humphries remarked.

"That is very likely, and I trust it is so," observed Harry, "However," he continued, "I shall take steps on Monday next, to find out where Mrs. Wentworth is now residing."

On Monday the following advertisement appeared in the evening papers:

INFORMATION WANTED.

Any one knowing where Mrs. Eva Wentworth and her two children reside, will be liberally rewarded, by addressing the undersigned at this place. Mrs. Wentworth is a refugee from New Orleans, and the wife of a gallant soldier, now a prisoner of war. Jackson, -- 1862.

H. SHACKLEFORD.

It was too late. Extensively published as it was, Mrs. Wentworth never saw it. Her hardships and trials had increased ten-fold; she was fast drifting before the storm, with breakers before, threatening to wreck and sink into the grave the wife and children of Alfred Wentworth.

CHAPTER SIXTEENTH.
MR. ELDER DEMANDS HIS RENT -- NOTICE TO QUIT.

The money received by Mrs. Wentworth from Mr. Swartz, proved but a temporary relief for her children and herself. A fatal day was fast arriving, and she knew not how to avert the impending storm. By a great deal of labor and deprivation she had heretofore succeeded in paying the rent of the room she occupied, although Mr. Elder had twice advanced the price. Now there was no hope of her being able to obtain a sufficient sum of money to meet the demand of that gentleman, who would call on her the following day in person, did she not call at his office and settle for at least one month's rent in advance. The month for which she had paid expired in three days, and she was apprehensive of being turned out, unless she could collect sufficient money to pay him. She knew not where to find the means. The room was stripped bare of furniture to supply the calls of nature; nothing but a mattress in one corner of the apartment, and a few cooking utensils remained. She labored day and night, to procure work, but all her efforts were unavailing. It appeared to her as if the Almighty had forsaken herself and children, and had left them to perish through want.

It cannot be that God would place his image on earth, and willingly leave them to perish from destitution. Many have been known to die of starvation, and the tales of wretchedness and woe with which the public ear is often filled attest the fact. Squalid forms and threadbare garments are seen, alas! too often in this civilized world, and the grave of the pauper is often opened to receive some unhappy mortal, whose life had been one scene of suffering and want. Philanthropy shudders and Christianity believes it to be a punishment, administered by the hand of God; that the haggard cause of the starved creature, who has thus miserably died, once contained the spirit of a mortal undergoing the penalty of Him, who judges mankind on high, and expiating through his heart-rending bodily agony, crimes committed in by-gone days.

This is not so in all cases. What mercy could we attribute to God, did He willingly entail misery upon the innocent, or punish them for the crimes of the guilty? Why call it a dispensation of Divine justice, that would condemn to weeks, months and years of wretchedness, the mortals He brought in the world himself? Who hath seen the hovel of the pauper; beheld its wretched inmates, heard their tale of woe, heard them tell of days passing without their having a crumb of bread to satisfy the cravings of hunger, or seen them in that last stage of destitution, when hunger brings on despair, until the mind wanders from its seat, and madness takes its place; heard the raving of the maniac, his frenzied call for bread, and his abject desolation, until death came kindly to relieve his sufferings, and felt not that the hand of God had never worked so much ill for His people? Is it profanity to say that the eye of God had wandered from them? We believe it; for the Book that teaches us of the Almighty, depicts him as a God of mercy and compassion. The eye of the Omnipotent is not upon the wretched. "He seeth all things," but there are times when His eyes are turned from those who endure the storm of a cold and heartless world, and He knows not of their suffering, until the Angel of Death brings their spirit before the Judgment seat.

God had not deserted the soldier's wife, but His eyes were turned away, and He saw not her condition. Thus, was she left unaided by the Hand of Providence. She felt her desolation, for as each day passed by, and her condition became worse, she knew that her prayers were unanswered. They reached not the ear of the Almighty, and the innocent children were allowed to participate of that bitter cup, which the chances of worldly fortune had placed before the unhappy family.

Three days sped away quickly, and the fatal morning arrived. She had no money to pay the rent, and the day passed away without Mr. Elder receiving a visit from her. She dared not to tell him of her position, but awaited patiently his arrival on the following day, for she well knew he would be sure to come.

The next morning saw him at her door, much annoyed at the trouble she gave him to call and collect the money. Mrs. Wentworth had nothing to say, nor had she a dollar to satisfy his demands.

"Good morning, madam," he said, as she opened the door to admit him, "I was much surprised at your not calling to pay the rent at my office on yesterday. I admire punctuality above everything else."

He entered the room, and cast his eyes on its empty walls. They did not satisfy him, for the absence of any furniture told the tale of the soldier's wife in a more graphic manner than words could have done.

"What does this mean?" he enquired.

"It means that necessity has compelled a mother to sacrifice everything to keep her children from starving," Mrs. Wentworth replied.

"Humph," said Mr. Elder. "This is singular. So, I suppose," he continued, addressing her, "you will say you have no money to pay your month's rent in advance."

"I have not a dollar this day to buy bread," she answered.

A frown gathered on Mr. Elder's brow, as he remarked: "I suppose you recollect the arrangement made between us when you first hired the room from me."

"What arrangement was that?" she enquired in an absent manner.

"That on you failing to pay the rent, I should have the power to resume possession of the room, without giving you notice to leave."

"I recollect," she said.

"Well, in accordance with our arrangements, I shall require that you vacate the room to-day, as I can procure another tenant, who will be able to pay the rent promptly."

"Do you mean that I must leave to-day," she asked.

"Yes," he replied, "I desire to have the room renovated at once."

"Where can I go to without money," she enquired, in a tone more like as if she was addressing herself than speaking to him.

"I really cannot tell my good, woman," he answered, "I am sorry for your position, but cannot afford to lose the rent of my room, I am compelled to pay my taxes, and support myself by the money I receive from rent."

"I cannot leave to-day," Mrs. Wentworth cried in a despairing tone. "I cannot leave to-day. Oh, sir! look at my child lying on that wretched bed, and tell me, if you can have the heart to turn me out, homeless, friendless and alone."

"My good Woman," he answered. "I cannot help your misfortunes, nor can I do anything to assist you. If you can pay the rent, I have no objection to your remaining, but if you can not, I will be compelled to get another tenant who will be able."

"Sir," she remarked, speaking slowly. "I am a woman with two children, alone in this State. My husband and protector is now pining in a Yankee prison, a sacrifice on the altar of his country. Let me ask you as a man, and perhaps a father, to pause ere you turn a helpless woman from the shelter of your property. You appear wealthy, and the sum charged for the rent would make but little difference to you, if it was never paid. Oh! do not eject us from this room. My child lies there parched with fever, and to remove her may be fatal."

"There is no necessity for any appeals to me," he replied. "If I were to give way to such extravagant requests in your case, I should be necessitated to do so in others, and the result would be, that I should find myself sheltering all my tenants, without receiving any pay for house rent. The idea cannot be entertained for a moment."

"Let your own heart speak," she said, "and not the promptings of worldly thoughts. All those who rent your houses are not situated as I am. They are at home among friends, who will aid and succor them, if ever necessity overtook them. I am far away from home and friends. There is no one in this town that I can call upon for assistance, and even now, my children are without food for want of funds to purchase it. Do not add to my wretchedness by depriving them of shelter. Let me know that if we are to die of starvation, a roof, at least, will cover our bodies."

He looked at her with unchanged countenance. Not even the movement of a muscle, denoted that his heart was touched at her pathetic appeal. His expression was as hard and cold as adamantine, nor did a single feeling of pity move him. He cared for nothing but money; she could not give him what he wanted, and too sentiment of commiseration, no spark of charity, no feeling of manly regret at her sufferings entered his bosom.

"Be charitable," she continued. "I have prayed night after night to God to relieve my necessities; I have walked the town through and through in the effort to procure work, but my prayers have been unanswered, and my efforts have proven unavailing. At times the thought of the maelstrom of woe into which I am plunged, has well-nigh driven me to madness. My brain has seemed on fire, and the shrieks of the maniac would have been heard resounding through the walls of this room, but my children would come before me, and the light of reason would again return. But for their sake I should welcome death as a precious boon. Life has but every charm for me. In the pale and alternated woman before you, none could recognize a once happy wife. Oh, sir!" she continued, with energy; "believe me when I tell you that for my children's sake alone, I now appeal. Hear me, and look with pity on a mother's pleadings. It is for them I plead. Were I alone, no word of supplication would you hear. I should leave here, and in the cold and turbid waters of Pearl River, find the rest I am denied on earth."

"This is a very unaccountable thing to me," said Mr. Elder. "You make an agreement to leave as soon as you fail to pay your rent, and now that that hour has arrived, instead of conforming to your agreement, I am beset with a long supplication. My good woman, this effort of yours to induce me to provide a home for your family at my expense, cannot be successful. You have no claim upon my charity, and those who have, are sufficiently numerous already without my desiring to make any addition. As I mentioned before, you must either find money to pay the rent, or vacate the room."

"Give me time," she said, speaking with an effort; "give me but two days, and I will endeavor either to obtain the money, or to procure somewhere to stay."

Mr. Elder knit his brows again as he answered. "I cannot give you two days, for I intend renting the room by to-morrow. You can, however, remain here until this evening, at which time you must either be prepared to leave, or find money to pay for the rent."

"It is well," she replied. "I will do as you say."

"Then you may expect me here this evening at dusk," he said, and turning towards the door left the room muttering; "when will I ever get rid of this crowd of paupers, who, it is always my luck to rent rooms to."

"God of Heaven aid me!" exclaimed Mrs. Wentworth, as she closed the door in the receding form of Mr. Elder, and sank on her knees before the bed on which Ella lay in a high fever.

CHAPTER SEVENTEENTH.
THE EJECTMENT.

Mrs. Wentworth knew not where to go to procure money to pay the rent, and when she asked Mr. Elder to give her time to procure either the means of paying him, or to procure another place to stay, she did so only to avert the threatened ejectment for a brief period. Nor did she know where to procure another shelter. There was no one in the town that she knew from whom she could have obtained a room to rent, unless the money was paid in advance.

After Mr. Elder's departure, she fell on her knees and prayed for help, but she did so only from habit, not with the belief that an Omnipotent arm would be stretched out to aid her. There she knelt and prayed, until the thought of her sick child flashed across her brain, and rising, she stooped over and enquired how she felt.

"The same way," answered Ella. "I feel very hot, and my throat is quite parched."

"You have got the fever, darling," said Mrs. Wentworth. – "Is there anything I can do for you?"

"Nothing," replied Ella, "except," she continued, "you could get me something sweet to take this bitter taste from my mouth."

A pang shot through Mrs. Wentworth's heart as she replied, "I cannot get anything just now. You must wait until a little later in the day."

She spoke sadly, for it was a deception that she was practicing upon her child, when she promised to gratify her wishes at a later hour.

"Never mind," observed Ella. "Do not trouble yourself, my dear mother, I do not want it very badly."

The little girl defined the cause of her mother's not acceding to her request at that moment, and she had no desire to cause her additional pain, by again asking for anything to moisten her parched lips, or remove the dry and bitter taste that the fever had caused.

Mrs. Wentworth had at last found out that Ella was sick. -- Not from any complaint of the child, for the little girl remained suffering in silence, and never hinted that she was unwell. -- But she had become so weak that one morning, on endeavoring to rise from the bed, she fell back and fainted from exhaustion, and on her mother's chafing her forehead with water for the purpose of reviving her, discovered that Ella had a hot fever. She was very much alarmed, and would have called a doctor, but knowing no medical man who would attend her child without remuneration, she was necessitated to content herself with what knowledge she had of sickness. This had caused the money she had remaining in her possession to be quickly expended.

The little girl bore her illness uncomplainingly, and although each day she sunk lower and felt herself getting weaker, she concealed her condition, and answered her mother's questions cheerfully. She was a little angel that God had sent to Mrs. Wentworth. She was too young to appreciate the extent of her mother's wretchedness, but she saw that something was wrong and kept silent, and she lay there that day sick. There was no hope for the child. Death had marked her as his prey, and nothing could stay or turn away his ruthless hand from this little flower of earth. Stern fate had decreed that she should die. The unalterable sentence had been registered in the book of Heaven, and an angel stood at her bedside ready to take her to God.

The day passed over the wretched family. Ella lay on the bed in silence throughout, what appeared to her, the long and weary hours; the little boy called every few minutes for bread, and as his infant voice uttered the call, the agony of Mrs. Wentworth increased. Thus was the day passed, and as the dusk of evening spread its mantle over the town, the soldier's wife prepared to receive her summons for ejectment. She was not kept waiting long. No sooner had the darkness set in, than Mr. Elder, accompanied by another man, opened the door and entered the room.

"Well," he said, "have you succeeded in procuring money to pay the rent."

"I have not," Mrs. Wentworth answered.

"I suppose you have made arrangements to go somewhere else then," he remarked.

"No," she replied. "My child has been ill all day long, and I was compelled to remain here and attend to her wants."

"That is very unfortunate," Mr. Elder remarked, "for this gentleman," pointing to the stranger who accompanied him, "has made arrangements to take the room, and will move into it to-night."

"Will he not wait until the morning," she enquired.

"I do not know," he replied. "Will you," he asked, speaking to the man, "be willing to wait until to-morrow before you take possession?"

"Bo jabers! I've got to leave my owld room to-night, and if I cannot git this, I must take another that I can get in town," answered the man, who was a rough and uneducated son of the Emerald Isle.

"That settles the matter, then," observed Mr. Elder. "You will have to leave," he continued, addressing Mrs. Wentworth. "You will perceive that I cannot lose a tenant through your remaining in the room to-night."

"Och!" said the Irishman, "if the lady can't lave to-night, shure ah' I will take the other room, for be jabers I wouldn't have a woman turned out of doors for me."

"You need not fear about that, my good friend," remarked Mr. Elder. "Does the room suit you?"

"Yes! It does well enough for myself and my children," was the answer.

"Then you can consider yourself a tenant from to-night," Mr. Elder said. "Go and bring your things here. By the time you return I shall have the room vacated and ready for you."

"Jist as you say, yer honor," replied the man, as he bowed himself from the room.

"And now, my good woman," remarked Mr. Elder, "you will perceive the necessity of removing your children and whatever articles you may have here to some other place at once. I cannot be induced to grant any further time, and lose tenants by the operation."

"Great God, sir!" exclaimed Mrs. Wentworth, "where am I to go to? I know of no place where I can find a shelter this night. You cannot, must not, force me to leave."

"I trust you will not put me to the necessity of having you ejected by force," remarked Mr. Elder. "You are fully aware that by the arrangement entered into between us, when you first rented the room, that I am doing nothing illegal in requiring you to leave. You will save me both trouble and pain by doing as I have requested."

"I cannot," she replied, pressing her hands to her forehead, and then bursting into tears she exclaimed appealingly: "For the sake of God have pity, sir! Let not your heart be so hardened, but turn and befriend a soldiers wretched wife. There is scarce a beast but contains some touch of feeling, scarce a heart but vibrates in some degree, and beats with a quicker pulsation at the sight of poverty and misery. Let me hope that yours contains the same feeling, and beats with the same sorrow at the miserable scene before you. Look around you, sir, and see the destitution of my family; go to the side of that lowly bed and press your hand upon the burning brow of my child; call that little boy and ask him how long he has been without food, look at a wretched mother's tears, and lot a gracious God remove the hardness from your heart, and drive us not homeless from this roof. Think not that the ragged, woman who now stands before you, weeping and pleading, would have thus supplicated without a cause. There was a time when I never dreamed of experiencing such suffering and hardship, such bitter, bitter woe. Oh! sir, let pity reign dominant in your heart."

He was unmoved. Why should he care for the misery of strangers? Was he not of the world as man generally finds it? The exceptions to the rule are not of this earth. They occupy a place in the celestial realms, for, if even they may have committed sins in early life, their deeds of charity blots out the record, and they enter Heaven welcomed by the hosts of angels who dwell there, while their absence from this creates a void not easily filled.

Mr. Elder answered her not for several minutes. He stood there with his arms folded, silently gazing upon the thin form of Mrs. Wentworth, who, with clasped hands and outstretched arms, anxiously awaited his decision. But he gave no promise of acquiescence, no hope of pity, no look of charity in his features -- they looked cold, stern, and vexed.

There she stood the picture of grief, awaiting the words that would either give her hope or plunge her forever into the fathomless depths of despair. The eyes of the soldier's wife were turned on Mr. Elder with a sad and supplicating look. In any other but the cold, calculating creature before her, their look might have moved to pity, but with him nothing availed; not even a struggle for mastery between humanity and brutality could be seen, and as she gazed upon him, she felt that there was no chance of her wishes being gratified.

Her little son clung to her dress half frightened at the attitude of his mother, and the stern and unforbidding aspect of Mr. Elder. Ella strove to rise while her mother was speaking, but fell back on her bed unable to perform the effort. She was, therefore, content to be there and listen to the conversation as it occurred between Mr. Elder and her mother. Her little heart was also tortured, for this had been the first time she had ever heard such passionate and earnest language as was depicted in Mrs. Wentworth's words.

At last Mr. Elder spoke, and his words were eagerly listened to by Mrs. Wentworth.

"This annoys me very much," he said. "Your importunities are very disagreeable to me, and I must insist that they shall cease. As I told you before, I cannot afford to lose tenants in an unnecessary act of liberality, and through mistaken charity. The fact is," he continued in a firm and decisive tone, "you 'must' leave this room to-night. I will not listen to any more of your pleading. Your case is but the repetition of many others who fled from their homes and left all they had, under the impression that the people of other States would be compelled to support them. This is a mistaken idea, and the sooner its error is made known the better it will be for the people of the South, whose homes are in the hands of the enemy."

"Then you are determined that my children and myself shall be turned from the shelter of this room to-night," she enquired, dropping her hands by her side, and assuming a standing attitude.

"You have heard what I have already said, my good woman," he replied. "And let me repeat, that I will listen to no further supplications."

"I shall supplicate to you no more," she answered. "I see, alas! Too well, that I might sooner expect pity from the hands of an uncivilized Indian than charity or aid from you. Nor will I give you any trouble to forcibly eject me."

"I am very glad to hear it," he rejoined.

"Yes," she continued, without noticing his words, "I shall leave of my own accord, and there," she said, pointing to Ella, "lies my sick child. Should exposure on this night cause her death, I shall let you know of it that you may have some subject, accruing from your heartless conduct, on which to ponder."

Slowly she removed all the articles that were in the room, and placed them on the sidewalk. There were but few things in the room, and her task was soon completed.

"Come, darling," she said as she wrapped up Ella in a cover-lid and lifted the child in her arms, "come, and let us go."

Mr. Elder still stood with folded arms looking on.

"Farewell, sir," she said, turning to him, "you have driven a soldier's helpless wife and children from the roof that covered them into the open streets, with none other than skies above as a covering. May God pardon you as I do," and speaking to the little boy who still clung to her dress, she replied, "Come, darling, let us go."

Go where? She knew not, thought not where. She only knew that she was now homeless.

The clouds looked as serene, the stars twinkled as merrily as ever, and the moon shed as bright a light upon the form of the soldier's wife, as she walked out of that room, a wanderer upon the earth, as it did on scenes of peace and happiness. The Ruler of the Universe saw not the desolate mother and her children; thus, there was no change in the firmament, for had He gazed upon them at that moment, a black cloud would have been sent to obscure the earth, and darkness would have taken the place of light.

CHAPTER EIGHTEENTH.
THE RESTING PLACE -- ANOTHER VISIT TO MR. SWARTZ.

The mother and her child walked on in silence. Mrs. Wentworth knew not where to go. From her heart the harrowing cry of desolation went out, and mingled with the evening air, filling it with the sound of wretchedness, until it appeared dull and stifling. But she knew not this, for to her it had never appeared pleasant. For weeks past her cup of misery had been filling, and as each drop of sorrow entered the goblet of her life, so did all sense of what was happy and lovely depart from her heart. She was, indeed, a breathing figure of all that could be conceived miserable and unhappy. The flowers that bloomed in the Spring time of her happy years, had withered in the winter of her wretched weeks, and over the whole garden of her life, nothing but the dead and scentless petals remained, to tell of what was once a paradise of affection -- a blooming image of love.

As she walked on, she discovered that the child she carried in her arms had fainted. She paused not for consideration, but observing a light in a small cabin near by, she hurriedly bent her steps towards it, and entered through the half-opened door. It was the home of an aged negro woman, and who looked up much surprised at the intrusion.

"Here, auntie," Mrs. Wentworth said hastily, "give me some water quickly, my child has fainted."

"Goodness, gracious, what could ha' made you bring dem children to dis part of de town dis time o' night," exclaimed the old negress, as she hastened to do the bidding of Mrs. Wentworth, who had already placed the inanimate body of Ella on the negro's humble bed.

The water being brought, Mrs. Wentworth sprinkled it upon the face of the child, but without avail. Ella still remained motionless, and to all appearances lifeless.

"Great Heaven!" exclaimed Mrs. Wentworth, "my child cannot be dead!"

"Top a bit, mistis, an' I will fix de little gal for you," said the old negro, hobbling, to the bedside, with a small bottle filled with camphor in her hand. "Dis stuff will bring her to. Don't be afeard, she ain't dead."

Pouring out some of the stimulant in one hand, the kind-hearted old woman bathed Ella's face with it, and held the bottle to her nostrils, until a sigh from the child showed that she still lived. After a few seconds she opened her eyes, and looked up to her mother, who was, bending with anxious countenance over her.

"Dar now," said the old negro in a tone of satisfaction, "did not I tell you dat de sweet little child was libbing."

"Thank you, old woman, God in Heaven bless you!" exclaimed Mrs. Wentworth, as she clapped the old woman's hand in her own.

"Berry well, berry well," was the answer of the negro, "you welcome misses."

There, in the cabin of that good old slave, the soldier's wife heard the first voice of kindness that had greeted her ears for months. From the hands of a servile race, she had received the first act of charity, and in a land like this. In the performance of that kindness, the old slave had done more to elevate herself than all the philanthropists and abolitionists of the North could have done. Could the cursed race, whose war upon the South have seen this act, they would have conceded to her people the justice of their right to slavery, when such a slave as this existed.

"What make you come to dis part ob town to-night, missis," asked the negro, after a few moments of silence.

"Nothing, nothing, my good woman," replied Mrs. Wentworth hastily. She could not let a slave know of her trials and misery.

"Poh ting!" ejaculated the old woman in a compassionate tone, but too low for Mrs. Wentworth to hear her. "I 'spec her husband been treatin' her bad. Dem men behave berry bad sometime," and with a sigh she resumed her silence.

The soldier's wife sat by the bedside, on one of the rude chairs, that formed a portion of the furniture, and remained plunged in thought. A deep sleep had overtaken Ella, although her breathing was heavy, and the fever raged with redoubled violence.

"Mother can't I get something to eat?" asked her little son. His words woke his mother from her thoughts, but before she could reply, the old negro had forestalled.

"Is it some ting you want to eat, my little darling," she enquired, rising from her seat, and going to a little cupboard near the door of the room.

"Yes granny," he answered, "I am quite hungry."

"Bress your little heart," she remarked, giving him a large piece of bread. "Here is some ting to eat."

Taking the child on her knees, she watched him until he had completed eating the food, when putting him down, she opened a trunk, and pulled out a clean white sheet, which she placed on a little mattress near the bed.

"Come now," she said, "go to bed now like a good boy."

The child obeyed her, and was soon enjoying a refreshing sleep.

"Where will you sleep to-night, auntie," asked Mrs. Wentworth, who had been a silent observer of the old woman's proceedings.

"I got some tings 'bout here; missis, dat will do for a bed," she answered.

"I am sorry I have to take away your bed to-night," remarked Mrs. Wentworth, "but I hope I will be able to pay you for your kindness some time."

"Dat's all right," replied the old negress, and spreading a mass of different articles on the floor, she crept in among them, and shortly after fell asleep, leaving Mrs. Wentworth alone with her thoughts, watching over the sleeping forms of her children.

The next morning the old woman woke up early, and lighting fire, made a frugal but amply sufficient breakfast, which, she placed before her uninvited guests. Mrs. Wentworth partook of the meal but slightly, and her little son ate heartily. Ella being still asleep, she was not disturbed. Shortly after the meal was over, the old negro left the cabin, saying she would return some time during the day.

About nine o'clock, Ella woke, and feebly called her mother. Mrs. Wentworth approached the bedside, and started back much shocked at the appearance of her child. The jaws of the little girl had sunk, her eyes were dull and expressive less and her breath came thick and heavily.

"What do you wish my darling," enquired her mother.

"I feel quite sick, mother," said the little girl, speaking faintly and with great difficulty.

"What is the matter with you?" Mrs. Wentworth asked, her face turning as pale as her child's.

"I cannot breathe," she answered, "and my eyes feel dim. What can be the matter?"

"Nothing much, my angel," replied her mother. "You have only taken a cold from exposure in the air last night. Bear up and you will soon get well again."

"I feel so different now from what I did before," she remarked. "Before I was so hot, and now I feel as cold as ice."

Mrs. Wentworth put her hand upon the face of her child. It was indeed as cold as ice, and alarmed the mother exceedingly. She knew not how to act; she was alone in the cabin, and even had the old negro been at home, she had no money to purchase medicines with. She was determined, however, that something should be done for her child, and the thought of again appealing to Mr. Swartz for assistance came into her mind.

"Perhaps, he will loan me a small sum of money when he learns how destitute I am, and that my child is very ill," she said musingly, and then added: "At any rate I will try what I can do with him."

Turning to Ella, Mrs. Wentworth said: "Do you think you could remain here with your brother until my return. I want to go out and get something for you to take."

"Yes, mother, but do not be long," she replied. "I will try and keep brother by me while you are away."

"Very well," said Mrs. Wentworth, "I shall make haste and return."

Admonishing her little son not to leave the room during her absence, Mrs. Wentworth was on the point of leaving the room when Ella called to her: "Be sure to come back soon, mother," she said. "I want you back early particularly."

"Why, my darling?" enquired her mother.

"Why, in case I should be going to--" Here her voice sunk to a whisper, and her mother failed to catch what she said.

"In case you should be going to, what?" enquired Mrs. Wentworth.

"Nothing, mother," she replied. "I was only thinking, but make haste and come back."

"I will," her mother answered, "I will come back immediately."

Choking the sob that rose in her throat, Mrs. Wentworth left the room and proceeded towards Mr. Swartz's office. Her visit was a hopeless one, but she determined to make the trial. She could not believe that the heart of every man was turned against the poor and helpless.

What a world is this we live in! We view with calm indifference the downfall of our fellow-mortals. We see them struggling in the billows of adversity, and as our proud bark of wealth glides swiftly by, we extend no helping hand to the worn swimmer. And yet we can look upon our past life with complacency, can delight to recall the hours of happiness we have past, and if some scene of penury and grief is recalled to our memory, we drive away the thought of what we then beheld and sought not to better.

What is that that makes man's heart cold as the mountain tops of Kamtschatka? It is that cursed greed for gain -- that all absorbing ambition for fortune -- that warps the heart and turns to adamant all those attributes of gentleness with which God has made us. The haggard beggar and the affluent man of the world, must eventually share the same fate. No matter that on the grave of the first – "no storied urn records who rests below, while on the grave of the other,

335

we find in sculptured marble long eulogies of those who rest beneath, telling us not what he was, but what he should have been." Their end is the same, for beneath the same sod they "sleep the last sleep that knows no waking," and their spirits wing their flight to the same eternal realms, there to be judged by their own merits, and not by the station they occupied below.

If there are men in this world who cannot be changed by wealth, Swartz was not of the number. What cared he for the sighs of the desolate, the appeals of the hungry, or the tears of the helpless? His duty was but to fill his coffers with money, and not to expend it in aimless deeds of charity. He looked upon the poor just as we would look upon a reptile -- something to be shunned.

It was indeed a wild hallucination that induced Mrs. Wentworth to bend her steps towards his office. Could he have seen her as she was coming, he would have left his room, for the sight of the mendicant filled him with greater horror than a decree of God declaring that the end of the world had come.

CHAPTER NINETEENTH.
AN ACT OF DESPAIR.

Mrs. Wentworth reached the store of Mr. Swartz and entered. The clerk looked at her in astonishment. She was unrecognizable. Her dress was ragged and dirty; the hands and face that once rivalled the Parian marble in whiteness, were tanned by toil, and lay shriveled and dried. Her hair was disheveled and gathered up in an uncomely heap on the back of her head. She looked like the beggar; she had become.

"Some beggar," the clerk said, in a contemptuous tone, as he advanced towards her.

"Is Mr. Swartz in?" enquired Mrs. Wentworth in a husky tone.

"What do you want with him?" he demanded in a gruff voice.

"I desire to see him privately, for a few moments," she answered.

"If it is charity you have come to beg, you may as well save yourself the trouble," observed the clerk. "This house don't undertake to support all the beggars in Jackson."

As his brutal words fell on her ear, a spark of womanly dignity filled her breast, and her eyes kindled with indignation. She looked at him for a moment sternly and silently, until her gaze caused him to turn his countenance from her, abashed at the mute rebuke she had administered. The pride of by-gone days had returned, with the unfeeling remarks of the clerk, and Mrs. Wentworth again felt all the bitterness of her position.

"I did not say I was an applicant for charity," she said at last. "All I desire to know is, if Mr. Swartz is in."

"I believe he is," replied the clerk. "Do you wish to see him, ma'am."

His tone was more respectful. Even poverty can command respect at times, and the threadbare garment be looked upon with as much difference as the gorgeous silken dress. It was so at this moment.

"Yes, I desire to see him," answered Mrs. Wentworth. "Be kind enough to inform Mr. Swartz that a lady has called upon him."

As she used the word "lady," the clerk elevated his eyebrows, and a smile of pity stole over his features. Lady! Could the miserable looking object, who stood before him have any claim to the title. Poor woman! She knew not that the outward form of woman is the only recognized title to the term. What though the mind be filled with the loftiest sentiment, and stored with the richest lore of learning. What though the heart be purer than the snow which covers the mountain tops, can they ever claim a position among the favorites of fortune, when accompanied by beggary? Philanthropists, and philosophers tell us they can, but the demon, Prejudice, has erected a banner, which can never be pulled down, until man resumes the patriarchal life of centuries ago, and society, the mockery by which we claim civilization was built up, is removed from the earth, and mankind can mingle with each other in free and unrestricted intercourse.

That day will never come.

But to return to our story. The clerk looked pityingly at Mrs. Wentworth for a moment, then walked to the door of Mr. Swartz's office, and knocked.

The door was opened.

"There is a 'lady' here who wants to see you on private business," he said with emphasis.

"Shust tell de lady I will see her in a few minutes," replied the voice of Mr. Swartz, from the interior of the room.

The clerk withdrew, after closing the door, and advanced to where Mrs. Wentworth was standing.

"Mr. Swartz will see you in a few moments, he said."

"Go back for me, and tell him my business is urgent, and will admit of no delay," she answered.

Her thoughts were of the little girl, who lay ill on the bed in the negro's cabin, and to whom she had promised to return quickly.

The clerk withdrew, and announced her wishes, to his employer.

"Vell," said Mr. Swartz. "Tell her to come in."

She walked up to the door, and as she reached the threshold it opened and Mr. Elder, stood before her. She spoke not a word as he started from surprise at her unexpected appearance. She only gazed upon him for a while with a calm and steady gaze. Hastily dropping his eyes to the ground, Mr. Elder recovered his usual composure, and brushing past the soldier's wife left the store, while she entered the office where Mr. Swartz was.

"Oot tam," he muttered as she entered. "I shall give dat clerk te tevil for sending dis voman to me. Sum peggar I vill pet."

"I have called on you again, Mr. Swartz," Mrs. Wentworth began.

Mr. Swartz looked at her as if trying to remember where they had met before, but he failed to recognize her features.

"I don't know dat you vash here to see me pefore," he replied.

"You do not recognize me," she remarked, and then added: "I am the lady who sold her last piece of furniture to you some time ago."

He frowned as she reminded him who she was, for he then surmised what the object of her visit was.

"Oh!" he answered, "I recollect you now, and vat do you vant?"

"I have come upon the same errand," she replied. "I have come once more to ask you to aid me, but this time come barren of anything to induce you to comply with my request. Nothing but the generous promptings of your heart can I hold up before you to extend the charity I now solicit."

"You have come here to peg again," he observed, "but I cannot give you anything. Gootness! Ven vill te place pe rid of all te peggers?"

"I cannot help my position," she said. "A cruel fortune has deprived me of him who used to support me, and I am now left alone with my children to eke out the wretched existence of a pauper. Last night I was turned out of my room by the man who left here a few

338

seconds ago, because I could not pay for my rent. One of my children was sick, but he cared not for that. I told him of my poverty, and he turned a deaf ear towards me. I was forced to leave, and my child has become worse from exposure in the night air."

"And vot have I cot to do mit all dis," he enquired.

"You can give me the means of purchasing medicine for my sick child," she replied. "The amount thus bestowed cannot cause you any inconvenience, while it may be the means of saving life."

"Dis never vill do," Mr. Swartz said, interrupting her. "My goot woman, you must go to somepody else, I can't give away my monish."

"You have got a plenty," she persisted, "you are rich. Oh, aid me! If you believe there is a God above, who rewards the charitable, aid me, and receive the heartfelt blessings of a mother. Twenty dollars will be enough to satisfy my present wants, and that sum will make but little difference to a man of your wealth."

"Mine Cot!" he exclaimed, "If I make monish, I work for it, and don't go about begging."

"I know that," she answered, "and it is to the rich that the poor must appeal for assistance. This has made me come to you this day. Let my desire be realized. Aid me in saving the life of my child who is now lying ill, and destitute of medical attendance."

He could not appreciate her appeal, and he again refused.

"I can't give you any ding," he answered.

"There is a virtue which shines far more than all the gold you possess," replied Mrs. Wentworth. "It is in man what chastity is in a woman. An act of charity ennobles man more than all the fame bestowed upon him for any other merit, and his reward is always commensurate with his works. Let this virtue move you. The ear of God cannot always be turned against my prayers to Him, and the hour must surely come, when my husband will be released from prison, and be enabled to repay any kindness you may show his wife and children. Let me have the money I have asked you for. Oh, sir!" she continued, falling on her knees before him, "believe the words I speak to you, and save my child from the hands of death. But a short time ago I left her gasping for breath, with cold drops of perspiration resting on her brow, perhaps the marks of approaching dissolution. She is very ill, and can only recover through proper treatment. Place

339

it in my power to call a physician and to procure medicines, and I shall never cease to bless you."

He moved uneasily in his chair, and averted his head from where she was kneeling, not because he felt touched at her appeal, but because he felt annoyed at her importuning him for money.

"Here my voman," he said at last. "Here is von tollar pill, dat is all I can give you."

She looked at the note in his extended hand, and felt the mockery.

"It will not do," she answered. "Let me have the amount I have asked you for. You can spare it. Do not be hardened. Recollect it is to provide medicine for the sick."

"I can't do it," he replied. "You should be shankful for what you get."

His motive in offering her the dollar, was not from a charitable feeling, it was only to get rid of a beggar.

"Oh God!" she groaned, rising from her knees, and resting her elbow on an iron safe near by. "Have you a heart?" she exclaimed wildly, "I tell you my child is ill, perhaps at this moment dying, aid me! Aid me! Do not turn away a miserable mother from your door to witness her child die through destitution, when it is in your power to relieve its sufferings, and save it, so that it may live to be a blessing and solace to me. If not for my sake, if not for the sake of the child, let me appeal to you for charity, for the sake of him, who is now imprisoned in a foreign dungeon. He left me to defend you from the enemy -- left his wife and children to starve and suffer, for the purpose of aiding in that holy cause we are now engaged in conflict for. For his sake, if for no other, give me the means of saving my child."

He did not reply to her passionate words, but simply rang a bell that stood on the table before which he was seated. His clerk answered the summons.

"If you vont quit mithout my making you," he observed to Mrs. Wentworth in a brutal tone, "I must send for a police officer to take away. Gootness," he continued, speaking to himself, "I pelieve te voman is mat."

"Save yourself the trouble," she replied, "I will leave. I am not yet mad," she added. "But, oh, God! the hour is fast approaching when madness must hold possession of my mind. I go to my child - - my poor dying child. Oh, Heaven, help me!"

As she moved her hand from the safe, she perceived a small package of money lying on it. She paused and looked around. The clerk had withdrawn at a sign from Mr. Swartz, while that gentleman was gazing intently at the open pages of a ledger, that lay before him. For a moment she hesitated and trembled from head to foot, while the warm blood rushed to her cheeks, until they were a deep crimson hue. Swiftly she extended her hand towards the package, and grasped it; in another instant it was concealed in her dress, and the act of despair was accomplished.

"God pity me!" she exclaimed, as she left the room and departed from the scene of her involuntary crime.

Despair had induced her to commit a theft, but no angel of God is purer in mind than was the Soldier's Wife, when she did so. It was the result of madness, and if the Recording Angel witnessed the act, he recorded not the transgression against her, for it was a sin only in the eyes of man; above it was the child of despair, born of a pure and innocent mind, and there is no punishment for such.

"Thank God, I have the means of saving my darling child," exclaimed Mrs. Wentworth, as she bent her steps towards a druggist's store. Entering it, she purchased a few articles of medicine, and started for the old negro's cabin, intending to send the old woman for a physician, as soon as she could reach there.

Swiftly she sped along the streets. Many passers by stopped and looked with surprise at her rapid walking. They knew not the sorrows of the Soldier's Wife. Many there were who gazed upon her threadbare habiliments and haggard features, who could never surmise that the light of joy had ceased to burn in her heart. Their life had been one long dream of happiness, unmarred, save by those light clouds of sorrow, which at times flit across the horizon of man's career, but which are swiftly driven away by the sunshine of happiness, or dissipated by the gentle winds of life's joyous summer.

And the crowds passed her in silence and surprise, but she heeded them not. Her thoughts were of the angel daughter in the negro's lonely cabin. To her she carried life; at least she thought so, but the inevitable will of Death had been declared. Ella was dying.

The eye of God was still turned from the widow and her children. He saw them not, but his Angels, whose duty it is to chronicle all that occurs on earth, looked down on that bright autumn day, and a tear fell from the ethereal realms in which they dwelt, and rested upon the Soldier's Wife.

It was the tear of pity, not of relief.

CHAPTER TWENTIETH.
THE DYING CHILD.

After the departure of Mrs. Wentworth, the little girl lie still upon the bed, while her little brother played about the room. Nearly one hour elapsed in silence. The breath of the child became shorter and harder drawn. Her little face became more pinched, while the cold drops of perspiration rose larger on her forehead. Instinct told her she was dying, but young as she was, death created no terrors in her heart. She lay there, anxious for her mother's return, that she may die in the arms of the one who gave her birth. Death seemed to her but the advent to Heaven, that home in which we are told all is goodness and happiness. She thought herself an Angel dwelling with the Maker, and in her childish trustfulness and faith almost wished herself already numbered among the Cherubs of Paradise.

The old negro returned before Mrs. Wentworth, and walking to the bedside of the child, looked at her, and recognized the impress of approaching death. She felt alarmed, but could not remedy the evil. Looking at the child sorrowfully for a moment, she turned away.

"Poh chile," she muttered sadly, "she is dyin' sho' and her mammy is gone out. Da's a ting to take place in my room."

"Granny," said Ella feebly.

"What do you want my darlin' chile," answered the old woman, returning to the bedside.

"See if mother is coming," she requested.

The old woman walked to the door, and looked down the street. There was no sign of Mrs. Wentworth.

"No missy," she said to Ella, "your mammy is not coming yet."

"Oh, I do wish she would come," remarked the little girl.

"Lie still, darlin'," the old woman answered. "Your mammy will come back directly."

The child lay still for several minutes, but her mother came not and she felt that before many hours she would cease to live.

"Look again, granny, and see if mother is coming," she again requested, and in a fainter tone.

The old woman looked out once more, but still there was no sign of Mrs. Wentworth.

"Neber mind, darlin' your mammy will cum directly," she said, and then added. "Let me know what you want and I will git it for you."

"I don't want anything, granny," Ella answered, and remained silent for a moment, when she continued: "Granny ain't I going to die?"

The old negro looked at her for a moment, and a tear stole down her withered features. She could not answer, for ignorant and uneducated as she was, the signs which betoken the parting of the soul from the body, were too apparent, not to be easily recognized.

"Poh chile," she muttered, as she turned her head and brushed away the falling tear.

"Answer me, granny," said Ella. "I am not afraid to die, but I would like to bid mother good-bye, before I went to Heaven."

"Don't tink of sich tings chile," observed the old woman. "You is sick now only; lie still and you will soon see your mother."

The time sped swiftly, but to the dying child it seemed an age. She lay there; her life breath ebbing fast, waiting for her mother, that she may die in her arms. Angels filled the lowly cabin, and held their outstretched arms to receive the spirit of a sinless babe, as soon as it would leave the mortal clay it animated. Soon, soon would it have been borne on high, for the rattle in the child's throat had almost commenced, when a hurried footstep was heard at the door, and Mrs. Wentworth, pale and tired entered the room.

The hand of Death was stayed for a while, for the presence of the mother started anew the arteries of life, and the blood once more rushed to the cheeks of the dying. Ella held out her arms as her mother approached her, with some medicine in her hand. As she gazed upon her child, Mrs. Wentworth started back, and uttered a faint exclamation of anguish. She saw the worst at a glance, and placing aside the medicine, she seized her child's extended hands, and bending over her, pressed her darling daughter to her heart.

"Here aunty," she said, as soon us she had released Ella, "Here is some money, run and call a physician at once."

The old negro took the money and moved off.

343

"Tell him to come instantly," she called out after the negro. "It is a matter of life and death, and there is no time to lose."

"Too late, too late! poor people," said the old woman, as she hurried on her mission of mercy.

It was too late. No science on earth could save Ella from death, and none on high save the Infinite Power, but He knew not of it. His eyes were still turned away from the Soldier's Wife and her children.

Mrs. Wentworth remained silent, looking at her child as she gasped for breath. Of what use was the money she had committed a crime to obtain? Of what avail were her supplications to God? It were thoughts like these that passed rapidly through her mind, as she speechlessly gazed at the fast-sinking form of her child. Ella saw her agony, and tried to soothe her mother.

"Come nearer to me, mother," she said. "Come near and speak to me." Mrs. Wentworth drew near the bedside, and bent her face to the child.

"What do you wish, darling?" she asked.

"Mother, I am dying -- I am going to Heaven," Ella said, speaking with an effort.

A smothered sob, was the only response she met with.

"Don't cry mother," continued the child. "I am going to a good place, and do not feel afraid to die."

Shaking off her half-maddened feeling, Mrs. Wentworth replied. "Don't speak that way, darling. You are not going to die. The physician will soon be here, and he will give you some thing which will get you better."

Ella smiled faintly. "No, mother, I cannot get better; I know I am going to die. Last night, while sleeping, an angel told me in my dream, that I would sleep with God to-night."

"That was only a dream, darling," Mrs. Wentworth replied, "you will get well and live a long time."

As she spoke the old negro returned, accompanied by a physician. He was one of these old-fashioned gentlemen, who never concern themselves with another's business, and therefore, he did not enquire the cause of Mrs. Wentworth, and her family being in so poor a dwelling. His business was to attend the sick, for which he expected to be paid; not that he was hard-hearted, for, to the contrary, he was a very charitable and generous man, but he expected that all persons who required his advice, should have the means of paying for the same, or go to the public hospital, where they could be attended to free of charge. His notions were on a par with those of mankind in general, so we cannot complain of him.

Approaching Ella, he took her hand and felt the pulse which was then feebly beating. A significant shake of the head, told Mrs. Wentworth that there was no hope for her child's recovery.

"Doctor," she asked, "will my daughter recover?"

"Madam," he replied, "your child is very, very ill, in fact, I fear she has not many hours to live."

"It cannot be," she said. "Do not tell me there is no hope for my child."

"I cannot deceive you, madam," he replied, "the child has been neglected too long for science to triumph over her disease. When did you first call in a medical practitioner?" he added.

"Not until you were sent for," she answered.

"Then you are much to blame, madam," he observed bluntly. "Had you sent for a physician three weeks ago, the life of your child would have been saved, but your criminal neglect to do so, has sacrificed her life."

Mrs. Wentworth did not reply to his candid remarks. She did not tell him that for weeks past her children and herself had scarcely been able to find bread to eat, much less to pay a doctor's bill. She did not tell him that she was friendless and unknown; that her husband had been taken prisoner while struggling for his country's rights; that Mr. Elder had turned herself and her children from a shelter, because she had no money to pay him for the rent of the room; nor did she tell him that the fee he had received, was obtained by theft -- was the fruit of a transgression of God's commandments.

She forgot all these. The reproach of the physician had fallen like a thunderbolt from Heaven, in her bosom. Already in her heart she accused herself with being the murderess of her child. Already she imagined, because her poverty had prevented her receiving medical advice, that the accusing Angel stood ready to prefer charges against her for another and a greater crime, than any she had ever before committed.

"Dying! dying!" she uttered at last, her words issuing from her lips, as if they were mere utterances from some machine. "No hope -- no hope!"

"Accept my commiseration, madam," observed the physician, placing his hat on, and preparing to depart. "Could I save your child, I would gladly do so, but there is no hope. She may live until nightfall, but even that is doubtful."

Bowing to Mrs. Wentworth, he left the room, in ignorance of the agony his reproach had caused her, and returned to his office. Dr. Mallard was the physician's name. They met again.

Ella had listened attentively to the physician's words, but not the slightest emotion was manifested by her, when he announced that she was dying. She listened calmly, and as the doctor had finished informing her mother of the hopelessness of her case, the little pale lips moved slowly, and the prayer that had been taught her when all was joy and happiness, was silently breathed by the dying child.

"Mother," she said, as soon as Dr. Mallard had left the room. "Come here and speak to me before I die."

"Ella! Ella!" exclaimed Mrs. Wentworth wildly. "Did you not hear what the physician said?"

"Yes, mother," she answered, "but I knew it before. Do not look so sad, come and speak to me, and let me tell you that I am not afraid to die."

"Ella, my darling child," continued Mrs. Wentworth in the same strain. "Did you not hear the physician say it is my neglect that had caused you to be dying?"

"I heard him mother, but he was not right," she replied.

"Come nearer," she continued in an earnest tone. "Sit on the bed and let me rest my head on your lap."

Seating herself on the bed, Mrs. Wentworth lifted the body of the dying child in her arms, and pillowed her head on her breast. The old negro was standing at the foot of the bed, looking on quietly, while the tears poured down her aged cheeks. Mrs. Wentworth's little son climbed on the bed, and gazed in wonder at the sad aspect of his mother, and the dying features of his sister.

"Mother," said the child, "I am going to Heaven, say a prayer for me." She essayed to pray, but could not, her lips moved, but utterance was denied to her.

"I cannot pray, darling," she replied, "prayer is denied to me."

The child asked no more, for she saw her mother's inability to comply with her wishes.

The little group remained in the same position until the setting sun gleamed through the window, and shed a bright ray across the bed. Not a sound was heard, save the ticking of the old-fashioned clock on the mantel piece, as its hands slowly marked the fleeting minutes. The eyes of the dying child had been closed at the time, but as the sunlight shot across her face she opened them, and looked up into her mother's face.

"Open the window, granny," she said.

The old woman opened it, and as she did so, the round red glare of the sun was revealed, while the aroma of thousands wild flowers that grew beneath the window, entered the room, and floated its perfume on the autumn air.

"Mother," said the dying child.

Mrs. Wentworth looked down upon her child.

"What is it darling," she asked.

"Let brother kiss me," she requested.

Her little brother was lifted up and held over her. She pressed a soft kiss upon his lips.

"Good-bye, granny," she said, holding out her hand to the negro.

The old woman seized it, and the tears fell faster, on the bed than they had hitherto done. Her humble heart was touched at the simple, yet unfearing conduct of the child.

"Mother, kiss me," she continued. "Do not be sad," she added, observing her mother's pale and ghastly countenance. "I am going to a world where no one is sick, and no one knows want."

Stooping over her dying child, Mrs. Wentworth complied with Ella's request, and pressed her brow in a long and earnest kiss. She had not spoken a word from the time her child requested the old woman to open the window, but she had never for an instant, ceased looking on the features of her dying daughter, and she saw that the film was fast gathering on her eyes.

After her mother had kissed her, Ella remained silent for several minutes, when suddenly starting, she exclaimed: "I see them, mother! I see them! See the Angels coming for me - Heaven mother -- Angels!" A bright smile lit her features, the half-opened eyes lit up with the last fires of life; then as they faded away, her limbs relaxed, and still gazing on her mother's face, the breath left the body.

There was a rush as of wind through the window, but it was the Angels, who were bearing the child's spirit to a brighter and a better world.

CHAPTER TWENTY-FIRST.
THE INTRUSION.

As soon as the breath had left her child's body, Mrs. Wentworth removed the corpse from her lap and laid it on the bed; than standing aside of it, gazed upon all that remained of her little daughter. Not a tear, not a sigh, not a groan denoted that she felt any grief at her bereavement. Except a nervous twitching of her mouth, her features wore a cold and rigid appearance, and her eye looked dull and glassy. She spoke not a word to those around her who yet lived. Her little boy was unnoticed, no other object but the dead body appeared to meet her view.

There are moments when the fountains of grief become dried up. It was so with Mrs. Wentworth. The sight of her dead child's face -- beautiful in death -- for it wore a calm and placid exterior, too life-like for death, too rigid for life, awoke no emotion in her bosom; nor did the knowledge that the infant would soon be placed in the grave, and be forever hidden from the gaze she now placed on it so steadfastly, cause a single tear drop to gather in her eye, nor a sigh to burst from her pale and firmly closed lips. And yet, there raged within her breast a volcano, the violence of whose fire would soon exhaust, and leave her scarred and blasted forever. At that moment it kindled with a blaze, that scorched her heart, but she felt it not. Her whole being was transformed into a mass of ruin. She felt not the strain on the tendrils of her mind; that her overwrought brain was swaying between madness and reason. She only saw the lifeless lineaments of her child -- the first pledge of her wedded affection -- dead before her.

It came to her like a wild dream, a mere hallucination -- an imagination of a distempered mind. She could not believe it. There, on that lowly bed, her child to die! It was something too horrible for her thoughts, and though the evidence lay before her, in all its solemn grandeur, there was something to her eye so unreal and impossible in its silent magnificence that she doubted its truthfulness. The old negro saw her misery. She knew that the waters which run with a mild and silent surface, are often possessed of greater depth, than those which rush onward with a mighty noise.

"Come missis," she said, placing her hand on Mrs. Wentworth's shoulder. "De Lord will be done. Neber mind. He know better what to do dan we do, and we must all be satisfy wid his works."

Mrs. Wentworth looked at the old woman for a moment, and a bitter smile swept across her countenance. What were words of consolation to her? They sounded like a mockery in her heart. She needed them not, for they brought not to life again the child whose spirit had winged its flight to eternity, but a short time since.

"Peace old woman," she replied calmly, "you know not what you say. That," she continued, pointing to the body of Ella, "that you tell me not to mourn, but to bend to the will of God. Pshaw! I mourn it not. Better for the child to die than lead a beggar's life on earth."

"Shame, shame missis," observed the old woman, very much shocked at what appeared to her the insensibility of Mrs. Wentworth. "You musn't talk dat way, it don't do any good."

"You know not what I mean, auntie," Mrs. Wentworth answered in a milder tone. "Why did I come here? Why did I bring my child ill and dying from a shelter, and carry her through the night air, until I found a home in your lonely cabin? Do you know why?" she continued with bitterness. "It was because I was a beggar, and could not pay the demands of the rich."

"Poh lady!" ejaculated the old woman. "Whar is your husband."

"My husband?" she replied. "Ah! where is he? Oh, God!" she continued wildly. "Where is he now while his child lies dead through destitution, and his wife feels the brand of the 'thief' imprinted upon her forehead? Why is he not here to succor the infant boy who yet remains, and who may soon follow his sister? Oh, God! Oh, God! that he should be far away, and I be here gazing on the dead body of my child -- dead through my neglect to procure her proper medical attendance; dead through the destitution of her mother."

"Nebber mind, missis," observed the old negro soothingly, "De chile is gone to heaben, whar it won't suffer any more."

"Peace!" exclaimed Mrs. Wentworth passionately. "Do not talk to me of Heaven. What has God done to aid me in my misery? Has he not suffered me to feel the pangs of hunger, to see my children deprived of bread, to permit me to stain my whole existence with a crime? The child is gone to Heaven. Aye! There her sinlessness and innocence might give her a welcome, and she may be happy, but the blank left in my heart, the darkness of my mind, the cheerless and unpropitious future that unveils itself before my aching eyes, can never be obliterated until I am laid in the grave beside her, and my spirit has winged its flight to the home where she now dwells."

She spoke slowly and earnestly, but her words were of despair not of grief. Motioning to the old woman that she desired no further conversation, Mrs. Wentworth again fixed her gaze upon the dead features of her child. On them she looked, until the tablet of her memory contained but one impress, that of her daughter's face. All records of past suffering, all anxiety for the present, all prayer for the future, were driven away, and solitary and alone the image of the dead child filled their place, and in that lone thought was concentrated all that had transpired in her life for months past. It was the last remaining bulwark to her tottering mind, and though it still held reason dominant, the foundation of sanity had been shaken to such an extent that the slightest touch and the fabric would fall from its throne and crumble to dust at the feet of madness. But this was unknown to God. He who knoweth all things still kept his eyes away rom the mother and her children.

"Dead! dead!" said, Mrs. Wentworth, swaying her body to and fro. "My angel child dead! Oh, God!" she continued, passing her hand across her brow. "That I should live to see this day, that this hour of bereavement should ever be known to me. Oh! that this should be the result of my sufferings, that this should be the only reward of my toils and prayers."

The blood rushed to her face, and her whole form trembled with an uncontrollable agitation; her bosom heaved with emotion, and the beatings of her heart were heard as plain as the click of the clock on the mantlepiece. Stooping over the dead body she clasped it in her arms, and pressed the bloodless and inanimate lips in a fond embrace. It was the promptings of a mother's heart. She had nursed the child when an infant, and had seen her grow up as beautiful as the fairies so often described by the writers of fiction. She had looked forward for the day when the child would bloom into womanhood, and be a blessing and a comfort in her old age. All these were now forever blighted. Not even the presence of her son awoke a thought within her that the living remained to claim her care and affection. He was but a link in the chain of her paternal love, and the bonds having been broken she looked on the shattered fragment and sought not to unite what yet remained in an unhurt state.

When she rose from her stooping posture her face had resumed its cold and rigid appearance. Turning to the old negro who was looking on in silent wonder and grief, she enquired in a calm tone: "Have you any of the money left that I gave you this morning?"

"Yes, missis," she replied. "I got some left."

"How much is it?" asked Mrs. Wentworth.

"Twelve dollars," she answered, counting the notes that she had taken from her pocket.

"Will that be enough to pay for a coffin for my child?" Mrs. Wentworth enquired.

"I don't know, but I spect it will do," replied the old negro.

"To make sure that it will be enough," observed Mrs. Wentworth, "here is some more money to pay for it." As she spoke, she handed several notes to the old woman. "And now," she continued, "I want you to go out and order a coffin, as I want the child to be buried to-morrow morning."

"I spec I better get de parson to preach over de poor chile," remarked the old woman, who was a strict member of the church, and very superstitious in relation to the evils that would accrue from a departure from all that is laid down in religious tenets.

"Yes, yes!" Mrs. Wentworth replied. "But there is no necessity of going for him this evening, wait until early in the morning, that time will do well enough."

The old woman curtsied and moved out of the room. Arriving in town she entered an undertaker's shop and enquired if he could furnish a coffin by the next morning. On his answering in the affirmative, she paid him twenty dollars, the amount charged, and hastened back to her cabin. The interest manifested by this old woman, was that usually shown to all persons in distress by the faithful slave of the South. She had not even learned Mrs. Wentworth's name, but the sight of her sad and haggard features, as well as the death of Ella, had awaken a feeling of sympathy for the unfortunate family; thus, we see her obeying the orders of her accidental guests, without making any objections. But to return to the dead.

As soon as Mrs. Wentworth was left alone, her face assumed its natural appearance, and the rigid expression it had hitherto worn was dispelled. Opening a bundle, she had brought front her room, she took out a white dress. It was one of the few remaining articles of clothing she possessed, and had only been saved at the earnest solicitation of the little Ella. It was her bridal robe; in that she had walked up to the altar and plighted her troth to the loved husband who was now a prisoner and far away. The first and last time she had worn it was on that day, and as she gazed on it the memory of the past rushed upon her. She thought of the hour when, as a blushing bride, she leaned on the proud form of her lover, as they walked together in the sacred edifice to register those vows that bound them in an indissoluble tie, and unite their hearts in a stronger and holier love than their lover's vows had done. Then she know not what sorrow was. No gift of futurity had disclosed to her the wretchedness and penury that after years had prepared for her. No, then all was joy and happiness. As she stood by the side of her lover her maiden face suffused with blushes, and her palpitating heart filled with mingled felicity and anxiety as she looked down on the bridal dress that covered her form. No thought, no dream, not even a fear of what after years would bring to her, stirred the fountain of fear and caused her a single pang. And now -- but why trouble the reader with any further remarks of the past? That is gone and forever. We have seen her tread the paths in which all that is dismal and wretched abides; we have seen herself and her children lead a life, the very thought of which should cause us to pray it may never be our lot. Words can avail but little. They only fill the brain with gladness for a while to turn to horror afterwards. We have but to write of the present. In it we find misery enough, we find sorrow and wretchedness, without the hand of compassion being held forth to help the miserable from the deep and fearful gulf with which penury and want abound.

The wedding dress was soiled and crumpled; the bunches of orange blossoms with which it was adorned, lay crushed upon its folds -- a fit appearance for the heart of the owner--It looked like a relic of grandeur shining in the midst of poverty, and as its once gaudy folds rested against the counterpane in the bed, the manifest difference of the two appeared striking and significant.

For a moment Mrs. Wentworth gazed upon this last memento of long past happiness, and a spasm of grief contracted her features. It passed away, however, in an instant, and she laid the dress across the dead body of her child. Drawing a chair to the bedside, she took from her pocket a spool of thread, some needles and her scissors. Selecting one of the needles, she thread it, and pinning it in the body of her dress, removed the wedding gown from the body of her child, and prepared to make a shroud of it. Rapidly she worked at her task, and before darkness had set in, the burial garment was completed, and the body of Ella was enclosed in the last robe she would wear on earth.

The body of the dead child looked beautiful. The snowy folds of the dress were looped up with the orange blossoms which Mrs. Wentworth had restored to their natural beauty. On her cold, yet lovely brow, a wreath of the same flowers was placed, while in her hand was placed a tiny ivory cross, that Ella had worn around her neck while living. The transformation was complete. The dress of the young and blooming bride had become the habiliments of the dead child, and the orange blossoms that rested on its folds and on the brow of Ella, were not more emblematical for the dead than they had been for the living.

"Oh! how pretty sister looks," exclaimed the little boy, who could not comprehend why the dead body lie so motionless and stiff. "Wake her up, mother," he continued, "she looks so pretty that I want her to stand up and see herself."

Mrs. Wentworth smiled sorrowfully at her son's remarks, but she did not remove her features from the dead. The saint-like expression of her child, and the placid and beautiful face that lay before her devoid of animation, had awoke the benumbed feelings of affection within her. A bright light flashed across her brain, and the long pent-up tears, were about to flow, when the door was widely opened, and a dark shadow spread itself over the body of Ella. Checking her emotion, Mrs. Wentworth looked around and beheld the figure of Mr. Swartz, accompanied by two police officers.

She spoke not a word at first, for in an instant the cause of his visit was known. One look she gave him, which sunk into the inmost depths of his soul; then turning to the dead child, she slowly extended her hand and pointed to it.

"There," she said at last. "Look there," and her face again wore its former colorless and rigid aspect.

CHAPTER TWENTY-SECOND.
IMPRISONMENT OF THE SOLDIER'S WIFE.

We must now take a glance back at the time that Mrs. Wentworth committed her act of despair in taking the package of money from the safe. Mr. Swartz, as we stated, was then gazing intently at the open pages of his ledger, and, in her leaving the room hurriedly, did not take any other notice of her, than mere glance. He then resumed his calculations, nor did he rise from his seat for nearly three hours afterwards, so intent was he on the books before him. Rising up at last, he walked to the safe, and observing that the package of money was gone, called out to his clerk, who quickly answered the summons and entered the room.

"Vere is dat package of money I had on de safe dis morning?" he enquired, as soon as the clerk had entered.

"I have not seen anything of it, since I gave it into your hands this morning at nine o'clock," the clerk replied.

"Vell, I put it on top of dis safe," observed Mr. Swartz, "and I forgot to lock it up, ven Mr. Elder came in, and kept me talking nearly two hours, den de beggar came in and remained for a long time. After dat I vas busy mit the ledger, and didn't think of it."

"Perhaps you have placed it somewhere else, and cannot recollect where," remarked the clerk, who was apprehensive that Mr. Swartz would charge him with having stolen the money.

"No, I didn't," answered Mr. Swartz, "De monish vas put down on de top of the safe, for I remember putting it down here myself," he added, pointing to the spot where the money had been.

"You had better search about before you make certain of that," said the clerk. "See if it is not in your pocket, you may have placed it there, and at the same time believe that you placed it on your safe."

"Mine Cot!" answered Mr. Swartz, "I tell you I put the package on de safe. See here," he continued, searching his pockets, and emptying them of whatever they contained. "Don't you see dat de monish is not in my pockets. It vas on de safe und unless somebody removed it, it never could have gone away."

"You should be certain, sir, before you insist that you placed it on the safe," remarked the clerk. "Look in the draw of your desk, it may have been placed there as well as any other place."

With a gesture of impatience Mr. Swartz opened the drawers of the desk, and removing everything they contained searched carefully among the large number of papers for the missing package. It was not there however, and turning to the clerk who was standing near by, he pointed to the table to indicate the fact of its absence among the papers he had taken from the drawers.

"I told you it vash not tere," he remarked. "Somebody has taken te monish, and, py Cot! I vill find out who has got it."

"Don't be so hasty in your conclusions, sir," said the clerk. "Let us search the room carefully, and see whether it has not been mislaid by you. It will never do," he added, "to charge anybody with having taken the money, when it may be lying about the room."

"Vere can it pe lying?" asked Mr. Swartz angrily. "I tell you it vash on te safe, and tere ish no use looking anywhere else."

"That maybe so, sir," replied the clerk, "but if you will give me permission, I will search the room well before you take any further steps in the matter."

"You can look if you like," observed Mr. Swartz, "but I know tere ish no chance of your finding it, and it ish only giving yourself trouble for noting."

"Never do you mind that, sir," the clerk answered. "I am willing to take the trouble."

Removing the books from the top of the safe he carefully shook them out, but the package was not among them. He then replaced them and turned the safe round, with the hope that the money might have fallen under it. The same success, however, attended him, and he was compelled to renew his efforts. Everything in the room was removed without the package being found. After a minute and diligent search, he was compelled to give up the work in despair, and ceasing he stood trembling before Mr. Swartz, who, he momentarily expected, would charge him with having committed a theft. But for this fear he would never have taken the trouble of upsetting and replacing everything in the room, but would have been perfectly satisfied for his employer to sustain the loss.

"Vell!" said Mr. Swartz. "suppose you ish satisfied dat te monish ain't here."

"Its disappearance is very singular," replied the clerk. "If, as you say, the package was laid on the safe and never removed by you, somebody must have taken it away."

"Of course, somepody tock it," remarked Mr. Swartz. "How te tevil could it go mitout it vash taken away py somepody?"

"Do you suspect any one of having stolen it," asked the clerk, turning as white as the shirt he wore.

"Did you ever come near de safe to-day," asked Mr. Swartz, abruptly.

"Me, sir?" said the now thoroughly frightened clerk. "No, I— No sir -- I -- never came further than the door each time you called to me."

"I can't say dat Mr. Elder vould take it," observed Mr. Swartz, "and all I remember now dat you didn't come anyvere near de safe, I can't tink who could have taken the monish."

Assured by his manner that Mr. Swartz had dismissed all idea of charging him with the theft, the clerk's confidence returned, and he ceased stuttering and trembling.

"Do you think the woman who was here could have taken it?" he enquired, and then added: "The last time I entered this room while she was here, I remember seeing her standing near the safe, with her elbow on the top."

"By Cot!" exclaimed Mr. Swartz, striking the table with his hand. "She must be de very person. She vanted me to give her monish, and she must have seen de package lying on the safe and taken it avay."

"It is no use wasting any time then," said the clerk, "you must endeavor to find out where she stays, and have her arrested this evening."

"Vere, can I find her house?" asked Mr. Swartz.

"You will have to track her," answered the clerk. "The first place you had better go to is Elkin's drug store, for I saw the woman enter there after leaving here."

Mr. Swartz made no reply, but taking up his hat he walked out of his office, and proceeded to the drug store. The druggist, who had noticed the wild and haggard appearance of Mrs. Wentworth, informed him, in reply to his enquiries, that such a person as the one he described had purchased several descriptions of medicines from him, and on leaving his store, she had walked up the street. This being the only information that the druggist could give, Mr. Swartz left the store, and after many enquiries discovered where Mrs. Wentworth resided. He immediately returned to his store, and mentioned his discovery to the clerk.

"You had better go at once and take out a warrant against her for robbery;" remarked the clerk, "and take a couple of policemen with you to arrest her."

Starting to the City Hall, Mr. Swartz took out a warrant against Mrs. Wentworth for larceny, and procuring the assistance of two policemen, he started for the old negro's cabin, determined to prosecute the thief to the utmost extent of his power and the law. Having informed our readers of his conduct on discovering that his money had been stolen, we will continue from where we left off at the close of the last chapter.

Mrs. Wentworth on perceiving Mr. Swartz and the two policemen, had pointed to the dead body of her child, and pronounced the solitary word, "there," while her face became cold and expressiveless.

Involuntarily looking in the direction pointed out by Mrs. Wentworth, the three men started with awe as their eyes fell upon the beautiful face of the dead child. One of the policemen, who was a devout Catholic crossed himself, and withdrew from the entrance of the door, but the other policeman and Mr. Swartz quickly shook off all feelings of fear that had passed over them.

"Here is de voman," said Mr. Swartz, pointing to Mrs. Wentworth. "Dis is de voman who shtole mine monish."

As he spoke, she turned her face towards him, but the mute anguish of the mother did not cause a sentiment of regret to enter Mr. Swartz's heart, at the part he was acting towards her.

"Arrest her," continued Mr. Swartz, "I vant you to take her to de jail, where she can be examined, and to-morrow morning I can have her up before de Mayor."

"Not to-night," exclaimed Mrs. Wentworth in a hollow voice. "Leave me with the dead body of my child; after she is buried you can do as you please with me."

"I knows better tan to do dat," observed Mr. Swartz, "by to-morrow morning you vould be a pretty far avay from Shackson."

"I will not move from this cabin an inch further than to the burial ground," replied Mrs. Wentworth, "but if you fear it is my intention to escape, let one of your policemen remain here and watch me tonight."

Mr. Swartz stepped to the threshold of the door, and consulted the two men on the possibility of complying with her request, but one refused through superstition, while the other declined in consequence of his being on the night watch.

"I can't agree to your vishes," said Mr. Swartz, as soon as the conference was over, and he returned to the bedside. "De policemen vont remain here."

"Then do you trust me," she replied. "By the holy name of God, I implore you not to tear me from the body of my child, but if that name has no weight with you, and as I perceive it is useless to appeal to you by the sacred tenets of Christianity, let me pray you, that as a man, you will not descend to such brutality as to force me from the dead body that now lies before you, and deprive me of performing the last sad rites over her. In the name of all that is humane, I plead to you, and, oh, God! let my supplications be answered."

"Dere is no use of you talking in dat vay to me," said Mr. Swartz in a coarse and brutal tone. "It vas in de same sthyle dat you vent on dis morning, ven you vas begging me, and den you afterwards shtole my monish."

As he finished speaking, the old negro entered the cabin, and perceiving the intruders, enquired the cause of their presence. The Catholic who was an Irishman, briefly explained the object of their visit to the astonished old woman, who never conceived for a moment that Mrs. Wentworth had been guilty of theft.

"De Lor!" she exclaimed, as soon as her informant had concluded his remarks. "Who would'a believe it? Poh people, dey is really bad off," and she hurried to Mrs. Wentworth's side.

Mrs. Wentworth had paid no attention to the colloquy between the old negro and the policeman; she was engaged in appealing to Mr. Swartz, not to remove her to jail that night.

"You must have some feelings of humanity within you," she was observing. "You must have some touch of pity in your heart for my condition. Do not send me to jail to-night," she continued in an earnest tone. "If your own heart is steeled against the sorrows of a helpless and wretched woman; if the sight of that dead face does not awaken a spark of manly pity within you, let me entreat you, by the memory of the mother you once had, not to tear me from the body of my child. The hours of night will pass of rapidly, and by the dawn of morning my daughter shall be buried."

This was the first touch of feeling she had manifested, and though no tears bedewed her cheeks, the swelling of her bosom and the anguished look she wore, told of sorrow more terrible than if tears had come.

The wretch was unmoved. He stood there, not thinking of the solemn and heart-rending scene before him, but of the money he had lost, and the chance of its being found on the person of Mrs. Wentworth.

"Do your duty, policemen," he said, without appearing as if he had heard her remarks.

"It is well," she said, and walking up to the bedside of her dead child, she lifted the body until it almost assumed a standing position. "Farewell child, farewell forever!" she continued, covering the lifeless face with kisses. "See this!" she said, turning to the men, "see the result of beggary and starvation. Look upon it, you have had it in your power to save me from this desolation, and rejoice in your work. Here, take me," she added, laying down the corpse. "Take me from the presence of the dead, for if I remain gazing at it much longer, I will indeed go mad."

Walking up to the old woman, Mrs. Wentworth continued. "Auntie, I leave my child's body with you. See that it is buried and mark the spot where it rests, for oh! I feel that the day is not far distant when my weary head will rest in peace at last, when that time arrives, I desire to be buried by the remains of her who now lies there. For the little boy who is here, keep him Auntie, until his father claims him, and should his father never return, take him before some man high in position, and tell him that a wretched mother leaves him to the care of his country, as a memento of one of the patriot band who died in her service."

The old negro fell upon her knees before the speaker, and burst into tears, while even the rude policemen were touched by her remarks, Mr. Swartz alone remained unmoved, the only feeling within him was a desire that the work of confining her in jail should be completed.

"And now one last farewell," continued Mrs. Wentworth, again embracing the corpse. Another instant and she was out of the room followed by the three men, and they proceeded in the direction of the jail.

The old negro fell on her knees by the side of the bed, burying her head in the folds of the counterpane, while the tears flowed freely from her eyes. The little boy nestled by her side sobbing and calling for his mother.

"Don't cry chile," said the old negro, endeavoring to console him. "Your mammy will come back one of dcse days," then recollecting the words of Mrs. Wentworth in reference to him, she took him in her arms, and continued, "poh chile, I will take care ob you until your father come for you."

Thus did the good-hearted slave register her promise to take care of the child, and her action was but the result of the kind treatment she had received from her owner. She had been taken care of when a child by the father of her present owner, who was no other than Dr. Humphries, and now that she had grown old and feeble, he had provided her with a home, and supported her in return for the long life of faithful service she had spent as his slave. The next morning at about nine o'clock, a hearse might have been seen in front of the old woman's cabin. Without any assistance the negro driver lifted a little coffin from the chairs on which it rested in the room, and conveyed it into the hearse. It then drove off slowly, followed by the old negro and the infant, and drove to the burial ground. There a short and simple prayer was breathed over the coffin, and in a few moments a mound of earth covered it. Thus, was buried the little angel girl, who we have seen suffer uncomplainingly, and die with a trusting faith in her advent to Heaven. No long procession of mortals followed her body, but the Angels of God were there, and they strewed the wood with the flowers of Paradise, which though invisible, wafted a perfume into the soul sweeter than the choicest exotics of earth.

From the grave of the child, we turn to the mother, to see if her sufferings died with the body of the Angel which had just been buried. They had not, for still the eye of God was turned from the Soldier's Wife, and he saw not the life of misery and degradation that she was leading.

CHAPTER TWENTY-THIRD.
THE COMMITTAL.

On the morning that Ella was buried, Mrs. Wentworth was carried before the Mayor, and charges preferred against her for robbery. The package containing the remainder of the money had been found on her person the night previous, and this evidence was brought forward against her.

"What are your charges against this woman, Mr. Swartz," began his Honor.

"Vell your Honor," replied that individual, "I vill tell dem in but few words. Dis voman called at my shtore yesterday, and begged me for monish. I gave her von tollar, but she vouldn't take it, and after she left de shtore I found out dat a package of monish, dat was on de safe was gone, I den called mine clerk, and I look for de monish, and he looked for de monish, but ve neider of us find de monish. Den I say dat certainly somepody must take dish monish, and he say so too; den ve remember dat dis voman vas leaning against de safe, and he told me of it, and I remember too, and--"

"Explain your charges against the woman as briefly as possible, Mr. Swartz," interrupted the Mayor. "I have not time to stay here listening to a long round-about story."

"Von minute your Honor, von minute," replied the wretch. "I will soon finish de account. As I vas saying, I remember dat dis voman vas standing leaning by de safe and mine clerk tells me to go to de Trug Shtore, as de voman vent in dere, and I goes in de Trug Shtore, and Mr. Elkin he tells me dat de voman did come in dere and py some physic and dat she valk up de street, and I goes up de street and--"

"For goodness sake, Mr. Swartz, let me beg of you to conclude your remarks as soon as possible and not detain the Court with unnecessary statements," again interrupted the Mayor, "I see no use for you to repeat all that you did. Just come to the point at once and I will be able to decide whether this woman is to be committed or not."

"Shust von minute longer, your Honor," Mr. Swartz answered, "I vill finish directly. Vell, you see, I vent in te street, and I goes up te street, and I asks te beoples if tey see tis voman, and von of tem say he not see te voman, and I ask another and he not see te voman, and I ask anoter again and he not see te voman eider."

"If you are going to continue this nonsense all day let me know, and I will prepare myself to listen, as well as to return the other prisoners to jail until to-morrow," observed His Honor. "It appears as if you can never get through your tale. Speak quickly and briefly, and do not keep me waiting."

"Shust vait a little vile more nor not so musht," replied Mr. Swartz, and continuing his story he said, "I ask everybody if tey sees dis voman and dey say dey not sees te voman, and after I ask everybody, von man tell me dat he sees dis voman valk up de shtreet, and I go up de shtreet von little more vay and -"

"In the name of Heaven cease your remarks," exclaimed the Mayor, who had become thoroughly exasperated at the narrative of Mr. Swartz.

"Gootness," observed that gentleman, "did you not shay I vas for to tell vy I pring dis voman up?"

"Yea," replied His Honor, "but I did not expect you to give me a long narrative of all that occurred during the time while you were looking for where she lived."

"Veil, I vill soon finish," he remarked, "as I was saying, I goes up de shtreet von little more vays and I ask anoder man vere dis voman vas, and he shust look on me and shay he vould not tell noting to von tam Tutchman, and I go to von oder man and he show me von little log cabin, and I goes up dere softly and I sees dis voman in dere."

"All this has nothing to do with the charge you have preferred against her," the Mayor said, "let me know upon what grounds you prefer the charge of robbery against her."

"Vell, ven I sees her I valks pack to mine Shtore and I talks mit mine clerk, and he say I vas have to take out a varrant, and I comes to de City Hall and I takes out de varrant, and I takes two policemen and I goes to te cabin and finds dis voman dere, and she peg me not to take her to jail, but I vouldn't pe pegged and I pring her to jail."

"Mr. Swartz, if you don't conclude your remarks at once, I will be necessitated to postpone your case until to-morrow; I am tired of hearing your remarks, every one of which has been to no purpose. You say the package of money that you lost was found on this woman, and that she had been in your store the same day and had leaned against the safe on the top of which the money had been placed by you."

"Dat's shust it," replied Mr. Swartz. "Ven I go mit te voman to te jail te jail man search her and find te monish in her pocket, and it vas te same monish as I had stolen off te safe. But te monish vas not all dere; over tirty tollars vas taken out of it, and dat vas vat dis voman sphent, and I-"

"That's enough, Mr. Swartz," interrupted the Mayor. "You have said enough on the subject, and I will now proceed with the accused."

While Mr. Swartz was speaking Mrs. Wentworth remained as silent as if she had not heard a word he said. Her appearance was calm, nor was there anything remarkable about her except a strange unnatural brightness of the eye.

"Well, my woman," continued the Mayor, "what have you to say in extenuation of the charge."

"Nothing, Sir," she replied, "I have nothing to say in defense of myself. The money was found on my person, and would alone prove me guilty of the theft. Besides which, I have neither desire nor intention to deny having taken the money."

"What induced you to steal?" asked the Mayor.

"A greater tempter than I had ever met before," she replied. "It was necessity that prompted me to take that money."

"And you sphent tirty-tree tollers of it, py gootness," exclaimed Mr. Swartz, in an excited tone.

"As you acknowledge the theft," said the Mayor, "I am compelled to commit you to prison until the meeting of the Superior Court, which will be in four days from this."

Mrs. Wentworth was then committed back to prison, and Mr. Swartz returned to his store.

The spirit of the child had reached God and at that moment was pointing to her mother below. The day of rest is near.

CHAPTER TWENTY-FOURTH.
RETURN OF ALFRED WENTWORTH -- A STRANGER.

After long weeks of pain and illness Alfred Wentworth became well enough to return to the Confederacy. He was accordingly sent down by the first flag of truce that went to Vicksburg after his recovery, and two days after the committal of his wife arrived at Jackson, where he was warmly welcomed by Harry.

"I am delighted to see you, my dear friend," he exclaimed, shaking his hands warmly, "you have no idea the suspense I have been in since my escape, to learn whether you were re-captured. It would have reproached me to the last hour of my life had you been killed by those cursed Yankees."

"I came pretty near it," replied Alfred, smiling at his friend's earnestness.

"You were not hurt, were you?" enquired his friend.

"The slight matter of a few Minie balls, lodged in different parts of my body, is all the injury I received," he answered.

"I suppose that occasioned your not coming with the first lot of prisoners," Harry remarked.

"Yes," he replied, "when the cartel was arranged and orders were given for the prisoners to prepare for their departure from Camp Douglas, I was still suffering from my wound, and the doctors declared me unable to move for several days. An excited mind soon brought on fever, which so prostrated me that the days extended to weeks before I was able to leave the hospital."

"I am heartily glad to see you once more safe on Confederate soil, at any rate," observed Harry, and he added, "as I will insist upon your staying at my house while you are here, let me know where your baggage is, that I may hate it removed."

"I am staying at the Burman House, but what little baggage I possess is at Vicksburg."

"Then take a walk with me to the residence of Dr. Humphries," said Harry, "and I will introduce you to my betrothed."

"I thank you," Alfred replied, "but the present state of my wardrobe does not admit of my appearing before ladies."

"Pshaw," observed Harry, "that is the least part of the question. Let me know what you desire and I will get it for you directly."

"I have about seven hundred dollars in Confederate money with me," answered Alfred, "if you will show me some store where I can purchase a decent suit of clothes; that will be all I shall trouble you for."

"Take a walk with me to Lemby's clothing store and you will find a fine outfit there."

Drawing Alfred's arm in his, Harry conducted him to Lemby's clothing store, where a suit of clothing was bought. They then proceeded to the Bowman House and entered Alfred's room.

"My furlough is only for thirty days," Alfred remarked, while engaged in dressing himself, "and how I am to send in a letter to New Orleans and receive an answer before that time expires, I cannot conjecture."

"What do you wish to write to New Orleans for," asked Harry.

"Why, to wife," answered Alfred, "I think it is about time that she should hear from me."

"My dear friend," replied Harry, "your wife is not in New Orleans, she is in the Confederate lines."

"Where is she?" he enquired, eagerly.

"I could not tell you that," Harry answered, "but of one thing you may be certain, she is not in New Orleans."

"How do you know that?" he asked.

"Dr. Humphries purchased a negro girl the day before I returned; she gave her name as Elsy, and said she was belonging to Mr. Alfred Wentworth, of New Orleans. On being questioned why she had left the city, the girl said that her mistress with your two children had been forced to leave by Beast Butler, who would not allow her to go also, but that, being determined to follow your wife, she had ran the blockade and came into the Confederate lines."

"And did my wife sell her to anybody else?" enquired Alfred.

"Wait a moment, my dear friend, and I will tell you," Answered Harry. "The girl did not see her mistress at all, for she was arrested on her arrival in this city, and having no papers, as well as no owner, she was sold according to law, and was purchased by Dr. Humphries, at whose residence she is now. I would have told you this when we first met, but it slipped my memory completely."

"But where could my wife have gone to?" remarked Alfred. "I do not know of any person in the Confederate lines with whom she is acquainted, and where she can get the means to support herself and children I have not the least idea."

"That she has been to Jackson I am certain," Harry replied, "for no sooner did I hear what the girl had informed Dr. Humphries, than I endeavored to find out where she resided. I searched the register of both the hotels in this city and found that she had been staying at this hotel; but the clerk did not recollect anything about her, and could not tell me where she went to on her departure from this city. I also advertised in several newspapers for her, but receiving no information, was compelled to give up my search in despair."

"I thank you for your remembrance of me," observed Alfred. "This intelligence, however, will compel me to apply for an extension of my furlough, so that I may be enabled to find out where my wife and children are. I am very much alarmed at the news you have given me."

"I hope your wife and children are comfortably situated, wherever they may be; and could I have discovered their residence, I should have made it my duty to see that they wanted for nothing."

"I know it, I know it," said Alfred, pressing his friend's hand, and he continued, "you will favor me on our arriving at Dr. Humphries' by obtaining an interview for me with Elsy; I desire to know the cause of my wife's ejectment from New Orleans."

"As soon as you are ready let me know and we will start for the Doctor's," Harry answered, "where you will find the girl. Dr. Humphries told me that he intended returning her to you or your wife as soon as he discovered either of you. So, in the event of your finding out where Mrs. Wentworth lives, she will be promptly given up."

"No, no," Alfred remarked, hurriedly, "the Doctor has purchased her and I do not desire the girl unless I can return the money he paid for her. If you are ready to go," he added, "let us leave at once."

The two friends left the hotel and soon arrived at the residence of Dr. Humphries. The Doctor was not at home, but Emma received them. After introducing Alfred to her, and engaging in a brief conversation, Harry requested her to call Elsy, as he desired her to speak with his friend. The fair girl complied with his request by ringing the bell that lay on the table; her call was answered by the slave in person.

On entering the room Elsy made a low curtsey to the gentlemen, and looked at Alfred earnestly for a moment, but the soldier had become so sunburnt and altered in features that she failed to recognize him.

"Do you not remember me, Elsy?" enquired Alfred, as soon as he perceived her.

His voice was still the same, and running up to him, the girl seized his hand with joy.

"I tought I knowed you, sah," she exclaimed, "but you is so change I didn't remember you."

"I am indeed changed, Elsy," he replied; "I have been sick for a long time. And now that I am once more in the Confederacy, it is to find my wife and children driven from their homes, while God only knows if they are not wandering all over the South, homeless and friendless. Tell me Elsy," he continued, "tell me what caused my wife to be turned out of the city?"

In compliance with his request, the girl briefly told him of the villainy of Awtry, and the infamous manner in which he had acted towards Mrs. Wentworth. She then went on to relate that, failing to achieve his purpose, Awtry had succeeded in having her expelled from New Orleans.

"Did your mistress -- I beg pardon -- I meant, did my wife tell you where she was going to?" enquired Alfred.

"She told me to come to Jackson, after I told her I would be sure to get away from de city," answered the girl; "but de police ketch me up before I could look for her; and since I been belonging to Dr. Humphries, I has look for her ebery whar, but I can't find out whar she am gone to."

"That is enough," observed Alfred, "you can go now, Elsy, if I should want to see you again, I will send for you."

"I trust you may succeed in finding your wife, sir," Emma said as the girl left the parlor.

"I sincerely hope so myself, Miss Humphries," he answered, "but Heaven only knows where I am to look for her. It will take me a much longer time than I can spare to travel over the Confederacy; in fact, I doubt whether I can get an extension of my furlough, so that I may have about three months of time to search for her."

"It is singular that she should have told Elsy to come here to her, and not to be in the city," observed Emily.

"I am afraid that my wife has, through prudence, gone into the country to live; for, with the means I left her, she could not possibly have afforded to reside in any part of the Confederacy where prices rule so high as they do here. It is this belief that makes my prospect of finding her very dim. Harry says he advertised for her in several newspapers, but that he received no information from any source respecting where she lived. I am certain she would have seen the advertisement had she been residing in any of our cities."

"She may not have noticed the advertising column of the newspaper," put in Harry, "if ever she did chance to have a copy of one that contained my notice to her. Ladies, as a general thing, never interest themselves with advertisements."

"You are right," Alfred replied, "but it is singular that some person who knew her did not see it and inform her; she surely must have made some acquaintances since she arrived in our lines, and I am certain that there are none who do not sympathize with the unfortunate refugees who have been driven into exile by our fiendish enemy."

"I am sorry to say that refugees are not as favorably thought of as they deserve," Emma remarked. "To the shame of the citizens of our Confederacy, instead of receiving them as sufferers in a common cause, they are looked upon as intruders. There are some exceptions, as in all cases, but I fear they are very few."

"Your statement will only increase my anxiety to find my wife," answered Alfred, "for if the people act as unpatriotically as you represent, there is no telling if my unfortunate family are not reduced to dire necessity, although it is with surprise that I hear your remarks on the conduct of our people. I had thought that they would lose no opportunity to manifest their sympathy with those who are now exiles from their homes, and that idea had made me feel satisfied in my mind that my wife and children would, at least, be able to find shelter."

"I do not think anyone would refuse to aid your family, my dear friend," Harry observed, "although I agree with Miss Emma, that our people do not pay as much attention to refugees as they should; but the unfortunate exile will always find a sympathizing heart among our people. You may rest assured that, wherever your wife may be, she has a home which, if not as comfortable as the one she was driven from, is at least home enough to keep herself and her children from want."

Harry Shackleford judged others by the promptings of his own heart, and as he uttered these words of comfort to his friend, he little dreamed that Mrs. Wentworth was then the inmate of a prison, awaiting her trial for robbery, and that the crime had her committed through the very necessity he had so confidently asserted could never exist in the country.

"Will you take a walk to the hotel," enquired Alfred, after a few minutes of silence, "I desire to settle my bill with the clerk."

"Certainly," he replied, rising from his chair, "I desire to conduct you to my home."

"Good evening to you Miss Humphries," said Alfred, as he walked to the door with his friend.

She extended her hand to him as she replied, "Good evening, sir - allow me to repeat my wishes for your success in finding your wife and children."

Bowing to her in reply, he left the room, accompanied by Harry.

"Do you know, Harry," he observed, as they walked towards the Bowman House, "I have a strange presentiment that all is not well with my family."

"Pshaw," replied his friend, "you are as superstitious as any old woman of eighty. Why in the name of wonder will you continue to look upon the dark side of the picture? It is more likely that your family are now comfortably, if not happily situated. Depend upon it, my dear friend, the world is not so cold and uncharitable as to refuse a shelter, or a meal to the unfortunate."

Alfred made no reply, and they walked on in silence until the hotel was reached. On entering the sitting room of the Bowman House, the two gentlemen were attracted by the loud talking of a group of men standing in the centre of the room.

"There stands an Englishman who lately run the blockade on a visit to the Confederacy," observed Harry as they approached the group; "let me introduce him to you."

Walking up to where the Englishman was, Harry touched him lightly on the shoulder.

"How are you Lieutenant Shackleford," he said, as he turned and recognized Harry.

"Very well, Mr. Ellington," answered Harry, and then added, "allow me to introduce my friend Mr. Wentworth to you--Mr. Wentworth, Mr. Ellington."

As the name of Wentworth escaped Harry's lips the Englishman started and changed color, but quickly resuming his composure, he extended his hand to Alfred.

"I am happy to make your acquaintance, sir," he observed, and then continued, "your features resemble those of a gentleman I have not seen for years -- so much, indeed, that I could not repress a start as my eyes fell upon your countenance."

"I was rather surprised at seeing you start," observed Harry, "for I knew that you were not acquainted with my friend Mr. Wentworth. He was a prisoner at Camp Douglas -- the prison you have read so much about -- when you arrived in this country, and has only returned to the Confederacy within the last few days."

"A mere resemblance to one whose intercourse with me was not fraught with many pleasant recollections," remarked Mr. Ellington. "Indeed, your friend is so much like him, both in form and features, that I really imagined that he was my old enemy standing before me!"

"A singular resemblance," said Alfred, "and one which I am rejoiced to know only exists in form and features. And now," he continued, "allow me to ask you a question."

Mr. Ellington bowed an assent.

"Were you ever in this country before?" asked Alfred.

"Yes," replied Mr. Ellington, "I visited America a few years ago, but why do you ask?"

"Because your features are familiar to me," he answered, and then enquired, "Were you ever in New Orleans."

"No, sir -- no," replied Mr. Ellington, coloring as he spoke, "I was always afraid of the climate."

"The reason of my asking you," observed Alfred, "is because you resemble a gentleman with whom I was only very slightly acquainted, but who, like the party you mistook me for, has done me an injury which neither time nor explanation can repair, but," he added, "now I recollect you cannot be the party to whom I refer, for he was a Northern man, while you are an Englishman."

Before the Englishman could reply, a gentleman at the further end of the room called him by name, and, bowing to the two friends, he apologized for leaving them so abruptly, and walked off to where the call came from.

As soon as he left them Alfred went up to the clerk's office and paid his bill. The two friends then left the hotel and proceeded to Harry's residence.

"Do you know, Harry," observed Alfred, as they walked along, "I have an idea that Mr. Ellington is no Englishman, but that he is

Awtry, the scoundrel who caused my wife and children to be driven from New Orleans?"

"Why do you imagine such a thing?" asked Harry.

"Only because his features are very much like those of Awtry; and the start he gave when you pronounced my name half confirms my suspicion."

"I feel certain you are mistaken," Harry remarked. "He arrived at Charleston in a blockade runner a short time ago, and brought letters of introduction to many prominent men in the South from some of the first characters in England."

"That may be," Alfred answered, "still I shall keep my eye on him, and cultivate his acquaintance. If I am mistaken it will make no difference, for he shall never know my suspicions; but if I am right in my surmise, he shall answer me for his treatment of my wife and children."

"That you can do," said Harry, "but be cautious how you charge him with being a Yankee spy, and have certain proof of his identity before you intimate your suspicions to him." As he spoke, they reached their destination and the two friends entered the house.

Horace Awtry, for the Englishman was none other than he, under an assumed name, had ventured to enter the Confederate lines as a spy for Sherman, who was then getting up his expedition against Vicksburg. He would have left Jackson immediately after the meeting with Alfred, but upon enquiry he learned that Mrs. Wentworth's place of residence was unknown, and his services being needed near Vicksburg decided him to remain.

CHAPTER TWENTY-FIFTH.
THE TWO SLAVES -- THE GLIMMER OF LIGHT.

From the time of Mrs. Wentworth's arrest and imprisonment, the old negro had paid every attention to the little boy left under her care. Knowing that she would be likely to receive punishment for having a white child living with her, she had made several efforts to see her master, but each time she called, both the Doctor and Emma were absent. She was thus compelled to wait until some opportunity offered to turn the little boy over to her master, who she knew would promptly give him a home while he remained unclaimed by his lawful guardians. In her visits to Dr. Humphries' house the old negro had met Elsy, and being pleased with the appearance of the girl, had contracted quite a friendship for her, and on every opportunity would hold a conversation with her. Having called several times without seeing her master or Emma, Elsy enquired if she had anything of consequence to impart to the Doctor, as, if she had, she would inform him on his return home.

"Yes, gal," replied the old woman, "I got a leetle boy at my cabin dat was lef dar by him mammy, and I want de boss to take him away and put him in a better place den my room."

"What chile is it, Auntie?" enquired Elsy.

"I do' know what de name is," answered the old woman, "but a lady come to my cabin one-night wid a berry sick gal chile and de leetle boy, and next day de gal die, and in de ebening some police come and take away de lady because 'she 'teal money,' and dey lef de dead chile and de libing one wid me."

"Goodness sakes, Auntie," interrupted Elsy, "what did you do wid de dead chile?"

"Why, gal, I bury her next mornin," replied the old woman, "and de leetle boy bin stayin wid me eber since; but I don't want to keep him, for dis nigger hab no right to hab white chile a keepin to herself."

"You better see de Doctor, den," Elsy observed. "When he come in, I will tell him dat you want to see him patickler."

"Dat's a good gal," answered the old negro, "you tell him dat I want to see him, but don't tell him what I want him for -- I rader tell him dat mysef."

"Berry well, Auntie," she replied, "de Doctor will come in about dinner time, and as soon as he is done eatin I will talk to him about it. But do you tink he will bring de chile home, yah, and take care ob him?"

"Ob course he will," said the old woman, "he neber see any body want but he get him plenty and take care ob him."

"What kind a chile is de one you had at your cabin?" asked Elsy.

"Jes de lubliest baby you eber seed in your life," answered the old negro. "He is one ob de best children I eber had taking care ob."

"Don't he cry none for his mudder," enquired Elsy.

"Ob course he cry plenty de first day," she replied, "but afterwards he behabe well, for I promise him dat he mammy will come back soon. He am a rale good chile, and I would lub to keep him wid me all time, but I 'fraid de police will get ater me for habin him."

"Dat's so," remarked Elsy, "but you can take care ob him a'ter you tell de boss -- you can come here and stay."

"No, gal," she answered, "I can't leab me old cabin; I been libbing dar dese twelve years, and I got so used to it dat I can't sleep out ob it."

"Den I will take care ob de chile for you," said Elsy, "and you can come ebery now and den and see him."

"Dat's so," she, replied. "But tell me, gal," she continued, "whar you come from?"

"I come from New Orleans, Auntie," replied Elsy.

"What bring you to Jackson?" continued the old woman.

Elsy repeated the tale she had told Dr. Humphries and Alfred, and after she had concluded, the old woman clasped her hands as she exclaimed, "Sake alibe! what become ob your mistis and de childen?"

"I don't know, Auntie, but my New Orleans mass'r is here now, and I's been looking for dem."

"Why de lady and childen dat come to my cabin was from New Orleans too," observed the old negro.

"You say you don't know de name?" remarked Elsy.

"No, I forget," she answered; "but what name did your mistis hab?"

"Dey was name Wentworth," she replied.

"Wantworth -- Wentworth," repeated the old woman. "No, dat don't sound like de name ob de lady, but maybe I forget. What was de leetle gal name?" she added.

"Ella," replied Elsy.

"Dat's it," exclaimed the old negro, "dat's de berry name!"

"Den it was my mistis and her childen," answered Elsy, "and you say de police take her to prison for stealin."

"Yes, gal," she answered, "dey take her away from de dead body ob her chile and take her to prison for stealin."

"It ain't true," said Elsy, "my mistis is a born lady, and she wouldn't steal for anyting. I don't beliebe a word ob it."

"I don't beliebe neider," replied the old woman, "but for all dat, dey did carry her to prison because dey say she steal money."

"My poh mistis," remarked Elsy, bursting into tears, "I knowed dat some bad ting would happen to her -- and I was in town so long and neber eben sawed her."

"Poh lady," observed the old negro, "she look bery bad and sorrowful like, aldough she didn't cry when de chile die; but she tan up by de bedside and look 'pon de dead face widout sayin' a word -- it made me feel bad to see her."

"I must tell my master," said Elsy, "so dat he can go and take her out ob prison. It am a shame dat a lady like dat should be locked up in a prison, and Mr. Wentworth will soon take her out."

"You better not say anyting to your master about it, yet," observed the old woman. "See de Doctor and tell him; he will know what to do, and den he can tell de gemman all about it a'terwards."

"But you certain it am my mistis?" said Elsy.

"I ain't quite sure ob dat," she answered, "for de name sound different to de one I heard, and dats de reason I don't want you to say noting 'bout it till de Doctor enquire into de matter and find out. I must go now, gal," she added, "don't forget to tell de Doctor all 'bout it when he come home."

"I won't," replied Elsy.

The old woman then left the house and returned to her cabin, where she found the little boy amusing himself on the floor with some marbles.

Dr. Humphries, accompanied by Harry, returned home at the usual hour. After dinner Elsy requested him to speak to her for a few minutes -- a request which he promptly complied with.

"Well, my good, girl, what do you wish with me?" he enquired.

"Oh! sir," she replied, "I hab found out whar my mistis is."

"You have," answered Dr. Humphries, rather astonished at the intelligence, "where is she?" he added.

"In prison, sah," she replied.

"In prison!" exclaimed the Doctor, "for what?"

"I don'no, sah," she replied, "but I hear it is for stealing."

"Who gave you the information?" asked Dr. Humphries.

"It was your ole slave what libs in de cabin, up town," answered Elsy.

"And how did she learn anything about Mrs. Wentworth?" enquired Dr. Humphries.

"My Mistis went dere wid her chil'en, sah, and her little daughter died in de ole woman's cabin."

"Good God!" exclaimed the Doctor, "and how was it that I have heard nothing about it until now?"

"It only was a few days ago," replied Elsy, "and Auntie come here ebery day, but you and Miss Emma was not at home ebery time, and she only tole me about it dis mornin."

"Are you certain that the woman who has been carried to jail is your Mistress?" asked Dr. Humphries.

"No sah," she answered, "Auntie say dat de name am different, but dat de name ob de leetle gal am de same."

"And the little boy you say has been under the care of the old woman ever since," remarked Dr. Humphries.

"Yes sah," Elsy replied, "but she want you to take him away from her, so dat he may be under a white pusson, and das de reason why she been here wantin' to see you bout it."

"Very well," said. Dr. Humphries, "I will attend to it this evening; in the meantime, do you remain here and go with me to the cabin and see if the child is your Mistress'."

Elsy curtsied as she enquired, "Shall I tell my Master 'bout dis, sah?"

"No, no," replied the Doctor, "he must know nothing about it until I have arranged everything for his wife and removed her from prison. Be certain," he continued, walking to the door, "that you do not breathe a word about this until I have seen your Mistress and learned the reason of her imprisonment."

On returning to the parlor, where Harry and Emma were seated, Dr. Humphries called him aside and related what he had heard from Elsy. The young man listened attentively, and was very much shocked to hear of Mrs. Wentworth's being imprisoned for theft. He knew that Alfred was the soul of honor, and he could not conceive that the wife of his friend would be guilty of such an offense.

"It is impossible to believe such a thing," he said, after Dr. Humphries had concluded, "I cannot believe that the wife of such a man as Alfred Wentworth would commit an offense of such a nature; it must be someone else, and not Mrs. Wentworth."

"That we can find out this evening," observed the Doctor. "Let us first call at the cabin of my old slave and find out whether the child in her keeping is one of Mrs. Wentworth's children."

"How will we be able to discover," asked Harry. "It appears by your account that the boy is a mere infant, and he could hardly be expected to give an account of himself or his parents."

"I have removed any difficulty of that nature," replied Dr. Humphries, "Elsy will accompany us to the cabin, and she will easily recognize the child if he is the son of your friend."

"You are right," Harry remarked; and then continued, "I trust he may not be, for Alfred would almost go crazy at the knowledge that his wife was the inmate of a prison on the charge of robbery."

"I hope so myself, for the sake of your friend," said Doctor Humphries, "Mr. Wentworth appears to be quite a gentleman, and I should greatly regret his finding his wife in such an unfortunate position as the woman in prison is represented to be."

"I know the spirit of the man," remarked Harry, "he is sensitive to dishonor, no matter in what form or shape it may come, and the knowledge that his wife was charged with robbery would be a fearful blow to his pride, stern and unyielding as it is."

"If it is his wife, and she has committed a theft, I pity her, indeed; for I am sure if she is the lady her husband represents, nothing but the most dire necessity could have induced her to descend to crime."

"Ah, sir," replied Harry, "Heaven only knows if it is not through want. Alfred Wentworth feared that his wife was living in penury, for he knew that she was without adequate means. If she has unfortunately been allowed to suffer, and her children to want with her, what gratification is it for him to know that he was proving his loyalty to the South in a foreign prison while his wife and children were wanting bread to eat in our very midst?"

"It will indeed be a sad commentary on our patriotism," remarked Dr. Humphries. "God only knows how willing I should have been to serve the poor woman and her children had they applied to me for assistance."

"And I fervently wish that every heart in the State beat with the same feeling of benevolence that yours does," replied Harry. "However, this is no time to lament or regret what is inexorable; we must see the child, and afterwards the mother, for, no matter whether they are the family of Alfred Wentworth or not, the fact of their being the wife and child of a soldier entitles them to our assistance, and it is a debt we should always willingly pay to those who are defending our country."

"You are right, Harry, you are right," observed the Doctor, "and it is a debt that we will pay, if no one else does it. Do you return to Emma, now," he continued, "while I order the buggy to take us to the cabin."

Leaving Harry, Dr. Humphries went to the stable and ordered the groom to put the horse in the buggy. He was very much moved at the idea of a friendless woman being necessitated to steal for the purpose of feeding her children, and in his heart he sincerely wished she would not prove to be the wife of Alfred Wentworth. Harry's story of his friend's chivalrous conduct to him at Fort Donelson, as well as the high toned character evinced by Alfred during the few days acquaintance he had with him, had combined to procure a favorable opinion of the soldier by Dr. Humphries; at the same time, he could not conceive how anyone could be so friendless in a land famed for the generous hospitalities of its people, as the South is; but he knew not, or rather he had never observed, that there were times when the eye of benevolence and the hand of charity were strangers to the unfortunate.

There are no people on the face of the earth so justly famed for their charitable actions as that of the Confederate States. Before the unfortunate war for separation commenced, every stranger who visited their shores was received with a cordial welcome. The exile who had been driven from his home on account of the tyranny of the rulers of his native land, always found a shelter and protection from the warm hearts and liberal hands of the people of this sunny land; and though often times those who have received the aid and comfort of the South, shared its hospitalities, received protection from their enemies, and been esteemed as brothers, have turned like vipers and stung their generous host, still it passed it heedlessly and was ever ready to do as much in the future as it had done in the past. As genial as their native clime, as generous as mortals could ever be, those who sought the assistance of the people of the South would find them ready to accord to the deserving, all that they desired. It was indeed a glorious land; blooming with the loveliest blossoms of charity, flowing with the tears of pity for the unfortunate, and resplendent with all the attributes of mortal's noblest impulses. Gazing on the past, we find in the days of which we write no similitude with the days of the war. A greater curse than had fallen on them when war was waged on their soil, had fallen on the people of the South; all those chivalrous ideas which had given to her people a confidence of superiority over the North had vanished from the minds of those who had not entered the Army. It was in the "tented field" that could be found those qualities which make man the true nobility of the world. It is true that among those who remained aloof from active participation in the bloody contest were many men whose hearts beat with as magnanimous a pulsation as could be found in those of the patriots and braves of the battle-field; but they were only flowers in a garden of nature, filled with poisonous weeds that had twined themselves over the land and lifted up their heads above the purer plants, which, inhaling the tainted odor emitted by them, sickened and died, or if by chance they remained and bloomed in the midst of contamination, and eventually rose above until they soared over their poisonous companions, their members were too few to make an Eden of a desert, and they were compelled to see the blossoms of humanity perish before them unrewarded and uncared for, surfeited in the nauseous and loathsome exhalations of a cold and heartless world, without the hand of succor being extended or the pitying tear of earth's inhabitants being shed upon their untimely graves.

While they, the curse of the world, how was it with them? But one thought, one desire, filled their hearts; one object, one intention, was their aim. What of the speculator and extortioner of the South, Christian as well as Jew, Turk as well as Infidel! From the hour that the spirit of avarice swept through the hearts of the people, the South became a vast garden of corruption, in which the pure and uncorrupted were as pearls among rocks. From the hour that their fearful work after gain commenced, charity fled weeping from the midst of the people, and the demons of avarice strode triumphant over the land, heedless of the cries of the poverty stricken, regardless of the moanings of hungry children, blind to the sufferings it had occasioned and indifferent to the woe and desolation it had brought on the poor.

But all this was seen by God, and the voice of Eternity uttered a curse which will yet have effect. Even now as we write, the voice of approaching peace can be heard in the distance, for the waters on which our bark of State has been tossing for three years begins to grow calmer, while the haven of independence looms up before us, and as each mariner directs his gaze on the shore of liberty the mist which obscured it becomes dispelled, until the blessed resumption of happiness and prosperity once more presents itself, like a gleam of sunshine on a dark and cheerless road of life.

The eye of God is at last turned upon a suffering people. The past years of bloody warfare were not His work; He had no agency in stirring up the baser passions of mankind and imbuing the hands of men in each others blood, nor did He knowingly permit the poor to die of want and privation. He saw not all these, for the Eye which "seeth all things" was turned from the scene of our desolation, and fiends triumphed where Eternity was not, Hell reigned supreme where Heaven ruled not -- Earth was but a plaything in the hands of Destiny. Philanthropy may deny it -- Christianity will declare it heresy -- man will challenge its truth, but it is no less true than is the universe a fact beyond doubt, and beyond the comprehension of mortals to discover its secrets.

CHAPTER TWENTY-SIXTH.
THE RECOGNITION.

As soon as the groom had prepared the buggy, he announced to Dr. Humphries that it was in readiness. Calling Harry, who was again seated by the side of his betrothed, indulging in secret conversation, the Doctor went into the street where the buggy was.

"I will drive myself this morning, John," he remarked to the groom, "Mr. Harry will go with me."

"Berry well, sah," replied the groom, moving off.

Stepping into the buggy, followed by Harry, the Doctor took the reins in his hands and was about to drive off.

"Wait a moment," observed Harry, "has Elsy gone to the cabin?"

"No, I forgot all about her," answered the Doctor, "and I am glad you reminded me."

"You had better send for her at once, and give her orders to proceed immediately to the cabin," said Harry, "for without her we would be unable to know whether the child is that of Alfred Wentworth or of some other unfortunate soldier."

"Here, John!" called out Dr. Humphries after the retreating form of the groom, "come here to me."

The boy turned back and returned to the side of the buggy.

"Tell Elsy to come here at once," said the Doctor.

The boy moved off to comply with his master's order, and in a few moments returned, accompanied by Elsy.

"Do you go to the old woman's cabin," said Dr. Humphries, as soon as she had reached the side of the buggy, "and wait there until I arrive. There is no necessity to mention what I am going there for."

"Yes sah," replied Elsy, as she turned away to do her master's bidding.

"And now," remarked the Doctor, "we will go on and find out who these people are. But before we go, I had better purchase a few things that will relieve the necessities of the child."

With these words the Doctor drove off, and on arriving in front of a store, drew in the reins and, alighting, shortly after returned with several packages, which he placed in the buggy and, re-entering it, he drove to the cabin of the old slave. On arriving there, the Doctor and Harry found the old woman and the child seated in the room talking. The boy appeared quite contented, now that his grief at the loss of his sister and departure of his mother had subsided, and was laughing merrily when they entered. He was dressed very cleanly and neatly by the old slave, who had expended all her savings in purchasing suitable cloths for him, and his appearance excited the remark of the Doctor and his companion the moment they entered the threshold of the room and saw him.

"Good day sah," said the old negro, rising and curtseying as soon as the two gentlemen entered.

"God day, Auntie," said the doctor, "how are you getting on."

"Berry well," answered the old woman, and then added, "I'm mighty glad you come here dis day, for I want to talk wid you 'bout dis here chile."

"I have heard all about him, Auntie," said the Doctor, "and have come here expressly for the purpose of learning something about his parents."

"'Spose dat gal Elsy tell you," observed the old woman, snappishly, nettled because she had not the opportunity of telling her master the tale of Mrs. Wentworth and her children.

"Yes, Auntie," he replied, "Elsy told me, but not before I had asked her all about those unfortunate people, so you must not be mad with her."

"She might ha' waited till you see me befo' she say anyting about it," remarked the old woman.

"Never mind that, Auntie," replied the Doctor, who knew the old woman's jealous disposition and wanted to pacify her. "Has Elsy been here yet?"

"No sah," she replied, "I ain't seen her since mornin'."

"She will be here directly, then," he remarked, and seating himself the Doctor waited the arrival of Elsy.

"Come here my little man," said Harry, who had been sitting on the bed during the dialogue between the old slave and her master.

The child walked up to him and placed his arms on Harry's knees.

"What is your name," enquired the young man, lifting the child up on his knees.

"My name is Alf," he replied.

"Alf what?" asked Harry.

The child looked at him enquiringly, not understanding the question.

"What is your mother's name," continued Harry, perceiving that the boy was unable to answer his question.

"My ma's name is Eva," he answered.

"And your sister's?" asked Harry.

"My sister is named Ella," replied the child, and then added, mournfully, "but she is gone from here; they took her out in a little box and put her in the ground, and Granny says she is gone to heaven; and my ma," he continued, "some bad men carried away, but Granny says she will soon come back -- wont she?" And his innocent face looked up confidingly in Harry's.

"Yes, my boy," he answered, "your ma will soon come back to you."

"There appears no doubt of the identity of this family," remarked Harry to Dr. Humphries, after a short pause, "everything we have yet discovered indicates that Alfred Wentworth's wife and children have passed a fearful life since their expulsion from New Orleans."

"Poor woman and children," observed the Doctor, dashing away a tear, "could I have known their penury, I should have been only glad to relieve them, and even now, it is not too late for us to benefit this child and his mother. As soon as Elsy arrives here I shall remove the boy to my house and visit the mother in jail."

"I do not think it advisable to move the child until you have succeeded in obtaining the release of Mrs. Wentworth," answered

Harry. "His father may chance to see him, and, under the circumstances, would discover where his wife was; which discovery I desire to avoid as long as possible. The best thing that you can do is to leave the boy here for twenty-four hours longer, by which time bail can be procured for his mother, and I shall endeavor to silence the charge, so that there may be no necessity for a trial."

"May not Mr. Wentworth see the child and recognise him before we have accomplished his mother's release," enquired the Doctor.

"I do not think it likely," he replied, "Alfred will not visit so remote a vicinity, and the child need not be carried into the business portion of the city."

"I shall leave him here, then, as you think it advisable," remarked the Doctor; "it cannot injure him to remain in this cabin for a day longer, while it might lead to unpleasant discoveries should he be removed."

Harry and the old gentleman remained silent for some time, when Elsy entered the room. No sooner did the girl see the boy than she recognized her master's child, and taking him in her arms caressed him with all the exhibitions of affection the negro is capable of.

"Dis am Mas Alfred own chile" she exclaimed to Harry and the old gentleman, "and who would thought dat him would be libin' here."

"I supposed it was your master's child, my good girl," observed the Doctor, and then added, as he rose from his seat, "you can stay here with him until dark, when you had better return home; meanwhile, I do not wish you to let Mr. Wentworth know that his wife and child are in this city, nor do I wish you to take him out of this cabin. Come Harry," he continued, "let us go now and see the mother; she will be able to give us full details of her unfortunate life and to inform us of the cause for which she is in prison."

Leaving the cabin, the two gentlemen re-entered the buggy and drove to the Mayor's office. Finding him absent, they proceeded to his residence, and, after briefly narrating the tale of Mrs. Wentworth and her family, requested permission to visit her.

"Certainly, my dear sirs," replied Mr. Manship, such being the name of the Mayor, "take a seat while I write you an order of admittance."

In a few minutes the order to admit Dr. Humphries and his companion in the female's ward of the prison was written. Returning thanks to the Mayor, the two gentlemen started for the prison, and on showing the permit, were ushered into the cell occupied by Mrs. Wentworth.

"Good God!" exclaimed Harry, as he looked upon the squalid and haggard form of the broken-hearted woman, "this surely cannot be the wife of Alfred Wentworth."

Mrs. Wentworth had paid no attention to the visitors when they first entered, but on hearing her husband's name pronounced, rose from her crouching position and confronted the speaker. The name of the one she loved had awoke the slumbering faculties of the woman, and, like a flash of electricity on a rod of steel, her waning reason flared up for a moment.

"You spoke my husband's name," she said in a hoarse tone, "what of him?"

"He is my friend, madam," replied Harry, "and as such I have called to see you, so that you may be removed from this place."

"Thank you," she answered; "yours is the first voice of charity I have listened to since I left New Orleans. But it is too late; I have nothing now to live for. Adversity has visited me until nothing but disgrace and degradation is left of a woman who was once looked upon as a lady."

"There is no necessity for despondency, my good madam," observed Dr. Humphries. "The misfortunes which have attended you are such as all who were thrown in your situation are subject to. Our object in coming here," he continued, "is to learn the true cause of your being in this wretched place. Disguise nothing, but speak truthfully, for there are times when crimes in some become necessity in others."

"My tale is briefly told," she answered. "Forced by the cruelty of a villain to leave my comfortable home in New Orleans, I sought refuge in the Confederate lines. I anticipated that refugees would meet with a welcome from the more fortunate people of the South. In that I was disappointed; for when my means gave out, and every endeavor to procure work to feed my children had failed -- when I had not a dollar to purchase bread for my innocent babes, I applied for assistance. None but the most dire necessity would have prompted me to such a step, and, Oh, God! when it was refused --

when the paltry pittance I asked for was refused, the hope which I had clung so despairingly to, vanished, and I felt myself indeed a miserable woman. Piece after piece of furniture went, until all was gone -- my clothing was next sold to purchase bread. The miserable life I led, the hours spent with my children around me crying for bread -- the agonizing pangs which rent my mother's heart when I felt I could not comply with their demand – all -- all combined to make me an object of abject misery. But why describe my sufferings? The balance of my tale is short. I was forced out of the shelter I occupied because I could not pay the owner his rent. My oldest child was then ill, and in the bleak night wind, canopied by heaven alone, I was thrust, homeless, from a shelter owned by a man whose wealth should have made him pause ere he performed such an act. With my sick child in my arms I wandered, I knew not where, until I found she had fainted. Hurrying to a small cabin on the road, I entered and there discovered an old negro woman. From the lips of a slave I first heard words of kindness, and for the first-time aid was extended to me. Applying restoratives, my child revived and I waited until next morning, when I returned once more to ask for aid. A paltry sum was handed to me, more for the sake of getting rid of the mendicant than to relieve my distress. I felt that the sum offered was insufficient to supply the demands of my sick daughter and my starving boy. I was turning in despair away when my eye lit upon a package of money resting on the safe. For a moment I hesitated, but the thought of my children rose uppermost in my mind, and, seizing the package I hurried from the store."

"So, you did take the money," said Harry.

"Yes," she replied, "but it did me little good, for when the doctor was called, he pronounced my daughter beyond medical skill. She died that evening, and all the use to which the money was appropriated, was the purchase of a coffin."

"Then the - the --" said Harry, hesitating to use the word theft, "then, it was not discovered that you had taken the money until your child was dead and buried."

"No," she said, "listen -- my child lay enrobed in her garment of death, and the sun was fast declining in the west, when Mr. Swartz and two constables entered the room and arrested me. On my bended knees I appealed to him not to tear me from the body of my child. Yes," she continued, excitedly, "I prayed to him in the most abject manner to leave me until my child was buried. My prayers were unavailing, and from the window of this cell I witnessed a lonely hearse pass by, followed by none other than my infant boy and the kind old negro. Oh God! Oh God!" she went on, bursting into tears and throwing herself on the wretched pallet in the cell, "my cup of misery was then full, and I had drained it to the very dregs. I have nothing more to live for now, and the few days longer I have to spend on earth can be passed as well in a prison as in a mansion."

"Not so," interrupted Dr. Humphries, "I trust you will live many, many years longer, to be a guardian to your child and a comfort to your husband."

"It cannot be," she answered sadly. "The brain, overwrought, will soon give way to madness, and then a welcome death will spare me the life of a maniac. I do not speak idly," she continued, observing the look they cast upon her; "from the depths of my mind, a voice whispers that my troubles on earth will soon be o'er. I have one desire, however, and should like to see it granted."

"Let me know what that is," remarked Dr. Humphries, "and if it lies in my power, it shall be accorded to you with pleasure."

"Your companion spoke of my husband as his friend; does he know where he is at present, and if so, can I not see him?"

"I promise that you shall see your husband before many days. Until you are removed from this place, I do not think it advisable, but," continued Harry, "I shall, on leaving this place, endeavor to secure your release."

Mrs. Wentworth made no answer, and, speaking a few words of consolation and hope to her, the two gentlemen left the prison. The next morning Harry called on the Mayor and asked if Mrs. Wentworth could be bailed, but on his honor mentioning that her trial would come off the next day, the court having met that evening, he determined to await the trial, confident that she would be acquitted when the facts of the case were made known to the jury. On the same day he met Alfred Wentworth, who informed him that he was more strongly impressed than ever in the belief that the pretended Englishman was a spy.

"I will inform you of a plan that will prove whether you are right or not," observed Harry, when he had concluded. "Tomorrow at about three o'clock in the evening persuade him to visit the Court

House. I will be present, and if he is really the spy you imagine, will have full evidence against him."

"What evidence?" enquired Alfred.

"Never do you mind," he replied, "just bring him and there will be plenty of evidence found to convict him if he is a spy. By the way," he continued, "you said you suspected him to be the same man who caused your wife to be turned out of New Orleans?"

"Yes," Alfred answered, "but why do you ask?"

"Oh, nothing in particular," he replied, "only in the event his being Awtry, you will have a double motive in finding out whether he is a spy or not."

"You are right," observed Alfred, "but whether he is Awtry or not, I should deem it my duty to the Government to ferret out the true status of that man, and to have him brought to justice if he is really a spy. Your request to carry him to the Court House is a strange one, and I will cheerfully comply with it, although I cannot see how his being there will enable us to make the discovery."

"Leave that to me," answered Harry, "and content yourself with believing that I am certain it will prove whether he is an Englishman or a Yankee."

With that the two friends departed and Harry returned home much perplexed at the manner he had arranged for the husband and wife to meet.

CHAPTER TWENTY-SEVENTH.
TRIAL OF MRS. WENTWORTH -- THE ADVOCATE.

The morning for the trial of Mrs. Wentworth arrived, and at the hour of ten she appeared in the court. Her appearance was changed since we last saw her. The kind hearted daughter of Dr. Humphries had visited her the day before with a supply of clothing, and though her features retained their haggard and care-worn expression, none who looked upon her as she entered the court room could have failed to perceive that she was a lady and unlike a majority of females brought before a jury to answer grave charges. Her case did not excite any notice until she appeared, when the pinched and sharp face presented to the spectators, and the evidence her lady-like demeanor gave of her being a different subject from that usually presented, awoke a feeling of interest in the crowd, and many enquiries were made of the nature of the charge made against her.

None, however, could inform the inquisitors, and they awaited the reading of the charges.

As Mrs. Wentworth entered the room she cast a look at the jury box, and a shudder came over her as she perceived Mr. Elder sitting among the jurymen. She knew that he would not favor the dismissal of the case; but a gleam of hope presented itself in the person of Dr. Mallard, who she believed to be a good man, notwithstanding his abrupt and true remarks at the bedside of her dying child. These were the only two persons present she knew, save and except Mr. Swartz, who stood nearby, ready to give his evidence against her. But from him she expected nothing; nor did she intend to ask one word of favor or mercy. There was no disposition within her to sue for mercy, nor did she purpose denying or palliating her having taken the money.

After the usual delay, Mrs. Wentworth was placed in the prisoners' stand and the charges preferred against her. In his usual style Mr. Swartz proceeded to narrate his business connection with the accused, and stated that he had done everything he possibly could for her, but that, not satisfied with receiving his bounty, she had stolen his money. His story was given in a conclusive and plausible manner, and on his clerk certifying to what his employer had said, the chances for the accused appeared very dim. What added more to the evidence against her, was the conduct of Mr. Elder, who, rising from his seat briefly stated that, from his intercourse with her, he believed Mrs. Wentworth to be an unprincipled and dishonest woman.

"On what ground do you make that assertion, Mr. Elder?" enquired the Judge.

"As I stated before, in my intercourse with her," he replied.

"And may I ask of what nature your intercourse was?" asked the Judge.

"It would delay the court were I to state what business transactions have taken place between this woman and myself," answered Mr. Elder. "When I arose, it was simply to state my belief in her dishonesty."

"You should have appeared on the witness' box, if you desired to give evidence against the accused," remarked the Judge. "As it stands, your assertions cannot be taken as evidence against her. If you desire to appear as a witness for the accuser, say so, and I will then be prepared to hear what you may have to say."

"I have no such desire," replied Mr. Elder, seating himself.

"And now my good woman," said the Judge, turning to Mrs. Wentworth, who had remained a silent listener to all that had been said against her, "let me know what you may have to say against the charges brought against you. By your appearance and general demeanor, you have seen better days, and it is a source of regret that I should see any one bearing evidence of once living in a different sphere from the one you now occupy, brought before me on a charge of robbery. Let me now know what you have to say on this charge."

"I can say nothing," she replied.

"Well, then, do you plead guilty, or not guilty?" asked the Judge.

"Not Guilty!" thundered Harry, in an excited manner. He had been unavoidably delayed from accompanying Mrs. Wentworth to the Court House, and had just arrived. "Not guilty! I repeat, and, as counsel for the accused, I beg leave to make a few remarks."

"Certainly, Lieutenant Shackleford," answered the Judge, who knew Harry well.

The remarks of Harry, and his excited manner, awoke the waning interest in the case, and the crowd clustered closer round the railings.

"Your honor, and gentlemen of the Jury," began Harry, as soon as he had become calm enough to speak: "It is now nearly two years since I appeared in a civil capacity before a court of justice, and I had thought that while this war lasted my services would have been solely on the battle-fields of my country, and not in the halls where law is dispensed. But the case which I have appeared to defend, is so unlike those you ordinarily have before your honorable body, that I have, for a while, thrown off the armor of the soldier, and once more appear as the lawyer. You will pardon my apparent digression from the subject at issue, but as I see many looks of surprise at my seemingly strange conduct, I deem it but justice to myself that I should explain my motive for so acting.

It is now nearly two years ago that a soldier in a happy and comfortable home in New Orleans bade adieu to a fond wife and two promising children. As the tear-drop trickled down the cheek of his lovely and blooming wife, he whispered a word of comfort and solace to her, and bade her be cheerful, for the dark cloud which covered the political horizon of his country would soon be dispelled by the bright sunshine of liberty. But the tear that fell on her cheek was not of regret; for she felt that in leaving her he obeyed the call of his country, and was but performing a duty he owed to his native South. The tear was brushed away, and she smiled in his face at the glowing words of hope and comfort he spoke to her. They were full of promise, and as each syllable fell on her ear, they awoke an echo in her heart, until the love of the wife paled before the enthusiastic patriotism of the Southern woman, and the dangers of the battle-field became hidden before the vision of the honor and glory which awaited the patriot hero. Then she bade him adieu with a smile, and they departed, full of love and hope. Oh! gentlemen, let me take a glance back at the home and household war had then severed. Before our treacherous enemy had proclaimed war against us, this soldier's home was a model of earthly joy and felicity. It is true, there was no wealth to be found there, but there was a bright and more glorious gift than wealth can command; there was happiness, and this, combined with the love borne by this soldier for his wife, served to make them pass their years of wedded life in comfortable union. Years pass over their heads, and two children are sent to bless them, and they were cherished as priceless gifts. When the call to arms resounded through the South, this husband, like thousands of others, ceased his civil pursuits, and enlisted under the banner of his country. None but the purest and loftiest motives of patriotism, and a sense of duty, prompted him to the step; and though he knew that in so doing he would leave his wife deprived of her natural protector, and subject to privations, he thought, and with every right, that those who remained at home would shield a soldier's wife from danger, and he trusted on the means at his disposal to keep her from penury and destitution. After making preparation for his wife and children, he bade them adieu, as I have described already, and departed for Virginia, whose soil had already been invaded by the vandals of the North.

And now, gentlemen, lest you should think by my intimating that this soldier was not wealthy, I meant he was also poor in society, I will state that he and his wife held as high a position in the social circle of New Orleans as the most favored of fortune. His wife, this unfortunate lady, who now stands before you charged with theft, is the daughter of one who was once wealthy, but on whom adversity fell shortly before her marriage. Think not that the haggard and care-worn features before you were always such. There was a time, not long distant, when the bloom of youth and beauty could be seen in that sunken cheek and that sharpened face; but adversity has reduced one of God's fairest works to the wretched and unfortunate condition she is now in. Pardon my digression, for the tale I have to tell cannot be briefly recited; it is necessary that I shall speak in full, and though I may tire you by my lengthy remarks, you must hear them with patience, for they are necessary in this defence, and are equally needed to hold up to the scorn and contempt of every patriotic spirit in the land, two men who have disgraced their sex and entailed misery, aye, and degradation, on an unfortunate woman."

"If his honor, the judge, will permit me," interrupted Mr. Elder, "I should like to decline serving as a juryman on this case."

"Silence!" exclaimed Harry, before the judge could reply. "You are already sworn in, and I desire that you shall remain where you are."

"I cannot possibly excuse you, Mr. Elder," remarked the judge, in a tone of surprise, "the case has progressed too far already for any excuse. Continue, Lieutenant Shackleford," he continued, speaking to Harry.

"As I was observing," Harry went on, "this soldier departed for Virginia, and shortly after his departure, a villain, who had addressed his wife in former years and been rejected, assumed the sheep's garb and resumed his acquaintance with her. Many were the kindnesses he extended towards her, and the delicate manner in which he performed those little acts of courtesy, that lend a charm to society, disarmed any suspicion of his sincerity of purpose. But under the guise of friendship, the villain designed to overcome a lonely woman. With that subtlety and deception which every 'roue' possesses, he ingratiated himself in her confidence and favor until she began to regard him in the light of a brother. But the hour approached when the mask he had worn so long would be thrown aside and his unhallowed desires be avowed. The soldier was taken prisoner at Fort Donelson, and within four months after, New Orleans fell. Then the persecutions of the unprincipled villain commenced. A Northern man, he did not at the commencement of the war avow his sympathies to be with the people of his section, but, pretending friendship for the South, remained in our midst until

Butler and his infamous cohorts had gained possession of the city, when he proclaimed himself a Unionist, and gaining the favor of that disgrace to the name of man, was soon able to intimidate the cowardly or beggar the brave. One of his first attempts was to compel this lady to yield to his hellish passions. With contempt she spurned his offers and ordered him never more to cross the threshold of her house. Swearing vengeance against her, he left, and on the following morning she received an order to leave the limits of the city, that day, and prepare to enter the Confederate lines. The dangers which then threatened her, she deemed vanished, for she feared more to remain in the midst of our enemies than to enter our lines. The order was therefore received with joy, and she prepared to depart. Though a pang of sorrow may have filled her heart at being compelled to relinquish her comfortable home, though she saw before her days, weeks, months, perhaps years of hardship, not one feeling of remorse at having rejected the offers of a libertine, ever entered the mind of the soldier's wife. The time at length arrived for her to depart, and with her two children, a few articles of clothing, and a small sum of money, she was placed within our lines, far from any human habitation, and left to find a shelter as best she could.

To this city she bent her footsteps, and here she anticipated finding an asylum for herself and children. Gentlemen, we all well know that, unfortunately for our cause and country, the evils Speculation and Extortion, had spread their leprous wings and covered our land with destitution. To a man of this city, who, before the world's eye, appeared the Christian and the man of benevolence, but who in his dealings with his fellow-men, was as vile an extortioner as the most heartless; to this man she went and hired a room in which to find a shelter. Finding she was a refugee and fearing an evil day, he bound her down by law to suffer ejectment the moment she could no longer pay the rent. Ignorant of the weapon she placed in his hands, she signed the deed, and after paying a portion of the rent in advance, left him and assumed possession. Mark well, gentlemen, what I have said. In his action we find no Christianity -- no benevolence; nothing but the spirit of the extortioner is here manifested. There is no feeling of sorrow shown at her unfortunate position, no disposition evinced to shield the helpless mother and her babes. No! we find his actions narrowed down to the sordidness of the miser, the avariciousness of the extortioner. A feeling of surprise at such conduct may flit across your bosoms, gentlemen, and you may perchance doubt that I can show a man of this city, so bereft of charity, so utterly oblivious to all the better feelings of humanity, but I shall before long call his name, and give such evidence of the truth of my assertions, as will be beyond contradiction or doubt.

To another man the soldier's wife went for the purpose of purchasing a few articles of furniture. Of him I have little to say at present. It is true that without caring who and what she was, his merchandize was sold to her at the 'speculator's' price. But he had the right to charge whatever he pleased, and therefore I have nothing to say against him for that.

Weeks passed on, and the soldier's wife found herself without the means of purchasing food for her children. The hour had at last arrived when she was utterly destitute. In the meantime, her husband lay in a foreign prison, ignorant of the unhappy fate his wife was undergoing. Many are the nights we have walked to and fro on the grounds of Camp Douglas, and often has he spoken to me of his absent wife and children. I know him, gentlemen, and never in the breast of man beat a heart truer than his, nor in the minds of God's mortals were there ever finer and nobler impulses. While he was thus suffering confinement for his country's sake, his wife and children were here -- in our very midst, 'starving'! Aye, starving! Think of it, gentlemen -- that in the midst of those who were supposed to be friends -- the wife and children of a patriot were allowed to starve. Great God! is there on earth a spectacle so fearful to behold as 'starvation'? And is it not enough to evoke the wrath of the Infinite, when men, surrounded by all that wealth can afford, refuse to aid and succor their starving fellow creatures?

You may think that no man can be found who would refuse, but I tell you, gentlemen, that that man who now stands before you, was appealed to by this lady, the accused, after she had disposed of every piece of furniture in the room, save and except the bed on which her children slept. The appeal was rejected, and, despairing of help, she offered and sold to him the last remaining article of furniture. Here now is the picture. He could not lend or give her a paltry pittance; and why, forsooth? Because the money would not yield him a profit, and there was a chance of his losing it. But the moment she offered to dispose of the bed, he purchased it, for in it did the profit of the speculator lie hidden, and on it could he get his money doubled. Think not, gentlemen, that the tale you have listened to from him is the true one. It is a varnished and highly colored evidence, beneath which a wide extent of corruption can be seen, the moment its curtain is removed.

The pittance thus obtained serves but a short time, and they are again reduced to want. The eldest child -- a lovely daughter, is taken ill, and while lying on a heap of rags in a corner of the room, the man calls and demands his rent. The poor woman has no money to satisfy his demands and he orders her to leave. She appeals to him, points to her ill child; but her prayers are unavailing -- and in the hour of night she is thrust from the room, homeless, penniless, friendless! Yes! He -- that man who now sits in the jury-box -- he --Mr. Elder, the so-called 'Christian' and man of CHARITY -- he, ejected this helpless woman from the shelter and forced her to wander in the night air with her sick child -- her starving babes. He -- the 'extortioner'" continued Harry, with every feature expressing the utmost scorn, "turned her from the wretched home she had found here, and left her to die on the sidewalks, like the veriest beggar. No touch of pity for the child, no feeling of sorrow for the innocent angel, no thought of the patriot lingering in prison, ever entered the mind of the extortioner. There was nothing but 'self' then, nothing but the promptings of his own avarice, which could view with indifference the miseries of others, so long as they should redound to his own benefit and aggrandizement. I tell you that man dare not deny a word I utter. He knows that every one is true, and if my language could wither him with shame, could make him the detestation of the world, I would speak yet stronger, for pity to him is but contempt for those he has injured.

Thus, thrust out of home and shelter, the helpless mother conveyed her fainting child to a negro's cabin and there revived it. The next morning, she once more called upon her accuser and petitioned him for help. He again refused to aid her, although informed that the money was intended to procure medical aid for her sick child, until at last, wearied of her importunities, he handed her the pitiful sum of 'one dollar'! This was not sufficient for the purpose she desired, and she was about turning away in despair when her eye lit on a package of notes lying on the safe. Remember, gentlemen, what I have told you. She was penniless and friendless. Her child was ill and she had no means to procure medical aid. Her appeal for charity had been rejected, and can we blame her if she yielded to the tempter and took the money lying before her? We cannot. Look not on the act, gaze only on the provocation. If in hearts there dwells a shade of pity, an acme of sympathy, you cannot return a verdict of guilty. She is not guilty of theft! I unhesitatingly assert, that if to act as she has, and under the circumstances she acted, be theft, then such a thief would I become to-morrow; and in my own conscience, of the opinions of the world and confident in the forgiveness of an Almighty Father, would I commit such a theft as she has--just such an offence. I pleaded 'not guilty,' and it may surprise you that in the face of such a plea, I should acknowledge that she took the money. Again, I repeat my plea. She is not guilty of theft, and to you who have hearts to you who sympathize with the sufferings of a soldier's wife -- to you, whose wives and children may to-morrow be placed in a similar position - to you, I leave a verdict. But one word yet ere I am done.

The money which she took, to what use was, it placed? To purchase a 'coffin' for her child! To place the lifeless body of her daughter in its last home ere it is covered by the dust -- this, and this only, was the good which accrued from it. And, gentlemen, he -- Mr. Elder -- is the MURDERER of that child. As such I charge him, and as such I brand him to be. But for his brutality -- but for his avarice and selfish lust for gain, the mouldering corpse might now have been a blooming and happy child. And yet another word. When the so-called theft was discovered, and the accuser sought the accused, he found her by the bedside on which the dead child lay clothed in its last earthly garments. Disregarding her entreaties, she was torn from the corpse, thrust into prison, and the humble and servile hands of the negro were left to perform those sad rites which affection is ever the first to do. This is my tale, and -"

Here the excitement grew intense, and a strong feeling of indignation was manifested by the soldiers present against Mr. Swartz and Mr. Elder, and many threats were made to hang them.

CHAPTER TWENTY-EIGHTH.
THE VERDICT.
THE HUSBAND AND WIFE -- ARREST OF AWTRY.

It was some time before the police could restore order and quiet the excitement. At length complete silence was restored, and Harry continued:

"Such," he continued, "is the tale of this unfortunate woman, and the position in which she found herself placed should excite, a feeling of sympathy, and not induce you to punish her for an act which may be deplored but cannot be condemned. That she took the money is undeniable, but why did she take it? I have told you it was to save her child's life, and though that class of philosophers and ultra moralists who believe that there are no causes sufficient to justify her act, may declare her guilty of theft, let the promptings of your own hearts decide whether her position did not excuse, if it does not render her conduct undeserving of condemnation by a jury. But in claiming from you a verdict in favor of my client, I must take occasion to say, that your acquittal will not restore this lady to that position she formerly occupied, or remove from her mind the impress left there by an act which necessity, and necessity alone, caused her to perform. It will not restore to her the innocent child now lying mouldering in the grave, it will not reunite the broken links of affection, it will not ease the agony of the soldier when he discovers that his wife was the inmate of a prison, nor will it replace on its former firm base the mind of this unfortunate lady, which, like the pillars of some ancient edifice, totters beneath a weight of agonizing thought, soon, alas! I fear, to fall, a mass of ruin, in the vortex of insanity. The patriot soldier must return to find his daughter dead, his wife a maniac, and his only remaining child a dependent on the bounty of strangers. But one thing remains; he must turn from the spectacle thus presented and return to the battle-field a heart-broken and unhappy man. The spirit with which he formerly contended for the liberty of his country will have vanished and fled, for the remembrance of his family's fate must ever remain uppermost in his mind, and the reflections they will produce must leave a blighting scar, which no future kindness can remove, sympathy eradicate, or consolation destroy. I am done. On your good judgment and the strength of my assertions, which can be proven, if necessary, I rely for the acquittal of this lady."

As he concluded, the building shook with applause from the crowd, and Mr. Swartz and Mr. Elder trembled for their safety. Harry felt that the acquittal of Mrs. Wentworth was now secure, for the jury itself, sharing the popular feeling, gave expressions of approbation in many remarks. If the language of Harry had been simple, it had carried conviction to every soul, and all present, as they looked upon the accused, felt that her offense was fully atoned for by the chain of harrowing circumstances with which she had been bound. And for her -- the soldier's wife? She had remained a passive spectator of all that occurred. When the voice of her defender first broke on her ear, she turned and looked at him for a moment, then, as if indifferent whether his defense was successful or not, she turned her head away and listlessly gazed at the crowd. She cared not now for freedom and acquittal; she felt that the chords of reason were on the point of breaking, and but one thought, one desire, filled her mind, before they broke and madness held sway over her. It was to see that loved form, to gaze once more on those loved features, to be clasped once again in her HUSBAND'S arms. This was the sole thought, the only desire. All "fond records," all recollection of past years, all hope for future happiness, were obliterated, and nothing remained before her mind's eye but the soldier who had parted from her in New Orleans. Even the memory of her dead and of her living child had vanished, and if they were for a while brought to her mind, it was only in connection with the single desire which kept the chains of sanity united. The lineaments of every soldier in the crowd were closely and eagerly scanned, but there were none there who bore the slightest resemblance to him for whom she yearned. But still she peered into the assemblage, regardless of the efforts being made in her behalf, and it was not until the interruption narrated in the last chapter took place, that she manifested any interest in the proceedings of the court, and then it was merely by a gesture of surprise at the uproar. When Harry concluded and sat down, she again evinced astonishment, but not a syllable escaped from her lips.

After a few minutes the shouts of the crowd subsided, and at the request of the judge, silence was restored. His honor then addressed the jury.

"Gentlemen of the jury," he began, "the case before your notice has become, from one of apparent insignificance, one of intense interest and importance. A merchant of this city, well known to you all, both by his wealth and his long residence in your midst, appears before this court and accuses a woman of theft. She is arrested and every evidence of her guilt is found on her person; she does not deny the act, and is accordingly brought before you to be tried and sentenced, or acquitted, as you may, in your good judgment think best."

Overwhelming evidence is brought against her to-day, and no doubt of her having committed the theft exists. There appears little more for you to do than to find her guilty, and for me to pass the sentence. But before doing these, it is necessary that the accused shall have a defense. She is questioned, but informs the court she has nothing to say. At this stage of the proceedings, a gentleman well known to you as a rising lawyer of this place before the war commenced, and better known since then as a gallant and meritorious officer, appears as her defendant. You have heard his defense. The act of taking the money is not denied, but in his defense, he claims that it was committed through dire necessity. It is true that a defense of this nature is a somewhat extraordinary one, and is new in the annals of criminal law. Still, he has given you a tale of hardships and privations which he claims occurred in this city, and which, coming from any other source, may well be doubted. It is left for you to decide whether his claim for an acquittal shall be granted or not. In my remarks I do not intend to bias you one way or the other. What my opinions are will be given after your decision is announced. To you I look for that decision."

"If your honor will permit me," said Dr. Mallard, rising, "I will make a few remarks before the jury retires. The tale told by Lieut. Shackleford is correct so far as I know of it. I was called upon to attend on the sick girl mentioned in the defense, and found her in an old cabin, almost at the point of death. At the time it did not strike me as singular that a white family should be found living in such a hovel, but the tale I have just heard narrated has made me reproach myself for my blindness in not discovering that the unfortunate family were of greater respectability than can be found in the residents of log cabins. Impressed, therefore, with a firm belief in the truthfulness of the tale I have heard, I shall act accordingly."

With these remarks he resumed his seat, and in a few minutes the jury retired to decide on their verdict. Mr. Elder followed reluctantly, but had made up his mind to give consent to anything the majority should decide on. He was already apprehensive for his personal safety and was anxious to be at home again.

After a short absence the jury returned and announced they had decided on a verdict.

"What is that verdict, gentlemen?" inquired the judge. "Do you find this lady guilty or not guilty?"

"Taking all the circumstances into consideration," replied the foreman, "we find the prisoner NOT GUILTY of the charge."

For a moment the building shook to the very foundation, from the prolonged cheers of the spectators. It was not rejoicing at the escape from punishment of the guilty, that they applauded, but it was through heartfelt exultation at the acquittal of an unfortunate woman. It was the spontaneous outburst of Southern hearts, bleeding with sympathy for the oppressed and poverty-stricken soldier's wife, and swelling with indignation at the brutal and unfeeling conduct of Mr. Elder and Mr. Swartz.

Harry's eye moistened as he heard the shouts of applause, and a feeling of grateful emotion swept over him. He felt no gratification at his success in gaining her acquittal which did not spring from the loftiest and most disinterested motives. He rejoiced on account of Mrs. Wentworth and her child and the gallant soldier he had so proudly called his friend. He rejoiced to know that the fair fame of the soldier's wife stood untarnished, and that he could restore her to the arms of her husband, not as the inmate of a penitentiary, but as the acquitted accused, who had committed the act she was accused of, but was still considered by all who had heard of the case, free from crime, and pure and unstained as before the blighting handy of penury and suffering were stretched across her sorrow-beaten path.

"Madam," said the judge, when the cheering had ceased, "you have heard the verdict of the jury, acquitting you of the charge made against you by Mr. Swartz, although in your defense, it is acknowledged you did take the money, and the jury is cognizant of the fact. While your acquittal, in face of the evidence given, and your own acknowledgment as well as the acknowledgment of your counsel, may be somewhat deviating from the letter of the law, it is nevertheless in strict accordance with its spirit, and with pleasure I inform you that being acquitted you are no longer held a prisoner, but are free to go where you will. But before you leave, let me make a few remarks on this case, which in my judgment are called for by the circumstances, and which may appear again, in consequence of many parties being similarly situated. Although the jury has acquitted you, such acquittal must not be considered a license for others to go and do likewise. Where your case is one of necessity, another of a like nature may be caused through dishonesty. Your act is not applauded by thinking minds, nor did the jury intend to convey the impression that in acquitting you they considered you had performed a very meritorious act. To the contrary, they deplore the performance of a deed which cannot be thought of but with regret; at the same time, they took into consideration the deplorable position into which you were placed, and declare you innocent of 'theft'."

"Before closing my remarks," he continued, "I would call the attention of those present, as well as the people in general, to this case. Like this unfortunate lady, many refugees are sojourning in our midst. They should be received with welcome by those who are fortunate enough to live in peace and quiet in their happy homes. But such, I fear, is not always the case. Many respectable families who had been accustomed to all that wealth could afford, are now living, if not in absolute necessity, in very poor circumstances, and could have their position materially improved if the people of this State would offer them that assistance they need. It is not an act of charity to lend a helping hand to the refugee. We are bound together by a sympathy formed on the battle-field by the gallant men of every State now struggling side by side for our independence, and it is a matter of duty that the wives and children of the soldier shall not suffer during his absence. It is a sordid spirit that refuses to aid a helpless woman because she happens to be a refugee. This Confederacy is a home for all its sons and daughters, and when they abandon their native State, and, fleeing from a brutal enemy, come into our midst for safety and protection, we should welcome them as suffering patriots and cherish, them as they deserve. It is a hard struggle for a woman to abandon a home, surrounded by all the luxuries of life and in which happiness reigns dominant, to incur hardships and privations. In doing so her patriotism is severely tested, and nothing but the most exalted devotion to our country triumphs over her fears.

There is yet another subject I will speak on. The two men who have figured so conspicuously in this case as the cause of this lady's sufferings, cannot be allowed to pass unnoticed. Mr. Elder is a well known gentleman of this city and has hitherto borne an irreproachable character. Did he not stand silent when accused of inhuman conduct towards this lady, I should hesitate to believe him guilty of such an atrocity. But as his silence is indicative of guilt, the horrible nature of his act comes before us with great force, and we shudder to think that any one wearing the form of humanity could so far debase the mind as to turn a helpless woman and dying child from a shelter because she had not the means of paying her debt. In so doing, Mr. Elder has displayed the spirit of the extortioner, and must feel all the stings of conscience which haunt the mind of a murderer, should his heart be not too much hardened already. He has acted a worse part than a murderer, for the assassin kills his victim through revenge, or at the worst, for pay. Here, Mr. Elder -- a possessor of wealth and not needing the money -- turns a tenant from his roof because she is penniless. I say nothing against him for doing so, for it was an indisputable right of his, but when we view the brutality of the act -- when we think of the hardness of the heart that could not commiserate with the situation of Mrs. Wentworth -- that was deaf to the appeals of a mother -- blind to the illness of her child -- the soul sickens with horror at the knowledge that a mortal so debased – so utterly devoid of the instincts of humanity which govern a brute -- should exist on the earth. But the mask of religion is now torn from his face, and we see his own lineaments. Henceforth the scorn of all generous, minds will he receive, and turned from the respectable position he once held, must reflect on the inevitable exposure of the hypocrite some day, sooner or later. I shall leave him to the scorn and indignation of all good men. From them he will receive that punishment which his brutality, caused from his extorting spirit, deserves.

And for Mr. Swartz, the accuser of this lady, I can see but little in extenuation of his conduct. If his business is even illegitimate, there are so many speculators in the South that it should not cause surprise that his refusal to aid this woman necessitated her taking his money. The speculator cannot be expected to have a heart tender enough to perform a charitable act. The man who will speculate on the necessities of the people, is not likely to feed the hungry. It is too true that many good men have been drawn into the vortex of speculation, but these are few in number and are isolated cases.

Mr. Swartz has been among us long enough to imbibe the spirit and sentiments of our people, but from his action towards this lady, he does not seem to have profited by their example. A foreigner by birth, he has cast a stigma on his nation, for, with all their faults, I do not believe there is a more charitable people than the German. I have found it so, in many years of familiar intercourse with them. But his last act is the one deserving unqualified condemnation. To tear a mother from the bedside of her dead child -- to incarcerate her in a prison, while the hands of strangers were performing the last sad rites over the dead, is an act that Christianity could never believe, were the evidence not before us, too forcible for denial, too truthful for contradiction. It is an act that calls for withering rebuke, but we dismiss him with the belief that on the coming of that inevitable 'Hereafter', he will receive the punishment he so well merits.

My remarks are now concluded, and the prisoner is discharged from custody."

There was deep silence for several minutes, during which Harry looked anxiously in the crowd for his friend; but Alfred was nowhere to be seen. Mrs. Wentworth retained her passive look of indifference, and took no further notice of the curious crowd, which gazed upon her with hearts full of pity and commiseration. Once or twice she slowly raised her hand and pressed her forehead with it, as if it ached. But she spoke no word of complaint, nor did she give any other indication of suffering.

Harry was about to remove her from the court, when there was a bustle in the crowd, and the voice of Alfred was heard calling on those around him to give way. He was followed by Awtry, perfectly unconscious of the cause of his companion's agitation.

"Make room there, for God's sake," asked Alfred, pressing through the dense mass of men and women. "Follow me," he continued, speaking to Awtry.

The men nearest to him, perceiving his excitement, generally surmised the truth, and a low murmur ran through the room that it was the prisoner's husband, and a passage was quickly made to where Mrs. Wentworth was sitting.

Awtry heard the words, "it is her husband," and turned back with the intention of leaving, but his arm was quickly seized by Alfred, who, still concealing his intention, simply said, "Come on; I will find a passage for us." He hesitated an instant, but believing his appearance sufficiently disguised to prevent Mrs. Wentworth from recognizing him, he determined to risk proceeding, in the hope of escaping discovery.

At last Alfred was by the side of his wife -- the soldier had met her he loved for the first time in nearly two years. Silently and sadly, he gazed at her changed appearance, and the briny tears slowly trickled down the soldier's cheeks as he noted her sunken features. At last, he spoke.

"Eva!" he said, in a voice that trembled with emotion, "my wife! My darling wife! do you not know me?"

His voice, full of love, sounded in her ear like the sweetest music ever played by the angels of God. At the sound of her name, she turned round and looked anxiously in his face -- a moment more, and he had scarcely finished speaking, before she had thrown herself in his arms.

"Alfred! my husband!" she murmured, as she pillowed her head in his bosom, "at last -- at last!"

"Oh, Heavenly Father!" exclaimed Alfred, raising her head and gazing fondly at the wan and emaciated features of his wife, "is this' all I find?"

His words were those of anguish, wrung out from a tortured heart. It was not so he expected to meet his wife.

"Rise, darling," he continued, "rise, and let us leave this place – let us go where friends are." She rose up, and leaning on his arm, moved off, when he suddenly confronted Awtry, who had stood with anxious and palpitating heart for the closing of the scene. "Stay awhile, dearest," Alfred went on, as soon as he perceived Awtry, "Look at this man -- do you know him?"

Mrs. Wentworth looked at him for some time, but failed to recognize Awtry. "I do not know him," she said, shaking her head.

"This is very strange conduct on your part, Mr. Wentworth," said Awtry, believing himself safe.

"Ha!" exclaimed Mrs. Wentworth, "it is his voice. It is Awtry –
there he is -- I know him now," and she fainted in her husband's
arms.

"Seize that man!" thundered Harry, who was standing near
Alfred, "he is a spy."

In an instant, Awtry was secured and hurried of to prison. Mrs.
Wentworth was conducted by Harry and her husband to Dr.
Humphries', where we leave them for a while.

CHAPTER TWENTY-NINTH.
THE EYE OF GOD -- THE MANIAC WIFE.

Pardon us, kind reader, for digressing for a while from the sad tale
it has been our lot to give you, to remark on the strange fancies
which govern the minds of a large majority. So inscrutable do the
works of the Almighty appear, that we believe all the ills of this
world are evoked by Him for some good end. In a measure this is
correct. When sinful mortals are burdened with sorrow and
affliction, we can recognize in them the chastening hand of God, for
under such weight of suffering the soul is apt to pass through
purified of the blackness and corruption which darkened and
rendered it odious to the good. Here we see the benefits accruing
from trouble and distress. We behold the sinner being punished for
his transgression, and to the righteous and good, these afflictions are
welcomed as the saving of one more soul from the grasp of hell. But
how is it when the innocent suffer? It is not the work of the Eternal.
High up in the celestial realms, His eyes are turned towards earth to
punish the guilty and reward the innocent, and in His works, we find
no instance where the hands of adversity and suffering have fallen
upon those who deserved reward. Where the guiltless are found
suffering, He relieves their necessities, and brings them once more
that happiness which they deserve on earth.

Why shall it be always said that when a home of happiness is in
an instant hurled from the summit of earthly felicity and buried in
the dark gulf of adversity, that such is the work of God? If that home
is contaminated by grievous sins, there is justice in the claim, but
where the transgressions are not heavier than those good men
commit, it cannot be, for the God who reigns above seeks to build
up, and not to destroy, unless there is no other way of punishing the
sinner but by the infliction of the heaviest penalties. We have

painted a soldier's wife, if not free from sin, at least innocent of crimes which are calculated to bear upon the conscience and cause remorse or fear; we have pictured her two children, pure and unsinful, for it cannot be said that mortal can sin in infancy. We have shown them plunged in direst misfortunes, and is there not force in the question when we ask if their months of penury and suffering were the works of the God of Mercy and Righteousness?

It cannot be. The innocent do not suffer by the hands of God, while the guilty revel in all the wealth and affluence that this earth bestows. How many men are there who live in ease and comfort, while their souls are burdened with sins? The hypocrite, the liar, the thief, the murderer; all, and by hundreds they can be counted, appear to the world *"A combination and a form, indeed, Where every god did seem to set his seal,"* but in whose souls the fires of hell rage with remorseless fury. But their afflictions are not known to man. The eyes of the world gaze not on them, when the mind is racked by the conflict of sin. We see not their sufferings; we know not the pangs they feel; we only recognize them by the outward appearance. They live, surrounded with all that can make mortal happy, save the happiness of a clear conscience. In this world they prosper, and many gain the applause and commendation of their fellow mortals. What are their sufferings? They are unknown to man, though remembered by God. And if punishment comes at last, it is just and merited, nor do we regret that sin is scourged by the avenging hand of a Savior.

But while we witness the guilty reveling in wealth and affluence, how often are the innocent plunged in want? Aye, myriads of times. We know not of them, but over the land there are hundreds of our fellow mortals whose days are but a repetition of suffering. Famine and sickness have stalked in the midst of hundreds who are innocent of crime, and reduced them to the last brink of despair. Is this the work of God? Forbid it, Heaven! that the charge should be made. There is no ground on which to assert that the Ruler of the Universe -- the God of Righteousness -- the Lord of Mercy, would thrust the innocent into woe -- would blast their earthly prospects -- would dash the cup of happiness from their lips, and leave them to perish through Famine and Disease -- while men steeped in crime, whose consciences, if read, would show an appalling blackness of guilt -- while they, we say, escaped from earthly punishment and enjoyed all the good of this world! On Earth, as in Heaven and Hell, man is divided into two bodies, Angels and Fiends. Both are known to the Almighty, and it is only when His eyes are turned from the good that Fiends triumph. Only then -- it is not His work -- it cannot and can never be.

And now, kind reader, you may think that the writer is either a lunatic or a madman to advance a doctrine which claims that God – the Infinite -- the Everlasting -- the Omnipotent -- the Inscrutable, would turn awhile from the good and survey them not -- allow them to suffer. We are neither the one nor the other. Perchance our doctrine is a mere vagary; still, as we glance over our country and see the scenes daily enacted, we cannot believe they are the work of an Almighty Father. When our maidens are ravished by the hated foe and despoiled of that Virtue held sacred in Heaven, is it the work of God? When the creeping babe is immolated by the savages of the North, is it a dispensation of Providence? When the homesteads of the people are given to the flames and the cursed army of Abolitionists exult at their demolition, does the hand of our Heavenly Father direct the work of destruction? When our temples are profaned by the bacchanalian orgies of the Northern hordes, does the Infinite invite them to desecrate His altars? They are not His works -- they never were. These acts which the Christian world shudders at, are the machinations and promptings of Hell, and the Fiends who dwell therein triumph for a while where the Eye of God is not.

But the Eye of God is not always turned away from His suffering people. The cry of the wretched is borne to His ear by the angels, and Mercy, Charity and Goodness descend to Earth and sweep away the incarnate spirits infesting it. In this we behold the Greatness and Righteousness of God, for though He may see not our hardships for awhile, the cry of the Innocent will ascend to Heaven; their sufferings will be obliterated, and if even on earth they gain not happiness, in those realms where sinless Angels abide, all past woes, all past years of want, all former wretchedness, are removed and forgotten, in an eternity of peace and celestial felicity.

And so, it was with the soldier's wife whose sad trials we are narrating to the reader. The spirit of the angel daughter had winged its flight to the Savior, and the little invisible hand pointed to its mother on earth below, and the Son of God supplicated the Father to relieve the miseries of the innocent. We have shown how this was done. The good of earth was the medium of salvation, and her trials are at an end.

Yes, they are at an end! But with them, when she fell fainting in her husband's arms on recognizing Awtry, the light of reason expired, and the soldier's wife was a maniac.

They bore her gently to the residence of Dr. Humphries, and there all that medical science could perform was done, and every attention was lavished upon her. But it was of no avail; madness had seized the mind of Mrs. Wentworth, and the doctor shook his head sadly as he gazed upon her. Days passed on, and still she continued in this state.

"I fear she will only recover her reason to die," observed Dr. Humphries to Harry. "Could her constitution sustain the frenzied excitement she now labors under, I would have some hope, but the months of wretchedness she has passed through, has so weakened her frame that nothing remains but a wreck of what was once a healthy woman."

"This is bad news," remarked Harry, "and I fear it will have a sad effect upon Alfred. I have been overcome with sympathy at observing his silent grief at the bedside of his raving wife, and several times I have heard him mutter, 'never mind, my darling, you will soon recover, and then we will be happy.' Unfortunate man! Could there be the slightest possibility of saving his wife, I am certain you would not despair."

"I do not yet despair," replied the doctor, "although I fear very much her case is hopeless. I have sent for Dr. Mallard and Dr. Purtell; when they have seen Mrs. Wentworth, we will have a consultation, and I trust some good will accrue from it. By the way," he continued, changing the conversation, "have you heard what has become of the supposed spy arrested in the court house?"

"I heard on yesterday that his trunks had been searched, but nothing had been discovered in them, beyond the fact that he was Mr. Awtry, and not an Englishman, as he pretended to be."

"Have they discharged him?" inquired the doctor.

"Oh no;" Harry replied, "the fact of his assuming a false character was deemed sufficient evidence to keep him in prison until further discoveries are made."

"It is very likely, then, that he will eventually pay the penalty of his crimes," observed the doctor.

"Yes; and I trust it will not be long before he suffers death," Harry answered, and then added: "I am not bloodthirsty, nor do I favor the hoisting of the black flag, as so many appear desirous of doing. But for a wretch like Awtry, I have not the slightest pity, and would hear of his execution with pleasure. If even there is no proof discovered of his being a spy, his brutality to Mrs. Wentworth merits punishment, and if only for that, I should desire to see him hung or shot. However, I have no fear but that the fact of his being a spy will be discovered, for several of the most expert detectives in the service are on the search for the necessary evidence to convict him."

"And which evidence I trust they will soon discover," remarked the doctor. "Like you, I am averse to a war of extermination, but when instances like the one before us are brought to our notice, an outraged and indignant people demand satisfaction and should have it accorded to them."

"Ah! my dear sir," replied Harry, "while Awtry's outrage on Mrs. Wentworth deserves condemnation and punishment, he is not solely the guilty cause of her sufferings. From the moment she reached our lines, it was the duty of the people of this city to aid and succor her. Had this been done, her daughter may have been alive this day. Unfortunately, the philanthropic and charitable were idle and waited until such cases came to their notice. Had they looked for them, Mrs. Wentworth never would have fallen into the hands of unprincipled speculators and extortioners, and would have been spared the load of affliction which has now periled her life."

"You are right, Harry," said Dr. Humphries. "It is our duty to search for the unfortunate poor, and not to wait until they appeal for assistance. There are many destitute women and children in our midst who have been driven from their once happy and prosperous homes by the hated Yankees. Among them are many high-toned and respectable families, whose pride shrinks from begging for bread, and who now live a life of penury and starvation rather than become the mendicant. And if even they bury delicacy at the mandate of stern Want, they are so apt to be refused assistance by the heartless, that they imagine all of our people alike, and fearing further refusal, shrink with natural horror from a second rejection."

"This can be prevented," observed Harry. "Let the benevolent make it a business to find out the suffering who are worthy of assistance, and let such aid be given, not as charity, but as a duty we owe those who have remained faithful to our cause, and abandoned their homes rather than submit to the enemy. By so doing, we not only alleviate hardships, but we render the soldier happy and contented to serve his country. The knowledge that his family is protected by those at home, and supplied with all that is necessary, will remove from his mind all anxiety for their welfare. It will, besides, grasp them from the clutches of the wretches who are speculating and extorting, and will not only be an act of everlasting honor to those who perform this good work, but will aid our cause as much as if the parties were serving in the field. Many a man who now lies in the deserter's dishonored grave, would have been this day sharing the glory of his country and been looked upon as a patriot, had not his starving wife and children forced him in an evil hour to abandon his post and go to them. It is true, there is no excuse for the deserter, but where the human affections are concerned, it is but natural that the soldier will feel solicitous for the comfort of his wife and children."

"Something of that sort should, indeed, be done," remarked the doctor, "and I believe there are many in our midst who would cheerfully aid in this good work. I cannot believe that the majority of our people are such inhuman characters as Elder and Swartz. It is true that these men have a monopoly in our midst, so far as wealth is concerned, but it would be wrong to blame the majority for the crimes of a few."

"The majority, if even good and charitable, are to blame," replied Harry, firmly, "for if they outnumber the miserable creatures whose sole thought is to amass wealth from the sufferings of our country, it is their duty to thwart such desires by every possible means, and it could be done were the proper steps taken. But they have heretofore displayed an indifference almost criminal, and appear to participate in the unworthy prejudice against refugees. Forgetful that they may to-morrow be similarly situated, they lend a moral, if not an active aid, in the oppression of this unfortunate portion of our people, and are perfectly careless whether want and misery overtake them or not. We must not forget that these refugees are as much entitled to a home in this as in their own State. Their husbands, fathers and brothers are fighting to protect us from subjugation, and if we are unmindful of the comfort of their relatives, it not only entails disgrace upon our name, but renders us deserving of a similar fate, and worse treatment."

"I agree with you," said the doctor, "and so far as I am concerned, everything that can be done for them shall be performed, and -"

Here a knock at the door interrupted the conversation. Harry opened it, and Drs. Mallard and Purtell were announced.

"Good morning to you, gentlemen," said Dr. Humphries, as soon as they entered. "I am very glad you have answered my call so promptly. The case I desire you to see is one of great seriousness, but I withhold any opinion until you have seen the patient and expressed your ideas about it."

"I suppose it is the lady who was accused of theft," said Dr. Mallard.

"Yes sir," answered Harry, "it is the same person."

"I observed her features very attentively during the trial," remarked Dr. Mallard, "and so convinced was I that she would soon be insane, that I determined, in the event of her being found guilty, to have her released and placed under my care on that plea. Is she raving?" he added inquiringly of Dr. Humphries.

"Yes," replied that gentleman, "but in her ravings she makes no allusion whatever to her wretched life of the past few months. She fancies herself at home in New Orleans again, and as all was then happiness with her, so does everything appear to her mind the reflex of her past days."

"We had better see her now," said Dr. Purtell, "for the sooner something is done towards restoring her reason the better."

"Certainly," answered Dr. Humphries, "walk this way," he continued, leading them toward Mrs. Wentworth's chamber.

At the door he was met by Emma, who had been watching by the bedside of the maniac all the morning.

"Walk easily," she whispered as the three gentlemen appeared at the door. "She is now calmer than ever, but the slightest noise will excite her again."

The medical gentlemen entered the room with noiseless steps, and remained for several minutes watching the sleeping sufferer. Her emaciated features were flushed from excitement and her breathing was hard and difficult. In her sleep, she softly murmured words which told of happy years that were past and vanished forever and could never more return. The broken sentences told of love and happiness, and a deep feeling of sympathy stole into the breasts of her hearers as they listened to her ravings. Alfred was sitting by the bed looking on the wreck of his wife, and when the doctors entered, he arose and briefly saluted them. To their words of condolence, he made no reply, for his heart was bitter with grief, and he felt that consolatory language was a mockery, and however well meant and sincere it may have been, it could not relieve the agony he felt at witnessing the destruction of his family's happiness. Oh, let those alone who have felt the burning of the heart when it was wrung with agony, appreciate the misery of men struck down from the pedestal of earthly joy and buried in the gulf of wretchedness. We have known homes where the heart beat high with joy, and life promised to be a future of happiness and peace where the fairest flowers of affection seemed to bloom for us, and over our pathway floated its perfume, while before our sight, its loveliness remained undiminished until that fatal delusion, Hope, intoxicated the senses and made us oblivions to reality. A brief spell -- a charm of short duration, and the hallucination is dispelled, only to leave us seared and blasted, almost hating mankind, and wearing the mask of the hypocrite, leading a double life, to hide the sears left by unsuccessful ambition, or disappointed aspiration. What were death itself compared with the misery of finding, when too late, that the hopes and happiness we deemed reality, were but a shadow, not a substance, which lingered for a while and left us to curse our fate.

And yet it is but life -- one hour on the pinnacle, the other on the ground. But to our tale.

After remaining by the bedside for several minutes, the doctors were about to leave, when Mrs. Wentworth awoke from her sleep, and gazed with an unmeaning look upon the gentlemen. She recognized no one - not even her husband, who never left her, save when nature imperatively demanded repose.

The doctors requested that Alfred and Emma would retire while they examined the patient. In accordance with their wishes, they did so, and Alfred, entering the balcony, paced up and down, impatient for the result of the consultation. The door of Mrs. Wentworth's chamber remained closed for nearly half an hour, when it opened, and Drs. Humphries, Mallard and Purtell issued from it, looking grave and sad.

The heart of the husband sank as he looked at their features.

"Let me know the worst," he said, huskily, as they approached him.

"We will not deceive you," replied Dr. Mallard, "your wife, we fear, will remain a maniac while her strength lasts, and then –" here he paused.

"And then-" replied Alfred, inquiringly.

"We fear she will only recover her reason to die" continued Dr. Mallard in a tone of sympathy.

"God help, me," uttered the soldier, as he sunk on a chair and buried his face in his hands.

After a few more words full of sympathy and condolence the two doctors left, and shortly after Dr. Humphries dispatched a servant to bring the little boy from the old negro's cabin.

"His presence may rally Mr. Wentworth," the doctor observed to Harry. "Since the consultation he has remained in the same seat, and has never once visited the room of his wife. Something must be done to rouse him from his grief, otherwise it will be fatal to his health."

"The presence of his son may be beneficial," said Harry, "but I do not believe the child can while him away from the sorrow he has met with. It has been a hard -- a fatal blow, and has fallen with fearful effect upon my poor friend."

In about an hour the servant returned with the child. He had been neatly dressed in a new suit of clothes and looked the embodiment of childish innocence.

Taking him by the hand Dr. Humphries led him into the balcony where Alfred still sat with his face buried in his hands, deep in thought and racked with grief.

"Here," said the old gentleman, "here is your son. The living and well claim your attention as well as those who are gone and those who suffer."

Alfred raised his head and gazed at the child for a moment.

"My boy," he exclaimed at last, "you are the last link of a once happy chain." As he spoke he pressed the child to his bosom, and the strong-hearted soldier found relief in tears.

CHAPTER THIRTIETH.
DEATH OF THE SOLDIER'S WIFE.

The presence of his child lightened but did not remove the grief of Alfred Wentworth. The love he bore his wife may be likened to the love of the eagle for liberty. Cage it, and the noble bird pines away; no longer allowed to soar on high, but fettered by man, it sickens and dies, nor can it be tamed sufficiently to become satisfied with the wires of a cage. So, it was with the soldier. His love for his wife was of so deep and fathomless a nature, that the knowledge of her being a maniac, and only returning to reason to die, changed the current of his nature, and from being a friendly and communicative man, he became a silent and morose being. The world had lost its charms, and the blank left in his heart, the sear upon his mind, the agony at knowing that his wife -- his pure and peerless wife, had been compelled from her necessities to take that which was not her own, could never be filled, never be healed and never be eased.

A wife! We know not from experience what it means, but there is a something, an inward voice, which tells, us that a wife is the holiest gift of God to man. A wife! what is it? A woman to cherish and protect, to give the heart's affection to, and to receive all the confiding love with which her bosom is filled. The partner of your happiness -- the source of all that makes man good and binds him to earth; the solace of woes, the sharer of joys -- the gentle nurse in sickness, and the fond companion in health. Oh! there is a something in the name, which thrills the heart, and makes it beat with emotion at the sound of the word. Amid the cares and pleasures of man, there can be no higher, no worthier desire than to share his triumphs with a wife. When Ambition tempts him to mount yet higher in this earthly life, and take his stand among the exalted men of genius, who so fitting to be the partner of his fame as the gentle woman of this world, and when disappointed in his aspirations, whcn the cold frowns of a callous world drive him from the haunts of men, who so soothing as a Wife? She will smoothen the wrinkles on his forehead, and by words of loving cheer inspire him with courage and bid him brave the censure and mocking of the world, and strive again to reach the summit of his desires. A Wife! There is no word that appeals with greater force to the heart than this. From the moment the lover becomes the Wife, her life becomes a fountain of happiness to a husband, which gushes out and runs down the path of Time, never to cease, until the power of the Invisible demands and the Angel of Death removes her from his side. Age meets them hand in hand, and still imbued with a reciprocity of affection, her children are taught a lesson from herself which makes the Wife, from generation to generation, the same medium of admiration for the world, the same object of our adoration and homage. We write these lines with homage and respect for the Wife, and with an undefined emotion in our hearts, which tells us they are correct, and that the value of a Wife is all the imagination can depict and the pen indite.

And to lose one! Oh! what sorrow it must awaken -- how the fountains of grief must fill to overflowing, when the companion of your life is torn from you by the hand of Death! No wonder, then, that the heart of Alfred Wentworth bled with woe, and he became a changed man. What cared he longer for this world? Almost nothing! But one thing urged him to rally his energies and meet the blow with fortitude whenever it should come. It was the knowledge that his little boy would need a father's care. This made him not quite oblivious to this world, for though his life would be in the front, so soon as he returned to the battle-field, there were chances for his escaping death, and his desire was to live, so that the child might grow up and remind him of his wife. No, not remind! As fresh as the hour when love first entered his heart for her -- as plain as the day he led her to the altar and registered his vows to Heaven -- and as pure as herself, would his memory ever be for her. Time can soothe woes, obliterate the scars left by grief, but the memory of a dead wife can never be extinguished in the mind of a husband, even though her place in his heart may be filled by another. She must ever be recollected by him, and each hour he thinks of her, so will her virtues shine brighter and more transparent, and her faults, if any, become forgotten, as they were forgiven. But we weary the reader with these digressions, and will proceed to close our narrative.

Three additional weeks passed, and still Mrs. Wentworth remained insane, but her insanity being of a gentle character, Dr. Humphries would not permit her to be sent to the lunatic asylum, as her husband advised. It is true, he desired it more for the purpose of avoiding being the recipient of any further favors, than because he thought it necessary. This morbid sensitiveness shrank from being obligated to a comparative stranger like the doctor, and it was not until the old gentleman absolutely refused to permit Mrs. Wentworth to leave the house, that he yielded his assent to her remaining.

"As you insist upon it," he remarked, "I make no further opposition to her remaining, but I think it an imposition on your benevolence that your home shall be made gloomy by my wife being in it."

"Not in the least gloomy, sir," replied the doctor, "nor do I think it the slightest imposition upon my benevolence. Were it only to repay the debt Harry owes you for the preservation of his life, I should insist upon her not being removed. But I deem it a duty we owe to our suffering fellow mortals, and as long as she remains in her present state, so long will she be an inmate of my house, and everything that can lighten and ameliorate her unhappy condition shall be deemed a pleasant business to perform."

"I do not doubt it, sir," said Alfred, grasping the doctor's hand and shaking it heartily, "believe me, the attention of your daughter, Harry and yourself, has been the oasis in my present desert of life, and though in a few short weeks I expect all will be over, and she will no longer need your care, the memory of your kindness in these gloomy times of sorrow, shall ever remain unfading in memory, and shall always be spoken of and thought of with the greatest gratitude."

"No gratitude is necessary," answered the doctor as he returned the pressure of Alfred Wentworth's hand, "I consider myself performing a sacred duty, both to God and to humanity, and no gratitude is needed for the faithful performance of the same."

"No, no sir," interrupted Alfred, hastily, "it is no duty, and cannot be looked upon as such -- at least by me."

"Well, well," remarked the doctor, "we will not argue about that. I only wish it were in my power to do more by giving you assurance that your wife will recover, but I fear very much she never can."

"How long do you suppose she will linger?" asked Alfred sadly.

"I cannot tell," replied the doctor, "Her strength has been failing very rapidly for the past week, and I do not think she can last much longer."

"Could nothing be done to keep her alive, if even it were as a maniac?" he inquired, and then added, and as he spoke, repressing the emotion he felt, "Could she but live, it would be some solace to me, for then I should have her with me, and by procuring a position in some of the departments, be enabled to remain with her; but the idea of her dying -- it is that which saddens me and almost makes me curse the hour I left her. My poor, darling wife!"

The last words were uttered as if he were speaking to himself, and the tone of sorrow in which he spoke touched Dr. Humphries deeply.

"Bear with fortitude the dispensations of a Divine Providence," said the old gentleman. "If He has willed that your wife shall die, you must bow humbly to the decree. Time will assuage your grief and remove from your mind, this sad -- too sad fate that has befallen her."

"If you think that time can assuage my grief," replied Alfred, "you greatly underrate the strength of my affection. When a mere stripling, I first met my wife, and from that hour all the affection I possessed was hers. Each day it grew stronger, and at the time I left New Orleans with my regiment, the love I bore my wife, and for her, my children, could not have been bartered for the wealth of California. She was to me a dearer object than all else on earth, and more-"

He could speak no longer, so overcome was he with emotion. Once more wringing the doctor's hand, he left the room and entered the chamber of his wife.

"Unhappy man," exclaimed the doctor, when he was alone, "his is, indeed, a bitter grief, and one not easily obliterated."

With these words the kind-hearted old gentleman retired to his study, greatly moved at the misfortunes of the family he had been brought in contact with.

The furloughs granted to Alfred and Harry had been renewed on the expiration of the time they had been granted for, but on the representation of Dr. Humphries, had been renewed. At the time the above conversation took place, they were again nearly expired and Harry determined to appeal to the government once more for a second renewal. Accordingly, he took the cars for Richmond and obtaining an interview with the Secretary of War, he represented the condition of Mrs. Wentworth, and exhibited the certificates of several doctors that she could not survive two months longer. For himself, he requested a further renewal of his furlough on the ground of his approaching marriage. With that kindness and consideration which distinguished Gen. Randolph, his applications were granted, and leaves of absence for Alfred and himself for sixty days longer were cordially granted.

With the furloughs, he arrived from Richmond the same evening that the conversation related above took place between the doctor and Alfred, and on the return of his friend from his wife's chamber, he presented him with his leave.

"You are indeed a friend," remarked Alfred, "and I can never sufficiently repay the kindness you have shown me. But before this furlough expires, I do not suppose I shall have any wife to be with."

"Why do you speak so?" inquired Harry.

"She cannot last much longer," he replied. "Although unwillingly and with sorrow I am compelled to acknowledge that every day she sinks lower, and to-day her appearance denotes approaching dissolution too plain, even for me to persuade myself that such is not the case."

"I cannot tell you I hope you are mistaken," observed his friend, "for I feel that such language can never lighten nor remove your sorrow. But be assured that I deeply sympathize with you in your affliction."

"I know it," he answered. "Would to heaven all in the South were like you. It might have been different with my poor wife, and my angel girl might have been alive this day. However, it was not their duty to succor and protect my family, and I have no right to complain because they lent her no helping hand. I alone must bear the weight of my affliction, and from the misery it causes me, I devoutly trust none of my comrades may ever know it. Here your betrothed comes," he continued, observing Emma at the door. "I will leave you for the present, as I suppose you wish to speak with her and I desire to be alone for a while."

"Do not let her presence hasten your departure," said Harry. "She will be as happy in my company while you are here, as if no third person was present."

Alfred smiled faintly as he replied: "Her presence alone does not impel me to leave, but I desire to be alone for a time. My mind is very much unsettled, and a few moments of solitary thought will restore it to its wonted quietude."

Rising from his seat, he bade Harry adieu, and bowing to Emma, who entered at the moment, left the house and bent his steps toward his lodgings. Dr. Humphries had invited him to be a guest at his house, but he politely but firmly declined the invitation, at the same time his days were spent there with his wife, and it was only in the evening he left, to take a few moments of rest. From the time he discovered his wife, and she was carried to Dr. Humphries' residence, he had never been to any other place than the doctor's or his lodgings.

Four days after Harry's return, he was seated with Emma in the parlor conversing on the subject of his marriage, which the fair girl desired put off until after Mrs. Wentworth's death, which her father told her could not be postponed many weeks. Her lover endeavored to combat her resolution, by declaring that while Alfred would always get a furlough if his wife was still alive at the expiration of its time, he could neither ask nor expect to obtain any further extension. They were in the midst of a warm discussion, when Dr. Humphries entered. He had just come from Mrs. Wentworth's room, and appeared exceedingly sad.

"How is Mrs. Wentworth this morning, father?" inquired Emma, as the doctor entered, and observing his mournful expression, she added, "What is the matter."

"Mrs. Wentworth has recovered her reason, and is dying," he replied.

"Poor Alfred," observed Harry, "this hour will not take him by surprise, but it cannot fail to add to his grief."

"Has he been here this morning," asked the doctor.

"Not yet," answered Harry, "but," he continued, looking at his watch, "he will soon be here, for it is now his usual hour of coming."

"I trust he will not delay," said Dr. Humphries "for his wife cannot last three hours longer."

"In that event, I had better go and look for him," Harry observed "he never leaves his lodgings except to come here, and there will be no difficulty in finding him."

Rising from his seat, he took up his hat and departed for his friend. Before he had gone two squares he met Alfred, and without saying anything to him, retraced his steps to the doctor's window.

"My friend" said Doctor Humphries as Alfred entered, "the hour has come, when you must summon all your fortitude and hear with resignation the stern decree of the Almighty. Your wife is perfectly sane this morning but she is dying. On entering her chamber a while ago, I found her quite composed and perfectly sensible of the life she had passed through. Though she did not recognize me, an intuitive knowledge of who I was, possessed her, and her first request was that you should be sent to her. Your little boy is now with her and she awaits your arrival."

Taking Alfred by the hand and followed by Harry, the doctor led the way to the chamber of the dying wife. The child was sitting on the bed with his mother's arms around his neck. Emma, Elsie, and the old negro were standing at the bedside looking sorrowfully at Mrs. Wentworth. As soon as her husband entered, they made way for him to approach.

"Alfred, my husband" exclaimed Mrs. Wentworth, extending her arms, "I am so glad you have come that I can see you once more before I die."

"Eva, my heart strings are torn with agony to see you thus" he replied raising her gently and pillowing his head on her bosom, "Oh! My wife, that this should be the end of all my hopes. What consolation is there left to me on earth when you are gone."

"Speak not so despairingly" she answered, "It were better that I should die than live with a burning conscience. My husband, the act for which I have been tried, still haunts me, for here on earth it will ever be a reproach, while in Heaven, the sin I committed will be forgiven through the intercession of a divine Savior."

"Perish the remembrance of that act!" answered her husband. "To me my darling wife it can make no difference, for I regret only the necessity which impelled you to do it, and not the act. Live, oh my wife, live and your fair fame shall never suffer, while your husband is able to shield you from the reproaches of the world. Though the proud may affect to scorn you, those in whose hearts beats a single touch of generosity will forgive and forget it, and if even they do not, in the happiness of my unfaltering affections, the opinions of the world, can be easily disregarded."

"It cannot be" she answered, "I am dying Alfred, and before many hours, the spirit will be resting in heaven. To have you by my side ere my breath leaves my body, to grasp your hand, and gaze on your loved features ere I die, removes all my unhappiness of the weary months now past, and I leave this world content."

"Oh, my wife" said Alfred, "Is this the end of our married life? Is this the reward I reap for serving my country! Oh, had I remained in New Orleans, the eye of the libertine would never have been cast upon you, and you would have been saved from the grasp of the heartless speculator and extortioner. What is independence compared with you, my wife? What have I gained by severing the ties of love and leaving a happy home, to struggle for the liberty of my country? A dead child -- a dying wife -- a child who will now be motherless; while I will be a wretched heart-broken man. Better, far better, had I resisted the calls of my country, and remained with you, than to return and find my happiness gone, and my family beggared, and tossing on the rough billows of adversity, unheeded by the wealthy, and unfriended by all."

"Speak not so, my husband," she answered, "my sufferings may be the price of independence, and I meet them cheerfully. Though in my hours of destitution, despair may have caused me to utter words of anguish, never, for a moment, have I regretted that you left me, to struggle for your country. If in my sufferings; if in the death of my child; if in my death; and if in the destroying of our once happy family circle, the cause for which you are a soldier is advanced, welcome them. Woman can only show her devotion by suffering, and though I cannot struggle with you on the battle-field, in suffering as I have done, I feel it has been for our holy cause."

"Eva, Eva," he exclaimed, "do all these give you back to me? Do they restore my angel daughter? Do they bring me happiness? Oh, my wife, I had hoped that old age would meet us calmly floating down the stream of Time, surrounded by a happy family, and thanking God for the blessings he had bestowed upon me. When I first led you to the altar, I dreamed that our lives would be blended together for many, many years, and though I knew that the 'Lord giveth and the Lord taketh away,' and that at any time we may die, I never thought that the end of our happiness would be brought about in such a way as this. You tell me it is the price of Independence. Aye, and it is a fearful price. When you are laid in the cold grave aside of Ella, and I am struggling in the battle-field, what is there to inspire me with courage, and bid me fight on until liberty is won? And when it is at last achieved, I cannot share the joy of my comrades. I have no home to go to, and if even I have, it is desolate. No wife is there to welcome me, no daughter to thank me, but I must take my orphan boy by the hand, and leading him to your grave, kneel by its side and weep together on the sod that covers your remains."

There was not a dry eye in the room. All wept with the husband, and even the dying woman could not restrain the tears.

"Alfred," she said, "do not weep. My husband, up there, in Heaven, we will meet again, and then the desolation on earth will be more than repaid by the pleasure of eternal joy. Let not my death cause you to falter in your duty to the South. Promise me, my husband, that through all changes you will ever remain steadfast and loyal to her sacred cause. Look not on the cruelty of a few men as the work of the whole, and remember that if even you are not made happier by the achievement of independence, there are others you assist in making so, and other homes which would have been as desolate as yours, but for you and your comrades' defense. Promise me, Alfred, that so long as the war lasts, you will never desert the South."

"I promise," he replied.

"There is now but one thing that gives me thought," she continued, her voice growing weaker each moment, "our little boy."

"Shall have a home so long as I live and his father is serving his country," interrupted Dr. Humphries. "Rest easy on that subject, madam," he continued, "it will be a pleasure for me to take care of the boy."

"Then I die happy," said Mrs. Wentworth, and turning to her husband she said with difficulty, "Farewell, my husband. Amid all my trials and sufferings my love for you has ever been as true and pure as the hour we married. To die in your arms, with my head on your bosom was all I wished, and my desire is gratified. Farewell."

Before her husband could reply her reason had vanished, and she remained oblivious to all around her. Her eyes were closed, and the moving of her lips alone told that she yet lived.

"Eva! darling! Wife!" exclaimed Alfred passionately "Speak to me! Oh, my angel wife, speak one word to me ere you die. Look at me! say that you recognize me. Awake to consciousness, and let me hear the sound of your voice once more. Wake up my wife" he continued wildly, "Oh for another word -- one look before you are no more."

His wild and passionate words reached the ear of the dying woman, and her voice came again, but it was the dying flicker of the expiring lamp. She slowly opened her eyes and looked up in the face of her husband.

"Alfred -- husband, happiness" she murmured softly, then gently drawing down his head, her lips touched his for an instant, and the soldier's wife embraced her husband for the last time on earth.

Releasing his head Mrs. Wentworth kept her eyes fixed upon those of her husband. Their glances met and told their tale of deep and unutterable affection. The look they gave each other pierced their souls, and lit up each heart with the fires of love. Thus, they continued for several minutes, when Mrs. Wentworth, rising on her elbow, looked for a moment on the grief struck group around her bed. "Farewell," she murmured, and then gazing at her husband, her lips moved, but her words could not be heard.

Stooping his ear to her lips, Alfred caught their import, and the tears coursed down his cheek.

The words were, "My husband I die happy in your arms."

As if an Almighty power had occasioned the metamorphosis, the countenance of the dying woman rapidly changed, and her features bore the same appearance they had in years gone by. A smile lingered round her lips, and over her face was a beautiful and saint-like expression. The husband gazed upon it, and her resemblance to what she was in days of yore, flashed across his mind with the rapidity of lightning. But the change did not last long, for soon she closed her eyes and loosened her grasp on her husband's neck, while her features resumed their wan and cheerless expression. Nothing but the smile remained, and that looked heavenly. Alfred still supported her; he thought she was asleep.

"She is now in heaven," said Doctor Humphries solemnly.

Yes, she was dead! No more could the libertine prosecute her with his hellish passions; no more could his vile and lustful desires wreak their vengeance on her, because of disappointment. No more could the heartless extortioner turn her from a shelter to perish in the streets. No more could the gardened and uncharitable speculator wring from her the last farthing, nor could suffering and starvation tempt her any more to commit wrong. No -- she is in heaven. 'There' the libertine is not and can never be. 'There' she will ever find a shelter, for 'there' the extortioner rules not. There the speculator can never dwell, and in that holy abode suffering and starvation can never be known. An eternity of happiness was now hers. To the home of the Father and to the dwelling of the Son, her spirit had winged its flight, and henceforth, instead of tears, and lamentations the voice of another angel would be heard in Paradise chanting the praises of Jehovah.

Yes, the eye of God was turned upon the soldier's wife, and she was made happy. Her months of grief and misery were obliterated, and the Almighty in his infinite goodness, had taken her to himself -- had taken her to Heaven. The spirit of the mother is with the child, and both are now in that home, where we all hope to go. In the ear of the soldier, two angels are whispering words of divine comfort and peace, and as their gentle voice enter his heart, a feeling of resignation steals over this mind, and kneeling over the dead body of his wife he gently murmurs,

"Thy will be done oh God!"

Every voice is hushed, every tear is dried, and the prayer of the soldier ascends to Heaven for strength to hear his affliction. The eye of God is now upon him, and He can minister to the supplicant.

CHAPTER THIRTY-FIRST.
CONCLUSION.

The dead was buried. The hearse was followed by a large concourse of Dr. Humphries' friends, who were brought there by the sad tale of the trials of the Soldier's Wife. The funeral service was read, and after the grave was closed many grouped around Alfred and offered their condolence. He only bowed but made no reply. The body of Ella had been previously disinterred and placed in the same grave which afterward contained her mother, and on the coffins of his wife and child Alfred Wentworth took a last look. When the service was over, he turned away, and accompanied by Harry returned to the dwelling of the doctor, where, with his boy on his knees, he conversed.

"My furlough does not expire for forty days," he observed, "but I shall rejoin my regiment in a week from this time. The object for which it was obtained being no longer there, it is only just that I shall report for duty."

"You must do no such thing," answered Harry, "I wish you to remain until your leave expires."

"Why?" asked Alfred, in a tone of surprise.

"Well, the fact is," said Harry, "I will be married in thirty days, and it is my urgent desire that you shall be with me on my marriage day, as a guest, if not as a friend."

"I can make but a poor guest," he replied. "My heart is too full of grief to willingly join in the mirth and happiness such festivities bring with them. You must therefore excuse me. I should indeed start at once did I not desire to find a place to leave this child."

"You need not trouble yourself about him," remarked Harry, "the doctor assured your wife that he should take care of the boy, and I feel certain he will be a father to him during your absence. Nor will I excuse your absence at my wedding, for I do not see why you should object if I desire it, and Emma, I know, will be very much pleased at your presence. So, offer no excuses, but prepare yourself to remain."

"As you appear so much to desire it," he answered. "I will remain, but I assure you I feel but little inclined for such pleasure at the present time, particularly a wedding, which cannot fail to bring up reminiscences of a happy day, not so long gone but that it still remains in my memory, as fresh and vivid as when I was an actor in a similar occasion."

"Let not such thoughts disturb you," said Harry, "let the Past bury the Past. Look forward only to the Future, and there you will find objects worthy of your ambition, and if you will pursue them, they will serve to eradicate from your mind the harrowing scene you have just passed through. Believe me, Alfred," he continued, "it will never do to pass your days in vain regrets at what is passed and vanished. It serves to irritate and keep open the wounds in our lives, while it never soothes the afflicted, nor gives us a moment of peace. Let the present and future alone occupy your thoughts. They will give you food for reflection, sufficient to bury all former unhappiness, and to entail upon you a return of that earthly joy you once possessed."

"Your remarks are correct in theory, my friend," replied Alfred, "but they cannot be put into practice. Sooner can the Mississippi river be drained of its waters than the inexorable Past be obliterated from the mind of man. It must ever remain in his memory, and though at times it may lie dormant, the slightest event will be all that is necessary to awake it into life. The cares of the present may deprive it of active participation in the mind; anxiety for the future may prevent the mind of man from actively recurring to it, but it still remains indelibly imprinted on the memory, and though a century of years should pass, and the changes of Time render the Present opposite to the Past, the latter can never be forgotten. Think not that coming years can render me oblivious to my present affliction. They may make dull the agony I now feel, and perchance I will then wear as bright a smile as I did in years ago, but the remembrance of my wife and child will never be blunted; no, nor shall a shade cross over my heart, and dim the affection I had for them, while living, and for their memory now that they are in the grave."

Alfred was right. The words of Harry were a theory which sounds well enough for advice, but which can never be placed into practice. The Past! who can forget it? The Present, with its load of cares; with its hours of happiness and prosperity; with its doubts and anxieties, is not sufficiently powerful to extinguish remembrance of the Past. The Future, to which we all look for the accomplishment of our designs -- the achievement of our ambitious purposes -- cannot remove the Past. Both combined are unequal to the task, and the daily life of man proves it so.

The Past! what a train of thought does it suggest! Aye, the Past, with its pleasures and misfortunes. It haunts our consciences, and is ever before our eyes. The murderer, though safely concealed from the world, and who may have escaped punishment by man for years, still has the Past to confront and harass his mind. Penitence and prayer may lighten, but can never remove it. Surrounded though he be with health and happiness, the demon of the Past will confront him ever, and make his life wretched. Oh, what a fearful thing is that same Past, we hear spoken of lightly by those whose lives have been along a smooth and flowery track over the same, and unmarked by a single adversity or crime. A single deviation from the path of honor, integrity and virtue, and as years roll on the memory of those past hours will cause bitter self-reproach, for it will be irremovable. So, with past happiness as it is with misery and crime. The beggar can never forget his past joys in contemplating the present or hoping for the future, but it must ever remain a source of never-failing regret and the fountain of unhealable wounds.

The Past! -- but no more of it, as we write the recollection of past happiness and prosperity, of past follies and errors rise up with vividness, and though it is never forgotten, burns with a brighter light than before.

Several days after his conversation with Harry, Alfred received a message from Dr. Humphries requesting him to meet that gentleman at ten o'clock the same morning at his residence. Accordingly, at the appointed hour, he presented himself to the Doctor, by whom he was received with great cordiality and kindness.

"I have sent for you, Mr. Wentworth," began the doctor, as soon as Alfred was seated, "to speak with you on a subject which interests you as well as myself. As you are aware, I promised your wife when she was dying that your remaining child should never want a home while I lived. This promise I now desire you to ratify by gaining your consent to his remaining with me, at least until he is old enough not to need the care of a lady."

"You have placed me under many obligations already, Dr. Humphries," replied Alfred, "and you will pardon me if I feel loath to add another to the already long list. I have already formed a plan to place my child in the hands of the Sisters of Charity at Charleston, by whom he will be treated with the greatest kindness, and with but small expense to myself. You must be aware that as a soldier my pay is very small, while I have no opportunity of increasing my salary by engaging in any mercantile pursuit. Such being the case, and as I could not consent to your defraying the expenses of the child, I think it better for him to be where I shall need only a small sum of money to pay all needed charges. At the same time let me assure you of my sincere gratitude for your generous offer."

"I will not hear of your objections, my good friend," said the doctor; "it is my desire that you allow me to adopt the boy, if only in part. My daughter will shortly be married, as you are aware, and then I shall be left alone. I possess ample means, and would not accept a dollar in return for the expenses incurred for the child, while his presence will be a source of happiness to me. Already I have formed an attachment for him, and it will only be gratifying my sincere wish if you will give your consent. Believe me, I do not ask it for the purpose of laying you under any obligations, or from any charitable motive, but from an earnest desire for him to remain with me. Let me hope that you will give your consent."

"I scarcely know what to say," answered Alfred, "for while I feel a natural delicacy in giving my consent, my heart tells me that the child will be far more comfortable than if he were at the convent."

"Why then do you not give your consent in the same spirit the offer is made," observed the doctor. "My dear sir," he continued, "let no false idea of delicacy prevent you from giving your consent to that, which cannot fail to render your child happy and comfortable."

"I cannot give a decided answer to-day," said Alfred. "You will give me time to consider your offer -- say a week. In the meantime, I have no objection to my child remaining with you until my mind is decided upon what course I shall pursue."

"I suppose I must be satisfied to wait" answered doctor Humphries, "but let me trust your decision will be a favorable one." As I remarked before, I desire you consent, from none but the purest motives, and I hope you will grant it.

*　　*　　*　　*　　*

The sad tale with which we have endeavored to entertain the reader is over. To the writer it has been no pleasant task, but the hope that it may prove of some service, and of some interest to the public has cheered us in our work, and disposed us to endure its unpleasantness. Apart from the dearth of literary productions in the South, we have believed that a necessity existed for a work of this nature, and with such belief we have given the foregoing pages to the people, in the hope that it may prove, not merely a novel to be read, criticized and laid aside, but to be thought over, and its truth examined, in the daily lives of hundreds in our midst. It is true, that with the license of all writers we may have embellished misery 'as a whole' to a greater extent than reality, but if it is taken to pieces no exaggeration will be discovered, and each picture drawn herein will be found as truthful as our pen has depicted.

As the reader may desire to know what become of the principal characters remaining, we anticipated their desire, by making enquiry, and learned the following facts, which we give to make this work as complete as possible.

Thirty days after the burial of Mrs. Wentworth, a large assemblage of gaily dressed ladies and gentlemen assembled at the residence of doctor Humphries to witness the marriage of Emma.

The party was a brilliant one; the impressive ceremony of the Episcopal church was read, and Harry Shackleford was the husband of Emma Humphries. The usual amount of embracing and congratulation occurred on the occasion, after which the party adjourned to the dining room, where a sumptuous supper had been prepared, and which was partaken of by the guests with many compliments to the fair bride and bridegroom, while many toasts were offered and drank, wishing long life, health and prosperity to the young couple. The party lasted to a late hour in the night, when the guests dispersed, all present having spent their hours in gaiety and happiness.

No, not all, for apart from the throng, while the marriage ceremony was being read, was one who looked on the scene with a sad heart. Clad in deep mourning, and holding his child, by the hand, Alfred Wentworth standing aloof from the crowd saw Emma and his friend united as man and wife with deep emotion. It had been only a few years before, that he led his wife to the altar and the reminiscences of the present awoke, and stirred his grief, and brought back upon him, with the greatest force, his sad bereavement. A tear started to his eyes, as he thought of his present unhappiness, and he turned aside, to hide his emotion from the crowd. Dashing the tear away, he offered his congratulation and good wishes to the newly married couple, as he thought, with calmness, but the quiver of his lips as he spoke, did not pass unperceived by Harry, and as he clasped the extended hand of his friend, a feeling of sympathy, which he could afford even in his happiness, crept over him.

Shortly after his marriage, Harry returned to his command, and is now the Lieutenant Colonel of his regiment, having been promoted to that honorable position for gallantry exhibited on many battle fields. When last we heard of him, he was on furlough, and with his wife in Alabama, where they now reside, he having removed to that State a short time previous to the fall of Vicksburg. So far, his wedded life has been one of unalloyed happiness, and we can only wish that it may continue so, through many long years. To his wife, though she has not been a very prominent character in this book, we tender our best wishes for the continuance of that happiness she now enjoys, and trust the day will soon arrive when her husband will have no farther need to peril his life in defence of his country, but turning his sword into a plough, be enabled to live always with her, and to require no more "furloughs."

Shortly after his daughter's marriage and removal to Alabama, Doctor Humphries found Jackson too lonely for him to reside at. He therefore, removed into the same State, where he possessed a plantation, and is now residing there, beloved and respected by all who know him. The unfortunate life of Mrs. Wentworth, and the sad fate of herself and the little Ella, did not fail to make him actively alive to the duties of the wealthy towards those who were driven from their homes by the enemy, and compelled to seek refuge in the States held by the Confederate government. Every time a refugee arrived at his locality; he visits the unfortunate family with a view to finding out the state of their circumstances. If he discovers they are in need, relief is immediately granted, and the parties placed above want. By his energy and perseverance, he has succeeded in forming a society for the relief of all refugees coming into the country, and as President of the same, has infused a spirit of benevolence in the members, which promises to become a blessing to themselves as well as to the wretched exiles who are in their midst.

The little Alfred is still with the Doctor, and is a source of much pleasure to the old gentleman. It was only after the greatest persuasions possible that his father consented to his remaining, but being overcome by the argument of the Doctor and Harry as well as the solicitations of Emma, he at last gave his consent, feeling at the same time that his boy would be happier and fare more comfortable than with the Sisters of Mercy, who, from their austere and religious life, are ill suited to rear an infant of such tender years. The boy is happy and can every evening be seen setting on the knees of Doctor Humphries, who he calls "grandfather" and indulging in innocent prattle. He has not yet forgotten his mother and sister, and very often he enquires of the Doctor if they will not come back to him at some future time. On these occasions the old gentleman shakes his head, and tells him that they are gone to heaven where he will meet them at some future time, if he behaves like a good boy. Enjoying good health and perfectly happy, although anxious for the termination of the war, and the achievement of our independence, we leave this worthy gentleman, with the hope that he may long live to receive the blessings and thanks of those who are daily benefited by his philanthropic benevolence.

The good old negro and Elsie accompanied the Doctor to Alabama, and are now residing on the Doctor's plantation. The old woman still resides in a cabin by herself, for no amount of persuasion could induce her to stay at the residence, but every day she may be seen hobbling to the house with some present for the little Alfred. The clothes which little Ella died in, and the remainder of the wedding gown, are kept sacredly by her, and often she narrates, to a group of open-mouthed negro children, the sad tale of the soldier's wife, embellishing, as a matter of course, the part she had in the eventful drama. Her kindness to Mrs. Wentworth and Ella, was not forgotten by the soldier, and before he left for the army, she received a substantial reward as a token of his gratitude. She often speaks of Ella as the little angel who "was not feared to die, case she was a angel on earf."

Notwithstanding he had yielded to so many offers of the Doctor, Alfred would not consent to receive Elsa from him, unless he paid back the sum of money given for the girl. This he could not do at the time, and it was decided that she should remain as the slave of Doctor Humphries, until he could refund the amount. She is now serving exclusively as the nurse of the little boy, and is as happy and contented as any slave in the South. Her attachment to the child increases daily, and nothing in the world could induce her to forego the pleasure of attending to her wants. The old negro and herself are often together, conversing of the unfortunate family of her former master, and their remarks teem with sympathy and abound with the affection felt by every slave for a kind and indulgent owner. Although of a servile race, we leave these negroes, regretting that in the hearts of many of our white people the same generous feelings do not exist. It is sad to think that, with all the advantages of birth, education, and position, there should be found men of Caucasian origin, who are below the negro in all the noble attributes of mankind. But there are many such, and while they do not elevate the servile race, they lower, to a considerable degree, the free born and educated.

Vicksburg fell on the fourth day of July, 1863, and the anniversary of American independence was celebrated by the Yankees in a Southern city which had cost them thousands of lives to capture. A few days after the surrender, the enemy advanced on Jackson, and compelled General Johnston to evacuate that city, to save his army. These are matters of history, and are doubtless well known to the reader. After retaining possession a short time, the Yankees retreated from the place, but not before they had given another proof of the vandalism for which they have been rendered infamous throughout the civilized world, by setting the city on fire. Luckily only a portion of the town was destroyed, and we could almost rejoice at being able to write that among the many buildings burnt were those belonging to Mr. Elder. Did not the homes of many good and worthy men share the same fate, we would almost attribute the destruction of his property to the righteous indignation of God. He lost every residence he possessed, and as the insurance companies refused to renew, from the aspect of affairs, on the expiration of his policies, the loss was a total one, and reduced him to almost beggary. With a few negroes he reached Mobile and is now living on the income their labor yields. His brutal conduct had reached the Bay city, before the fall of Jackson, and on his arrival there, instead of receiving the sympathy and aid of the generous hearted people, he was coldly met and all rejoiced at his downfall. Those, in that city, who in heart were like him, might have offered assistance, did they not fear that such conduct would lead to suspicion and eventuate the exposition of their enormities. His punishment is the just reward for his iniquities, and we record almost with regret that he is not reduced to abject beggary. Though we are told to "return good for evil" and to "forgive our enemies," we cannot in the case of Mr. Elder do either, but would like very much to see the Mosaic law of "an eye for an eye and a tooth for a tooth" put in force, and in this wish those who are even more charitable than ourselves will coincide.

Swartz is now in Augusta, Georgia, living in ease and affluence, like the majority of Southern speculators. The lesson he received from his uncharitableness, has not benefited him in the slightest degree. He still speculates on the wants of the poor, and is as niggardly to the needy. Though loyal to the Confederacy, we believe his loyalty only caused from his being the possessor of a large amount of Confederate funds, but perhaps we judge him wrongfully. At any rate, he has never done any act, either for the government or for individuals to merit praise or approbation. In justice to the

Germans of the South, we would state that when his conduct towards Mrs. Wentworth became known, they generally condemned him. As we observed in a former chapter, kindness and benevolence is the general trait of the Germans, and we would not have it supposed that Swartz is a representative of that people. The loss sustained by Mr. Swartz, by the fall of Jackson, was comparatively insignificant, and therefore he has felt no change of fortune. The punishment that he merits, is not yet meted to him, but we feel certain that it will be dealt to him at the proper time.

Further investigation and search resulted in the discovery of sufficient evidence to convict Awtry of being a spy. When brought before the court martial convened to try him, he displayed considerable arrogance, and obstinately persisted in declaring himself a British subject. With such plausibility did he defend himself, that the court was at first very much puzzled to decide whether or not he was a spy, for every evidence brought against the prisoner was explained and made insignificant by his consummate skill in argument, and it was only by the opportune arrival of a detective with the most decided proof of his guilt, that he was condemned to death. Awtry received the sentence of the court with haughty indifference, and was led back to prison, to await death by hanging. On the morning of his execution, the courage and obstinacy which had sustained him from the day of his arrest, gave way, and to the minister who edited upon him, he made a full confession of his having been sent to Mississippi as a spy for Sherman, and that he had already supplied that yankee General with valuable information of the strength and capacity of Vicksburg for resistance. He was very much humiliated at being condemned to death by hanging and made application for the sentence to be changed to shooting, but the military authorities declined acceding to his demand, and he was accordingly hanged on the branches of a tree near Jackson. A small mound of earth in an obscure portion of the Confederacy is all that is left to mark the remains of Horace Awtry. The libertine and prosecutor of Mrs. Wentworth is no more, and to God, we leave him. In His hands the soul of the dead will be treated as it deserves, and the many sins which stain and blacken it will be punished by the Almighty as they deserve. Black as was his guilt, we have no word of reproach for the dead. Our maledictions are for the living alone, and then we give them only when stern necessity demands it, and when we do, our work of duty is blended with regret, and would be recalled were it possible, and did not the outraged imperatively demand it. To our Savior, we leave Awtry. Before the Judge of mankind, he will be arraigned for his guilty acts on earth, and the just voice of the Father, will pronounce on him the punishment he merits.

But one more character remains for us to notice. Three or four times in the last twelve months a man dressed in the uniform of a Lieutenant of the Staff, and wearing a black crape around his arm, may have been seen with a little boy kneeling by the side of a grave in the cemetery of Jackson, Mississippi. The grave contains two remains, but is covered over with one large brick foundation from which ascends a pure and stainless shaft of marble, with the following inscription on its snowy front:

SACRED

TO THE MEMORY OF

MY WIFE AND CHILD,

EVA AND ELLA WENTWORTH.

"Their troubles o'er, they rest in peace."

1863.

A.W.

As our readers must perceive, the stranger and child, are Alfred Wentworth and his little boy. About four months after the death of his wife, he was appointed Inspector General of a Louisiana brigade with the rank of first Lieutenant, and being stationed for a while near Jackson, paid frequent visits to the city, and never failed on such occasions to take his son to the grave of his wife and child. There, kneeling before the grave, the broken-hearted soldier would offer up a prayer to God for the repose of the souls of those beneath the sod. The tears which fell on the grave on such visits, and watered the last resting place of the loved ones were the holiest that ever flowed from the eyes of man--they were the homage of a bereaved husband to the memory of a pure and spotless wife, and an angel daughter. Alfred is still alive, and has passed unharmed through many a hard-fought battle. Those who know not the tale of his family's sufferings and unhappy fate, think him moody and unfriendly, but those who are acquainted with the trials of the soldier's wife, regard his reserved and silent manners with respect, for though the same sorrows may not darken the sunshine of their lives, their instinct penetrates the recess of the soldier's heart, and the sight of its shattered and wrecked remains often cause a sigh of sorrow, and a tear of commiseration. Let us trust that a merciful God in His divine wisdom, may alleviate the poignant grief of the soldier, and restore him to that happiness he once possessed.

And now kind reader, we bid you a last farewell; but ere the pages of this book are closed, let us speak a word to you, for those unfortunates who abandon their homes on the approach of the enemy to seek refuge in the Confederate lines. Many -- alas! too many of its citizens consider the term "refugee" synonymous with that of 'beggar.' In this idea we err. It is true they are in many instances, reduced to penury, but in their poverty are as different from the mendicant as the good are from the bad. Many of these refugees have lost their homes, their wealth -- their everything to retain their patriotism and honor. Some of them adorned the most polished circles in their midst, and many held an enviable position in the State of their nativity or residence. For their country, for our country, for your country, the brave abandoned all they possessed, preferring to live in want among the people of the South, than to revel in luxuries in the midst of our enemies. Seek these exiles. Look upon them as suffering Confederates, and extend the hand of friendship and assistance to all who are in need. Let the soldier know that his wife and children are provided for by you. It will cheer him while in camp, it will inspire him in battle, and if he falls by the hand of the enemy, the knowledge that those he loves will be cared for, will lighten the pangs of Death, and he will die, happy in the thought of falling for his country. Oh! kind reader, turn your ear to the moaning of the soldier's wife -- the cries of his children, and let your heart throb with kindness and sympathy for their sufferings. Relieve their wants, alleviate their pains, and earn for yourself a brighter reward than gold or influence can purchase -- the eternal gratitude of the defenders of our liberties.

Farewell! if a single tear of sorrow, steals unhidden down your cheek at the perusal of this sad tale -- if in your heart a single chord of pity is touched at its recital -- we shall have been fully rewarded for the time and labor expended by us. And if at some future day you hear of some soldier's family suffering; sympathise with their afflictions and cheerfully aid in ameliorating their condition, by giving a single thought of "THE TRIALS OF THE SOLDIER'S WIFE."

FINIS.

APPENDIX

In presenting a work of this nature to the reader, the Author takes the opportunity of making an apology for the errors, typographical and otherwise, which may be found therein. The difficulties under which he labored in procuring the publication of the book at this time, when the principal publishers of the South are so busily engaged in publishing works written in foreign parts, and which cost them nothing but the expense of publication, and the procuring of them through our blockaded ports. The book which our readers have just completed perusing, is filled with many errors; too many, in fact, for any literary work to contain. The excuse of the Author for these, is, that at the time the book was in press he was with the Army of Tennessee performing his duties, which prevented him from reading the proof sheets and correcting all mistakes which crept in during composition. The party on whom devolved the duty of reading the proof performed his work as well as could be expected, for, in some instances, the errors were the fault of the Author, and not that of the printer, who labored under many disadvantages in deciphering the manuscript copy of the book; the greater part of which was written on the battle-field, and under fire of the enemy. It is thus that in the first page we find an error of the most glaring character possible, but which might have been the Author's, as well as the printer's omission. Thus, the Author is made to say that the 'aristocracy' of New Orleans were "well known by that elegance and etiquette which distinguish the 'parvenu' of society." Now the intention, as well as the words of the author, represented the 'aristocracy' in quite a different light. That line should have read "that elegance and etiquette which distinguish 'the well-bred' from the 'parvenu' of society, etc." Nevertheless, the whole sense of the sentence is destroyed by the omission of the 'italicized' words, and the reader is left to infer that the aristocracy of New Orleans are the 'parvenu' of society; rather, we must admit, a doubtful compliment, and quite in accordance with the following words, which go on to speak of "the vulgar but wealthy class of citizens with which this country is infested." Now we do not pretend for a moment to believe that our readers would imagine that we meant the sentence quoted in the sense it appears, and they may, perhaps, pass it over without noticing the errors complained of; but when such errors should not exist, they become a source of much annoyance to the author, and could they have been rectified before it was too late, they should never have appeared in print. In fact, after discovering that an error of so gross a nature existed in the first pages of the book, the author would have had the entire "form" reprinted, had not the extravagant price of paper, and its great scarcity, precluded the possibility of such an idea being carried into effect. The errors, therefore, remain, and for them we would claim indulgence, although readily admitting that none is deserved.

And now we desire to say a few words relative to the work you have just completed reading. It may appear to you a wild and extravagant tale of hardships and privations which existed only in the imagination of the author. Were your supposition correct, we should rejoice, but unfortunately, every day brings us scenes of poverty that this work lacks in ability to portray, in sufficient force, the terrible sufferings borne by thousands of our people. In the plenitude of our wealth, we think not of poor, and thus we cannot tell or find out the hundreds of poverty-stricken wretches who cover the country. Our natures may be charitable even, but we only give charity where it is asked for, and await the coming of the mendicant before our purses are opened. By these means alone do we judge the extent of suffering in the land, and, not hearing of many cases of penury, or receiving many applications for assistance, we believe that the assertions of great want being among the people are untrue, and we purposely avoid searching for the truth of such assertions. The design of the author, in this little book, has been to open the eyes of the people to the truth. If he has painted the trials of the soldier's wife more highly colored than reality could permit, it has been because he desired to present his argument with greater force than he could otherwise have done; and yet, if we examine well the picture he presents; take it in its every part, and look on each one, we will find that it does not exaggerate a single woe. We have seen far greater scenes of wretchedness than those narrated herein; scenes which defy description; for their character has been so horrible that to depict it, a pen mightier than a Bulwer's or a Scott's would be necessary.

The tale which the reader has just finished perusing is taken from scenes that 'actually occurred' during the present war -- except, perhaps, that part which relates the tearing of the mother from the bedside of her dead child. In every other respect all that is narrated in the foregoing pages are strictly true, and there are parties now in the South, who, when they read this work, will recognize in themselves, some of the characters represented herein. The Author would rejoice, for the sake of humanity and civilization if the tale he has written was only a fiction of his own imagining; but did it not contain truths the work would never have been written. No other object than that of calling attention to the vast misery and wretchedness which at the present time of writing abounds in the South, prompted the Author to pen the pages which you have perused. He has witnessed them himself; he has seen the soldier's wife absolutely starving, and from a slender purse has himself endeavored to relieve their necessities. To present before the world the fact that there are thousands in our midst who are in 'absolute beggary', has been the object of the writer, and to call on those who are able to do so, to aid these unfortunates, is his purpose. This book is an appeal to the Rich in favor of the Poor. It is the voice of Humanity calling upon Wealth to rise from her sluggish torpor and wrest the hungry and threadbare victim from the grasp of Famine, and drive desolation from our midst. If this call is answered; if the wealthy awake to their duty and save the wretched beings who are in our midst, then the Author will have gained a richer reward than all the profits accruing from this work. He will have been more than rewarded by the knowledge that he has been the instrument, through which charity has once more visited the South, and swept oppression and want from our land. Such scenes as those we daily witness were never seen, even in the mildest form a few short years ago. Prior to the war there was scarcely a beggar in the South, and from one end of the country to the other could we walk without hearing the voice of the mendicant appealing to our benevolence. How changed now! In every city of the South the streets are filled with ragged boys and girls stopping each passer by and asking aid. It is a disgrace to humanity and to God, and that such things should be in our land, whose sons have exhibited such heroism and devotion. Many of these beggary are the sons and daughters of our soldiers -- of our honored dead and heroic living. To the soldier who lies beneath the sod a martyr to his country's cause, their sufferings are unknown; but if in Heaven he can witness their penury, his soul must rest ill at peace and weep for those on earth. To the soldier, who is still alive and struggling for our independence, the letter that brings him news of his wife's and children's poverty must bring him discontent, and render him unwilling to longer remain in the army and struggle for liberty while they are starving. How many times have not desertion taken place through this very cause. In Mississippi we witnessed the execution of a soldier for the crime of desertion. On the morning of his execution, he informed the minister that he never deserted until repeated letters from his wife informed him of her wretched condition; informed him that herself and her children were absolutely starving. He could no longer remain in the army; the dictates of his own heart; the promptings of his affection triumphed and in an evil hour he deserted and returned home to find her tale, alas! too true. He was arrested, courtmartialed and 'shot'. He had forfeited his life by his desertion and bore his fate manfully; his only fear being for the future welfare of that wife and her children for whom he had lost his life. When he fell, pierced by the bullets of his comrades, was there not a murder committed? There was, but not by the men who sentenced him to death. They but performed duty, and, we are charitable enough to suppose, performed it with regret. The murderers were the heartless men who are scattered over the land like, locusts, speculating on the necessities of the people, and their aiders and abettors are those who calmly sat with folded arms, and essayed not to aid his family. Rise, O my readers and aid the poor of our land. Let your hearts be filled with mercy to the unfortunate. Remember that

> "The quality of mercy is not strain'd
> It droppeth, as the gentle rain from heaven
> Upon the place beneath; it is twice blessed,
> It blesseth him that gives and him that takes:
> 'Tis mightiest in the mightiest; it becomes
> The crowned monarch better than his crown:"

and in performing an act of charity you bless yourself as well as the one who is benefited by such charity.

We shall now close our remarks with the hope that the reader will appreciate the motive which prompted the writing of this book. As will be seen, it has no plot -- it never was intended to have any. The Author intended merely to write a simple narrative when he commenced this work, and to place before the public in the most agreeable form of reading, a subject of vital importance to the Confederacy, and to impress upon the minds of the wealthy their duty to the poor. He knows not whether he has succeeded in the latter hope, and he could have wished that some other pen had taken up the subject and woven it into a tale that could have had a better and more lasting effect than the foregoing is likely to have. Nevertheless, he trusts that all his labor is not lost, but that some attention will be paid to his words and a kinder feeling be manifested towards refugees and the poor than has hitherto been shown. If this be done then nothing but the happiest results can follow, and the blessings of thousands, the heartfelt blessings of thousands on earth, will follow those who aid in the work of charity, called for by the present emergency, and from the celestial realms the voice of God will be heard thanking His children on earth for their kindness to their fellow mortals.

*   *   *   *   *

For the publication of this work the Author has to thank the kind proprietor of the "Atlanta Intelligencer," Col. Jared I. Whitaker. To this gentleman is he indebted for being able to present the work to the public, and to him does the Author extend his sincere thanks. In Col. Whitaker the Confederacy has one son who, uncontaminated by the vile weeds of mortality which infest us, still remains pure and undefiled, and, not only the obligations due from the author are hereby acknowledged, but as one who has witnessed the whole souled charity of this gentleman, we can record him the possession of a heart, unswayed by a sordid motive. To this gentleman are the thanks of the author tendered, with the wish that he may live many long years to reap the reward due to those, who, like himself, are ever foremost in deeds of charity and benevolence.

END OF APPENDIX.

PHOTOGRAPH and ILUSTRATION CREDITS

Maj. Alexander St. Clair-Abrams by Gary Schermerhorn, Page 4

Adm. David Farragut at New Orleans, Library of Congress, Page 8

Gen. Benjamin Franklin Butler, Library of Congress, Page 10

Gen. Mansfield Lovell, Library of Congress, Page 10

Col. William Temple Withers, Library of Congress, Page 12

Gen. William Wing Loring, Florida Memory, Page 12

Capt. Samuel Jones Ridley, Library of Congress, Page 12

Gen. Carter Littlepage Stevenson, Library of Congress, Page 12

Gen. James Longstreet by Robert A. Grenier, Page 18

Edward Alfred Pollard, Library of Congress, Page 22

Pres. Davis and His Administration, Author Collection, Page 23

Jefferson Davis by Robert A. Grenier, Page 25

Joanna St. Clair-Abrams, Historical Society of Tavares, Page 30

Alex Abrams Roster Slip, Author Collection, Page 30

Gen. Ulysses Simpson Grant by Robert A. Grenier, Page 34

Gen. William Tecumseh Sherman by Robert A. Grenier, Page 34

Gen. Edmund Kirby-Smith by Robert A. Grenier, Page 34

Atlanta Intelligencer Office, Library of Congress, Page 38

Vicksburg (Three Photographs), Library of Congress, Page 130

New York Herald Field Headquarters (Two Photographs),
Library of Congress, Page 132

James G. Bennett Sr., Library of Congress, Page 134

New York Herald (Three Photographs), Library of Congress
Page 138

ACKNOWLEDGMENTS

I am very grateful to everyone who assisted me in bringing the remarkable story of Major Alexander St. Clair-Abrams back from the lost pages of American history. There are many outstanding organizations, education and research centers, federal, state, and local museums, historical societies, archives, and libraries to thank, including the Historical Society of Tavares, Tavares Public Library, City of Tavares, Lake County Historical Society, Central Florida Railroad Historical Society, Pine Castle Historical Society, Jacksonville Historical Society, Jacksonville Public Library, Rollins College, University of Central Florida, University of Florida, Flagler College, Florida Memory, State Archives of Florida, New Georgia Encyclopedia, Emerging Civil War, Digital Library of Georgia, Newspapers.com, Find-A-Grave Memorial, The Prairie School Traveler, Harness Racing Museum and Hall of Fame, Vicksburg National Military Park, United States Navy, and the Library of Congress

My appreciation to the gifted artists who contributed their artwork, including David Campos, Shirley Cannon, Iddir Aoujil, Gary Schermerhorn, and my dad, Robert A. Grenier.

I am very grateful to Richard "Rick" Lee Cronin for writing the Introduction for this book and for his efforts in preserving Central Florida history.

A special thank you to Tavares Public Library reference librarian Marli Wilkins-Lopez for her research, editing and proofreading.

This book was made possible by the support and encouragement of my parents, Mary and Bob Grenier, Alma N. Grenier, and God!

BIBLIOGRAPHY

Ackerman, Joe A. Jr., and Ackerman, Mark J.
Jacob Summerlin: King of the Crackers 2004

Andrews, J. Cutler *The South Reports the Civil War* 1970

Brown "The Parson Brown Orange"
The Florida Historical Society Quarterly July 1951

Cronin, Richard Lee *Tavares: Darling of Orange County,
Birthplace of Lake County* 2020

Crouthamel, James L. *Bennett's New York Herald and the Rise of
the Popular Press* 1989

Eaton, Clement *A History of the Southern Confederacy* 1954

Fielder, Herbert *A Sketch of the Life and Times and Speeches of
Joseph E. Brown* 1883

Grady, Henry Woodfin *The Complete Orations and Speeches of
Henry W. Grady* 1910

Grenier, Bob *Woodlea: Life on the Lake of the Dancing Sunbeams,
Second Edition* 2010

Hain, Pamela Chase *Murder in the State Capitol* 2013

Kennedy, William T. *History of Lake County*, 1929

Loquasto, Wendy S. *Celebrating Florida's First 150 Women
Lawyers* 2000

Peet, E. A. *Biography of Henry Holcomb Duncan* undated

Pollard, Edward A. *Southern History of the War* 1977

Simes, Walter P. *About Some Lakes and More in Lake County*
1995

Tenny, Llyod S. *Florida Growers and Shippers League* 1915

Wehr, Paul W. *Dateline: Pine Castle* 2014

SELECTED INDEX of PEOPLE

NOT INCLUDED ARE ST. CLAIR-ABRAMS'
SEIGE OF VICKSBURG and THE TRIALS OF THE SOLDIER'S WIFE

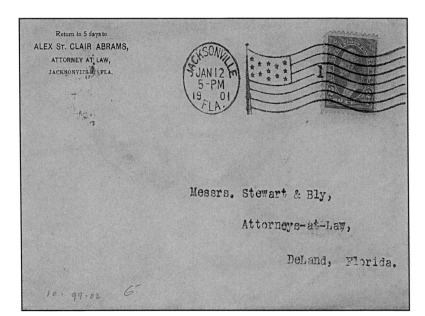

JACKSONVILLE
JAN 12
5-PM
19 01
FLA.

Messrs. Stewart & Bly,

Attorneys-at-Law,

DeLand, Florida.

10. 99-02   6

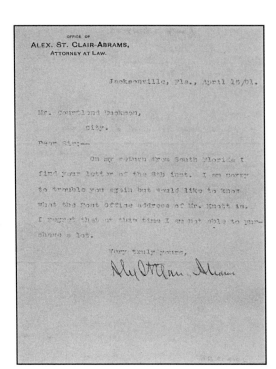

OFFICE OF
ALEX. St. CLAIR-ABRAMS,
ATTORNEY AT LAW.

Jacksonville, Fla., April 15/01.

Mr. Courtland Buckman,

City.

Dear Sir:—

On my return from South Florida I
find your letter of the 8th inst. I am sorry
to trouble you again but would like to know
what the Post Office address of Mr. Knott is.
I regret that at this time I am not able to purchase a lot.

Very truly yours,

Alex St Clair Abrams

446

Bob Grenier was born in Chicago, Illinois, and grew up in the Chicago suburb of Northlake. He moved to Lake County, Florida, in 1985. Bob has authored several books on Florida history, including *Florida's Forgotten Pioneer: The Gallant Captain Melton Haynes* and *Woodlea: Life on the Lake of the Dancing Sunbeams*, as well as books for Arcadia Publishing's Images of America series – *Tavares; Leesburg; Central Florida's Civil War Veterans;* and *Central Florida's World War II Veterans.* Bob edited and published the book *From Farm to Flight to Faith: My Story of Survival in the Skies During WWII* by Bernie DeVore.

Bob served twenty years on the board of directors of the Lake County Historical Society that included multiple terms as president. He is a retired Curator and Exhibit Designer of the Lake County Historical Museum and is very active in historical and memorial preservation projects and events.

Bob worked for Walt Disney World's engineering and facilities for twenty-five years and served as a Vice Mayor and Councilman for the City of Tavares.